Radical Moves

Radical Moves

Caribbean Migrants *and the* Politics of Race *in the* Jazz Age

LARA PUTNAM

THE UNIVERSITY OF NORTH CAROLINA PRESS
Chapel Hill

© 2013 THE UNIVERSITY OF NORTH CAROLINA PRESS

All rights reserved. Designed by Sally Fry. Set in Minion and Scala Sans by
Integrated Book Technology. Manufactured in the United States of America.
The paper in this book meets the guidelines for permanence and durability of
the Committee on Production Guidelines for Book Longevity of the Council
on Library Resources.

The University of North Carolina Press has been a member
of the Green Press Initiative since 2003.

Library of Congress Cataloging-in-Publication Data
Putnam, Lara.
    Radical moves : Caribbean migrants and the politics of race in the jazz age /
Lara Putnam.
        p. cm.
    Includes bibliographical references and index.
ISBN 978-0-8078-3582-1 (cloth : alk. paper)—
ISBN 978-0-8078-7285-7 (pbk. : alk. paper)
1. Blacks—West Indies, British—Migrations—History—20th century. 2. West
Indians—Migrations—History—20th century. 3. Blacks—Social conditions—20th
century. 4. West Indians—Social conditions—20th century. 5. Blacks—Politics
and government—20th century. 6. West Indians—Politics and government—20th
century. 7. Anti-imperialist movements—History—20th century. 8. West Indies,
British—Emigration and immigration—History—20th century. 9. Emigration and
immigration—Political aspects—History—20th century. 10. Racism—Political
aspects—History—20th century. I. Title.
F2131.P88 2013
972.905'2—dc23   2012031385

A section of chapter 2 appeared previously in Lara Putnam, "Rites of Power
and Rumors of Race: The Circulation of Supernatural Knowledge in the Greater
Caribbean, 1890–1940," in *Obeah and Other Powers: The Politics of Caribbean
Religion and Healing*, ed. Diana Paton and Maarit Forde (Durham, N.C.:
Duke University Press, 2012), 243–67. Reprinted by permission.

cloth   17 16 15 14 13   5 4 3 2 1
paper   17 16 15 14 13   5 4 3 2 1

To Miriam, Gabriel, Alonso, and Eleanor Wren

Contents

Illustrations, Maps, and Tables

TABLES

Acknowledgments

My gratitude belongs first and foremost to the extended family who have made it possible to raise four children, conduct research, and write semi-coherent sentences at the same time, especially Amy Crosson, Elsa Perez, Mario Perez, Bob Putnam, Christin Campbell Putnam, Jonathan Putnam, Rosemary Putnam, Therese Tardio, and Doug Wible.

Funding in support of the research presented here came from the Central Research Development Fund, the School of Arts and Sciences, the Center for Latin American Studies, the University Center for International Studies, the Nationalities Rooms Fellowships Program, and the Department of History, all of the University of Pittsburgh; the Vicerrectoría de Investigación of the Universidad de Costa Rica; and an ACLS/SSRC/NEH International and Area Studies Fellowship. Even with such support, this research would not have been possible without generous souls who opened their homes: Norma and Dale Anderson, Fred Butcher, Bob and Raffaella Nannetti, and Ethel Shoul. The support and enthusiasm of Annette Insanally and the Latin American–Caribbean Centre of the University of the West Indies at Mona has been crucial to me as to so many scholars.

Portions of this research were presented at conferences at Tulane University, the German Historical Institute, the University of the West Indies at Mona, Newcastle University, the Newberry Library, the University of Chicago, the Cornell University Anthropology Colloquium, the University of California, Los Angeles, the Committee on Global Thought at Columbia University, and the University of Delaware; to Carnegie Mellon's "Recognition of Migrants" Working Group, the University of Pittsburgh's Caribbean Reading Group, and John Soluri's 2011 graduate seminar; and at meetings of the American Historical Association, the Association of Caribbean Historians, the Society for Caribbean Studies, the Association for the Study of the Worldwide African Diaspora, and the Latin American Studies Association. Many thanks are due to the organizers, commentators, and questioners at each of those venues.

I have benefited greatly from comments on earlier versions of material contained here by George Reid Andrews, Nigel Bolland, Dain Borges, Louis Chude-Sokei, Paul Eiss, Maarit Forde, John French, Donna Gabbaccia, Jorge Giovannetti, Larry Glasco, Glyne Griffith, Lowell Gudmundson, Marc

Hertzman, Dirk Hoerder, Pat Manning, Wayne Marshall, Scott Morgenstern, Harvey Neptune, Diana Paton, Shalini Puri, Jonathan Putnam, Roger Rouse, Rob Ruck, Nico Slate, Klive Walker, Andrew Weintraub, Michael O. West, and Justin Wolfe. Soili Buska, Sharika Crawford, Jorge Giovannetti, Julie Greene, LaShawn Harris, and Franny Sullivan have all shared sources they knew would interest me. Ileana D'Alolio, Rachel Gately, Carolyn Just, Heidi Lozano, and Doug Wible provided stellar research assistance. Huberth Vargas drew beautiful maps. At UNC Press, Elaine Maisner's early enthusiasm was crucial; Caitlin Bell-Butterfield kept me on track; and Jay Mazzocchi provided superb and patient copyediting.

Special thanks are due to some long-term interlocutors for conversations that always push me to recognize how much more there is to know: Moji Anderson, Sueann Caulfield, Harvey Neptune, Diana Paton, Roger Rouse, Rebecca J. Scott, and Nico Slate. George Reid Andrews, Nigel Bolland, Jonathan Putnam, and an anonymous reviewer for UNC Press read the manuscript in its entirety; to say that their input was invaluable falls short.

This project has benefited from the intellectual excitement of the University of Pittsburgh's Department of History, where intersections of Atlantic, Latin American, transnational, and world history are debated among some of the finest scholars at work in each field. Among many colleagues to whom thanks are due, I must single out George Reid Andrews and Alejandro de la Fuente. Working closely with Reid and Alejandro in graduate advising and journal editing alike has been an extraordinary education.

To Doug Wible, for his willingness to join me in multiple madcap adventures—down the Orinoco by motorboat, through the streets of Cumaná on foot at midnight, down West Virginia Route 39 on a KTM 990 Adventure, and into parenthood in the midst of it all—something deeper than gratitude is due. This book would not exist in its current form without him. Additional moral support in Pittsburgh has come from the TRC, the Salon of Thursday Dinners, Wendy Goldman, Scott Morgenstern, Lisa Tetrault, and the Eiss/Friedman family.

Finally, my son Alonso would like me to use these acknowledgments to acknowledge that Mike Tomlin is awesome. I am happy to do so. I will also acknowledge that sharing my life with Miriam, Gabriel, and Alonso Perez-Putnam has been an incomparable trip. If anyone reading this far has never met them in person, all I can say is I'm very sorry for you. They're exceptional people. If their baby sister, Eleanor Wren, grows up to be anything like them, we are blessed indeed.

Note on Sources

This project has relied heavily on the interwar press. The *Kingston Daily Gleaner* was consulted via newspaperarchive.com and the *Pittsburgh Courier* and *New York Times* via the ProQuest Historical Newspapers database. All Port Limón papers quoted (including the *Times*, the *Searchlight*, and the *Atlantic Voice*) were consulted on microfilm in the Biblioteca Nacional de Costa Rica in San José, Costa Rica. All Barbados papers quoted (in particular, the *Weekly Herald*) were consulted on microfilm at the National Library of Barbados in Bridgetown. All Trinidadian papers quoted, including the *Daily Mirror* and the *Weekly Guardian*, were read in bound copies at the National Archive of Trinidad and Tobago in Port of Spain. The *Panama Tribune* was consulted in loose copies at the Museo Afroantillano in Guachipali, Panama City; microfilmed issues for some years are now available through the New York Public Library. The Salvation Army's *West Indies War Cry* was consulted at the Salvation Army's Territorial Headquarters in Kingston, Jamaica. The *Panama American* and *Bluefields Weekly* are held in microfilm at U.S. libraries and were consulted via interlibrary loan.

Further research was conducted at the Archivo Nacional de Costa Rica, the Archivo Nacional de Panamá, the Institute of Jamaica, the Jamaica Archive, the Barbados Archive, the National Library of Trinidad and Tobago, the National Archive of Trinidad and Tobago, the National Archives of the United Kingdom, the U.S. National Archive II, the Archivo Nacional de Venezuela, the Biblioteca Nacional de Venezuela, the Archivo Histórico de Guayana, the Archivo Histórico de Sucre, and the Archivo del Ministerio de Relaciones Exteriores de Venezuela. I am grateful to the staffs of all of these collections for their unfailing generosity and patience.

Introduction

Louise Helen Norton was born in the fishing village of La Digue on the eastern Caribbean island of Grenada in 1897, at the end of two generations in which tens of thousands of Grenadians had sailed off to seek opportunity "in foreign"—over 10,000 on the goldfields and cacao farms of Venezuela and larger numbers still on the British island of Trinidad. In the years just after Louise's birth, it was Panama instead that drew thousands of Grenadians to try their luck. When the hemisphere's economies rebounded after the Great War, Grenadians had accumulated enough capital, savvy, and connections to travel farther afield. Louise was no exception. At twenty, she traveled to Montreal to join an uncle who was already there. She found work as a servant and found support in a new community group, Marcus Garvey's Universal Negro Improvement Association (UNIA), which fused the ethics of fraternal love familiar to her from the lodges back home with ringing calls for solidarity among black people the world over. These ideas echoed observations that Louise and the Caribbeans that she knew in Montreal made every day, as they navigated an unforgiving world in which their skin color and accents marked them as outsiders for the first time in their lives.

Through the UNIA, Louise met Georgia-born Earl Little, a Baptist lay preacher and fervent Garveyite. They married in 1919 and relocated to Philadelphia, home by then to some 2,000 British Caribbeans. Louise and Earl would have seven children over the course of a decade in which the couple organized for the UNIA—and faced threats from resentful whites—everywhere they went. Their fourth child, Malcolm Little, born in 1925, is better known today as Malcolm X.[1]

Sometimes the experiences and ideas of not-very-powerful people in not-very-prominent places generate very powerful change. I study working-class men and women who left their islands of birth at the margins of the British Empire at the dawn of the twentieth century to seek work in ports and plantations at the leading edge of a new empire, the informal empire of the United States. Those ports and plantations were mainly located within the borders of Spanish-speaking republics—places like Panama, Costa Rica, Cuba, the Dominican Republic, and Venezuela. By the time Louise Norton left for Montreal, scores of thousands of British islanders were turning northward, too, toward New York City most of all.

At the start of the twentieth century, politicians in circum-Caribbean receiving societies had accepted the arrival of tens of thousands of British West Indian workingmen and -women as a temporary expedient, a short-cut on the path to "national" development of marginal territories within their domains. But export economies contracted in the 1920s and 1930s, and "national" workers' demands for job protection grew. A rising cadre of populist politicians sought to ban the arrival of English-speaking Afro-descendants and, sometimes, to kick out those already there.

The confluence of nativism, populism, and race-based border making that British Caribbean migrants confronted was not an isolated or region-specific phenomenon but rather part of a nearly global trend. The interwar years saw the internal commitments and external permeability of sovereign states fundamentally remade. Matters of political membership—the kinds of rights and privileges that people were able to claim from the states that claimed to govern them—were transformed. This was the culmination of linked economic, sociodemographic, and ideological trends. Industrialization and urbanization had spurred labor organizing and had increased working people's ability to pressure employers and politicians. New attention to the potential (and threat) of the masses spurred new sciences like demography and biology. Intellectuals drew elements from these emerging disciplines to forge a newly "scientific" racism, which helped rejustify social hierarchies in the face of surging democratic claims.

These developments crystallized first in Western Europe and the United States and have generally been studied there. But they were not limited to those locales. An international system was emerging in which states interacted with each other, compared themselves to each other, and learned from each other's mistakes, all in pursuit of recognition as sovereign equals. From the empires of East Asia to Latin American republics only recently emerged from colonial status, politicians and labor organizers and intellectuals watched and listened, remaking state structures and ideologies accordingly. How could the experiences and ideas of a few hundred thousand Afro-Caribbean emigrants be relevant to this international macropolitical shift? One might imagine the opposite to be true. From the point of view of one imperial state (the British Empire), one neoimperial state (the U.S. government), and many republican states (of the Spanish-speaking circum-Caribbean), black Caribbean workers were utterly marginal. They had few de facto political rights on their islands of origin, fewer still in the lands where they sojourned.

And yet they believed themselves to be at the center of all things. Specifically, they believed themselves to be at the center of linked processes they recognized as fundamental to the modern world: the transformation of race, of nation, and of empire. Believing, they made it so. First, they accurately saw themselves as being at the forefront of the creation of a newly self-conscious and self-active collective: "Our People," "the Great Negro Race." Second, they accurately perceived themselves as living in a moment of fundamental redefinition of the relation of people to government, as the demands that could be made by members of national communities expanded and the boundaries of national membership hardened. British Caribbean sojourners—long present yet now "alien," so similar yet now "unassimilable"—forced awkward clarifications of that national romance. Did African ancestry make individuals unfit for citizenship in modern republics—and would white elites make that argument out loud, in front of native-born Afro-Panamanians, Afro-Cubans, and Afro-Americans who were being promised full citizenship to come in those same years?

Third and finally, the men and women of the British Caribbean migratory sphere saw themselves as standing at the center of an unprecedented crisis of empire itself. The mobility rights of British subjects of color were under attack, and Britain seemed to have nothing to say about it. Where were the universal British rights that island schoolbooks had lauded? Denouncing their treatment as "British objects" rather than "British subjects," sojourners warned that divisions of caste and tribe had been the downfall of Rome. In a new world of nativist states, where could these natives-out-of-place demand their own native rights?

Believing that their exclusion and their aspirations mattered to the modern world in the making, British Caribbeans remade that world. In dance halls and revival meetings, in street talk and political tracts, they created radical new ways of thinking about themselves, their communities, and their rights. "Race" was fundamental to much of this thinking—just as it was to debates from Münich to Memphis in the same interwar era. But what did race mean? What determined the boundaries of peoplehood? And how could "a people" of color advance in a white-supremacist world? Multiple answers were proposed from within the circum-Caribbean migratory sphere. Some were explicit, in the form of manifestos and organizations; others were implicit, symbolized or embodied in ritual and rumors, music and moves. The popular cultures of black internationalism that emerged from this broad-based debate include Garveyism, Rastafarianism, and "regge" dances to the irresistible rhythms that made this the Age of Jazz.

With good reason, this migratory world and this historical moment were the point of origin not only of Marcus Garvey (b. Jamaica, 1887) but a whole pantheon of prominent black internationalists, including Hubert Harrison (b. St. Croix, 1883), W. A. Domingo (b. Jamaica, 1889), Claude McKay (b. Jamaica, 1889), Richard B. Moore (b. Barbados, 1893), Amy Jacques Garvey (b. Jamaica, 1895), Amy Ashwood Garvey (b. Jamaica, 1897), Eric Walrond (b. British Guiana, 1898), C. L. R. James (b. Trinidad, 1901), George Padmore (b. Trinidad, 1902), Una Marson (b. Jamaica, 1905), Eric Williams (b. Trinidad, 1911), Claudia Jones (b. Trinidad, 1915), Harry Belafonte (b. New York, 1927), and George Lamming (b. Barbados, 1927). Indeed, of the forty key "political leaders" from across "Africa and the Diaspora" whom Hakim Adi and Marika Sherwood selected as central to "Pan-African History" from 1787 to the present, fully one-fourth were born in the British Caribbean during the years covered here and came of age in the heyday of the circum-Caribbean migratory sphere.[2] But black internationalism was not restricted to political leaders, nor to eloquent authors, nor to the print public sphere. The border-crossing spread of black-identified music and dance in this era (under names like jazz, calypso, mento, rumba, and *son*) reflected a different kind of black internationalism, one that was generated and spread by people of varied ages and stations, young working-class men and women most of all.

One consequence of the shift from tracking a few leaders to exploring the cultural ferment of the world they came from is that it transforms our understanding of the gender profile of black internationalism. Once we set aside the Great Man theory of history that still shades some accounts of political change in the African diaspora, we see active women everywhere. This is true even with regard to formal organizations once we look at the level of local and regional activists. These were UNIA organizers like Malcolm X's mother, Louise; orators like Garvey lieutenant Madame de Mena (born to British West Indian parents in Nicaragua ca. 1890); and labor leaders like International Ladies' Garment Workers' Union firebrand Maida Springer (born to British West Indian parents in Panama in 1910). But it becomes even more true when we turn away from formal institutions to observe popular culture. Every circum-Caribbean newspaper had sizeable numbers of female readers and published letters from women correspondents on issues of the day— which is not surprising, given that literacy was higher among women than men everywhere across the region. Every migrant's family included aunties and grannies and sisters willing to speak their minds. And every dance hall had just as many women as men making up the couples that shimmied and shay-shayed their way across the floor.

Why this place, and why this time? Specific characteristics of the circum-Caribbean migratory sphere made its encounter with this moment in the evolution of the international nation-state system particularly generative—and generative of formulations that would be found useful and relevant up until the present day. Caribbean migrants in this era encountered essentialist paradigms of collective identity at their most exclusionary. These paradigms fused ideas about blood and character, cultural inheritance and biological destiny. Yet migrants' travels showed them the shifting nature of the supposedly essential categories on which the paradigms depended. Having experienced multiple racial formations firsthand—knowing that what counted as "white" and the consequences of being "black" varied from place to place, even though such divides were treated as gospel in each setting—migrants recognized both the fictitiousness of race and its very real weight in the modern world.

Meanwhile, in the interwar era, the extensive circulation of people combined with an intensified circulation of media, making it possible for individual experiences in far-flung locales to add up to cohesive intellectual and cultural movements. The emergence of a circum-Caribbean/transatlantic black press gave migrants a panoramic view of the rise of antiblack discrimination worldwide. The popular cultures of black internationalism that came out of this moment all wrestled in their own ways with the core tension between essentialist and constructivist paradigms. Was membership in "the Negro race" a matter of who you were born or who you chose to be? Was the essence of modern jazz about African rhythms from the past or creative musicianship in the present? Interwar thinkers from all over the ideological map—from white supremacists to Fabian socialists—agreed with W. E. B. Du Bois's 1900 claim that the problem of the twentieth century was the problem of the color line. But was that line dictated by God, or biology, or the capitalist system? What kinds of line crossings might be politically productive, or gloriously rude? These were the questions that the cultural and intellectual production of the circum-Caribbean migratory sphere addressed. Just as the underlying dilemma has remained fundamental to political collectives and self-understanding up to the present, the cultural products of that time and place have remained "good to think with" for successive generations.

DEFINITIONS AND DESIGNS

Pioneering journalist Roi Ottley (himself the Harlem-born son of Grenadian parents) defined "black nationalism" in 1940 as the "group solidarity . . . form[ed] as Negroes developed new racial sentiments and loyalties" that cut across "class lines," bringing in turn "a growing *world* consciousness, expressed in feelings of racial kinship with colored peoples elsewhere in the world."[3] Do black nationalism and black internationalism necessarily go together, then? Are they even two separate things? I suggest that the terms are most helpful if we use them to point us toward different (but potentially complementary) scales on which to think about racism, and different (though potentially complementary) strategies of response.

Black nationalism holds that within a racist society, black people's primary political allegiance should reflect racial solidarity. Black nationalists seek to create structures to channel that allegiance, either within existing systems (for instance, by founding race-based political parties) or by transforming systems (for instance, by building new institutions under black community control). Whether primary allegiance to race is or is not compatible with alliance along lines of class (populism, socialism, communism) has been actively debated across the black Americas for the past century. Meanwhile, black internationalism analyzes racial subordination as a part of systems that function on a supranational scale. Black internationalists prioritize responses that target those systems as a whole, which usually requires communication and alliance across political boundaries, be they national or imperial.[4]

Following these definitions, many black nationalists were also black internationalists, and some black internationalists were also black nationalists. The two approaches could well be mutually reinforcing, but they did not everywhere and always coincide. Some black-nationalist activists and organizations appear in the account that follows, but I make no pretense to capture all of them or build an argument about the conditions that generated them.[5] Rather, it was black internationalisms that were generated, I will argue, with extraordinary intensity by the intersection of the circum-Caribbean migratory sphere with emerging populisms and international mobility control.

Benedict Anderson famously defined the nation as a specific kind of imagined collective: "An imagined political community . . . imagined as both inherently limited and sovereign."[6] Black internationalisms are inherently "political" in a broad sense, for they have invariably imagined their collective with reference to inequalities of access to power. But unlike Anderson's "nation," the communities that black internationalists have imagined have been explicitly defined by their *lack* of sovereign status. Whether the imagined collective should *aspire* to sovereign status—and by what means that might be attained—has been one focus of debate among black-internationalist thinkers and activists. Just where the limits of the imagined community might lie is another.

Thus, initiatives that sought to create an institutional structure for coordination among peoples of African ancestry have comprised an important subcategory of black internationalisms, but they were neither the totality of black internationalism nor its necessary destiny. In this book, I will reserve the term "Pan-African" to refer to organized movements that sought to build institutional structures connecting New World populations of African ancestry to the continent of Africa.[7] These included the Pan-African Association, founded by (Trinidadian) Henry Sylvester Williams in London in 1900; the Universal Negro Improvement Association, founded by (Jamaican) Marcus Garvey in Kingston in 1914 and New York in 1917; and the Pan-African Congresses, convoked by (North American) W. E. B. Du Bois in Paris in 1919 and over the decades that followed. The stories of these initiatives have merited a wealth of recent scholarship. While you will find some mention of these organizations in the pages that follow, my own focus is elsewhere: on the myriad black internationalisms that flourished in popular culture in the same era. This broader cultural outpouring was, I will argue, the vital context for the spread of organized Pan-Africanism in the same era. And as I have foreshadowed above, I will argue that this broader surge of black internationalisms occurred in the interwar Greater Caribbean for very specific reasons.

Because the interwar surge of black internationalism drew on connections that spread from multiple sites, no one regional vantage on this story is complete. This book reconstructs the circum-Caribbean piece of circuits whose impact in 1910s to 1930s Harlem has been captured by Winston James, in 1920s Harlem and 1930s London by Minkah Makalani, in 1930s Britain by Susan Pennybacker, and in 1930s Paris by Brent Hayes Edwards.[8] The patterns of circulation of the era mean that many of the people who play prominent roles in those accounts began their days moving between the tropical places I study—and that many of the debates they protagonized in Harlem or Paris echoed back to the nonmetropolitan yet deeply cosmopolitan islands and rimlands they came from.

My contribution is to trace the story of one set of connected peripheries and the black internationalisms that emerged from them or bounced back to them. Stories of other networks from the peripheries—like those that linked West African and British ports, or those that tied southern African mining towns to sending communities from Botswana to Bombay—are necessary counterparts to the story I tell here.[9]

In addition to centering my inquiry on a particular circuit of tropical locales whose modernity has not always been recognized, I aim to capture the collective understandings and cultural creations of a wide range of people in those places. This book will not tell you much about influential émigré activists—important as they were—but it should tell you a good deal about where they were coming from, literally and figuratively. Anthropologist Charles Carnegie has argued that "to adequately theorize the formation and practice of a black diaspora requires the ethnography of nonmetropolitan sites that were and are part of the diasporic circuit; requires, moreover, that we get at the voices and experiences not just of literary and political figures but of the anonymous and unlettered who provide them with community and succor."[10] I hope this book serves as one piece of that needed ethnography.

Meanwhile, the "Jazz Age" of the 1920s and 1930s was not only epochal in the history of black internationalism; it was also the beginning of the end of empire. How exactly this happened—how the lived experiences of colonial subjects in the years that Michael West and William Martin have tagged the "global White Thermidor" translated into the social mobilizations and collective imaginings that would undermine British imperial rule after World War II—is part of my story here. Again, I find that the experiences and ideas of British Caribbean migrants—not just leaders and activists, but unremarkable men and women doing their best to live unremarkable lives—formed a crucial driver. As worldwide economic crisis deepened over the 1930s, politicians in migratory destinations such as Panama, Cuba, and Venezuela promoted the expulsion of black "foreigners" as a response to economic straits and labor unrest. Repatriation, whether merely threatened or violently enacted, made the filiation and rights of British Caribbeans abroad a matter of urgent debate. As former emigrants and their children poured back to Jamaica, Barbados, and other islands, the ideas of race, nation, and native entitlement they had developed in response to populist compacts and state racism abroad came with them. Both the Labour Rebellions of 1934–39 and political demands in their aftermath bore the mark of ideologies limned in the republics of the Greater Caribbean.

This book argues, then, that the making and unmaking of the circum-Caribbean migratory sphere over the first four decades of the twentieth century was key to the emergence of globally influential black internationalisms and to the course of British Caribbean decolonization, in each case as conditioned by a broader and more fundamental international shift in the relationship of states to "their" people. When observed from the perspective of working people in North Atlantic democracies, that shift looks like a fundamentally domestic matter, and one to be lauded: this is the emergence of what

T. H. Marshall famously termed "social citizenship."[11] Within Latin America, it was populist coalitions combining middle-class leaders with mobilized laborers and peasants that, where they managed to gain power, redefined the role of the state in social provisioning. Populist leaders bulwarked their rule by channeling (or coercing) mass support; they often sought to use the new state muscle to claim for nationals like themselves a larger role in economic sectors that foreign capital had dominated.

The populist era encouraged new consideration of populations of African and indigenous ancestry within the nations' boundaries. The 1920s and 1930s saw the rise of *indigenismo* in Mexico and the Andes, the flowering of Afrocubanismo in Havana, and Gilberto Freyre's reframing of the "*senzala*" (barracks) of the slaves as well as the "*casa-grande*" (big house) of the masters as seminal to Brazilian character. Nations were being redefined along with states. New cultural borrowing was part of the shift—and, just as with the contemporaneous Harlem Renaissance, has been the object of debate, as some scholars stress the agency of black-culture creators while others emphasize exoticization or exploitation. Either way, uneven but real material gains also registered. With some of the barriers to black and brown advancement eroding, the rising tide of populist compacts lifted most boats.[12]

But the relationship of populism to race and racism was complicated. The newfound mission to integrate and advance "our" Indians or blacks was often described as predicated on action to halt the infusion of nonwhite "blood" from without. The denunciation of certain elements of scientific racism and the erection of new forms of state racism routinely went hand in hand. A nationalist intellectual like Laureano Vallenilla Lanz could declare in a single breath in 1930 that "theory built exclusively on the racial factor is completely discarded by science" and that in his beloved Venezuela, the admixture of "African blood" had prevented the smooth fusion of "the white" and "the Indian," hampering "the creation of the bonds necessary to unite our *pueblos* in a common ideal of nationality and *patria*."[13] Unifying *pueblos* for collective progress required both biological and cultural mixing. As we shall see, in the interwar Americas, demographic, cultural, labor-market, and geopolitical arguments were all marshaled to argue that foreign blacks must not be allowed to mix in. The term "mestizo" had long signaled mixed indigenous and European ancestry in Latin America, and I will often refer to the above complex of ideas and programs as mestizo populism. Where the exclusion of people considered foreign by birth or ancestry became central to the definition of the national community, I will speak of "xenophobic populism" as well.

The label fits many places, including the interwar United States. For the other side of "social citizenship" was that expansion of the possibilities for popular claims making within states generally went hand in hand with a hardening of borders without. The pattern transcended any particular national or racial ideology. Nations newly embracing mestizo identity built exclusionary barriers in this era. Nations that insisted they were "white-men's democracies" did too. Indeed, these same few decades of the interwar era saw the worldwide spread of elements of international migration control that have endured up to the present day. These elements include the two-tiered mobility system with different rules for "tourists" (those who can demonstrate wealth in their lands of origin) and "immigrants" (the presumptive identity of those who cannot); the extension of "family" preferences for certain kin relations (legal husbands and wives) and not others (consensual partners, siblings); and the divide between those noncitizen residents who are accorded basic civil protections and others who, because of their entry status, color, or particular birthplace, can make no claims that the receiving state considers itself bound to respect.

Modern border control was new, and it hurt. Attending to the ruptures experienced and denounced by interwar Caribbean migrants makes visible the radical nature of the changes instituted by nation-states in this era. In the United States as elsewhere, the new mobility control system was erected with the explicit goal of race-based exclusion as well as labor-market protection. While explicit racial goals disappeared from immigration policies in the United States and elsewhere by the end of the 1940s, the mechanisms that achieved race-based exclusions remained largely in place. Tracing the changing experiences of Caribbean migrants across the interwar era shows us the origin of the legal structures and systematic illegalities that shape cross-border movement in the Western Hemisphere today.

Born in tandem with the nation-state in the nineteenth century, the discipline of history built methods and concepts to tell stories of national peoples as coterminous with national territories. A century later, black-internationalist intellectuals were among the first to develop methods and concepts for reconstructing critical histories of supranational systems instead. These pioneering works by C. L. R. James, Eric Williams, and Walter Rodney have been reacclaimed in recent years as scholars seek better ways to study connections across borders over time. Rethinking our presumptions about which "places" have narratable pasts is one component of this process.[14] For this book, I have structured my inquiry around circuits significantly larger than states and centered my research on communities significantly smaller.

The former permit me to notice when ideas, sounds, moves, and people from one place have an impact in another; the latter lets me gain some understanding of the layers of local meaning that made those ideas or moves worth borrowing, and transformed them along the way.

The conclusion that emerges from a research strategy delimited by circuits of movement rather than national or imperial boundaries is not that states do not matter. On the contrary, this is the story of how hard states worked to *make* themselves matter, to create a world in which frontiers of language, culture, mobility, and authority indeed became coterminous. The states we will observe did not succeed in that project of homogenization, but they did succeed in employing more bureaucrats and making migrants' lives more precarious. States also succeeded in excluding noncitizens from the new social commitments that citizens won in this era—even when workers born elsewhere were permitted, with a sly wink, to cross over borders and work. Thus, a methodology designed to reconstruct the history of connections across boundaries turns out to offer new insights into the nature and weight of the boundaries themselves.[15]

In sum, this book reconstructs three fundamental stories and argues that their outcomes were mutually contingent, that is, that none of the three would have happened as it did in the absence of the other two. Migrants circled the Caribbean. Strengthening states built new systems of mobility control. Black internationalisms flourished in print and popular culture. I have already begun to lay out the argument that black internationalisms were shaped by the experience of migration on the one hand and exclusionary populism on the other. But the claim of mutual contingency also implies that restrictive laws did not simply fall upon Caribbeans like bolts from the blue, outcomes of distant and exogenous trends. If migrants had not made the choices they did, state policies would not have evolved as they did either.

If the migratory control systems that emerged included systematic illegalities and deniable violence—and they did—this resulted in part from on-the-fly adaptation by states to the strategies that migrants developed to duck state power and get on with their lives. While the documentary record is full of stories of state sanctions and abuse, the oral record is just as full of stories of evasion: brother after brother passing through Ellis Island under cover of a single Harlem birth certificate; patois-speaking higglers from northeast Venezuela returning from Trinidad with a month's worth of hats and lace tucked under their skirts. And the ports and towns of the circum-Caribbean today are full of third-generation immigrants who consider themselves first-class citizens of the republics of their birth. A reconstruction of the story of migration control in the Americas that takes their stories seriously is more complex and less linear, yet it may offer useful grounds for thinking about the future that past has bequeathed us.

CHAPTER OUTLINE

Chapter 1 lays out the broad contours of the circum-Caribbean migratory system from the second half of the nineteenth century through the first decades of the twentieth. Who went where when, how long did they stay, and where did they head next? How did Caribbeans mold kin practice and associational life to support these traveling lives? What kinds of labor relations did migrants face and how did these compare to the kinds of coercion and recompense native-born working people encountered? Finally, what considerations shaped states' actions toward migrants in this era? I analyze the dynamic triangle formed by sending state policies, receiving state policies, and migrants' maneuvers through the case study of eastern Venezuela, where Venezuelan authorities, British officials, and tens of thousands of Windward Islanders argued over what kinds of prerogatives dark-skinned imperial subjects could claim abroad. This chapter introduces the unusually disparate settings where the book will "take place" and establishes the range of state policies impacting mobility *before* the new international system coalesced in the interwar years.

The expansion of a Caribbean-wide labor market driven by cyclical foreign investment created a world of uncertain opportunity and uneven risk. Chapter 2 turns to the realm of popular culture, reconstructing the practices through which migrants sought spiritual succor and supernatural protection. When we attend to popular practice rather than elite rhetoric, connections between Anglophone, Francophone, and Hispanophone populations become clear. Outside observers saw only black people and black magic and asserted that "obeah," "voodoo," or "fetishism" demonstrated the grip of barbarous African tradition on Caribbean minds. In contrast, primary sources reveal a region-wide ritual complex equally engaged with the healing practices and supernatural techniques of the contemporaneous North Atlantic: patent medicines, tarot cards, mystic "Eastern" lore. Popular fears of malevolent assault captured the vulnerability of Caribbeans in the modern economy. Fusing Christian evangelism, Afro-descended cosmologies, and modern esoterica, Caribbean spiritual practice had a radical potential that radicals at the time could not see. On the contrary, like other middle-class British Caribbeans, black-internationalist leaders from Harlem socialists to Marcus

Garvey himself denounced the "superstition" and even the "African barbarism" of popular religiosity. But in the 1930s, hard-pressed believers would create racialized religious movements more radical than anything those leaders had conceived.

It was the cascade of antiblack mobility bars in the interwar era, I argue, that generated such race-conscious responses. Chapter 3 examines the anti-immigrant measures enacted in the 1920s and 1930s, using internal government correspondence from around the region to reconstruct the actual implementation of sometimes slippery laws. Hundreds of letters sent to U.S. consuls in Jamaica and Barbados by would-be migrants seeking desperately to reunite with relatives in the Unites States offer an unprecedented window onto the individual and societal impact of shifting regimes of mobility control. In the space of a single decade, the circum-Caribbean world of relatively free mobility was fractured by a series of new laws that made the right to enter, the right to work, and the right to stay contingent on the color of one's skin. Legal sanctions went hand in hand with extralegal pressures. Migrants paid bribes, stowed away, and risked physical violence as never before.

Circum-Caribbean governments were eager partners rather than grudging passengers on the anti–colored immigrant bandwagon. Latin American populists did not merely copy foreign models of xenophobic exclusion; they innovated new forms, including nationality quotas applied to specific workplaces rather than total entries as in the United States. Laws were not always obeyed and sometimes could be evaded; de facto and de jure rights and protections diverged. But across the board, the shifts made migrants more vulnerable to violence and more dependent on employers. Anti-immigrant violence was fiercest where anti-immigrant states had the least institutional power, a pattern that reached its tragic apogee in the massacre of tens of thousands of Haitians and Haitian-descended Dominicans in the border region of the Dominican Republic. Meanwhile, xenophobic populism elsewhere spurred nativist agitation in Jamaica and Trinidad, where Chinese and Syrian shopkeepers drew the ire of those with no power to exclude them.

This was the panorama against which black internationalisms flourished, as British Caribbeans abroad confronted new possibilities of "nations" as well as new powers of states. Chapter 4 argues that a vibrant circum-Caribbean/transatlantic black press played a crucial role in showing migrants these hemispheric, imperial, and global trends. Observing a world where the political stakes of race were higher than ever, migrants formulated new notions of race-based solidarity, with divergent diagnoses and consequences. Some understood race as a matter of biology and blood. Others argued that the international arrangement of political and economic power—and the shared oppression that it guaranteed—drove the common plight of people of color. The question of where the British Empire fit into that international arrangement seemed ever more pressing. In the early twentieth century, British Caribbeans abroad had both embraced empire (volunteering for duty and sending donations to help Britain in the Great War) and questioned it. As imperial abandonment of colored subjects' mobility claims became undeniable by the late 1920s, columnists and correspondents in rimland communities urgently sought new possibilities for sovereignty and for voice. In a world of racialized nation-states, what state spoke for the Negro race?

The black-run circum-Caribbean newspapers where these questions were asked were vitally important, but print culture was not the sole venue of black internationalism. Chapter 5 reconstructs the creation of new forms of music and dance by Caribbeans on the move, with special attention to Kingston, Harlem, Panama, and Port Limón, Costa Rica. Where the previous chapter traced developments in the print-based public sphere, here instead an equally transnational performative realm takes center stage. The protagonists of this chapter are younger, less respectable, sometimes downright vulgar—and having a blast. Out of a rich array of rhythms, conventions, and aesthetics, Caribbean migrants created sounds, steps, and social practices that were themselves then borrowed and reworked from site to site. Labels like jazz, mento, *son*, and calypso came to associate specific rhythms and styles with iconic locales: New Orleans, Jamaica, Cuba, and Trinidad. But when we use primary sources to reconstruct the range of music actually danced, we find not insular "traditions" but extraordinary variety. Jazz Age music was generated in dance halls where patrons and players alike brought an extraordinarily rich musical experience to bear. This was as true of the elegant "casinos" of Harlem as it was of the streets of Port Limón, and I present extensive evidence of the role of Caribbean entrepreneurs and audiences in shaping the swing music and dance for which renaissance Harlem became known.

Musicians' travels and fans' eager embrace of new music and moves generated a supranational black performative realm, an embodied rather than discursive space that functioned sometimes in tandem and sometimes in tension with the print-centered public sphere. In the United States, Jamaica, Panama, and Limón alike, the prominence of music and dance innovated by black musicians and black dancers sparked hot debate. How did the moral imperatives of race consciousness play out on the stage of popular culture? What was the relationship of Negro progress to modern pleasures? Facing external racism, community leaders preached self-help and respectability.

Middle-class editorialists decried any public practice that could be seen by outsiders as evidence of sexual looseness. But young people here as elsewhere made irresistible rhythms and flashy moves the core of an exuberant youth culture. Some community leaders denounced the "Regge Dances" young people organized in Port Limón as indecent displays of vulgar sexuality, the antithesis of racial uplift. But others saw local talent as part of a race-wide triumph that had Negro artists at the forefront of modern culture internationally.[16]

Even as the crisis of the circum-Caribbean migratory sphere drove new calls for worldwide racial solidarity, the straitened years of the 1930s brought harbingers of imagined communities far smaller and shrinking fast. Chapter 6 examines deportation and return migration from Panama, Venezuela, Cuba, and elsewhere and the consequences for island communities. Systematic hostility from abroad drew no coordinated response from the islands. On the contrary, lines of division became visible in new ways. British bureaucrats and island elites disavowed responsibility for West Indians born abroad to unmarried parents and banned entry by deportees born on other British islands, common imperial subjecthood be damned. Back on the islands, new leaders preached, and new followers took to the streets. Returnees would be key protagonists of social movements that rocked Jamaica, including the birth of Rastafarianism and the 1938 Labour Rebellion. In Barbados, Trinidad, and Guiana, labor leaders came disproportionately from among those born elsewhere. Change was afoot. But the very processes that undermined imperial rule narrowed the possibilities of postimperial belonging. The independent island states that emerged from decolonization would bear the imprint of the conflictive politics of color, culture, and class of the interwar Greater Caribbean.

SCHOLARLY CONTEXT

The academic dialogues with which this book engages fall into three broad clusters: writings on the development of black internationalism; histories of Caribbean migration; and research on the transformation of citizenship into social good and systematic barrier.

Over the past decade, the flourishing of African diaspora studies and the "transnational turn" in history and American studies have intersected to generate a wealth of interest in black internationalism. Scholars of literature have followed the lead of Paul Gilroy's *Black Atlantic* and analyzed the work of canonical black authors as reflecting specific moments of transatlantic or transhemispheric connection.[17] Others have drawn attention to the border crossings that shaped a wider array of less-well-known political thinkers, underlining the disproportionate impact of British Caribbean sojourners in this realm.[18]

This recent interest complements the existing tradition of scholarship on Marcus Garvey and the UNIA, while sitting in a slightly awkward position in regard to that scholarship and to Garvey himself. In part, this reflects the fact that Garvey was in his lifetime a deeply polarizing figure, nowhere more so than among leading black internationalists. By the definitions sketched above, Garvey was both a black nationalist and a black internationalist. But he differed from his contemporaries, liberal integrationists and radical anti-capitalists alike. He was not interested in working for change within the U.S. political system (although after his deportation in 1927, he would form a political party in Jamaica and work from that base). He also rejected the class-based international alliances that his black-internationalist radical peers pursued.[19] While Garvey's analyses of racism and imperialism could have provided common ground with other progressive leaders of color, in practice, one after another ended up alienated from the man and his plans.

Garvey's disputes meant that from the start, assessments of his legacy were mixed, even among those who shared his antiracist agenda. Their contemporary writings judged Garvey a demagogue whose important message to the masses was doomed by his personal failings.[20] Not until the 1960s and 1970s would a new generation of scholars—less hostile to separatist black nationalisms and seeking historical antecedents for the black internationalisms once again under way—reassess Garvey and Garveyism with more sympathetic eyes.[21] Garvey became an icon of early twentieth-century black nationalism and internationalism alike. Ironically, then, the past decade's renewed interest in early twentieth-century black internationalism has brought new and sympathetic attention to some of Garvey's fiercest critics, even as it has also enhanced interest in Garveyism itself.

Most recently, research has focused on grassroots Garveyism, tracing the origins and consequences of popular involvement in the UNIA at different sites as distinct from the rise and fall of Garvey himself.[22] Nowhere was grassroots Garveyism stronger than in the circum-Caribbean migratory sphere. Over half of the 271 UNIA branches located outside the United States were in just four countries: Cuba, Panama, Trinidad, and Costa Rica, precisely the four largest destinations for British Caribbean emigrants in that era.[23] Largest destinations, that is, other than the United States, and there too the immigrant presence in the UNIA was crucial. A recent estimate suggests that in the

UNIA's formative years in New York, two-thirds of male activists and two-fifths of female activists were British Caribbean immigrants.[24]

Thus the 2011 publication of the first volume in the Caribbean series of *The Marcus Garvey and Universal Negro Improvement Association Papers* is especially welcome. The overall project of which this volume forms a part has been an extraordinary endeavor, led by general editor Robert Hill and channeling four decades of investigation, erudition, and hard-won funding into a dozen volumes of meticulously annotated documents. The 800 pages of primary sources in the most recent volume reveal the myriad roles Garveyism came to play in the Greater Caribbean, fueled by the passionate dedication of tens of thousands of men and women. It was "a West Indian movement of diasporic consciousness; a Caribbean-wide nationalist movement; a redemptive social movement; a fraternal movement and friendly society; a movement aimed at moral reformation; a racial-irredentist movement; and an African American protest movement against racial injustice in America—all of them, interacting simultaneously and sometimes in dizzying combination."[25]

Precisely because others are studying Garvey and Garveyism wisely and well, I have directed the bulk of my research elsewhere, while nevertheless capturing, I hope, the pervasive integration of Garveyism into the popular cultures and communication networks that I profile. As the introduction to the above volume argues, the UNIA was central to British Caribbean overseas communities—and vice versa: "In coming to think of and understand themselves as a group that was culturally and ethnically distinct from the wider social milieu, diasporic West Indians gravitated to the UNIA as a major vehicle of group expression. Without the emigrant base, the Garvey moment would never have arisen and flourished to the extent that it did."[26] And yet despite this centrality, or perhaps because of it, Garveyites in British Caribbean communities could be as polarizing as Garvey himself. On the need for black unity in the face of white racism, there was strong agreement; on strategies and tactics, there was none. Just tracing grassroots debates over Garveyism at the sites I explore would be a book in itself, but this is not that book.

Rather, the present book seeks to contribute to the broadest understanding of black internationalisms as encompassing a multitude of ways of analyzing the world and reaching out in response: explicitly political movements and apparently apolitical music and dance, rational print debate and apparently irrational religious visions. Garveyism, for all its breadth and variety, was only one part of that much broader whole.

Next, the present volume seeks to add to a growing body of research on intraregional migration, which argues for placing the marginal spaces and margin-crossing people of the Caribbean at the center of its story. Region-wide analyses of British Caribbean migration began being written at the end of the period we are studying, based on colonial demographic data, entry and exit records, and island laws and debates.[27] Recent decades have seen these complemented by a wide array of case studies reflecting in-depth research in receiving-society archives and, in some cases, oral history, including works on Panama,[28] Costa Rica,[29] points northward in Central America,[30] Cuba,[31] and New York.[32] This book uses those valuable monographs alongside fifteen years of original research in archives across the region to reconstruct the multisited circuits of the eastern and western Caribbean, tracking the expansion and contraction of flows whose drivers were never limited to a single here and there. Primary research has been particularly crucial for the case of Venezuela. Mass British West Indian migration to Venezuela predated that to any of the western and northern destinations listed above and outnumbered all of them until U.S. Panama Canal recruitment began in 1903. Yet not a single monograph in any language focuses on British West Indian migration to Venezuela per se.[33] Therefore, I synthesize here research at the Archivo General de la Nación and the Archivo del Ministerio de Relaciones Exteriores (Caracas), the Archivo Histórico de Guayana (Ciudad Bolivar), and the Archivo del Ejecutivo del Estado de Sucre (Cumaná) in order to sketch the broad contours of Caribbean migration to Venezuela.

All of the above monographs offer insights into the national impact of Caribbean immigration and the community formation that followed. Recent collective efforts have pushed even further, attempting region-wide panoramas of the social, cultural, and intellectual formations that circum-Caribbean migration wrought. Such works see "the dexterity, versatility, and matter-of-factness with which Caribbean peoples put their border savvy to work" as fundamental to "historical knowledge and cultural practice" in the region.[34] I hope my reconstruction of popular cultures and political imaginaries at the moment when borders were remade helps to historicize this crucial insight. The contours and consequences of Caribbean border savvy have changed over time in fundamental ways, in response to changes in the nature of borders themselves.

Finally, this story from the mobile peripheries speaks to a scholarship born and raised in the North Atlantic core: the dialogue among sociologists, historians, and political theorists over the evolution of citizenship. In the past decade, scholars of immigration history, labor history, and state formation converged in reexamining the mid-twentieth-century transformations each of their fields had marked. They discovered that the separate processes were inextricably linked. Over the nineteenth and twentieth centuries, the duties that states shouldered toward their populaces shifted, as did the means of identifying those who belonged and keeping out those who did not. The new formulations of citizens' entitlements reflected local struggles, labor struggles in particular, but were also shaped by an emerging international system and the efforts of political elites to position themselves within it.

The story of the making of outsiders is thus also the story of the making of insiders and of the naturalization of the barriers—ideological, institutional, physical—between them. Early research exploring these processes in Western Europe was followed by monographs that tracked the shifting legalities of access to citizenship in the United States.[35] Other studies have traced the making of citizenship's boundaries in a waning empire rather than rising republics, exploring migration restriction and political belonging in the British dominions in the first half of the twentieth century and in Great Britain after World War II.[36] Most recently, scholars have turned to new sources and methods to illuminate the international connections that shaped the development of regimes of borders and rights.[37]

The stakes of understanding are high. Current events push onto front pages the sometimes-tragic systematic illegalities of border control and reveal the anger fueled by systems that deny longtime residents a route to rights. How do citizens' security and the precarity of "guest workers" relate?[38] And how does the trajectory of citizenship in colonial metropoles relate to the paths of political and civil rights in the polities that decolonization created? I hope the present volume can add to these discussions, in part by stretching our scope of observation beyond the U.S.–Western Europe–"white dominion" nexus. Finally, this study aims to bring the new scholarship on boundaries and rights into dialogue with old and new scholarship on the comparative dimensions of race in the Americas. In interwar Latin America, concern over the impact of African ancestry could drive public-health investment, labor laws aiding populations of color, denunciations of U.S. imperialism, and antiblack immigration bans—all by the same regime. The nuanced lines of Latin America's "racial democracies" could look stark indeed when viewed by "aliens" of color. In turn, the supposedly clear-cut U.S. structure of race and rights confronted black migrants with many shades of gray.

A NOTE ON TERMINOLOGY

My use of the term "black" throughout this book is anachronistic. In the years under study, this label sounded patronizing at best, aggressively insulting at worst. "There is no greater insult among Aframericans than calling a black person black," wrote Jamaica-born Claude McKay in 1932. "That is never done. In Aframerican literature, perhaps, but never in social life. A black person may be called 'nigger' as a joke in Aframerica, but never 'black,' which is considered a term of reproach in the mouths of colored people quite as contemptuous as 'nigger' in the mouths of whites."[39] The term embraced by most English speakers of African ancestry in the era that I study was "Negro." Yet modern readers will not hear in those syllables the dignity and pride with which they were uttered at that time. The term "coloured" was also sometimes used, with the complication that in some places, particularly Jamaica, "coloured" designated mixed ancestry and light skin in contradistinction to the darker majority. At times in the pages that follow, I will use terms such as Afro-descended, Afro-Caribbean, or Afro–North American. But I hesitate to do so routinely because it seems that would risk naturalizing a paradigm of group commonality anchored in shared continental—"African"—ancestry. As we will see, some Afro-descended activists in this era embraced exactly that paradigm. But not everyone did. Other formulations emphasized instead the common experience of racist discrimination as central to the forging of "Our People." Under the circumstances, when writing about people who would have called themselves Negro, I will generally describe them as "black."

Meanwhile, another categorical term in routine use at the time was "British West Indian." This phrase, too, sounds ideologically suspect to modern ears, harking as it does to an imperial geography that classed regions by their cardinal direction from Europe: East Indies that way, West Indies there. Though conscious of that legacy, I use the term here. It was indeed shared imperial rule that united British West Indians, even as island of origin, language, genealogy, class, or color might divide them. How this shared imperial rule mattered to them and others, and how that changed over time, are empirical questions that I attempt to answer in the pages that follow.

One   Migrants' Routes, Ties, and Role in Empire, 1850s–1920s

If you were leaving your home on an eastern Caribbean island in the 1870s or 1880s, you were probably heading south. Perhaps you boarded an inter-colonial steamer in Bridgetown, your passage buying you the right to jostle for space on the open forward deck, amid scores of men and women from Martinique off to seek work at the gold mines of Venezuela. If a storm came up, as it often did, daybreak would find all of you unpacking boxes and bundles, hanging carefully stitched skirts and elegant hats out to dry before landfall in St. Vincent. Or perhaps you boarded the Royal Mail packet in St. George's, Grenada, looking up once more at the town layered in the curve of the volcanic crater, "rows of red-tiled roofs gleaming in the sun one above the other, nodding palms and flowering trees between them." By afternoon you would reach the Gulf of Paria. The dark sierras of Venezuela spread to the right, the green mountains of Trinidad to the left. The rocky cliffs of the Dragos islets loom above on either side as your ship passes through to the gulf.[1]

Then days or a week in Port of Spain, waiting for a returning cattle boat on which to purchase passage across the Gulf of Paria and up the muddy brown current of the mighty Orinoco River. Paddle-wheel riverboats claim the main channel; dugout canoes hug the mangrove-lined banks. Patois and English and Spanish sound around you on deck. In three days, Ciudad Bolivar appears, two-story commercial houses lining the riverfront, customs agents and porters (some from your very island) bustling to and fro. You might find room in a lodging house run by "a good old Barbadoes woman," as one Englishman did in 1869. He was surprised by the conversations he heard, though you would not have been. Mother Saidy's "was a sort of reunion for all the niggers from the British West India Islands," he wrote, "where they met to discuss affairs private and political. It was most amusing to see what pride they took in being British subjects, and the contempt in which they held their dark brothers of the Main" (that is, Venezuela).[2] To this English-man, the political opinions of black Caribbeans abroad seemed "amusing," no more. But sojourners' allegiance mattered in this era, and not only to sojourn-ers themselves.

This chapter introduces the places that came to form part of the circum-Caribbean migratory sphere and the people who made it so. Histories of receiving-society enterprises that employed British Caribbeans in this era routinely refer to "imported Jamaican workers." But to think of Caribbean sojourners as commodities imported by employers is inaccurate. The number of British Caribbeans traveling to any given destination under contract was always smaller than the number who made the trip at their own expense and under their own authority. Certainly, they went where employers wanted them. Labor-market disparities drove emigration: scarce options here, higher wages there. But migrants' economic decision-making reflected an evolving social panorama shaped by those who went before. Transnational networks of kith and kin determined which opportunities would-be migrants heard about, what resources they could mobilize to get there, and who they could fall back on if plans went awry. Migration remade the human geography of the nineteenth-century Greater Caribbean because migrants made it so.

The mobile world that reached its zenith in the early 1920s had its origins three generations before, at the end of slavery. As Caribbean freedpeople and their children sought opportunity and autonomy, two fundamental strategies emerged to lessen dependence on the plantations where they or their parents had labored as slaves: people headed either into the hills or out to sea. Efforts in the first direction created what later scholars tagged "reconstituted peasantries," as hundreds of thousands of Afro-Caribbeans turned to growing provisions and export crops (cocoa, bananas) on land they purchased, inherited, or held in common with extended family. The seaborne strategy began with small-scale and seasonal movement between adjacent islands or nearby territories. Separate migratory circuits developed in the eastern and western Caribbean, linking Barbados, Trinidad, Guiana, Venezuela, and the Windward Islands in the east and Jamaica and the rimlands of Central America and Colombia in the west.

As U.S. investment in infrastructure and export agriculture surged at the end of the century, movement intensified. Work on the Panama Canal under U.S. government control brought eastern and western circuits together for the first time: scores of thousands of Barbadians joined thousands of "small islanders" and over 100,000 Jamaicans who traveled to or through the isthmian port of Colón. Cuba's interwar sugar boom created another wave of opportunity, drawing 150,000 or more British West Indians, mostly from the western Caribbean. The sugar plantations of the Dominican Republic drew eastern Caribbean migrants in a parallel process. Meanwhile, the expanding economies of the southeastern Caribbean set hundreds of thousands of migrants in motion—some from far away, like the many scores of thousands of South Asians who reached Trinidad and Guiana from British India under contracts of indenture; others from nearby, like the scores of thousands of Windward Islanders who traveled to and through Trinidad and Venezuela in the same years.

Relying on word of mouth, mails, money orders, and cheap deck passage, migrants kept in touch. In addition to kin ties, British Caribbeans created a rich associational life, founding churches, lodges, and mutual aid societies with branches across the region. Did they find the prosperity they sought? Migrants encountered or created a huge range of work relations. The degree of coercion they faced varied enormously, determined less by which nation they were in than by where they were within it. Port cities, squatter hinterlands, plantation zones, and jungle camps each offered a characteristic mix of opportunities and pressures. In order to understand why, we must look at the intersection of local politics and geopolitics, asking what laws and what logic governed sending- and receiving-state attitudes to the Afro-Caribbeans crossing their borders. Subsequent chapters will argue that interwar political shifts ruptured the circum-Caribbean migratory sphere, with intensely generative consequences. This chapter lays out what the "before" had come to look like, so that you will understand just how different the "after" was.

THE MAKING OF A MOBILE WORLD: CIRCUM-CARIBBEAN MIGRATION FROM THE MID-NINETEENTH CENTURY TO THE EARLY 1920S

The complexities of nineteenth-century migrations are well illustrated by the range of routes into and out of Venezuela, the Spanish-speaking nation that received more British West Indian immigrants than any other until construction of the Panama Canal under U.S. sponsorship began in 1904. In the Windward Islands and adjacent continental rimlands, the eighteenth century had seen borders move across people even more often than people had moved across borders. Imperial possession of these territories shifted back and forth, as France, Spain, Holland, and Great Britain vied for position on both the European continent and the Caribbean Sea. Only Barbados, with its flourishing sugar plantations well garrisoned, remained British throughout. Struggles against slavery—and the empires' halting efforts to abolish or reimpose it—sent fugitive slaves or fearful slave owners across imperial borders as well. By the 1820s, Guadeloupe and Martinique were consolidated as French possessions; the other Windwards (Dominica, St. Lucia, St. Vincent, and Grenada), Trinidad, and Guiana (including Demerara, Berbice, and Essequibo) as British colonies; and the continental territory west of Guiana as the now-independent Republic of Venezuela. Yet commercial circuits and family networks continued to cut across these nominal boundaries, and French patois-speaking Caribbeans of African ancestry moved with ease between Venezuela's northeast coast and the nearby islands. The coastal ports of Cumaná, Carúpano, and Güiria were all far easier to reach from Port of Spain than from Caracas, as was Ciudad Bolivar, the Orinoco River port through which all exports from Venezuela's western Andes, central plains, and southern jungles traveled to the Atlantic.[3]

Gold was discovered in the sparsely settled lands south of the Orinoco delta in 1849, the very year of the better-known California strike. Almost all of the eager prospectors and would-be entrepreneurs drawn to the strike's site, El Callao, were British West Indians. Some traveled overland from Guiana, others by sail from Grenada, St. Vincent, and the other Windward Islands to Port of Spain and then southward by steamer or sloop. By the 1890s, it was estimated that more than 7,000 Dominicans resided in Venezuela, while many more had gone and returned—this out of a total island population that remained under 27,000 in 1891.[4] As gold mining and rubber tapping boomed and contracted in turn, the British Caribbean population in El Callao and points south and west topped 5,000, creating constant demand for provisions and supplies. British West Indian settlers around Ciudad Bolivar, similarly estimated at over 5,000 souls at the end of the nineteenth century, grew foodstuffs, raised mules, and profitably provisioned the camps to the south.[5]

In the same years, cocoa farming for export boomed on the Paria Peninsula to the north, pulling entrepreneurs and traders from locations as far afield as Corsica, Lebanon, and Spain. Carúpano, center of the cocoa trade, flourished. The first cable line between Europe and South America was anchored here in 1877 so that local buyers could adjust prices in line with the latest European market news. Those Paria residents who had arrived years before from nearby islands had often managed by the late nineteenth century to acquire smallholdings of their own and gain some prosperity as independent cultivators. Later arrivals more often found work as laborers on plantations owned by Corsican or Venezuelan merchants. Most of these British islanders, whether newly arrived or long resident, prosperous or poor, were Afro-descendant, patois-speaking men. In the same years, some 1,000 island-born women and men from Guadeloupe, Martinique, and the British Windwards labored as servants and artisans in Venezuela's capital, Caracas.[6]

Similar patterns of movement shaped the western fringes of Britain's Caribbean claims. Travel between Jamaica and Central America's Caribbean coast, long linked by the circulation of traders, turtlemen, and fugitives,

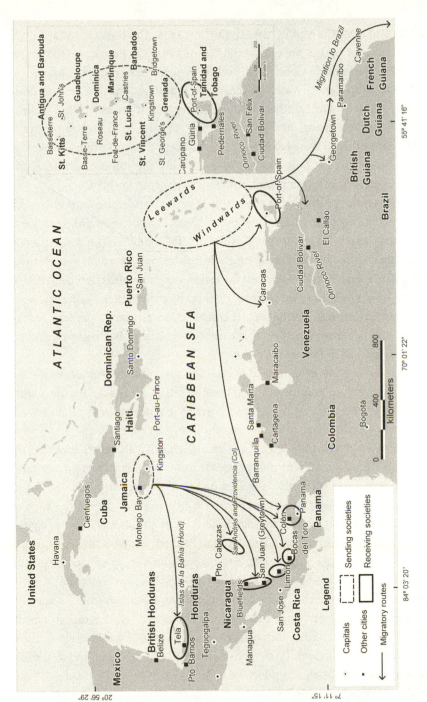

British Caribbean Migration, 1870s–1900s

accelerated after the end of slavery in the 1830s. The building of a railway across Panama by U.S. investors in 1850 relied upon Jamaican laborers, as did the Ferrocarril de Costa Rica, built from Port Limón up to Costa Rica's coffee-growing Central Valley in the 1870s. Abortive French efforts to build a canal across Panama in the 1880s drew scores of thousands from Jamaica to work on the diggings and scores of thousands more to seek opportunity in the boomtown service economy canal workers' demand drove.[7] Linked by bonds of empire and language to those running the show, Martinique and Guadeloupe, too, sent significant numbers to Panama in this era.

But it was not until canal construction resumed, under the aegis of the U.S. government, after 1903 that eastern Caribbean islands were linked to western Caribbean destinations in a significant way. The U.S. Canal Commission established its recruiting headquarters in Bridgetown in 1905. Some 20,000 Barbadian men left under contract for Panama over the next decade. Another 25,000 Bajans headed to the isthmus on their own dime in the same era, seeking their fortune outside the formal construction economy; perhaps half of these latter were women. Overall, nearly one-fourth of Barbados's working-age men worked in Panama in this era.[8]

Even during the exodus to Panama, the long-standing pattern of Barbadian emigration southward to Trinidad continued apace. The durability of highly specific migratory circuits is striking and utterly typical of what migration scholars have found for other places and times. People traveled to places where people they knew had already gone. In the years that St. Vincent and Grenada had sent many thousands to Venezuela, similar numbers of Barbadians had left instead for Trinidad (and smaller numbers for British Guiana and Brazil)—perhaps some 20,000 in the 1860s alone. The turn of the century found 14,000 Barbadians resident in and around Port of Spain; the population of Barbados's own capital, Bridgetown, was under 13,000 at the time.[9] Booming commerce to and through Port of Spain carried steady numbers of interisland hucksters and job seekers along on boats like the fifty-four-ton *Wild Rover*, which arrived from Bridgetown in November 1904 with a large cargo and forty-three passengers "packed like red herrings in a box." While many traveled back and forth over the course of a week, or a month, or a year, some stayed. Overall, in the two generations leading up to 1911, some 65,000 Windward Islanders relocated to Trinidad.[10]

Just as Port of Spain served as transport hub and commercial center for the eastern Caribbean, Kingston and Colón did so in the west. Already by 1908, four different steamship lines used Kingston as the nexus for routes linking northern Venezuelan, Colombian, and Central American ports to New York,

TABLE 1 Total Population of British Caribbean Colonies, 1891–1946

	1891	1911	1921	1936*	1946
Jamaica	639,491	831,383	858,118	1,139,000	1,321,054
Trinidad	218,381	333,552	365,913	448,000	557,970
British Guiana	270,865	289,140	288,541	333,000	359,379
Barbados	182,867	172,337	156,774	188,000	192,800
Windward Islands				210,000	
Dominica	26,841	33,863	37,059		47,624
Grenada	53,209	66,750	66,302		72,387
St. Lucia	42,220	48,637	51,505		70,113
St. Vincent	41,054	41,877	44,447		61,647
Leeward Islands				140,000	
Antigua	36,819	32,269	29,767		41,757
Montserrat	11,762	12,196	12,120		14,333
St. Kitts–Nevis	47,662	43,303	38,214		46,243
Virgin Islands	4,639	5,562	5,082		6,505
British Honduras	31,471	40,458	45,317	56,000	59,220

*Estimates from Malcolm J. Proudfoot, *Population Movements in the Caribbean* (Caribbean Commission Central Secretariat: Port of Spain, Trinidad, 1950), 20

Sources: George W. Roberts, *The Population of Jamaica* (Cambridge, UK: Conservation Foundation at the University Press, 1957), 330–31; Proudfoot, *Population Movements in the Caribbean*, 20.

Liverpool, Bristol, Havre, and Hamburg.[11] The growth of the banana trade reinforced these connections and made two U.S. ports—New Orleans and New York—integral to western Caribbean circuits. The Boston Fruit Company exported bananas to Boston and New York from Jamaica, Cuba, and Santo Domingo; Minor Keith supplied the same cities from Limón, Bocas del Toro, and northern Colombia; and Sam Zemurray and the Vacarro Bros. shipped to New Orleans from Honduras, Nicaragua, and Guatemala. The first two combined to form the United Fruit Company in 1898 and absorbed the latter in 1929. Not only did the banana business employ scores of thousands of workers on plantations, rail lines, and docks, but the "Great White Fleet" that cycled fruit to northern consumers ensured continuous service between ports for first-class passengers and cut-rate "deckers" alike. One cluster of routes ran from Panama northward along the Central American coast to

New Orleans and back via Havana; another ran from Santa Marta to Colón to Kingston and Port Antonio to New York, and back via Santiago de Cuba or Haiti.[12]

Thus sitting at the crossroads of the Caribbean, Jamaica supplied the great bulk of English-speaking black migrants to Central America and Cuba, and roughly half of those to the United States as well. Demographers estimate that Jamaica saw a net loss of 146,000 people to emigration in the last two decades of the nineteenth century and first two decades of the twentieth century. The total number of Jamaicans migrating was far greater, since seasonal and short-term migrants are not counted in net figures.[13]

As Panama Canal construction drew to a close and war in Europe sent sugar prices sky-high, migrant streams shifted northward to the Greater Antilles. The cane harvests of eastern Cuba became a bonanza for laborers from around the region. Thousands of Caribbean immigrants left jobless in Panama boarded steamers bound for Cuba.[14] Over 1,000 of the more than 7,000 British West Indians arriving in Cuba in 1916 reported that their last place of residence had not been their country of birth; in 1917 more than a quarter of the nearly 8,000 arrivals said the same.[15] Movement from Jamaica directly to Havana and Santiago de Cuba was even more intense than that from the rimlands. Jamaican officials recorded 60,000 departures for Cuba between 1919 and 1921 (coming from a total Jamaican population of under 860,000). Even after sugar prices tumbled from their vertiginous heights in that latter year, Cuba continued to attract thousands of Jamaicans each harvest, alongside smaller but growing numbers from Britain's eastern Caribbean colonies. Meanwhile, nearly 36,000 Haitians reached Cuba in 1920 alone, and migrants from Haiti would outnumber incoming British Caribbeans by at least 50 percent every year for the following decade.[16]

Both Jamaica and Barbados had sent small numbers of migrants north to Boston and New York from the 1870s onward, creating significant enclaves in each city by the turn of the century. As Panama Canal construction cycled Yankee dollars and ships through the Caribbean in unprecedented numbers, these small connections became large-scale migratory flows. The circuits then carried ever greater numbers northward as the Panama Canal workforce was demobilized beginning in 1913. Some 7,000 black immigrants to the United States in the first three decades of the twentieth century listed Central America as their last region of residence. The number of British West Indians who arrived after time spent in Cuba was even greater. In all, black immigration from the Caribbean to the United States averaged 3,500 per year from 1903 to 1913 and climbed to 5,000 per year from 1914 to 1923, dipping

TABLE 2 Jamaican Population and Estimated Net Emigration, 1881–1921

	Island Population at Start of Period	Net Emigration to Panama	Net Emigration to Costa Rica and Others	Net Emigration to Cuba	Net Emigration to United States	Net Emigration: All Areas
1881–1891	581,000	17,000				
1891–1901	639,000					
1901–1911	N/A	26,000[b]	10,000[a]		16,000[a]	69,000[a]
1911–1921	831,000	2,000	23,000	22,000	30,000	77,000

[a] Figure covers 1881–1911

[b] Figure covers 1891–1911

Source: George W. Roberts, *The Population of Jamaica* (Cambridge, UK: Conservation Foundation at the University Press, 1957), 51, 139.

during the peak harvest years of the Cuban sugar boom and rising when opportunities in Cuba shrank.[17]

Those arriving were men like Sam Burke, who left Barbados to cut cane in Cuba and then stowed away on a sugar freighter bound for the Domino refinery in Brooklyn in 1921. Within a few years, he had met and married young Bajan Adriana Carlyle, whose own passage to New York to live with her brother Winston had been paid for with a second brother's earnings in Panama. Sam and Adriana named their daughters Anita and Valenza Pauline to remind Sam of the Cuban Spanish he loved to hear, and they took in boarders—Clarice and Josephine, arrived from Barbados in 1923—to make ends meet. "White people like peas, and not one of them speaking the Queen's English!" thought Adriana upon arrival, yet the brownstone Brooklyn world she and Sam and thousands like them created was intensely Barbadian, and therefore tightly tied as well to Trinidad, Cuba, and Panama. (Valenza Pauline would grow up to chronicle that world, writing under her married name, Paule Marshall.)[18]

One can track the shifting migratory circuits through the shifting origins of remittances sent home. In 1911 the total value of postal orders reaching Barbados from Panama was over three times that of orders from the United States. In 1916 money arriving from the United States outpaced that from Panama for the first time. By 1919 the total remitted from the United States was four and a half times larger than it had been in 1911, while the total

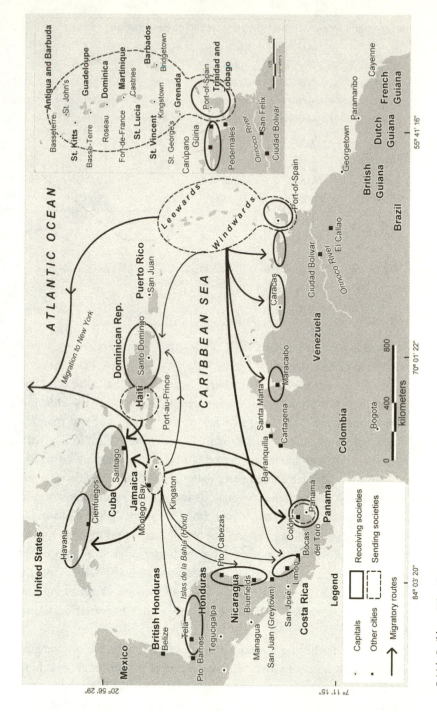

British Caribbean Migration, 1903–1924

from Panama was one-fourth what it had been in that year.[19] Emigration had become fundamental to Barbados's economy and demography alike. Despite declining death rates, the island population fell by 6 percent from 1891 to 1911 and a full 9 percent in the single decade from 1911 to 1921.[20]

In the southeast Caribbean, British rather than U.S. investment drove growth. Trinidad's more than 120,000 East Indians (by 1921, less than a third of them foreign-born and the rest locally born to immigrant parents or grandparents) were the mainstay of sugar plantations.[21] Similar numbers of East Indian immigrants and their descendants resided in British Guiana, farming rice or laboring in cane fields. New export enterprises depended on interisland circuits of labor supply. By 1921 the population of Trinidad included 17,000 Barbadians, 13,000 Grenadians, 10,000 Vincentians, and 7,000 other "small islanders"; British Guiana was home to 10,000 migrants from the same range of nearby origins.[22] Oil production began in Trinidad near the La Brea "pitch lake" in the first years of the twentieth century. By the 1920s, more than 10,000 Trinidadians and Windward Islanders labored on Trinidad's southern oil fields.

A receiving society for small islanders and South Asians, Trinidad was increasingly also itself a sending society vis-à-vis the Spanish republic only seven miles to the west. The depleted gold veins around El Callao now saw only small-scale work with pick and shovel, the steam-driven pumps that had run continuously in the 1870s and 1880s silently rusting nearby. But cocoa farms large and small on the Paria Peninsula still prospered. British Caribbeans still found work, too, as boatmen along the Orinoco, as stevedores on the docks of La Guaira, and as servants and chauffeurs in the burgeoning capital, Caracas.[23] Between 1914 and 1917, U.S. and British companies found major oil fields south of Paria and around Lake Maracaibo in the west, triggering a maelstrom of camp construction that would provide employ for thousands more British Caribbeans (and hundreds from the French and Dutch islands) by the mid-1920s.[24]

Migration to the United States was accelerating as well. In the United States as a whole in 1920, there were 50,000 Afro-Caribbean immigrants, living alongside some 55,000 of their U.S.-born children; a decade later, there were 72,000, with 83,000 U.S.-born children.[25] By 1930 one-third of the black populations of Manhattan (fundamentally, Harlem), Brooklyn, and Boston and two-fifths of those of Cambridge and Miami were made up of foreign-born blacks and their children.[26]

Where did they hail from? By far the largest numbers came from Barbados and Jamaica, with Bajans slightly outnumbering Jamaicans in both New

York and Boston—striking figures, given that Barbados's island population was one-sixth that of Jamaica in these years.[27] (A Barbadian paper estimated in 1925 that the island "receives 50 per cent more parcels from the USA than any other West Indian colony," and they may not have been far off.)[28] The third-largest group hailed from the Virgin Islands (purchased from Denmark in 1917, their residents granted U.S. citizenship in 1927). Trinidadians, Grenadians, Guianese, and Panama-born British Caribbeans appear in roughly equal numbers, each group perhaps one-sixth the size of either the Jamaican or Barbadian contingent. Leeward Island emigrants were few compared to the size of Manhattan but massive as a proportion of their sending societies: Antigua's population dropped by 8 percent between the 1911 and 1921 censuses, and St. Kitts-Nevis's by 12 percent.[29] The distinct western and eastern Caribbean migratory circuits remained visible in New York. Some five-sixths of Jamaicans in New York lived in Harlem, but Barbadians split evenly between Harlem and Brooklyn, and Trinidadian patterns hovered between the two.[30]

Jamaica-born, New York–based journalist W. A. Domingo described Caribbean migrants there in 1925 as a "dusky tribe of destiny seekers . . . eyes filled with visions of their heritage—palm fringed sea shores, murmuring streams, luxuriant hills and vales" who "bring with them vestiges of their folk life—their lean, sunburnt faces, their quiet, halting speech . . . their light, loose-fitting clothes of ancient cut telling the story of a dogged, romantic pilgrimage to the El Dorado of their dreams."[31] What Domingo's romanticized portrait of rural pilgrims in Gotham risks obscuring is the modernity and cosmopolitanness of the world from which British Caribbeans came. These "destiny seekers" were former canal workers who had danced the tango in the polyglot dancehalls of Colón and Havana; returning veterans of the British West Indies Regiment, whose experiences in the Great War had made their second-class status within empire painfully clear; and other men and women making their first voyage "to foreign" but whose dreams—and demands— had been shaped by the stories such sojourners told.

SENDING MONEY, STRETCHING TIES: CREATING A CONNECTED CARIBBEAN

In large part, it was island elites' unwillingness to adjust to free labor—to offer workers enough wages to persuade them to work; to bargain rather than impose terms of housing or days—that pushed Caribbean working people abroad. But how free were the labor relations they encountered when they did so? There is no single answer. Not only did the power exerted by employers vary, but whether migrants even *had* an employer varied. Some British Caribbeans abroad did work for wages, whether in cane fields or oil fields, as a stevedore in Colón or a doorman in Manhattan. Others carved out small farms of their own along the coasts of Honduras, Nicaragua, Panama, Colombia, or Venezuela; others worked as artisans or entrepreneurs. Female migrants overwhelmingly concentrated in this last category, taking in laundry, selling savories and sweets, running boardinghouses or brothels. And even if we look only at work for wages—something most every man traveling circum-Caribbean circuits did at some point in his life—we see great variation.

Those workers who left home under contract were pledged to stay where sent until the price of passage was repaid. This was true for South Asians reaching Trinidad and Guiana under contracts of indenture, as it was for Jamaicans hired to labor on the Ecuadoran railroad and Barbadians contracted by the U.S. government for Panama. In all of these cases, accusations by workers that they were treated as slaves were not uncommon. Conditions at the destination tended to be vastly worse than recruiting agents had promised—the labor heavier, the hours longer, the food meager, and the wages scant once debts were deducted. Particularly in those cases where the destination was a distant railway camp or plantation frontier and employers controlled all transport in and out, "free" labor might be only nominally free.

Such circumstances were most common in the late nineteenth century, when much labor demand was for infrastructure projects cutting across sparsely settled terrain, and when arriving migrants were the first of their kind to reach each destination; they had no welcoming community of compatriots awaiting them. Even after circum-Caribbean circuits swelled and networks of knowledge and support expanded, for those laboring for the sole employer in an inaccessible spot, coercive debt peonage remained common. One sees the pattern in the 1916 case of two brothers who fled from the mangrove camps on the Orinoco delta, where a U.S. concessionaire manufactured charcoal from harvested wood. The brothers told authorities at Carúpano that they had been cheated of wages and then beaten and had only barely escaped in a raft while overseers fired at them from the shore. Meanwhile, the company had telegraphed the same authorities to report that two insubordinate *negros* had tried to incite their fellow workers to revolt and then run off, and that the fugitives should be returned in chains to finish working off their debts. Each side, workers and employers, seemed quite confident authorities would agree that they were the aggrieved party.[32] In this case, no record exists of who guessed right. But as late as 1928, Venezuelan rural police were reminding contractors who held concessions for rubber extraction in the jungles west of El Callao to register the names of their workers at the start of each season, with the warning that if the paperwork was not filed in advance, "no request that workers be tracked down or obliged to work" would be heeded.[33] The odds that authorities in Carúpano sided with the mangrove workers over their bosses seem low.

Note, though, that none of this depended on workers' birthplace, skin color, or citizenship. Local Spanish-speaking working people faced debt peonage and employer abuses in all of these receiving societies as well. Indeed, by the 1920s most, though not all, of the crews collecting rubber and digging gold near El Callao were made up of Spanish-speaking Venezuelan nationals. For Spanish American citizens as for British Caribbean sojourners, travel to a remote work site was a gamble, a bet that wages promised would actually be paid and that exploitation would be bearable. The presence of competing employers, a nearby frontier offering a subsistence alternative, networks of support made up of friends or family from home: each of these raised the odds that workers might over the course of a laboring life come out a little ahead. To the extent that British West Indians in the Spanish-speaking circum-Caribbean could begin to rely on family lending rather than employer advances to pay for travel, could build communities in ports or railroad-line towns with easy access to cheap tickets out, and could access transnational social networks that opened doors elsewhere if local conditions got rough, they could be *better* off, on average, than the native-born workers around them—and sometimes they were.

At the individual level, there were successes and dashed hopes and everything in between, but overall the earnings of three generations of Caribbean men and women abroad made possible a slow expansion of opportunity for British Caribbean working people as a whole. And it did so in the teeth of island elites whose disinclination to raise wages or invest in public welfare remained unaltered. The Jamaican villages of Claude McKay's childhood at the start of the twentieth century were home to men like Mr. Andry, who had "pushed up out of the black-and-brown peasant people and emigrated to Central America as a barelegged lad" on the pence he earned catching mongooses for bounty and returned after thirty years to buy the best farmland in the district; former schoolteacher Jabez Fearon, who returned from Panama "a changed man after being so long free from semi-religious duties, a little dapper with a gait the islanders called 'the Yankee strut'"; "the dwarfish baker Patton," who beat all comers at wrestling "with the jiu-jitsu tricks he brought back from Colón"; and "shiny black Johnny Cross, who had arrived from Panama with eye-catching American-style suits and a gold watch and chains and rings of Spanish gold."[34]

Island cities, like villages, were transformed by migration. A clergyman visiting Port of Spain from Barbados in 1904 found himself in a cosmopolitan metropole suffused with small-town ties. Not only did everyone know each other, but everyone also knew *him*.

> The population is a very mixed one, English, French, Spanish, Coolie, Hindustani, and last but not least, Barbadians are everywhere met with. Of the latter there are crowds. Some twenty greeted me on my arrival, many of them men and women who said I had baptised them and seemed quite surprised that I did not recollect them. I had to remind them that when I performed that interesting ceremony for them, they were slightly different looking animals from what they are today. Many of them seemed to have dropped upon their feet. Clerks in stores, policemen, car conductors, and drivers are many of them from the place where flying fish abound.[35]

Bajans "dropped upon their feet" in Panama as well in the years when canal construction was booming and there was demand for services of all kinds. More than £83,000 in postal remittances reached Barbados from Panama in 1910 alone, and close to the same amount was transmitted through alternate routes.[36] Eric Walrond (himself born in British Guiana to a Barbadian mother and raised in Colón in the heyday of canal work) shows us the motley crowd at the British consulate in Colón. First in line was a "Negress who owned a fried fish and muffins stand on the Wharf Aux Herbes," who emptied twenty pounds in gold coins out of a dirty blue handkerchief onto the counter, along with a passbook to a Jamaican bank account, for the consul to process her deposit.[37] Friendly societies and insurance providers like the Jamaica Burial Scheme likewise served as vehicles for transnational savings and transfers.[38]

Ties and institutions that spanned multiple sites mattered a great deal to migrants' options, and migrants brought them into existence. With astonishing speed, British Caribbeans founded fraternal lodges, mutual aid societies, communities of worship, and English-language newspapers in Panama, Costa Rica, and elsewhere. Island branches of British fraternal orders as well as U.S. Afro-American fraternal orders abounded. The Independent United Order of Mechanics, the Loyal Order of Ancient Shepherds, the Lebanon Foresters, the Grand United Order of Odd Fellows, and the Independent Benevolent Order of Elks had chapters across the region, as did island-specific mutual

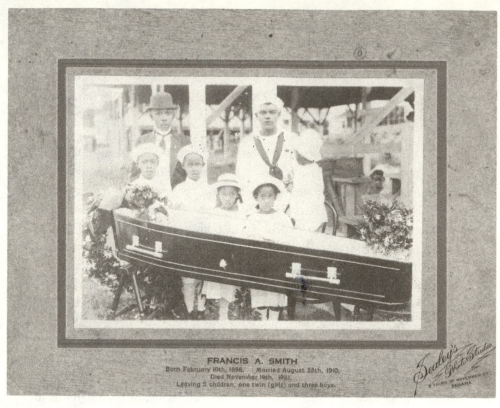

FRANCIS A. SMITH
Born February 10th, 1896.   Married August 28th, 1910.
Died November 19th, 1921.
Leaving 5 children, one twin (girls) and three boys.

Funeral card, Sealey's Photo Studio, Panama, 1921. Family of Mrs. Francis A. Smith, who died at age twenty-five, leaving five children. (George Westerman Collection, Schomburg Center for Research in Black Culture, New York Public Library)

associations from the Grenada Benevolent Society to the Sons and Daughters of Barbados.[39]

Newer than any of these, yet growing fastest of all, was the "Universal Negro Improvement Association" that a Jamaican migrant named Marcus Garvey founded in Kingston in 1914 and reestablished in New York three years later. The UNIA was a product of the migratory sphere. By 1914 Garvey had worked in Costa Rica, Panama, Ecuador, and England. It was the experience of seeing black people exploited in such similar ways in such different places, he would later say, that inspired him. His cofounder (and future wife) was the teenage Amy Ashwood, herself raised in Panama and only recently returned to Kingston. The organization they created combined global mission—"Africa for the Africans, at home and abroad"—with concrete local ties. Each chapter held weekly meetings, exhorted members to solidarity and self-help, and made newcomers welcome. Its spread offers a precise map of where migrants were. Within a decade, the UNIA had fifty-two chapters in Cuba, forty-seven in Panama, thirty in Trinidad, twenty-three in Costa Rica, eleven in Jamaica, eight in Honduras, seven in British Guiana, six in Colombia, five in Guatemala, five in Nicaragua, four in Barbados, two in the Canal Zone, and one in El Callao, Venezuela.[40]

Because social networks shaped flows and voluntary associations integrated new arrivals, this highly mobile world was anything but anonymous. Upon arrival in Baraguá, Cuba, two Jamaican laborers who had joined the Salvation Army in Panama began preaching Open-Air Meetings, built a wooden "Salvation Centre," and wrote to Salvation Army headquarters in Kingston for support.[41] The officer who was sent in response to the request reported: "I met in Cuba comrades from every [Salvationist] Corps I have been stationed at in the West Indies and on the Isthmus of Panama."[42] In a parallel vignette from the eastern Caribbean circuit, when Salvation Army brigadier Charles Smith visited the Dominican Republic in 1928 (in response to the petitions of one Hester O'Neal, who had rallied fellow Salvationists she found there from Barbados, St. Kitts, Antigua, and St. Thomas to begin preaching on the plantations), he "discovered among the dear people many of my own Converts and Soldiers of the Leeward and Windward Islands."[43]

A woman far from home, Hester O'Neal was not unusual. In the boomtown ports, opportunities for female earnings abounded. Women sold sweets or fruit on the docks; rented out rooms and cooked for boarders; offered companionship for cash or for love.[44] Though men outnumbered women among emigrants from every island, still scores of thousands of women left their home islands in this era. Some women traveled with male partners or to join them; others traveled with or to female kin or companions. Some women left children behind with relatives or placed as servants; others brought infants and children along.[45]

Large-scale migration was made possible by, and in turn reinforced, a flexible and fluid kinship system. By this era, "child-borrowing" had become a standard component of Caribbean kin practice, and it was common for children to be raised in households that included neither their mother nor father.[46] Miss D. was born around the turn of the century; her father died in 1914, and she had to raise her half siblings when their mother "did go foreign. And after she go foreign, she came back. She sick. She sick and dead, so me had to help mine the littler ones dem."[47] With many mouths to feed, even remittances from abroad might only cover school materials for a few years. Lucky boys might be apprenticed, girls sent into unpaid service to "learn" salable skills. "And sometimes," Miss D. reported, "they send them abroad after

Sweet venders in Kingston, Jamaica, ca. 1900. (Library of Congress Prints and Photographs Division, LC-USZ62-65561)

them get complete." Some wrote home on a regular basis, she explained, sending letters through the local parson if their parents could not read. "Plenty of them help them parents. And plenty die. And plenty never remember them parents. All various ways it go you nuh know."[48]

Those who wanted to remember could manage to keep connections alive over long distances and long years. Joshua Howell and his half brother left Kingston for New Orleans in the mid-1880s. Howell died in New Orleans in 1935, leaving "a small interest in some property," and his attorney wrote from there to the U.S. consul in Kingston for help. "Howell used to say that he had a sister and a brother back in Jamaica but whether or not they are living now, no one here knows. . . . They are colored people."[49] The consul published a note in the Kingston press, and within weeks the attorney had heirs to spare. "I am now in touch with eight or nine nieces and nephews of the decedent, who saw the ad and at once wrote me about their relationship to him. There can be no doubt of their being the right people because they have sent me letters in Howell's handwriting, written from here, which I recognize to be his hand."[50] Over the half century that Joshua Howell had lived in New Orleans, his brother and sister and their children had stayed in touch. Not only were letters written; letters were saved.

In sum, migrants—those who returned and those who kept going, those who sent help and those who were never heard from again—remade the geography of the Greater Caribbean in the first decades of the twentieth century. Their physical labor altered infrastructure and ecosystems, carving canals, laying rail, felling rain forest. Just as important, their social labor remade the routes along which knowledge, people, and resources traveled, tying villages to ports and ports to each other in networks of connection that cut across imperial and national lines.

CAPTURING CITIZENS AND CLAIMING SUBJECTS: THE CONSEQUENCES OF GEOPOLITICS FOR MIGRANTS ABROAD

I argued above that during the rise of the circum-Caribbean migratory system, the labor position of British Caribbeans abroad was not systematically worse than that of workers native to the lands where they sojourned. Like locals, they were highly vulnerable to employer abuses. As with locals, their friends, their feet, and occasionally their fists were the best guarantors they had. Like locals, foreigners might hope that if they escaped the mangrove swamps and reached Carúpano, authorities might take their side against abusive bosses. And like locals, in thus seeking allies among officials, they would sometimes get lucky and sometimes not.[51]

The context of work negotiations was shaped by migrants' position vis-à-vis multiple agents of the multiple states their lives spanned: London bureaucrats, colonial governors, British consuls, local police, municipal officials, regional *caudillos*, national leaders. Crucial to understanding migrants' experiences, then, are the logic and incentives of the international political system and the patterns of local politics. Together, these determined just what particular authorities would be willing to do for whom.

Territorial boundaries were anything but fixed in the era when our story began, and that matters a great deal. Imperial borders had shifted back and forth over the heads of Caribbean people multiple times in the eighteenth century. Nineteenth-century frontiers remained particularly ill-defined in those zones where, during the colonial period, indigenes, maroons, and other fugitives had managed to fend off the full grip of any one empire: Central America's Caribbean lowlands in the west and the jungles of the Guianas in the east. After independence, conflicting claims to these lands by the new Spanish American republics and the British Empire rested in part on the ability of each to prove that the local populace recognized their sovereignty and sought their protection. Rather than depicting dark-skinned foreign speakers in the borderlands as alien outsiders, then, Crown and congressmen alike espoused an expansive vision of who could become subject or citizen.

As island-born migrants found themselves caught up in Venezuelan civil wars over the first decade of the twentieth century, disputes between the British Foreign Office and the Venezuelan chancellery played out with each government reaching to claim sojourners as their own—even against sojourners' will. Venezuela passed laws that nationalized immigrants automatically after a few years' residence; Great Britain instructed migrants to ignore the law and insisted on diplomats' sovereign right to protect British subjects abroad whatever their color, language, or station and with or without documentation. This nominal stance did not translate into expeditious and color-blind service from British consuls for Grenadians, Barbadians, or Vincentians abroad. But it provided migrants with a lever, and they used it.

From the moment gold was discovered in El Callao, local authorities began jostling for position for themselves and the states they represented. In 1849 the Venezuelan governor of Guayana state wrote to his superiors in Caracas denouncing the local British consul, who "wishes to act like the magistrate here for subjects of his country." The consul fired off a self-righteous reply, accusing the governor of stripping sojourners' legitimate right to bear arms and of wielding the term *extranjero*—"foreigner"—as if it were an insult.[52] The core question, of course, was just who would turn out to be foreign here. The demarcation line between British Guiana and the Republic of Venezuela might fall on either side of the gold fields, depending on which state could make its claim effective. The dispute was fought out through diplomacy and then arbitration for the next half century. It all came down to what people were here, and whose people they were. As Venezuela's U.S.-based lobbyist stressed in 1896, by Great Britain's own confession, the British claim had "no basis but occupation."[53] Approximately none of the purported subjects on whom Britain's claim to "occupation" rested were of English ancestry, and more would have spoken French patois or indigenous languages than English creole, much less standard English.

In 1850 the same Venezuelan governor who had denounced the British consul's assertions with regard to "subjects of his country" urged superiors in Caracas to block the entry of further *libertos de las Antillas*—"Caribbean freedmen"—to the territory. Since race-based arguments for immigration restriction would be so common three generations later, it is worth pausing to note the argument he made. This was not about blood or biology but about character, power, and international consequences. Caribbean freedpeople were known to be "haughty, immoral, accustomed to vagrancy"—there was "no guarantee that they would submit to Venezuelan laws or authorities." A few thousand would be enough to "keep the entire Republic in alarm," not only because as "a mass with no partisan loyalty they could add to any domestic unrest" but also because "the specter of international demands [*reclamaciones*] would be constant. Do not doubt it! For we have our own painful experience, and can observe too the experience of other weak nations subject to the whim of the powerful. Concretely, powerful England has inspired terror for her recent claims [*pretensiones*] against Greece, which all Europe has denounced, as well as her acts against our own 'lesser authority.'"[54]

This reference to Greece was not happenstance, and that it sprang to the mind of this Venezuelan governor points to the centrality of the high politics of imperial representation to the reception of Caribbean migrants. What happened in Greece had resonated across Europe—and, as we will see in chapter 4, would remain a touchstone for British Caribbean thinkers in a very different geopolitical moment eighty years later. It was the case of Don Pacífico.

Don Pacífico was a Portuguese-speaking Jew, born in Gibraltar and thus a British subject, whose properties were attacked by an Athenian mob in 1847. When his efforts to gain redress through Greek courts failed, he appealed to Great Britain for help; Foreign Secretary Palmerston sent warships to seize Greek ships to compensate Pacífico's claims. Defending his action, Palmerston exhorted Parliament to "fully [recognize] the Right & Duty of the Government to secure to Her Majesty's subjects in Foreign States the full Protection of the Laws of those States."[55] His was an expansive version of both the where and the who of British rights. The attributes of a subject should inhere wherever the subject went and whoever the subject was. The question, Palmerston insisted in closing, was "whether, as the Roman, in days of old, held himself free from indignity, when he could say *Civis Romanus sum*; so also a British subject, in whatever land he may be, shall feel confident that the watchful eye and the strong arm of England, will protect him against injustice and wrong."[56]

Both the facts of the case and the words of the speech underlined the tenet that subjects' entitlements should hold regardless of rank, birthplace, ancestry, or culture. Palmerston denounced those critics who had "treated jocosely" the claims of impoverished Maltese, Ionians, and others who had sought redress for Greek abuses. British parliamentarians had roared with laughter "at the poverty of one sufferer, or at the miserable habitation of another; at the nationality of one injured man, or the religion of another; as if because a man was poor he might be bastinadoed and tortured with impunity; as if a man who was born in Scotland might be robbed without redress; or, because a man is of the Jewish persuasion, he is fair game for any outrage." Palmerston insisted that his vision of rights to which British subjects were universally entitled, and which they could make universally effective, matched "the principles . . . held by the great mass of the people of this country."[57] To judge by public reaction at the time, he was right. As one historian concludes: "Few sympathized with Pacífico himself, yet almost everyone applauded the evocation of the 'civis Romanus sum' principle."[58]

It was barely two weeks after Palmerston's speech that the governor of Guayana urged his superiors to bar West Indian freedmen from Venezuela—and leaked a copy of that letter to the press. Britain's chargé d'affaires in Caracas fired off a response. From the moment of emancipation, the freedpeople of the Caribbean had "acquired a perfect right to due protection from their Government," a right that was in no way diminished by their "color," their "former status," or "the meagerness of their resources and condition." "Her Majesty's Government will never permit any foreign state, on the pretext that they were once slaves, to administer to them justice in any measure different" from any other British subjects.[59]

The logic of expansion of the Roman Empire had insisted that populations of distinct ancestry, language, and religion could be absorbed into a functioning whole. The nineteenth-century adjudication of former Spanish fringes rewarded similar faith. For the new republic of Venezuela to claim the Orinoco delta and Guayana rain forests as her own, she would have to claim their inhabitants as potential citizens.[60] The claim to territory rested on evidence of popular allegiance. If that populace was nonwhite, so be it. The state that could claim them as belonging to its political community could claim their lands for its sovereign domain.

So, for instance, Lord Salisbury argued in 1880 that if Britain were to yield to Venezuela's proposed demarcation with Guiana, it "would involve the surrender of a province inhabited by 40,000 British subjects."[61] Venezuelan spokesmen scoffed. On the contrary, Venezuela's U.S. lobbyist argued that even the heart of the gold-mining region "contains no settlements even today. The [mines] are worked exclusively by negroes, who are hired on the coast and go up for three months at a time. There are no homes there, for they live in huts built in the Indian fashion or mere shanties, and no families and no permanent residents, unless that term be applied to a few negroes who have kitchen gardens, and perhaps a few foremen or officials whose duties keep them there."[62] The repetition of the racial label underlines the implicit argument. Surely these *negroes* could not be those subjects?

British commentators, in contrast, insisted that the people of the disputed borderlands were numerous, settled, and full subjects of the Crown. Promoter William Barry made a fact-finding trip from London in 1886. "The present population of the mines is principally composed of English subjects," he reported, "and all would hail gladly, and support energetically, a union with British Guiana or an independent state with free trade. If this country is opened up as Australia was, and similarly populated with an English speaking race, the [British] Government will be forced to interfere for the protection of its own subjects."[63] That the "English subjects" currently comprising the mines' population were not imitation Australians but Caribbeans of color is left as hazy as grammar allows. But Barry later made explicit that the subjects the Crown was duty-bound to defend were Caribbean: "The great influx of English subjects from Jamaica, and the other islands, and now, the persistent pressing forward of prospectors, in large numbers from Demerara will in time compel the English Government to take active steps to protect their own subjects, and to enforce their treaty rights."[64] The editors of Jamaica's *Daily Gleaner* argued likewise that the gold rush "rendered necessary the extension of British protection to the numbers of British subjects who flocked to the El Dorado from Trinidad and Demerara."[65]

Violence at the gold camps strengthened the claim that British expansionism was mere duty-bound protection of their own. In a letter to the *Port of Spain Gazette*, an English former mine supervisor decried the "nearly daily" murders of British subjects in El Callao. "Where is the oft-sung freedom of British subjects to travel where and when they wish, if on the frontiers of English Guiana and scant miles from Trinidad they are sacrificed at whim by Venezuelans?"[66] The author of this call to arms was Albert Nicholson, former head of one of El Callao's mines. At a moment of high tension in the zone, Nicholson had raised the British flag over his camp, then hauled it down as Venezuelan troops arrived to put down the strike turned secessionist movement. Nicholson fled, and the British West Indian laborers who had supported him found themselves in shackles.[67] The *Gleaner* editors, usually no fans of labor resistance, for once urged British Caribbeans to use force to enforce their rights: "In case the Venezuelans should attempt any armed demonstrations, the diggers, British and American, as many of them are, can be trusted to render a good account of the Venezuelan army."[68] William Barry concurred. The "miners have already on one occasion" attempted to take up arms against abuses, and "but for the incapacity and cowardice of their leader, who first provoked the outbreak"—that would be Nicholson—"they could successfully have resisted all interference."[69] Combative colored subjects here looked far better than pusillanimous white ones.

Relations remained tense in the region, with miners subject to forced exactions by venal officials and pressed into armies when warring factions swept through during the era's frequent civil wars.[70] Yet it seems clear that the potential attention of arbiters far away, and the presence of British consuls eager to intervene with regard to "their" people—in order to reinforce the claim that those people were truly full subjects of the Crown—made a difference. Coercive labor arrangements were less common than they might have been, and wages were higher as a result. One Englishman who worked as a mine boss during the 1880s gold boom wrote with grudging respect, "All the miners were niggers from the islands, not easy to manage, and asking absurd wages—I have heard of eighteen shillings a day."[71] Later travelers concurred that this was a place where the scarcity of labor actually translated into worker bargaining power. The only employees to be had were "West Indian coloured settlers and immigrants, often of a very low type, so that it is necessary to pay B 6.00 per day for the lowest class of unintelligent manual labour, and up to B 16.00 for skilled."[72]

Events from 1906 show that workers could gain some leverage even in precisely the circumstances I have described above as most consistently disempowering: travel under contract to a specific employer, to an isolated spot, in a land where local authorities routinely used force on behalf of local employers. Nine British recently arrived workers wrote from El Callao to the governor of Trinidad that conditions at the half-derelict mine were nothing like what they had been promised back in Port of Spain: "Men are killed and mutilated every week." They had been promised aboveground carpentering work, appropriate to their skills and paid by the day; on arrival, they were forced to work underground and were paid by depth drilled: "if we drilled only four or five inches we would get nothing." The overseer refused to let them seek better conditions in a different mine; they were still under contract of debt, he alleged, and sent police to force them back to work at gunpoint. They continued to protest; the overseer had them jailed for three days.[73]

The workers' complaints got high-level attention. The governor wrote to the Foreign Office in London and the Foreign Office to the British minister in Caracas. The British minister wrote a personal note to the Venezuelan minister of foreign relations, urging that instructions be sent to "Local Authorities" to resolve complaints in the zone and underlining the "gloomy picture of [workers'] sufferings" the Trinidadian governor had confirmed. The British minister also dispatched the British consul at Ciudad Bolivar, C. H. De Lemos, on the multiday journey by boat and mule train to El Callao.[74] The workers wrote again to Trinidad from El Callao, describing the "misery, the hardest of tasks," and the further abuses by police and magistrate they had faced once released from jail to work off their debt. One worker fell deathly ill; the company said it was no problem of theirs, and the man would have died but for the "kind people of our race and subjects lend[ing] a helping hand in giving to the sick man and others a morsel of bread."[75] Finally, advances repaid and freedom regained, they returned to Trinidad and complained to the governor in person. He wrote to the Foreign Office to reiterate his conviction of their "absolutely indefensible" treatment and the need for just recompense.[76]

In his eventual report, Consul De Lemos openly distinguished among British subjects in ways the public rhetoric of the imperial government strenuously avoided. "I found that the whites have at present no complaints whatever," he wrote, "and that the coloured subjects with a few individual exceptions are also at present quite satisfied." The latter, "Colonial British subjects from the West Indies," numbering some 5,000 to 6,000, were on balance glad to be there and earning. Doubtless some of the workers' complaints were justified, although De Lemos believed some ill treatment had been "provoked by want of discretion and unruly and impudent conduct" by the workers.[77] De Lemos assured his superiors that after a few days of conflict, the men in question had been let out of jail, had paid off their passage, and had even prospered: "They seem to have earned quite a substantial sum of money within a short period as, according to the two men interviewed by me, eleven out of the twenty originally imported had by December 24 already returned to Trinidad at their own expense and no doubt all of them carried money with them."[78] By January the British minister in Caracas reported to his superiors at the Foreign Office that the mines were quiet and several thousand British West Indians were busily at work. Clearly, the conditions under which some migrants labored in El Callao were wretched. Equally clearly, the position of British Caribbean migrants as the leading edge of Britain's territorial claims gave workers leverage to gain a hearing, and they used it as best they could.

In a world in which foreign nationals carried the backing of foreign states, receiving-society governments might prefer to naturalize sojourners, turning aliens with allies into sons of the soil—of whom much could be demanded with impunity. Military impressment, in particular, was an ongoing issue. During the 1903 British blockade, explained a British official in Caracas in a private note to superiors, "recruiting for the Venezuela army was very active, and practically all Venezuela labourers and artisans seem to have been impressed. Among these would, no doubt, be many negroes." Some of these were now claiming redress as British subjects. "None of these men have any proof of British nationality. They come to Venezuela without any sort of papers, and in consequence, but for their assertion, there is no proof whatever of their origin, so that, in case of general conscription in time of war, the Venezuelan officers can hardly be blamed for taking them."[79] For public consumption, however, the British stance was that all self-proclaimed British subjects' rights to imperial protection were absolute—a necessary posture, given that the Crown's "duty" to support British subjects had been Great Britain's declared justification for the 1902–3 blockade of Venezuela on behalf of jilted London bondholders.

The logic of pulling resident foreigners into the subordination of citizenship reached its apex with Venezuela's *Ley de Extranjeros* of 1903, which mandated automatic naturalization after twenty-four months of residence. The law was careful not to offer new political rights that might give those naturalized some political scope in their new nation. The British minister in Caracas marveled at the audacity.

> The Law appears to be an attempt on the part of the Venezuela government to deprive foreigners within the territories of the republic, as soon as they have been in the country for two years, of their nationality of origin, and of the advantages which that nationality might confer, without giving them any option or election in the matter, or any complete national status in exchange for that which they will lose. It rigorously excludes them from any share in the public life of Venezuela . . . and compels them, on pain of expulsion, to agree to bear all the burdens that Venezuelans have to bear (except military service and forced loans during revolutions) and to forego resort to diplomatic intervention.[80]

Foreign Office staff fell over themselves citing treaties to which Venezuela was signatory that the proposed law violated. It was simply unacceptable. The British minister made a formal "general protest against the law as a whole" to the Venezuelan president, and British consuls and sojourners alike were instructed to ignore its provisions.[81]

For a decade, no effort was made to implement the 1903 law's controversial mandate. But in 1914 the Venezuelan government began to demand not only passports or visas but also certificates of good conduct for entry, alleging the authority of the 1903 law. The Foreign Office instructed consuls in Venezuela to tell arriving British Caribbeans that Venezuelan authorities had no grounds to demand such a certificate. Venezuelan authorities also tried to require entering foreigners to sign a declaration ceding all right to call on British representatives in case of dispute; the Foreign Office insisted that "His Majesty's Government did not recognize the right of" Venezuela to remove British subjects' rights, signature or no signature.[82] As late as 1914, then, the Foreign Office sought to maintain the maximal interpretation of how tightly the right to imperial protection and prerogative of cross-border mobility adhered to British subjects abroad—even colonial subjects of color.

CONCLUSION

The workers from Trinidad concluded their second petition from El Callao to the British minister: "Most respectfully Sir should we be left in the hands of these people we will be no more Britons and surely we know wherever a grief are our Government is ready to share its power."[83] Similar rhetoric filled petitions to British consuls in Cuba, the Dominican Republic, and Panama alike, in this era and subsequently. Did the workers really have faith in empire's embrace? By the late 1920s, the notion that the British government would treat black emigrants' travails as a call to arms—that there was such as thing as "*our* Government . . . ready to share its power"—was so transparently false that jokes about British Caribbeans being not "British subjects" but rather "British objects" became wry standards within émigré communities.[84] But in 1906, in an international context in which Great Britain still sought to extend empire's domain on the basis of empire's subjects' inviolate rights, the words had some pull.

Another vignette from northeast Venezuela less than a decade later offered a rumbling of things to come. It also confirmed common knowledge of certain key facts: that migrants' degree of vulnerability abroad depended in part on the stance of their sending state and that sending-state commitments depended on race (even if parliamentary perorations denied it) and were highly vulnerable to shifting metropolitan priorities. In 1914—as the Great War convulsed Europe—an exile invasion threatened the Gomez regime. Led by the Ducharne family, whose money had been made in cacao and trade on the Paria Peninsula, rebels sailed from Trinidad to the eastern tip of the peninsula and used it as their rebellion's base.[85] When government troops retook the area in 1915, they were merciless with locals thought to have supported the rebels. Scores of Trinidadian, Grenadian, and Vincentian workers were whipped or beaten, their goods were seized, and their houses were burned. A Trinidadian doctor examining two decades later one Joseph Mitchell, arrested in this moment, found that Mitchell's body still bore "scars and signs" from the torture he had suffered—beaten with the flat of a sword, forced to wear "grillos" on both legs, and "put in the 'Tortol' for 15 minutes," that is, hung "by his testicles with a rope tied around it."[86]

Some men escaped to Carúpano on foot and sought out the British consul and Venezuelan civilian officials to plead for help for those, like Mitchell, still imprisoned. They reported that the Venezuelan troops beating them had laughed at their pleas and protests: "The troops told us that the British Government is currently too busy to worry about a bunch of *negros* and that if we think we can get any reparation that we should go ahead and try."[87] And indeed, the British government was very busy sending young Britons and Canadians to their deaths in Flanders fields and on Gallipoli's shores; and indeed, the abused colonials' complaints yielded few results, despite the local consul's efforts.

This chapter began by looking at the macroeconomic and technological shifts that generated demand for workers in new places in and around the Greater Caribbean in the late nineteenth and early twentieth centuries. We saw that evolving practices of community and kinship made it possible for islanders to move outward, making the most of the earnings opportunities that new investment in transport, bananas, and sugar opened. We then shifted to examine a different context that also shaped migrants' position: the expansive ambitions of a British Empire aiming to consolidate its rimland presence in the wake of Spanish American independence. Particularly in the mineral-rich borderland of Venezuela and Guiana, immediate interests as well as the broader principle were at stake. Where territorial boundaries would be drawn depended in part on the ability of rival states to demonstrate residents' historic and ongoing allegiance. Against this backdrop, British Caribbeans abroad could leverage some support from their status as full-fledged British subjects, and states (both sending and receiving) understood emigrants' "rights" as a key component of their own geostrategic maneuvering.

Two   Spirits of a Mobile World
Worship, Protection, and Threat at Home and Abroad, 1900s–1930s

The sound of prayer is everywhere in firsthand accounts of the circum-Caribbean migratory sphere. Crowded decks echoed with supplications when seas grew rough and rung with hosannas as ports drew near. "Every time you hear a bell [in Cuba], is Salvation Army or a [Garveyite] talking about Africa," remembered one Jamaican returnee.[1] If you paused at every Port of Spain housefront where cries of worship could be heard, you would never get home at night—or so quipped a judge in 1920 as he sentenced five women to hard labor for holding a "Shouter" revival.[2] Ira Sankey's Methodist hymnal was part of the kit of every decker, and in every port, stevedores sang Sankey hymns as they worked. The sound of Bocas del Toro at night, wrote British traveler Winifred James, was "half a hundred niggers singing the bananas into the holds and talking religion in between the loads."[3]

Salvation mattered deeply in this place and time, and theology was too important to leave to the professionals. The boatmen piloting Anglican bishop Herbert Bury in and out of mangrove swamps along the Central American coast engaged him in solemn religious debate for hours every night under the stars.[4] The first known publication by Marcus Garvey is a letter to the *Times* in Limón, Costa Rica, written while he worked on a nearby banana plantation in 1911. It dealt neither with race nor politics but with the "pseudo gospel pounders" currently drawing crowds in Port Limón. (Garvey had no sympathy for the local Bedwardites and "mial men"—two Afro-Jamaican Revival groups—but he leapt to defend the Catholic Church as a "glorious institution.")[5] Why were there so many gospel pounders? This was a world in which common people took seriously the responsibility to listen for messages from God and to preach themselves if that was what dreams, visions, or intellect guided them to do. A Barbadian character in the *Trinidad Weekly Guardian*'s humor column explained the prevalence of street preachers in an immigrant neighborhood of Port of Spain thus: "Alyuh Bajans alwis waun fuh put moh exterpertashuns pun de scriptures and dat's why dose prophets dus live down deay so."[6] "Putting more interpretations upon the Scriptures" was a right and a duty for locals and sojourners alike. The circum-Caribbean migratory sphere was a space of constant religious creation.

Christian traditions old and new were not the only spiritual practices that gave succor to migrants as they traveled, and were remade along the way. Working in a framework rooted in West African ontologies, Caribbean peoples had developed practices of healing and protection—and, rumor had it, assault—worked by ritual specialists through herbs, baths, bundles, and divination. Most migrants understood their world to be suffused by invisible powers that they themselves would only access for good but that others might harness for malevolent ends. Outsiders used the terms "obeah," "voodoo," "black magic," or "witchcraft" to designate all such practices and took them as proof that African savagery lived on in local minds. But Caribbean people themselves were more likely to call the kinds of protection or help they sought "Science," "work," or "cure" and reserve the term "obeah" (or "hex" or "humbug") to designate cases where those same powerful forces were used to harm rather than heal.

While outside observers and local elites saw magical practice as confirmation of the moral and intellectual gulf between white people and black, there is no evidence that early twentieth-century Caribbeans saw their encounters with the supernatural through the lens of race. Parents in rural Trinidad did not think that their children were at risk from night-flying, blood-sucking soucouyants because the children were black, or because the potential soucouyants were black; they feared for their children because children were children and soucouyants were soucouyants.

Belief in the spirit world fissured Caribbean societies along lines of class rather than race—separating "the classes" from "the masses," in the language of the times.[7] The East Indian and Afro-Caribbean masses shared many ideas about nonmaterial threats and what to do about them; men and women of the classes would sooner eat their proper, imported hats than consult an obeahman. We should not be surprised, then, that Afro-Caribbean intellectuals, including black internationalists, had no sympathy for the "superstitions" and "immorality" of popular spiritual practice. Those Caribbean intellectuals who would take a pioneering role within the U.S. Socialist and Communist Parties went further, rejecting church worship, too, as deceptive and retrograde. Pan-Africanist radicals' impatience with popular religion placed them firmly at odds with the very religious black masses for whom they hoped to speak.

This chapter begins by describing the wide range of Christian movements that circulated with migrants in and around the Caribbean at the start of the twentieth century. Migrants spread new versions of the gospel into new lands, taking European- or North American–led evangelical movements in directions those northern leaders might never have imagined. We then turn to the realm of quotidian spiritual practice known as "Science" or "obeah." Practices of supernatural manipulation served as a kind of lingua franca across the Greater Caribbean, providing grounds for meaningful encounter between sojourners and locals of widely varied origin. Far from being the archaic remnant of African tradition, Science/obeah grew as part of the modern world, with supernatural specialists incorporating new knowledge from patent medicine to spiritism to Victorian mysticism. We then follow worship and protection north, examining the wide-ranging spiritual entrepreneurship of Caribbean migrants in New York. Finally, we examine the attitude of black-internationalist leaders toward popular spiritual practice. From upright journalists to Harlem radicals, they were uniform in decrying spirit work and unorthodox "cults" as foolish and backward. Their own programs for social transformation had no room to recognize that religious innovation had long been a vital source of oppositional politics in the British Caribbean, as impassioned individuals spread visions of justice to come.

One caveat before we begin. This chapter is about popular beliefs—where they converged, how they changed, why they mattered. And yet there was no such thing as unitary "popular belief," not within a single linguistic region, not on a single island, not even in a single room. There were individual Caribbean people, and they believed different things. Henry Neblett was tried in Tobago in 1904 on charges of "practicing obeah" by crafting a bundle of shroud and coffin wood at a wake. "When I saw him nailing up those things I was afraid," testified the dead woman's mother. "I am afraid up to now. I believe it was obeah and I am still afraid." In contrast, a man who was standing by the dead woman's corpse when Neblett nailed the assemblage to the wall testified that he was not afraid at the time, although nevertheless he admitted: "I don't like it at all." Still another woman, who heard Neblett speak the dead woman's name before striking the first nail, reported no unease: "I do not understand the meaning of this thing. . . . I was not afraid . . . for I don't know the sense of it."[8] Living in the same neighborhood at the same historical moment, these working-class Tobagans had completely different ideas about the nonmaterial powers that did or did not permeate their world. They were not the puppets of an overarching "culture"—they created it, every day, and they spoke in many voices.

COLLECTIVE WORSHIP ON THE GO: CHRISTIAN MISSIONS, REVIVALS, AND PROPHETS

The panorama of worship within British Caribbean sending societies as emigration took off was extraordinarily complex. On these islands, over the course of preceding centuries, enslaved Africans of varied origin had been forced to remake spiritual practice under grave conditions, and they and their free descendants had incorporated different streams of Christian ideas, symbols, and rites in different ways. The end of the slave trade brought new inputs, African and Christian alike. Nineteenth- and twentieth-century mobility brought together divergent traditions grounded in partially shared African pasts—as when Afro–North American immigrants in Jamaica and Trinidad introduced the enthusiastic Christianity developed by slave communities in the U.S. Second Great Awakening, or as when Central Africans arriving under indenture reinforced particular forms of spirit work in postemancipation Jamaica. Such reencounters had multiple and far-reaching effects.

Over the course of the eighteenth century, outreach by Capuchins, Carmelites, Dominicans, and Jesuits among the enslaved in the French islands of the eastern Caribbean had been inconsistent but widespread. When Dominica, St. Lucia, St. Vincent, Grenada, and Trinidad ended the late eighteenth-century wars under British control, their peoples remained largely Catholic. In the core British sugar islands of Barbados and Jamaica, in contrast, the Anglican Church had long ministered to white residents, but planters had balked at any efforts at education or conversion that might seem to endow the enslaved with personhood or rights.[9] Significant evangelizing among Jamaica's enslaved did not begin until a Virginia-born, free black Baptist preacher, George Liele, arrived among other refugees from the American Revolution to the north. He trained local men of color, who in turn became deacons of spreading "Native Baptist" congregations.

In the wake of this precedent, European-based Protestant missionary groups—Baptists, Moravians, Wesleyan Methodists—redoubled missions to the enslaved on Jamaica and other British islands. The established Anglican Church found itself hustling to catch up, fearful that the Nonconformist groups, increasingly tied to abolitionism in Europe, would work to undermine slavery in the colonies. Despite the missionaries' largely sincere efforts to uphold the slave system, slaves and freedpeople used the rhetoric and social spaces of Christian ritual to do the opposite. Enslaved creoles brought together in chapel by the London Missionary Society led a revolt in Demerara in 1823; Native Baptists were at the forefront of rebellion in Jamaica in 1831–32.[10]

We know far less of the parallel story of how particular African traditions were promulgated by individual visionaries or reworked in collective practice in different settings across the region. There are glimpses. Within Trinidad, a small group of Muslim "Mandingos" maintained their identity, worked to purchase freedom, and proselytized among others.[11] Even in Jamaica, where Nonconformist missionaries had been most active, less that one-tenth of the 300,000 slaves freed upon final abolition in 1838 were claimed by the missionaries as church members.[12] Over the following generation, the concepts and practices sustained by the other nine-tenths (and by many of the formally churched one-tenth as well) would be combined with elements of Christian traditions to form a range of Afro-Jamaican religious practice.

The end of slavery spurred new migratory streams, introducing new faith traditions and remaking old ones. Largest in number were the scores of thousands of East Indians reaching Trinidad and Guiana, the great majority of them Hindu yet with thousands of Muslims among them. But midcentury also brought tens of thousands of Africans to the islands under contracts of indenture, the majority of whom had been "freed" from Portuguese, Brazilian, or Cuban slave ships by the Royal Navy. As late as the 1880s, there were over 5,000 Africa-born individuals in British Guiana, over 4,000 in Jamaica, and over 3,000 in Trinidad. In Jamaica, Africans who arrived in the 1840s generated the Kumina ritual complex, centered on drumming, dancing, and spirit possession; from its base among indentured Africans and their descendants in St. Thomas, Kumina would cross-pollinate surrounding, more Christian traditions over the following generations.[13] In Trinidad, midcentury Yoruba immigrants combined spirit possession with elements of Catholic ritual, creating a version of Orisha-work with strong resonances to *Santería* in Cuba and *vodoun* in Haiti.[14]

Postemancipation Jamaica witnessed an extraordinary awakening of the spirit. Attendance at Baptist, Methodist, and Anglican services rose even as "Myalism" swept the island in the 1840s and 1860s. Myal bands formed around charismatic leaders, catching the spirit in their own bodies in order to combat "obeah," malevolent sorcery. Elite observers saw the Myal "outbreaks" that developed from what began as Nonconformist revivals in 1860 and 1861 as travesties of Christian teachings. Participants, in contrast, insisted they were purifying the faith and defending the island. Arrested for disturbing the peace, one myal group chanted in protest: "We no mad; who say we mad? It the Lord Jesus Christ. We dig out all dem badness. Ush, ush, ush."[15] Myal would evolve into Jamaica's Zion Revival complex, in which small bands of mainly female worshippers sought possession by the Holy Ghost through circular dance and exaggerated breathing, using the spirits' power to heal the afflicted. This was not an exclusive faith: one might rely on the healing that Revival Mothers offered and still worship devoutly at an orthodox Christian church. (Church fathers disagreed.)[16]

Zion Revival shared much with the Afro-Christian worship traditions that emerged in the postemancipation eastern Caribbean, including those that would come to be labeled Shakers in St. Vincent and Spiritual Baptists or Shouters in Trinidad. These too were groups whose leaders' authority came from experience of the holy—in dreams or visions—rather than formal education. Worshippers here too dressed all in white, danced in circles to induce trances, and burned candles.[17] Whereas Zion Revival drew its Christian elements from the Native Baptist practice that grew out of Virginia-born George Liele's evangelizing, the Spiritual Baptist movement in Trinidad seems to have drawn in part on enthusiastic Christian worship introduced by the "Merikans," ex-slave soldiers, originally from the United States, who were resettled in Trinidad after serving Britain in the War of 1812. As a British missionary explained, what had begun in the 1850s as an encouraging Christian revival—"the Spirit of God was poured out on the people, and at all the stations numerous converts were baptized"—had gone terribly wrong. "An American negro introduced the wild and fanatical notions and practices so frequent in the camp-meetings of the Southern States. . . . Jumpings were mingled with prayers and the songs of the sanctuary degenerated into discordant shouts."[18] The arrival of Shakers from St. Vincent, responding to persecution there by following the many other Vincentians gone to Trinidad or Venezuela in those same years, further nourished Trinidad's Spiritual Baptist tradition.[19] Spiritual Baptists routinely risked physical punishment—by disapproving family, like the foster mother who flogged fifteen-year-old Amelia Bovell for sneaking out to "the 'Jumpers' meeting" in 1904, or by the state, as when Barbadian Martha Roach was sentenced to eighteen days hard labor yet again for keeping a Shouters' Meeting in Port of Spain in 1920—in order to come together and be filled with the spirit.[20]

Clearly, migrations of faithful people had consequences for faiths as well as for people. So what religions did British Caribbean migrants carry with them into foreign as large-scale emigration to the Spanish-speaking rimlands took off in the second half of the nineteenth century? Even at the level of formal Christian churches, the answer varies. In the eastern Caribbean, Barbados was heavily Anglican, Dominica and St. Lucia entirely Catholic, and St. Vincent split between Anglicans and Wesleyan Methodists (along with uncounted faiths like the Shakers); Plymouth Brethren were everywhere present in small numbers. In Trinidad, the East Indian population was largely Hindu, with a Muslim minority; the light and white elite largely Catholic; colonial bureaucrats Anglican; and the black peasantry Catholic, although with ever more Anglicans among them as Barbadians, Vincentians, and Grenadians kept coming.[21]

On the islands, the Anglican Church was run by and for "the classes" rather than the masses. But among British West Indians abroad, the classes were barely represented, and the masses made the Anglican Church their own. This is clear, for instance, in the account of Bishop Herbert Bury, who from 1907 to 1910 headed the diocese of British Honduras, which had expanded to include the Central American rimlands where British Caribbean communities were burgeoning. Anglican churches in the larger ports were led by ordained clergy, some of them Englishmen, others men of color of Barbadian or Jamaican birth. But the great majority of rimland Anglican communities were led by local lay "readers" whom the bishop would visit once a year at most. If working-class Afro-Caribbeans had not felt ownership of the Anglican Church in these lands, they would not have been so fiercely angry when, after the creation of the Canal Zone in 1904, its Anglican churches were ceded to the U.S. Episcopal hierarchy and Jim Crow segregation was imposed.[22]

Meanwhile, in the eastern Caribbean, the Dominicans, Vincentians, Martinicans, and Trinidadians drawn to El Callao in the 1850s would have been Catholic in their great majority, though sources contain no mention of organized worship during the gold-boom tumult. Not until 1907 did the Anglican bishop of Trinidad visit Venezuela, founding one congregation of "almost all coloured West Indians" in Caracas, another in Ciudad Bolivar, and a third among the 6,000 British subjects in El Callao.[23] Local memory there emphasizes that Anglican worship had begun a full generation earlier at the initiative of the faithful themselves. On the frontispiece of the yellowing *Book of Common Prayer* that Father Adams Delgado—himself the great-grandson of Trinidadian and Martinican immigrants—conserves for his flock, careful script records not only Canon Trotter's founding of the Church of the Redeemer in 1911 but also the "First Evening Prayer" led by one Timothy Rouse in September 1875.[24]

Migrants embraced other mainline Christian churches as well—some that they might have belonged to back home, others that they encountered abroad for the first time. Along the northern coast of Honduras at the start of the century, there were not only Anglican priests at four banana ports but also Brethren, Church of God, Baptists, and two African Methodist Episcopal Churches of Zion.[25]

The traditional denominations were not the ones growing the fastest, though, or praying the loudest. The dawn of the twentieth century brought to the Caribbean missions from several newborn evangelical faiths, including the Salvation Army, the Seventh-Day Adventists, and the Pentecostals. Considered anything but orthodox in their societies of origin, in the Caribbean these groups counted as relatively respectable by the mere fact of their white leadership. They held noisy outdoor meetings, drawing crowds with drums and fervent Hallelujahs that would have gotten Revivalists or Shouters rousted in a moment.[26] It was the religious enthusiasm of local converts that drove these missions, more than any blueprint from above. As Salvationist "officers" or Adventist "elders," Caribbeans of color spread the gospel in line with their own conceptions of the holy. The Salvation Army regularly sent Afro-Caribbean officers, women as often as men, to lead corps in Panama, Costa Rica, Honduras, and Cuba or run the Army's social institutions there.[27] Lay initiatives were common too. Jamaicans who had become Salvationists in Panama and then migrated to Cuba initiated the Army's work there; Salvationists from the Leewards did the same in the Dominican Republic.[28]

U.S. missionaries brought Pentecostalism to Jamaica and Pilgrim Holiness to Barbados in the same years; these too drew island masses into intense fundamentalist worship in myriad congregations soon led by local black preachers.[29] Other British West Indians encountered evangelicals in the Spanish American republics—like the itinerant midwestern missionary who sold five boxes of Bibles in English and one in Spanish in El Callao in 1915, holding "precious conversations" with West Indians "hungry" for the Word.[30] The outreach reflected the intersection of two currents within North America: burgeoning evangelicalism and boosterish U.S. expansionism in the wake of 1898 and the Panama Canal. Yet even if missionaries saw themselves as bearers of the White Man's Burden or agents of U.S. empire, the gospel they brought was turned to local ends.

Caribbean visionaries, too, struck out on their own to preach the word of God as they heard it. We catch glimpses only: of "The Barbados Prophet" who walked the streets of Port of Spain declaring "in a shrill and piping voice . . . that he was a prophet of the Lord who had journeyed to fair Iere to perform a mission of righteousness to the people of Woodbrook and to warn them of the wrath which would fall upon them if they maintained their evil ways";[31] or Jamaica-born Catherine McKendo, who took up "preaching and the spirits" around 1900 in Port Limón and found herself sued for divorce. The case spotlights divergent assessments of spiritual power and its manifestations. McKendo explained that she now lived from money that people gave her when she preached. Yet her husband saw her visitations differently: "Every time she is possessed," he "threatens her with a shotgun."[32]

Adjutant and Mrs. Da Costa and family, Jamaica-born Salvation Army missionaries, 1933. (Salvation Army International Headquarters, London, U K)

Some fifteen years earlier, another Jamaican emigrant down the coast in Colón had received a similar call to prophesize and preach. His name was Alexander Bedward, and for the next fifty years, his followers would flock to the Mona River on the outskirts of Kingston to be washed and healed by his powers—as many as 10,000 people at a time at the height of his movement. Just as Baptist deacon Paul Bogle had summoned Jamaican peasants to rebellion in 1865 with an apocalyptic vision of races at war—"skin for skin and colour for colour"—Bedward would preach race and resistance. The *Gleaner* reported one speech in 1895: "He referred to the black population as the 'black wall' and the white as the 'white wall' saying that the white wall had long enough oppressed the black wall and the time had now arrived when the black wall must knock down and oppress the white."[33] Another paper's account captures Bedward's biblical grounding of his racial vision: "Thanks to Jesus I am able to understand [the Bible], and I, servant of Jesus, will tell you. The Pharisees and Sadducees are the white men, and we are the true people. . . . The fire of hell will be your portion if you do not rise and crush the white people."[34] After a trial for sedition and brief remit to the insane asylum, Bedward returned to preaching. His rhetoric was less incendiary, but his sway was enormous. "Bedwardite" became a recognized Christian denomination across the western Caribbean. People traveled from Panama and beyond to be healed in his monthly immersions, and travelers found Bedwardite "evangelists" in Port Limón and elsewhere in Central America.[35]

Bedwardites were likely among the "6 or eight pseudo gospel pounders" denounced by Limón's English-language paper in 1911. But the editors' main complaint was with the Myal Revival currently under way in the port, with nighttime assemblies of 200 to 300 people in open yards, singing, "yelling at the top of their voice," and then entering trance states with loud groans. "This they claim to be seized by a holy spirit and while in this state they are said to be possessed of healing powers."[36] The editors treated the "mial meeting or ghost healing" on the rise in the port as both risible and dangerous, the same attitude the editors assumed with regard to the "obeahmen" whose profitable business in malevolent magic they denounced almost daily. Yet those seeking spirit possession in Limón's yards surely did not think of the two as similar, but rather locked in contention. Obeahmen "put ghosts" on victims (and therefore might be hired to take off ghosts by those who felt themselves hexed); Myal promised healing—healing of the ills caused by obeah in particular.[37]

The point goes to the heart of spiritual practice in the circum-Caribbean migratory world and unites the above discussion with what follows. The British Caribbean "masses" developed practices of collective worship against a background of presumptions about the presence of interventionist spirits, the possibilities of human ill will, the meanings of maladies, and the destiny of the dead. The spirit-work complex called Science or obeah formed part of the terrain in which worship traditions developed, and vice versa. That which we recognize as "religion" and that which is often called "superstition" were thus neither separate realms nor opposing points on a spectrum from Christian to African; they were dialectically connected. Thus a St. Lucian laborer in Panama might become "a religious man . . . [as] a thrust against the omnipresent obeah," joining not a Myal Revival but "the English Plymouth Brethren in the Spanish city of Colón."[38] Men and women like him did not cleave to the church because they found obeah risible; they cleaved because they found it real.

Thus in our exploration of the spiritual lives of Caribbean migrants, we turn now from religion to Science.

KNOWLEDGE OF AND FOR A MOBILE WORLD: SCIENCE AND OBEAH ACROSS DIVIDES

Outsiders depicted "obeah" as proof positive of African atavism, a legacy marking Caribbeans of African ancestry as uncivilized and maybe uncivilizable. Meanwhile, middle-class Caribbeans of color rejected this racialized reading, instead insisting that obeah reflected popular ignorance, "backwardness" that would have to be overcome for modern progress to begin. But as we shall see, obeah was neither delimited by ancestral origin nor divorced from modern life. Quite the contrary. The pursuit of protection through ritual Science brought together sojourners and settlers of many origins—Spanish-speaking *mestizos*, South Asians, and indigenes as well as creole- and patois-speaking British Caribbeans. And both the demand for healing and protection and the mechanisms through which they were sought showed these people to be firmly a part of the modern Atlantic world.

Debate has long raged among scholars over the extent to which the cultures of Afro-descended people in the Americas reflect the retention of African beliefs and practices (a position laid out by anthropologist Melville Herskovits in his 1941 *Myth of the Negro Past*) or are the results of cultural creation by Africans of disparate origins thrown together in the crucible of slavery (the "creolization hypothesis," forcefully argued by Sidney Mintz and Richard Price from the 1970s forward). The paradigms offer contrasting explanations for the commonalities found among diasporic peoples. Do they reflect African roots? Parallel responses to repressive systems? Or perhaps not Old World roots but New World routes—ongoing exchange rather than unidirectional diffusion? From the late 1920s, when Melville and Frances Herskovits searched for "Africanisms" in the backlands of Surinam, the spiritual lives of Caribbean people have been called on as evidence in these ongoing debates.[39]

The commonalities across space, time, language, and polity are indeed striking. S. T., who immigrated to Limon from Jamaica as a child in the second decade of the twentieth century, described years later the hex that had separated him from his second wife. A hex, he explained, "is a thing which is planted at the doorstep, a little bottle, it's planted beneath the doorstep and you are walking over the little bottle all the time."[40] In 1940s Brooklyn, Bajan matrons recounted the hex that killed a wayward girl back home: the "obeah man" took "rusty nails and feathers and broken glass and thing so" and "put in a bottle and bury it."[41] In the peninsula of Paria in the 1980s, *hechizos* were worked with bundles "known as *bojotes* elsewhere in Venezuela," prepared by ritual specialists and buried in the doorway of the home.[42] In El Callao today, ritual specialists called *vuduman* or *vuduwoman* work *brujería* or *óbea* by means of a bottle filled with grave dirt and surreptitiously acquired hair or nails, buried in the doorway of the target's home.[43]

The symbolism, logic, and ingredients of obeah practice surely did draw on knowledge that survived the Middle Passage. (In Benin, in coastal Venezuela, and in highland Costa Rica, if someone accidentally sweeps a broom over a single woman's foot they will joke that she will now never marry—mundane household lore whose specificity suggests West African women's knowledge shared at hearths on all shores of the Atlantic.[44]) Yet ground-level sources from around the Caribbean also show how innovation and exchange shaped the strikingly cohesive regional repertoire of magical practice. We see the impact of capitalist commerce and Victorian science as practitioners used tarot cards and colored candles; consulted *The Great Book of Magical Art, Hindu Magic, and East Indian Occultism* and the de Laurence guides sold by mail order from Chicago; and sent clients off to pharmacies to purchase patent medicines, oil of this, and powder of that.[45]

Thus one factor in the commonalities of obeah around the Caribbean was shared West African roots; a second was a shared engagement with the contemporaneous North Atlantic and the technologies of healing and knowledge for sale within it. Local sources also underline the degree of communication and borrowing under way, as not only people but products and prints circulated in ever greater numbers. Barbados-born William Young had "first heard of obeah about six months ago in Trinidad"; with this new knowledge, when he moved to Tobago and found himself unfairly castigated by his supervisor, Young suspected someone was "humbugging him at work" and sought out a local obeahman for help.[46] Commentators in the late nineteenth century played up the notion of traveling obeahmen. One traveler wrote in 1871 of a "sort of secret College, or School of the Prophets Diabolic," in St. Vincent, whose "emissaries spread over the islands, fattening themselves at the expense of their dupes."[47]

Again and again, we hear of the hiring of magical specialists across linguistic and cultural divides. Cases from both the eastern and western Caribbean demonstrate the thoroughgoing involvement of South Asian immigrants in the market for supernatural aid. Indeed, the only Jamaican *brujo* ever accused to the police of causing death by witchcraft in Limón was "John Gupi (culi)," identified by police as *jamaiquino*, whose place of birth was "Hindustan."[48] The spread of Science was a two-way street: Afro-Caribbeans also sought out and valued elements of Indian occult traditions—as did their metropolitan peers in this heyday of Orientalism, of course.[49] Meanwhile, in the eastern Caribbean there were fissures of language and culture between British West Indians as well. When Simon Joseph's three-year-old son disappeared in Tunapuna, Trinidad, in 1904, he traveled to the capital to consult a "female oracle" who "lives on a hill at Laventille at about five miles from Port of Spain"—"but the [oracle] spoke English. He only understood one word." Joseph, like many other Afro-Trinidadians in these years, spoke only French creole. This did not stop him from hiring the English-speaking oracle to help.[50]

Indeed, the heterogeneous French-English fringes of the eastern Caribbean seem to have been particularly generative of supernatural power, perhaps by their very heterogeneity. In outsiders' accounts, then as now, Haiti stood as the presumed epicenter of African black magic in the Caribbean. But in local sources, St. Vincent (home of the above-mentioned School of the Prophets Diabolic) and the other British-adopted former French islands seem more widely influential. Eric Walrond—himself born in Guiana in 1898 to a Barbadian mother and raised in Panama from the age of twelve—described gatherings of the "crust of Black Art idolators" in Colón—"Negroes from St. Lucia and Martinique . . . believers in the magic of obeah" who "would sit and chant old voodoo songs and dream and sip Maube and anisette."[51] The Jean-Baptiste mentioned above, who joined the Plymouth Brethren in Panama to keep his home safe from obeah, exemplified the fringes' contradictions: "Like a host of the native St. Lucian emigrants, Jean Baptiste forgot where the French in him ended and the English began. His speech was the petulant patois of the unlettered French black. Still, whenever he lapsed into His Majesty's English, it was with a thick Barbadian bias."[52]

A court case from Limón in 1903 offers us a glimpse of the role of obeah as a common vocabulary among Caribbeans of far-flung origin. A fistfight began when Serafín Clutero, from Martinique, accused his neighbors—Sofia Wilson of Mosquitia, Nicaragua, and her consensual partner, Daniel Glover, from Antigua—of working witchcraft against him by means of "a bundle with strange contents that he found in front of the door to his house." It was "a packet with small pieces of plantains cut in half, this is for creating animosity in one person regarding another, for it's used as witchcraft." Clutero immediately suspected Glover, for "that was his occupation": Glover had previously "offered me his services of witchcraft."[53] Here we have English and patois-speaking migrants from Martinique, Nicaragua, and Antigua selling, using, and fearing obeah on the Caribbean coast of Costa Rica. In the midst of their quarrel, what they do not disagree over is most significant: none doubted that a bundle that included sliced plantains placed in a doorway could create discord for the couple inside. In cases like these, we see supernatural practices functioning as a medium for communication across boundaries of language, origin, and empire. From the former French islands of the eastern Caribbean to longtime Anglophone settlements like Mosquitia in the western Caribbean, there was enough commonality in the underlying grammar and specific gestures of magical practice that newcomers could seek assistance, recognize threats, and offer services. It was neither roots nor routes alone that explains the spread of obeah, then, but rather the way they came together: reencounter.

As shifting patterns of employment and investment made international mobility ever more common in working-class lives, Caribbean people found in Science/obeah a source of power that was likewise not limited by jurisdictional boundaries. It could be used to speed migrants on their way or to tie them more tightly to home. In Kingston in 1921, a man nicknamed "Colon" and working out of the Hotel Colon (named for the preeminent boomtown of the previous decade) met four men about to head off for the Cuban cane fields and demanded money to "wash" them so they would be successful in that island.[54] In Port of Spain in 1920, Maria Ramcharan was arrested for using a pack of cards, "a lap board," "Altar Stations," and a crucifix to work obeah for Maria Thomas. Thomas testified that "she went there to hear about her husband who was at the oilfields and was not good to her. [Ramcharan] had charged her three shillings to see her business and $25 to get her husband to be as good to her as before."[55]

Supernatural recourse was well suited to the specific challenges of transnational kinship. Family obligations in the Caribbean as elsewhere were generally enforced through informal mediation. But the extraordinary mobility of the early twentieth-century Caribbean made this difficult. Family ties that were stretched between distant lands might remain intact. Then again, they might not. Social pressures could be attenuated by distance; people who wished to get lost could be lost. Like the faithless Mathilda of King Radio's 1938 calypso, who "take me money and run Venezuela," conjugal partners could put themselves beyond reach all too easily.[56] Could Science keep you where you did not want to be? Jamaicans Adina and David Ogilvie met in the Canal Zone in 1907; ten years and seven children later, they finally wed. A year later, when Adina was back in Jamaica looking after business for David, everything changed: "Suddenly he wrote to say my entire life has been revealed by God to him and that I have been bewitching him for the past nine years," and now "I am using acult means to take his life and that of an innocent woman who is caring him and if it was not for the woman he would have been dead already by my witchery." The accused, so careful to sign herself "(Mrs.) Adina Ogilvie," could see clearly the complications of kinship legalities in a mobile world. "My reason for sending you this letter," she wrote to the British consul in Panama City, "is because I hear that he is trying to get a divorce for me and I think it is possible that he may tell the courts over there that he do not know where to find me or anything that could cause them to think I cant be found."[57] Adina's attempts to mobilize formal protections seem to have brought no response from the consul. Perhaps the informal connections through which she "heard" in Yallah's Bay of her husband's legal maneuvering in Panama were more helpful, or perhaps her brothers, whom David had previously accused of "witchery," exerted pressure, occult or otherwise, on her behalf. Or perhaps Adina and her four surviving children just made do without further support.

Like buried bottles or *bojotes*, long-distance love magic transcended linguistic and national divides. In 1894 a self-described Cuban *brujo*, resident in San José, Costa Rica, claimed that seventeen-year-old Costa Rican Ester Bestard had told him she suspected that her Cuban husband planned to leave for Nicaragua; she sought "a *reliquia* [holy object] to keep him from abandoning her." (Ester's fears were understandable, given that her husband's brother had already "abandoned a shop he had in Limón, leaving his wife and daughters abandoned.") Another man, a Costa Rican artisan, testified that the same *brujo* had sold him "a composition that would serve to tie women, that is, make all the women you want fall in love with you." Ester's mother reported the *brujo* had offered to sell her "white water for tying men."[58]

Fears over women "tying" men through *brujería* appear in life histories composed in Limon by men of every origin. M. G. L., a Nicaraguan migrant, was threatened with a whip by a Costa Rican *compañera* around 1949 and only later learned that she had "tied" him "by means of a *bruja*" and thought she had him dominated.[59] When Costa Rican R. G. C. was working on a road-building project in Talamanca around 1950, all the men on the crew took indigenous women as temporary partners, but with some caution: "the *compañeros* would say, that *india* is going to tie you."[60] L. C. was born in the foothills south of Limón in 1916, his father Nicaraguan, his maternal grandmother indigenous Bribri, and his maternal grandfather a Jamaican immigrant. While collecting rubber on an abandoned United Fruit Company plantation in the 1950s, L. C. fell ill and began suffering hallucinations. A local healer revealed that the cause was a *daño* put on him by a jilted lover.[61] It is impossible to pin down the cultural coordinates of the hex that injured L. C., just as (but not only because) it is impossible to pin down the ethnicity of any of the people in his account. Such stories reveal the complicated mixture of parallels, common origins, mutual reinforcement, and ongoing borrowing that characterized popular belief in the Greater Caribbean.

CHILDREN AT RISK: POPULAR FEARS OF SUPERNATURAL ASSAULT

We have not yet mentioned the centerpiece of white people's claims about black people's black magic in the early twentieth-century Caribbean: the idea that black sorcerers sacrificed white children to use their blood for healing. Such claims were most prominent in regard to Cuban *brujos*, but they spilled over onto ideas about "voodoo" and obeah as well. Historians in recent years have explored the interplay of island politics, racial ideologies, and libels from afar that made such sacrifice tales useful for national elites and persuasive to metropolitan readers.[62] Here, I would like to read rumors of child sacrifice not for what they tell us about the racist imaginaries of the Cuban officials who pursued them or the British writers who relayed them. Rather, I want to read rumors of child sacrifice for what they tell us about popular belief within the communities where the rumors began.

The idea that black witches sought white babies in particular seems quite likely an invention of outsiders' racist fantasies, and a late invention at that: the first such claims came with the *niña* Zoila case in Cuba in 1904 and the death of Rupert Mapp in Monchy, St. Lucia, six months before.[63] Mapp was a Barbadian street urchin taken from Bridgetown by a St. Lucian man seeking to create a *main de gloire* (thieves' candle) following instructions from the medieval French *Petit Albert*. There were indeed poor white children running about the streets of Bridgetown, offspring of that island's "red leg" settlers, so it is possible that Mapp was in fact white, although only one early report made this claim.[64] But with that one exception, contemporary hubbub over Monchy—in newspapers across the region and mouth to mouth in ports like Colón—centered on the menace of obeah rather than whiteness or blackness.[65] Sacrifice tales' resonance among British Caribbeans did not depend on outsiders' obsession with race. Real people around the Caribbean believed themselves and their families to be vulnerable to malevolent forces—as indeed they were. Some believed their children in particular to be vulnerable

Children on a Dominica lime and cocoa plantation, ca. 1903. (Library of Congress Prints and Photographs Division, LC-USZ62-66913)

to supernatural attack. That the potential evildoers might happen, like them, to be black was irrelevant to their fears.[66]

Testimonies gathered as part of an inquest in San Fernando, Trinidad, simultaneous with the Monchy case, bear witness to these popular concerns. "On Friday an enquiry began touching the mysterious death of Calixte Joseph, a three year old child," reported the *Port of Spain Daily Mirror* on September 12, 1904.[67] The child had gone missing two weeks earlier, and efforts to locate him proved fruitless. Eventually his decomposing corpse was discovered at the bottom of a ravine some distance from town. As the coroner's inquest wore on, it became clear that many in the village—including the boy's mother, his father (the mother's estranged partner), neighbors far and near, and the police themselves—were convinced that the child had been kidnapped for evil magical ends.

Donnacien McKenty, owner of the yard where the boy and his mother lived, testified that Calixte, his godson, had followed him out of town that day, as often before. It was Calixte's habit "to go with me and leave me to go home by himself," explained McKenty, "as well as from place to place, returning home in the afternoon. I was very fond of him." The affection that united toddler and farmer comes through in McKenty's repetitions, the shared routines he describes. "I had been absent for some weeks, and when I came out I found the child standing in the street, and he was naked. The mother was not there that morning." As McKenty walked toward his cocoa groves, the woman accompanying him "told me 'look that child is coming behind us' and I said it was the child's habit to follow me and go back whenever he pleased."[68]

When it turned out that afternoon that the child this time had not gone back home as he pleased but was nowhere to be found, McKenty, frantic, led the searches. But rumor soon fastened suspicion on McKenty and his neighbors, the Edwardses. People heard a child crying from the Edwardses' house: neighbors sent the police in to search first one trunk, then another, then a third.[69] Edwards testified, "I have been constantly annoyed by these suspicious people in the district. Since the loss of the child they get up into trees and watch my place constantly." How did Edwards explain his neighbors' suspicions? "I am a Grenadian, and I married one of these girls and got a good amount of land, and they are annoyed, saying they would not leave me until I am in gaol, because I had come from too far."[70]

Thus one suspicion within the village was that Ma Edwards and her uncannily successful Grenadian husband had secreted the boy in a trunk in their home in order to eat the child's bones and flesh with McKenty. Once the body was found in the ravine, these particular rumors lost steam. But others abounded and indeed had guided police action, as defense attorney Scipio Pollard drove home at the inquest. Surely it was obvious, Pollard argued, that the child had simply wandered off the path "and unawares fallen into the ravine which was overgrown with brushwood and which was exactly the place where a child rambling through bush and cocoa would happen to fall into. That suggestion he thought was more reasonable than the one put forward by the police, i.e., that the child had been taken to get oil for racing purposes. Supt. Sergt. Corbin objected, and stated that the police had said nothing like that." Pollard retorted "that he had been informed that all the time they were losing here was at the behest of head-quarters, on account of some wild idea having reached them that children were killed at the time of the races for the purpose of getting the oil from the liver or some other part of their bodies to use on race horses so that the owners might secure wins."[71] Police had also excavated terrain where villagers claimed McKenty's son had dug for gold, the implication being that McKenty might have sacrificed Calixte to favor the search.

One hears echoes of an 1899 Dominica case, in which "a negro" was "charged with murdering a child in order to provide a human sacrifice for obeah or voodoo worship, in connection with a search for alleged hidden treasure."[72] The idea that racehorse owners sought human livers for supernatural aid echoed claims from other islands as well. And as we follow these rumors we begin to see that sacrifice tales—just like Science, above—were very much in dialogue with a modern, unequal world.

On the gallows in Grenada in 1905, an accused obeahman broke into a diatribe that, although framed in the press as a confession, in fact was a denunciation of elite depredations on the bodies of the poor.

> Many murders that have been heard of at Grenville have been done by decent and respectable young men of the parish; they are still walking about freely and have not been caught, but their hands are not clean—merchants, shopkeepers, race-horse owners, butchers, estate owners, labourers and almost all the flourishing men of Grenville are concerned in the blood of many poor people found dead, just to satisfy the purpose of obeah, either to get the liver or the blood or some other part of the body for evil practices.[73]

The San Fernando case reflected popular knowledge of the dangerous ends that might befall children who ran afoul of malevolent men. Calixte Joseph might have been locked in a trunk for later consumption, might have been dismembered and parceled out to a godfather who would eat his flesh and to neighbors who would gnaw his bones. His body fat might have been rendered to anoint a racehorse and ensure its owner's fortunes; his blood might have been shed so that treasure would be found. Everything in the testimonies suggests that each of these seemed a real and present threat to members of a village community that had just lost one young member and seemed bent on meting out justice to others within its fold.

Events in San Fernando encourage us to take more seriously reports from St. Lucia that same month, describing how, after the third man accused of killing Rupert Mapp was finally captured, 5,000 people thronged the police station and "for hours . . . stood waving sticks and flags and shouting themselves hoarse in denunciation of St Hill and in their joy at his capture."[74] Likewise, perhaps we should reconsider one traveler's 1871 claim that when an obeahwoman who had "ruled in a certain forest-hamlet of Trinidad" was finally entrapped by police and handed over to the magistrate, people of surrounding areas rose up—"just as if they had been French Republicans"—and tore down her hut. "Whether they did, or did not, find skeletons of children buried under the floor, or what they found at all, I could not discover."[75] The author's arch skepticism had the virtue of refusing to condemn the woman as a cannibal before the jury of metropolitan readers. But its ironic tone also distances him, and us, from what may have been a very real local conviction that skeletons would be found, long-mourned losses explained.

We need to take seriously popular belief that malicious supernatural agents threatened children in Caribbean communities, in part because those beliefs remind us just how vulnerable children really were in this time and place. Calixte Joseph, in a rural community full of kith and kin, lived a more protected life than many. Yet of course there was no one to stop him from wandering to the edge of a ravine, any more than anyone was there to stop James Providence, age eleven, from drowning the following month when he and a younger sibling were fishing for bait at Milford Bay; or to stop one-year-old Irene Jestina from being run over by the wheel of a public cart passing in the road in La Plaisance village a week later, when her mother had gone "to the back of the house" for water.[76]

Consider the precariousness of Rupert Mapp's life even before he had the misfortune of meeting Montoute Edmond—indeed the precariousness that made it possible for Montoute to acquire a child with such ease. Frederica King, the woman who fed Rupert "breakfast, tea and dinner" in exchange for his unpaid labor in her Bridgetown cookshop, reported that Rupert had met Montoute on the docks and rushed eagerly back to tell her "that the accused Montoute Edmond had asked him to go away with him and he would care him like a father." Montoute appeared in her shop later that day. As she explained in court, "I said to the accused: 'You are a Frenchman and the little boy is an English subject: you can't carry him away without giving some satisfaction.' The accused told me then, 'Why, the boy has told me that his father is locked up and his mother is dead.'" King's attempts to present herself as a proud champion of imperial filiation founder at that point: she let the boy go with the stranger.[77]

In such a world, where even those parents still alive and in residence necessarily left their children to face risks day after day, attributing senseless death to witchcraft might offer some kind of solace. We hear traces of this, perhaps, in the non sequiturs through which the mother of Calixte Joseph tried to reconcile her conviction that she was a good mother—that her son was loved and cared for—with the manner of his death, his body carrion for crows at the bottom of a ravine. "He was a favourite," she repeated, "but someone must have put him there, for the place where he was found, not even crabs could go there." Cross-examined, she insisted: "I am not always at home, but I can swear that my child did not go far from home."[78] And yet he did. Are we to wonder that when nine-year-old Samuel Flatts went missing in Port of Spain only weeks before Calixte, his father insisted first to the police and then to the press that the child was "secreted" by a particular individual "for some nefarious purpose"—and are we to wonder that police found no basis for response?[79] The loss of a child to a malignant enemy might just be easier to bear than the loss of a child for no reason at all.

Post hoc rumors of sacrificed children became, in outsiders' retelling, stories of race, flowing into the self-confirming circuits through which white certainty of African savagery was made. We cannot know how many of the rumors that became fodder for white accusations of black witchcraft in this era began life as rumors of victimization from within Afro-Caribbean communities, but we can mark the existence of such rumors and note their far-different message. Certain stories told in the turn-of-the-century Caribbean rang true to a North Atlantic audience. Other stories, enunciated on the gallows in Grenada or in a San Fernando courtroom—stories of poor children stolen by neighbors seeking gold or by rich men racing horses—spoke instead and insistently of Afro-Caribbeans made victim. These, though, were not the rumors that seized the attention of those authors and authorities whose own fears and beliefs determined which tales were retold in the transatlantic prints.

Press reports offer only glimpses of quotidian concerns and periodic terror, such as rumors of a nocturnal "death car" seizing Haitians for their blood in 1932: "Overridden by superstition, the humble classes of [Port-au-Prince] are panic-stricken over the 'death car' which is said to be running around the city kidnapping persons between the hours of 1 o'clock and 4 o'clock in the morning."[80] The possibility was hardly unthinkable, seventeen years into a U.S. occupation in which technology and mechanized transport had been used against Haitians in new and malevolent ways.[81] Indeed, the very correspondent who saw here "Superstition Still Rife in Haiti" noted in passing the violent campaigns by "legions of marines," the public's total lack of "confidence in the armed forces," and, most immediately, the nightly onslaught of "police-cars" that "patrol the city at great speed and in a reckless manner," enforcing new laws that banned women from the streets: "When a woman or man is caught and arrested, they cry out and people who hear the cries, do not hesitate to believe that it is the 'death car,' hauling away a person."[82] But such stories of bloodthirsty sorcerers in official vehicles, with their unmistakably black victims and inescapably modern means, were not useful to white readers on a transatlantic stage and were not repeated there.

In sum, rumors of child sacrifice seem to reflect fears widely shared between people of the islands and people of the rimlands, republican citizens and imperial subjects alike. As with Science/obeah above, it seems likely that this broad agreement reflected the convergence of multiple factors: shared West African heritage, common engagement with North Atlantic modernity, the spread of knowledge through both print and oral culture, and human universals.

The irony is that this strand of Afro-Caribbean belief held outsiders to be particularly menacing, and in an era of accelerating intraregional labor migration, the outsiders falling under suspicion were likely to be Afro-Caribbeans themselves.[83] Pa Edwards, above, escaped with only his reputation harmed. Others were not so lucky. In 1919 Jamaican Joe Williams was arrested in Regla, Cuba, for "attempting to kidnap a little white girl." Reactions were shaped by *brujería* reporting. The news came "close upon the frightful crime of the negro witches in Matanzas who, a few days ago, kidnapped a white baby girl, tore the heart out of her living breast and made a meal of it." So the people of Regla reacted. "Three thousand citizens" mobbed the jail, seized Williams, beat him, tied him to a horse's tail, and made it run. "When finally the exhausted horse came to a stop and the negro was cut loose from the animal's tail, he was dead and naked, the clothes having been torn from his body by the rough, stony streets." The good people of Regla remained, after the fact, "unanimous in their approval of the swift justice dealt," and the editors of the *Havana Post* took the occasion to praise the effectiveness of "Lynch Law" in the United States, expressing the chilling hope that the "swift retribution meted out in Matanzas and Regla" would have a similar "sanitary affect."[84] The lynching of Joe Williams in Regla in 1919 suggests the real violence a black stranger might face in a world where poor people of every ancestry had reason to feel vulnerable.

SPIRITS AND SALVATION AT THE NORTHERN FRONTIER: THE CARIBBEAN FAITHFUL REACH HARLEM

Louise Little—Malcolm X's mother—was born in Grenada two or three years before Calixte Joseph's birth in Trinidad and perhaps a year after Rupert Mapp's in Barbados. Like them, she suffered a youth shaped by death and departure: her mother died shortly after her birth, and her father, a Scots planter, wanted nothing to do with the child. Like Rupert and Calixte, Louise was a product of the patois fringes. She grew up speaking Grenadian French Creole and English and attended an Anglican school on a Catholic island. Despite her proper schooling, she knew there was more to the world than met the eye. "She always believed in all this West Indian stuff about spirits and dreams and things supernatural," recalled Malcolm years later.[85]

Unlike Rupert and Calixte, Louise lived to early adulthood. And then, like so many other Grenadians, and Barbadians, and Trinidadians, and Jamaicans, she headed north. Which spirits traveled with them? What faiths gave them direction?

As we have seen, unorthodox revivals in the eastern and western Caribbean alike had been linked to Afro–North American connections. So when British West Indians arrived in Harlem to meet African Americans from Georgia, South Carolina, and Virginia, it was the latest in a long history of religious divergence and reencounter. In part because of these swirling connections, the early twentieth-century Caribbean that migrants came from was a place of religious ferment, including both enthusiastic evangelicalism and Afro-Christian faiths that "shouted," danced, and summoned spirits. Jamaicans in Limón, St. Lucians in Panama, and Barbadians in Trinidad drew on and added to this spiritual ferment. Did British Caribbeans in New York City do likewise?

Absolutely not, according to Jamaican émigré W. A. Domingo: "There is a diametrical difference between American and West Indian Negroes in their worship. While large sections of the former are inclined to indulge in displays of emotionalism that border on hysteria, the latter, in their Wesleyan Methodist and Baptist churches[,] maintain in the face of the assumption that people from the tropics are necessarily emotional, all the punctilious emotional restraint characteristic of their English background."[86] "Emotional restraint" was a label rarely attached to Caribbean worship in the Caribbean. Yet it seems there was enough truth to Domingo's claim for it to be widely shared. "All the people from the islands were all Anglicans," one Panama-born immigrant remembered; African Americans laughed at islanders and their "high church" ways.[87] As in the Canal Zone, the Anglican faithful found themselves subsumed into Episcopal churches, although here with black ministers and no Jim Crow. St. Martin's, on Lennox Avenue, had over a thousand members within a few years of its 1928 founding, at least three-fourths of them British West Indian.[88] Catholic, Lutheran, and Wesleyan Methodist churches drew thousands more.[89]

The high-church tilt makes sense, given the class dynamics of circum-Caribbean migratory streams. In the early twentieth century, it was the sons and daughters of the islands' colored middle ranks who sought opportunity in Harlem. If not of "the classes," they were close enough to wish they were. Only after the Panama Canal and Central American banana booms had waned, leaving working-class Caribbeans with some cash and connections, did the masses head north in large numbers. And even then, U.S. literacy requirements barred the islands' rural poor. Those who set the tone for Caribbean life in interwar New York, then, came precisely from the sectors most eager to distance themselves from the islands' ecstatic, disreputable revivals. If there were Shouters or Myalmen or Bedwardites in Harlem, they stayed well hidden.

Migrants were religious innovators here as across the Caribbean: adage had it that "West Indians came to Harlem 'to teach, open a church, or start trouble.'"[90] But religious entrepreneurship was channeled in more orthodox directions. There was, for instance, James Humphrey, a Baptist minister from Jamaica who stopped in Harlem on his way to Africa in 1901 and was converted to Seventh-Day Adventism. Humphrey founded Adventist churches in Harlem, Brooklyn, and White Plains and eventually led black Adventists out of the church entirely over the issue of segregation.[91] Meanwhile, nearly a dozen British West Indies–born pastors filled the A.M.E. Zion hierarchy in New England, and British West Indian priests headed Episcopal churches "all the way from Boston to Palatka, Florida."[92] When future Pan African activist George Griffith reached Beaumont, Texas, from British Guiana in 1928, he found not one but two British West Indian clergymen in town; and Griffith, a YMCA stalwart back in Guiana, became a lay leader as well.[93]

And then there was Garveyism. In 1921 the UNIA's chaplain general, Antigua-born George Alexander McGuire, founded the African Orthodox Church (AOC) in Harlem, and by 1926 there were sixteen AOC congregations in New York alone.[94] But even for those who did not join the AOC, the UNIA's rhetoric, ritual, and mission made it a community of faith as much as a political movement. Think of Baptist preacher Earl Little and his Grenadian wife, Louise, spreading the gospel of Garveyism in the heartland. The "jumping and shouting" churches where his father preached felt alien, their son Malcolm recalled, but his parents' UNIA meetings pulled him in.[95] "The hour of Africa's redemption cometh," preached Earl Little. "It is in the wind. . . . One day, like a storm, it will be here."[96] Many years later, when challenged as to whether he had any core beliefs at all given his quick abandonment of Nation of Islam for Sunni orthodoxy, Malcolm would define himself by this faith: "I'm one and the same person, the son of a mother and father who were devoted Garveyites all of their lives."[97]

Christian tradition offered Garvey much to draw on, just as it had Alexander Bedward and other prophets of black vindication. Psalm 68, "Princes shall come out of Egypt; Ethiopia shall soon stretch forth her hands unto God," had long been read as a promise of redemption by African American churches.[98] The UNIA's 1921 *Universal Negro Catechism* gave the prophecy pride of place:

> Q. *What does this verse prove?*
> A. That Negroes will set up their own government in Africa, with rulers of their own race.[99]

But redeeming Christianity from its historical complicity with black subjugation was not simple. Garvey argued that "We Negroes" should worship the "one God of all ages" but do so "through the spectacles of Ethiopia." The Madonna and Child portrayed in black churches should be black, elaborated McGuire, and blacks should invert white tradition and imagine the devil as white.[100]

Other Garveyites sought theological revindication by going deeper than the Christian past. Rabbi Wentworth Arthur Matthew, born in Lagos to a Falashan father and Nevisian mother, founded the Temple of Commandment Keepers in Harlem in 1919. The congregation grew to claim some 1,000 members, most of them female, British West Indian, and Garveyite. Rabbi Matthew taught that all Africans in the Americas are lineal descendants of Abraham by way of Ethiopia: "You are descended from kings, and the white man knows it. It is his purpose to keep you ignorant of your past so he can exploit you."[101] Matthews's followers included immigrants like Jamaicans David and Annie Harvey, who met and married in Port Limón, Costa Rica, moved on to Panama and Cuba, and joined the Commandment Keepers in Harlem in the early 1920s. This utterly common trajectory, and the race-conscious theologies they encountered within it, would send them off in portentous directions. They followed Barbados-born Garveyite Rabbi Arnold J. Ford to Ethiopia after 1924 and returned to Kingston in 1930 to found a storefront mission, "The Israelites," that helped originate Rastafarianism, as we shall see in chapter 6.[102]

The Commandment Keepers presented themselves as religious conservatives—traditional Jews following traditional Jewish law. Yet by radically revising conventional history in order to upend racial hierarchies, they stepped onto the terrain where, in the eyes of outsiders, religion shaded into cult. And cults, observers insisted, abounded. Interwar Harlem was home to a "legion of mystics and medicine men" who called themselves "prophets and priests, shepherds, bishops, confessors and even sons of god," wrote Jamaica-born Claude McKay.[103] There were "Pentecostal Pilgrims, Orthodox Ethiopians,

Moorish Science Templars, Black Jews and many others, Christian and non-Christian," he concluded: "the black masses thrive upon heterodoxy."[104] But Harlem's embrace of global spiritual esoterica was more than just heterodox. Symbols from the East—decidedly nonwhite, and yet laden with Orientalist cachet—shook up inherited hierarchies of race.

Thus while middle-class black New Yorkers, immigrant or native born, pursued respectability through decorous worship in traditional denominations, the masses found solace in louder and outrageously modern faiths. With charismatic leaders, small groups, and eclectic ritual, this kind of worship shared much with the practices of spiritual protection that also abounded. It is unclear how involved British West Indians were with the "spiritualist churches," "cultists," "herb doctors, clairvoyants, and 'jackleg' preachers" of interwar Harlem.[105] Claude McKay, at least, saw Caribbean practitioners everywhere. They might "promote themselves as numerologists, magicians, oraculists, metaphysicists, or plain spiritualists. But under the high-sounding titles they are the same old delvers in West Indian obeahism and voodooism."[106]

There was a long history of contact between the Caribbean and the United States in the realm of supernatural practice, just as there was in the realm of Afro-Christian worship. New Orleans—like St. Vincent, a former fringe of the French empire—was a particularly important node. Practices of "conjure" and "hoodoo" spread from there across the South, including to the communities now sending migrants to Harlem by the thousands. So British Caribbeans encountered in New York a range of popular belief that at least resonated with home.[107] As in the rimlands, islanders' supernatural expertise was familiar enough to be meaningful, exotic enough to be valued. On the streets of Harlem, "East Indian Moslems peddled incense, oils, and teas. . . . West Indians vended pamphlets explaining the mysteries of voodooism. Of the home-grown varieties, there were fire-eating Rajah Rabo, dream-book author, and the voluptuous slant-eyed Madame Fu Futtam, a seeress of Negro-Chinese parentage."[108]

The passage suggests both the visibility and invisibility of British West Indians at the occult edges of Harlem life, for Madame Fu Futtam, although quite possibly of "Negro-Chinese parentage," was not "home-grown" at all but Jamaican by birth and apparently Panama raised.[109] In other words, she hailed from the same western Caribbean nexus that gave us Eric Walrond's "obeah-loving and obeah-hating" islanders, Alexander Bedward and his traveling devotees.[110] In Harlem, she turned her multicultural origins into an exotic package of arcane authority. Her published guide to deriving lottery numbers

Famed Harlem mystic Madame Fu Futtam (born Dorothy Matthews in Jamaica, 1905). (Photo by George Silk/Time-Life Pictures/Getty Images, published Life *magazine, May 1950)*

from dreams was a best seller for decades. Fu Futtam was also the wife of Sufi Abdul Hamid, a Massachusetts-born African American who changed his name, embraced Islam, sometimes claimed to be Egyptian, and, at the urging of a group of "Negro Moslems," became a labor organizer.[111] In 1933 Harlem, Hamid led a campaign against hiring discrimination that temporarily succeeded beyond what conventional radicals had thought possible.[112] Hamid exemplified the embrace of global religious esoterica described above, crafting a pseudo-Egyptian persona with which to rally black solidarity.

Meanwhile, another Jamaican seer who had spent time in Panama had set up shop on West 136th Street, just one block north of Sufi Abdul Hamid's street corner. His name was Leonard Howell. He called his business a tea room, although rumor had it he was an obeahman or a healer. He had Garveyite enemies and Garveyite friends.[113] In 1930 he would be deported to Jamaica and there encounter David and Annie Harvey, just back from Ethiopia. Howell is central to the history of Rastafarianism, as we will explore in chapter 6.

Amid all these larger-than-life characters flaunting their mysterious foreignness, it is easy to lose sight of the quotidian presence of the spirit world in ordinary immigrants' lives. Did duppies menace Harlem crossroads at night? Did Science help Barbadians in Brooklyn, clawing their way into middle-class respectability by working two jobs and pinching dimes till they screamed?

The answer of course is that there is no single answer, for as we warned at the outset, there was no single popular belief. Some Bajan matrons sallied down Atlantic Avenue with goat-feet charms under their frocks; others made fun of them for believing. Some people knew their neighbors must be working "strong strong obeah" to get ahead so. Others, fresh off the boat, already knew that "that obeah foolishness don work in New York."[114] Lives were changing, and it was unclear what would endure.

PAN-AFRICANISTS AGAINST AFRICANISMS

If there was one thing that was consistent around the Caribbean and across the decades, though, it was educated Caribbeans' impatience with lower-class culture. As Claude McKay wrote in 1940, "to the Harlem intelligentsia and the respectable church-goers the cults were local circuses."[115] To McKay, in contrast, the cultists and occultists were something far more significant: proof of African culture. "Educated Negroes" might "delude themselves that there is no difference between black folks' religion and white folks' religion," that any gap was merely a matter of education or class, but McKay, citing his own observations in West Africa, knew better. "The innumerable cults, mystic chapels and occult shops which abound in Harlem are explainable only by tracing back to the original African roots," he wrote. Africans' faith was necessarily "pervaded by occult imagery. The fetich gods rule their hearts and the secret ritual of jungle magic is evoked to appease the obscure yearnings of the mind, which civilized religion cannot satisfy."[116]

In attributing New World black culture to African roots, McKay's analysis echoed cutting-edge social science of the day. Pioneering Haitian ethnologist Jean Price-Mars's *Ainsi Parle l'Oncle* had been published a decade before, and, guided in part by Price-Mars's model, Melville Herskovits would publish *The Myth of the Negro Past* in 1941, just one year after McKay wrote. If McKay's tone above pretends detached authority, elsewhere he seconded Price-Mars's fervent conviction that popular culture held the key to Caribbean self-discovery and empowerment. "It's the common people," insists self-exiled Haitian intellectual Ray in McKay's 1929 novel *Banjo*, "who furnish the bone and sinew and salt of any race or nation." We hear McKay speaking back to Harlem's literati in Ray's debate with a Martinican student in Marseilles:

"If this renaissance we're talking about is going to be more than a sporadic and scabby thing, we'll have to get down to our racial roots to create it."

"I believe in a racial renaissance," said the student, "but not in going back to savagery."

"Getting down to our native roots and building up from our own people," said Ray, "is not savagery. It is culture."[117]

Celebrating cultural continuities across the African diaspora would become a centerpiece of black internationalism by the middle of the twentieth century. But in the interwar era, few of McKay's peers—from W. E. B. Du Bois on down—wanted to hear it. Rather, the Martinican student's response captured perfectly the position of middle-class leaders of color. Racial renaissance, absolutely. But no savagery. For long decades, British Caribbean intellectuals had been fighting a two-front battle in regard to the masses' spiritual practices—on the one hand, disputing white outsiders' claims that the African "atavisms" of Caribbean ritual proved Negroes unfit for self-government; and on the other hand, exhorting the masses to clean up their act.[118] A typical 1926 editorial in the West Indian–run section of the *Panama American* cited Africa as the root, popular belief as the problem, and education as the solution. West Indians on the isthmus saw malevolent witchcraft in every misfortune: "every case of death . . . every case of sickness, the losing or procurement of employment, the success or failure in business ventures and everything affecting the course of their lives." Such superstition, which originated "with the witch-doctors of darkest Africa," will "[continue] to retard our progress" until the masses realize that those selling protection are just "preying on the gullibility of the simpletons who put their trust in obeah."[119] Similar comments appeared continuously in the British Caribbean papers of Port Limón across the interwar years.

While the white-run newspapers of Jamaica and Trinidad generally mocked popular convictions, for the black-run rimland papers, belief in obeah was no joking matter. That "this blight on civilization still exists among our people" in these "enlightened times and places" was intolerable.[120] This particular editorial was penned by Sidney Young, a fervent black internationalist who sympathized with Garvey's goals, denounced Britain's injustices toward colored subjects, excoriated the brutality of the U.S. occupation of Haiti, monitored the disenfranchisement of nonwhites in southern Africa, and called constantly for the unity of black people worldwide. Neither he nor his fellow editors were simply saps parroting the colonizers' perspective. But Africa-derived ritual practice, whether Afro-Christian revivals or protective Science, had no place in the future of the modern Negro as they saw it.

The African past thus appears in two starkly different lights in the print culture these intellectuals produced. African legacies in Caribbean popular culture? Damaging embarrassments. African legacies of ancient empire? Required reading—literally. The black child of today needed to know "that his race founded great civilizations" and "was prolific in statesmen, scientists, poets, conquerors, religious and political leaders" back "when the white race was wallowing in barbarity or sunk in savagery and cannibalism," wrote Marcus Garvey, instructing UNIA chapters to make sure their young people read Jamaica-born journalist J. A. Rogers's inspirational history, *From Superman to Man* (1917).[121] Rogers's publications were part of a concerted effort, explained journalist Roi Ottley, to counter "the concept of the Negro as superstitious . . . religious, ostentatious, loud and musical."[122] Not surprisingly, then, Rogers hated Eric Walrond's *Tropic Death* (1926), with its fervid descriptions of "Black Art idolators" in "voodoo-stricken" Colón. He accused Walrond of peddling "the bizarre, the exotic, the sexy, the cabaret side of Negro life" for white readers in ways that no "self-respecting Negro" author would.[123]

Garvey's own position vis-à-vis Caribbean popular spirituality was complicated. As we have seen, he relied heavily on the Christian rhetoric and ritual most familiar to the masses. He called out white-dominated churches for their racism and inspired the birth of new denominations that seemed to some observers more cult than religion. Yet Garvey denounced the "immorality, obeah and all kinds of dirty things that are part of the avocation of a large percentage of our people" as fervently as any of the striving black-internationalist editors above.[124] And when in the early 1930s some of Garvey's followers put his call to reimagine God in the black man's own image into radically literal practice—declaring the divinity of Ethiopian monarch Haile Selassie, under his former name of Ras Tafari—Garvey hustled to distance himself. The Ethiopianist revivals led by returnees like David and Annie Harvey and Leonard Howell in Kingston in 1931 and 1932 were "driving a large number of [our people] crazy," wrote Garvey. The sway of new "religions that howl, religions that create saints, religions that dance to frantic emotion" revealed "ignorance and superstition" unchanged from Bedward's heyday.[125] (Garvey's view of Bedward had apparently not improved since his 1911 letter to the editor back in Port Limón.)

Meanwhile, the Caribbean radicals who made up the far left wing of McKay's "Harlem intelligentsia" had little sympathy for any religion, from the most established church through the most Afro-identified revival.[126] As we saw above, in 1924 W. A. Domingo had praised the "punctilious emotional restraint" of Caribbean immigrants in their Wesleyan Methodist and

Baptist churches. Yet apparently he did not find them restrained enough. On the contrary, in 1920 he had helped his fellow immigrant E. Ethelred Brown establish a Unitarian church in New York (after Brown's first attempt failed to catch on in Jamaica), responding to the need for "more rational" religion to counter rampant "superstition, ignorance, and fanaticism." The founders of Brown's congregation were a who's who of the socialist/communist strand of interwar pan-Africanism, which happened to be pervasively West Indian: Domingo, Grace Campbell, Frank Crossthwaite, Richard B. Moore, and Brown himself.[127]

But even rational and progressive Unitarianism would prove too much for the Communist International. Moore's father had been a Plymouth Brethren lay preacher in Barbados before his death left Moore an orphan at nine; Moore was converted by an American evangelist and preached for the Christian Mission before leaving Barbados in 1909. By the time he joined Brown's congregation a decade later, Moore was an atheist as well as a socialist and a founding member of the African Blood Brotherhood, working toward "the liberation of people of African descent all over the world." Moore was a frequent speaker in Brown's church, "exposing the role of religion as 'the opium of the people' and the Church as a force of capitalist-imperialist oppression," he later explained. And for all that, in 1929 he was ordered by Communist Party hierarchs to leave Brown's church and publically denounce "religion in all its forms"—because "atheism is an essential part" of the "clear-cut and homogeneous world outlook of Marxism." His fellow party members either preceded or followed him out the church door.[128] The Harlem radicals who have been the focus of well-deserved scholarly attention in recent years, in sum, were profoundly atypical of the British Caribbean migratory stream in one crucial particular: the secularism they were drawn or pushed to adopt.

Trying to advocate a radical politics divorced from spiritual belief, they were fighting an uphill battle. There were not many potential atheists in Harlem for these would-be fishers of men to fish among. Moreover, the radicals had cut themselves off from a truly radical tradition. Although the established churches had been bulwarks of the Caribbean plantocracy, unorthodox preachers had arisen again and again to blend spiritual, political, and economic demands, from Paul Bogle crying "skin for skin" at Morant Bay to Alexander Bedward inveighing the "black wall" to knock down and oppress the white. None of the disparate strands of Caribbean spiritual practice we have surveyed were primarily focused on political mobilization, and yet, forged as they were in response to deep injustice, all had the potential to turn in that direction.

Garveyism came closest to realizing this synergy. With or without the African Orthodox Church, Garveyism was pervaded with religion simply by dint of its integration into the civic life of the Caribbean masses. Supporters pulled the UNIA into communities in which salvation and spiritual protection had pride of place and found them all fully compatible. "Onward Christian Soldiers" rang out in UNIA halls, in fraternal lodges, and at cricket matches. "Garvey common over Cuba," reminisced the Jamaican returnee quoted at the start of this chapter. "Any time you hear a bell there, is Salvation Army or a man talking about Africa."[129] Although Garvey himself rejected religions that howl, or created saints, or danced to frantic emotion, Garveyism fit easily into a spiritual landscape that had room for all of these. And as we have noted, Garvey's call to view God "through the spectacle of Ethiopia" would lead in extraordinary directions.

New York–based radicals like Moore, Domingo, Cyril V. Briggs, and Hubert Harrison worked tirelessly to bring working people of color into oppositional politics. Their lobbying was crucial in getting the problem of racism onto the agenda of the Communist International, and they were unafraid to challenge that body when they saw the interests of black people around the world at risk. Yet despite it all, the black masses embraced Garveyism on a scale and with a fervor that the radicals' organizations never inspired.[130] One piece that set the radicals apart was their secularism. To the extent that the movements they advocated insisted on rejecting all faith, those movements would find skeptical response among those they most sought to reach.

Religion was becoming revolutionary, though, even without their help. As we explore in chapter 6, by the 1930s, new religious movements in both the United States and the Caribbean would make oppositional racial ideologies the core of extraordinary theologies.

CONCLUSION

This chapter has looked at the spiritual worlds of British Caribbeans at home and abroad in the first decades of the twentieth century. Collective worship covered a wide spectrum, from public and ecstatic to private and cryptic, from avowedly Christian to markedly less so. There was high-church Anglican propriety, enthusiastic evangelical Christianity, Revival bands and Shouter meetings; those who caught the Holy Ghost and others whose spirit work more resembled *vodoun* and *Santería*. All but the most orthodox agreed that divine intervention was not the only unseen presence impacting the material world.

Obeah became an object of contention in different ways: the classes accused the masses of believing in it; the masses suspected each other, or others, of using it for ill. Fear of witchcraft within Caribbean communities may have reflected convictions drawn from the West African societies from which great-grandparents had been torn. But witchcraft fears also had room for modern developments like horse racing and police cars. Stories of macabre consumption suggest entirely reasonable concern over outside interlopers' use of the bodies of the poor—and of children in particular—to enhance their already excessive powers. Tales of witches gave Caribbean people a language for denouncing their profound vulnerability in the modern world. And revival shepherds and prophets and obeahmen gave them guidance on what to do about it.

As migration accelerated over the first decades of the twentieth century, spiritual practice proved to travel well—from rural to urban to foreign and back again, from Trinidad to Panama to Harlem, providing grounds for exchange with locals each step of the way. The combination of shared African, and European, influences (roots) and repeated contact (routes) meant that around the region, collective worship and spiritual protection had enough commonality to make communication possible.

But there were lines that spiritual practice did not cross—indeed, lines that religion reinforced rather than breeched. These were lines of class within each society. Educated middle-class strivers insisted on the gap between their own religious lives and the less-reputable ferment around them. Just as we will find when we look at music and dance, popular cultural creativity in the spiritual realm was both race conscious and border-crossing. Yet this did not open the way for convergence with those pursuing black internationalism through respectable publishing or radical politics in the same years. Potentially parallel projects were divided by cultures of class.

Three   Alien Everywhere

Immigrant Exclusion and Populist Bargains,
1920s–1930s

The brownstones on 136th Street were elegant but crowded. A full forty-three people lived in four adjacent townhouses in 1920. They hailed from Grenada, St. Vincent, Barbados, St. Kitts, the Turks, Jamaica, and St. Marten, as well as from Virginia, North Carolina, Pennsylvania, Maryland, and Georgia. Each of them, like every resident up and down the block, was black. No. 225 was home to future journalist Roi Ottley, his parents and brother, and the dozen-plus boarders whose rent helped pay for the house. Roi's parents had been in the United States the longest, having come from Grenada back in 1904; lodgers Minna and Vinetta, Jamaican dressmakers who arrived in 1917 and 1918, were the most recent arrivals.[1] The streets of Harlem had become the crossroads of the Caribbean, and islanders kept pouring in. The slacking of the Cuban sugar boom after 1921 and the continued reduction of the canal workforce in Panama came just as the flow of European immigrants to the United States was stanched by new legislation. British Caribbeans, like all others born in the Western Hemisphere, could still enter the United States at will, as long as they could demonstrate literacy, good health, and the support of friends or relatives who would keep them from becoming a public charge. With neighborhoods like 136th Street waiting, this was little barrier.

Then: rupture. The U.S. Johnson-Reed Act of 1924, which for all other groups merely tightened prior limits, confronted British Caribbeans with an unprecedented and portentous break. For the first time, those born in "non-self-governing" (read: black-majority) colonies in the New World were placed under numerical limit, dependent on distribution of quota numbers from the annual allocation to Great Britain. As I will discuss in detail below, this nominally race-neutral rule functioned as a nearly total ban on immigrant visas for British Caribbeans. Total black immigration into the United States—counting arrivals from across the Americas and around the world, but comprised in its great majority of British Caribbeans—dropped from over 12,000 arrivals in the first six months of 1924 to under 800 in 1925.[2]

This chapter will ask how and why this seismic shift occurred and measure its consequences for lives on all sides of the remade borders. It offers a simultaneously comparative and connected history of migration restriction in the

United States, Latin America, and British Caribbean. For Johnson-Reed was merely the first among a series of new laws that radically restricted the entry and employment of black "aliens" around the region. The United States had long differed from Spanish America in explicitly disenfranchising on the grounds of partial African ancestry—"one drop of blood." Yet in this case, the United States excluded Afro-Caribbean immigrants without making mention of race, while circum-Caribbean republics explicitly added *la raza negra* to existing categorical exclusions. Meanwhile, in the British Caribbean, it was Chinese immigrants against whom systematic—although here, too, nominally race-neutral—bans were imposed in these years for the first time. The patterns have much to tell us about the shifting politics of race and belonging in the interwar Americas.

The fundamental trend was common not only to the United States, Latin America, and the British Caribbean but much more broadly. These years saw the rise of mestizo populism in Latin America, *völkisch* nationalism in Europe, and nativism in the United States—differing labels for a common phenomenon. Organized workers made demands on the state in the name of the nation, and states identified national destiny with the health and virtue of the working classes as never before. In country after country—industrialized North Atlantic and agro-exporting circum-Caribbean alike—the two sides forged an implicit bargain in which more robust social guarantees went along with new forms of exclusion that limited who had access to the new public goods.[3]

In the Spanish-speaking circum-Caribbean, these populist bargains were hampered by the outsized power of the transnational companies on whom export economies depended. Systematic illegalities riddled enforcement, so that powerful employers retained de facto access to a supranational labor market. Nevertheless, real gains were made by "national" labor in this era. Only in the British Caribbean, with no popular vote and elites who still did not identify the future of the polity with the well-being of the masses, were populist bargains not on offer. There, anti-immigrant politics couched in the language of incipient nationalism—Jamaica for the Jamaicans!—did not accompany but rather substituted for genuine social investment. More substantive state commitment to what British sociologist T. H. Marshall would label "social citizenship" remained, for black colonial subjects, undemandable.[4]

The similarity of restrictionist moves across the region reflects both shared circumstances—sociopolitical, like the rise of organized labor; economic, like the instability of key commodity prices in the 1920s and the export collapse after 1929—and direct connections. Some connections came via print circulation. Latin American, U.S., and Caribbean elites read the same expert authors on the relationship between national "stock" and social cohesion. Newspaper articles on Chinese vice were excerpted and reprinted. Other connections came from intentional institution-building, like the First Pan-American Conference of Eugenics and Homiculture, held in Havana in December 1927, at which U.S. eugenicists presented a "model immigration law" to delegates from across Latin America.[5]

But connections in the realm of quotidian practice were just as important. The emerging mobility-control regime demanded multilateral engagement from the get-go. The system depended on the existence of bureaucrats elsewhere who could generate or demand in one country documents being demanded or generated in another. Functionaries of Venezuela's *estado* Sucre, sweating in the governor's palace in the Caribbean port of Cumaná circa 1917, found themselves besieged with instructions and demands. There was a "Decree of the Spanish government on passports and other requisites for foreigners who travel to that kingdom," "Formalities that must be fulfilled by persons embarking for the Republic of Cuba," "Requisites needed to disembark in India," and "File on the new passports that the North American government is issuing." In parallel, and not surprisingly, a new "Order from the [Venezuelan] Minister of Interior Relations" forbade "entry into the territory of the State of foreigners who do not carry the necessary documents in conformity with the law." What self-respecting nation-state would not demand documentary obeisance in such an era?[6]

Not just politicians but also journalists and labor activists observed the race-based measures put in place by allies and rivals and urged their governments to follow suit. British Caribbeans seeking action against Chinese and Syrians did so with explicit reference to anti-Asian bans elsewhere in the British Empire (Canada and Australia in particular), as well as the antiblack bans in the surrounding republics.

One cannot fully explain the origins or course of interwar restrictionism, then, without placing the United States, the circum-Caribbean republics, and the British islands as part of the same story. And one certainly cannot explain the *results* of that restrictionism without observing at this regional scale. For the impact of a ban against black entry to Honduras would have been utterly distinct had Honduras been alone in barring its doors. Both in terms of the material suffering occasioned and the ideological shifts inspired, it mattered enormously that British Caribbeans found themselves defined as *negros* and banned for that reason at port after port after port. As we shall see in chapter 4, faced with this systematic assault, British Caribbeans looked to their "own" government for the kind of support that other sending states routinely provided their emigrants. As we shall see in chapter 6, what they got was the opposite. Britannia's expansive commitment to protect the rights of British subjects—whoever they were, wherever they went—turned out to be a thing of the past.

A HEMISPHERE NOT YET PARTITIONED: THE NORTHERN FRONTIER OF THE MIGRATORY SPHERE UP TO JUNE 1924

A pioneer in conceptualizing government as something "of," "by," and "for" the *pueblo* and the New World's largest recipient of immigrants in the nineteenth and early twentieth centuries, the United States was also a pioneer of the movement to revolutionize entry controls. Here, as elsewhere, Asians had been the first target. The U.S. Chinese Exclusion Act of 1882 had started a cascade of anti-Asian laws across the Americas; the 1917 Immigration Act extended Asian exclusion by creating an "Asiatic Barred Zone." With the 1921 Emergency Quota Act, the federal government moved to cap total entry and select among Europeans on the basis of supposed assimilability, with quotas proportionate to the numbers of each "national origin" reported by the 1910 U.S. Census.[7]

Like all others from the Western Hemisphere, British Caribbeans were exempt from any such categorical caps. Instead, like all emigrants under the system scholars have dubbed "remote control," they were prescreened at the point of departure by U.S. consuls, who extended visas based on proof of good character, good health, literacy, and prospects for economic independence (the "LPC," or "likely to become a public charge" clause).[8] By the early 1920s, these criteria had been standardized into a series of documentary requirements: passport, birth certificate, attestations of character from "respectable" figures at place of last residence, police records from same locale, letters of promised support from relatives or friends in the United States, and "show money" (from $20 to $50) in hand to display on arrival.[9]

The documentary demands themselves could be onerous, given the multisited trajectories from which travels to the United States were launched. As we have seen, it was precisely migrants' prior experience with labor abroad—in Panama and Cuba in particular—that generated the resources and connections necessary to travel northward. U.S. consular files from the early 1920s attest to gymnastics of international paperwork as Jamaicans and Barbadians trying to leave Cuba for the United States sought documents and authentications from Cuba, Panama, and British islands at once.[10] In this sense, Caribbean lives were a poor fit for the emerging exigencies of remote control. But the gatekeepers did what they could to help, and people managed.

That Caribbean kin practice routinely eschewed state and church sanction created some difficulties: documentary control presupposed state tracking of family ties.[11] Vernacular kin practices like long-term concubinage and child borrowing raised eyebrows among consuls but did not spark exclusion. Among those given visas to travel to New York in 1923, but flagged by the Kingston consul for extra questioning on arrival, were "CLEOPATRA E BECKETT: Is unmarried, is supported by a colored doctor by whom she has four children, the oldest of which is 13 years old"; and "MRS. MARY MOILE who is taking the minor to her father, states that she does not know anything about the mother of the child although she has taken care of the child for many years."[12] Faced with the complications of making family practice match U.S. authorities' documentary demands, it was sometimes easier to create documents that fit than go through the hassle of explaining the truth. Ada Alleyne took out a passport in her native Barbados in 1917, intending to return to Panama; the daughter who appeared on it as hers, she later explained, was actually the child of a friend, who had asked her to take the three-year-old to the child's father in Panama and then changed her mind. "I was taking it as my child in order to avoid any trouble," Alleyne explained.[13]

The bottom line was that up through 1923, both the letter of U.S. law and its implementation prioritized migrants' economic potential, as evidenced by literacy, health, cash, and networks of support. Jamaicans, Barbadians, and others connected to the circum-Caribbean migratory system had all of these, and consuls knew it. While some relatives sent formal affidavits of support, U.S. consuls readily accepted informal correspondence. A handwritten letter—"To Whom it May Concern: This is to inform you that I have known Jane Smalling for two years and she is very captable in receiving her sister Maud Smalling. Sined Theodora Richards"—could (and in this case did) suffice.[14] Indeed, the system worked with a smooth welcomingness that is almost painful in hindsight, given what would replace it. In July 1923 the U.S. consul asked the Jamaican press to publicize yet again the list of documentary requirements and to urge intending passengers to apply for a visa *no less than two weeks* (emphasis mine) before the intended date of departure to avoid any risk of delay.[15] That same month, the same consul reassured the *Gleaner* that not a single visa application had been refused in Kingston for a year or more: "Refusal" was "practically only made in the case of anarchists and persons in opposition to organized Governments, agitators and others who were considered actually dangerous."[16]

Thus even as hundreds of thousands of Europeans found themselves blocked by U.S. "emergency quotas" after 1921, British Caribbeans reached U.S. shores by the thousands. Still, the proportion of total immigrants who were of "African Black" race remained less than 2 percent of the total.[17] A drop in the bucket on a national level, British Caribbean immigration was so tightly focused that, viewed from certain street corners, it seemed a flood. Bound to island and rimland communities by densely overlapping ties, Harlem's stately, teeming blocks and Brooklyn's Red Hook flats were home to over 36,000 Caribbean immigrants in 1920 and absorbed some 24,000 more in the following three years.[18] The Harlem streets where Roi Ottley and friends had played in 1920 now made room for men like Eugene Ebanks, who arrived in 1920 and worked as a chauffeur; Eugene's future wife, Etheline, who followed two years after and found work as a servant; and his older brother Phelix, who came the following year and worked in a restaurant.[19]

Could hardworking men and women like Eugene and Etheline and Phelix be "actually dangerous" like the anarchists and agitators the Kingston consul kept from U.S. shores? Did New York–born children like Roi and Jerome menace the future of American democracy? Some thought so, and their voices were getting louder. Professional racist Lothrop Stoddard had warned in 1920 of the "momentous consequences that the introduction of colored stocks into white lands would entail," "far more" dire still than the "momentous changes" that even "near-related and hence relatively assimilable" European arrivals brought.[20] The 1921 legislation that limited arrivals from southern and eastern Europe but placed no numerical cap on Mexicans or Jamaicans—even less desirable by eugenicists' yardstick—seemed to some the height of folly.[21] The Commonwealth Club of California (CCC) not only commissioned studies of trends in "race stocks" within the U.S. population but also made sure the studies reached those whose decisions mattered. Because he "expected that the subject of Immigration will be brought further under the jurisdiction of the United States Consuls by future legislation," explained the head of the CCC's Section on Immigration in a letter to the U.S. consul in Kingston in 1923, he was enclosing a copy of the CCC's latest report on the impact of dysgenic immigration. "We believe it will repay a careful perusal and also will influence your action."[22]

An exchange that same year between the U.S. consuls in Bridgetown and Port of Spain reveals both the spread of this eugenicist case for race-based restriction and the persistence of alternative ways of thinking. The Port of Spain consul had taken the initiative to denounce to Washington the grave damage that the flood of Trinidadian emigrants whose visas he had no legal reason to deny would cause the United States. Asked for comment, the U.S. consul in Barbados disagreed on all points. He did not concur that "the black races in the West Indies are essentially inferior to the black races in the United States. Those from Barbados are rather noted for being industrious and making excellent servants." What mattered was economic rationality, not race: "If these people meet an industrial and social necessity in the United States I do not see whether it matters whether they are black or whether they are white." Any attempt to apply to the Caribbean the quota system that 1921 legislation had imposed on European emigrants "would prove most complicating to work out" and might exclude "many desirable people."[23]

Yet in thinking that black immigrants might still be "desirable," the Bridgetown consul was in a shrinking minority. Even moderate restrictionists like Yale sociologist Maurice Davie called the categorical exclusion of "darker-skinned races" the "one issue on which there is more or less of a national agreement. . . . We cannot assimilate the yellow, brown, and black races. . . . Their exclusion is indispensable to the welfare of the United States and its range should be extended."[24] The year was 1923.

STRIPPING RIGHTS WITHOUT SHEDDING— OR INVOKING—ONE DROP OF BLOOD: JOHNSON-REED IN THE COLONIAL CARIBBEAN

This was the context in which the Immigration Act of 1924 took shape. Prominent scientists and politicians argued for placing all of the Americas on a quota basis, but in the end, the desire of the Western agricultural lobby to maintain access to easily hired, easily deported Mexican laborers—and State Department concern that limits on Latin American entry would complicate diplomacy and trade—prevailed. National-origins quotas would not be created for the Americas.[25] What of steps to bar the "black race," like the Asiatic, through geographic or biophysical criteria? Davie's claim of "national agreement" on this score depended on a constrained view of whose opinion counted as national. Attempts by the U.S. Senate a decade earlier to declare black foreigners ineligible for immigration or naturalization (in reaction to the numbers of Jamaican former canal workers reaching Gulf ports circa 1913) had collapsed in the face of opposition from congressmen with Afro-American constituencies and vocal lobbying by the NAACP.[26]

No one sought to reopen this can of worms in 1924. Disavowing federal responsibility for U.S. Afro-Americans' de facto second-class citizenship was tricky enough already without entering open debate over whether black race categorically disqualified one from political rights. Thus nothing in the Johnson-Reed Act limited entry by those of "African" or "black" race per se. Yet with a single sentence, it rewrote the parameters of legal mobility for British Caribbeans: "Persons born in the colonies or dependencies of European countries situated in Central America, South America, or the islands adjacent to the American continents (except Newfoundland and islands pertaining to Newfoundland, Labrador, and Canada), will be charged to the quota of the country to which such colony or dependency belongs."[27]

Exactly how this new quota status would work was not clear, least of all to the officials charged with administering it. "Emigration of Jamaicans to U.S. Stopped," read the banner headline in the *Daily Gleaner* on June 14, 1924. Consuls on the island had ceased visaing passports, stranding masses of "young men and women" with relatives in the United States and passages already booked. "They will not be able to leave again."[28] Yet two weeks later, the *New York World* was assuring readers that "Labor Department officials pointed out today"—note: incorrectly—"that the British West Indian possessions occupy the same position under the act as does Canada, against whose citizens there is no bar whatever."[29] Meanwhile, the U.S. consul in Kingston offered smooth nonanswers to the public and worked frantically behind the scenes to get clarification about the new system he was supposed to be enforcing.[30] The "quota control officer" in the U.S. consulate in London seemed to be the authority in charge of what finally emerged as the key issue: the allocation of the 34,000 British annual quota slots among the dozens of U.S. consulates in the UK and colonies.

"We are having an average of seventy-five to eighty-five callers daily, who desire to go to the United States for permanent residence and from what I can gather from the instructions received, it cannot be determined whether Jamaica comes under the quota," wrote the Kingston consul to London. If it did, hundreds of quota numbers should be cabled immediately. "For your information, prior to June 30, 1924, this office was issuing in the neighborhood of thirty visas daily, for permanent residence in the United States, and on a rough estimate it is believed that there are at least two thousand people who desire to go to the United States for permanent residence at this present time."[31]

The telegraphed reply from London was a model of economy: ten visa numbers allotted to the Kingston consulate for the month of September.[32]

Surely, London had misunderstood? The Kingston consul repeated himself by return mail. At least 2,000 Jamaicans intended to relocate to the United States in this fiscal year. "For your information in nearly every case the applicant has from one to five children," the consul wrote, "and if I interpret the instructions properly, it will be necessary to issue a quota visa for each one regardless of the children's ages, and all will be counted against the quota. . . . Can I understand from the allotment made for September of ten numbers that Jamaica will only have one hundred for the entire fiscal year?"[33] The frosty reply from London quashed any undiplomatic identification with the newly excluded: "Upon consideration, no doubt, you will appreciate the fact that with a total available quota for Great Britain and Northern Ireland and various British Dependencies of 34,007 many thousands of persons must be disappointed this year."[34]

Across the Caribbean in Barbados, a similar drama was under way, as the news sunk in that a total of five (5) British quota numbers per month would be allocated to the consular district covering Barbados and Dominica, and none at all to the Leeward Islands.[35] Over 300 Barbadians who had received visas under the old system in the month of June alone now found themselves unable to embark. Merely applying the trickle of new quota numbers to this backlog meant that not a single new immigrant visa would be granted in Bridgetown for another five years.[36] The other sites from which British West Indians had routinely emigrated to the United States were similarly constrained: there were four British quota numbers per month for Panama, six for the Canal Zone, and ten for Colón, and these figures were cut by half three years later.[37] The outcome was as clear as the mechanism had been murky: in fiscal year 1925, only 462 people born in the British West Indies entered the United States under the British quota—and fewer than half of them were black.[38]

Through it all, the public position of U.S. officialdom was that race had nothing to do with it.[39] (Indeed, this was the private position as well, at least as far as State Department correspondence goes.[40]) Certainly, barring black entry was not the law's raison d'etre. Johnson-Reed reflected two core commitments for two distinct constituencies. Overall immigration would be further reduced, protecting wage levels for national workers; and the influx of the wrong kind of white person would be stemmed. British Caribbean commentator PROLETARIAT, writing to the *Gleaner* from New York in August 1924, captured the marriage of convenience between working-class populists and elite eugenicists. "Native-born labor" had gained bargaining power in the wake of the Great War and amid elite fears of "Bolshevists from Russia." Labor support then helped eugenicists get what they wanted: to "check the influx of Polish and Italian Roman Catholics, Russian and other Jews, and people of Slavic blood." That the new legislation allowed British Caribbeans to be barred was a fortuitous addition, from the perspective of those "believers in the theory of keeping out what is insolently and unscientifically regarded as inferior stock" who had been distressed over "the influx of nearly 10,000 coloured persons yearly."[41]

For British Caribbean observers, the plain result was to strip rights from British subjects of color alone, excluding Caribbeans while Canadians moved freely. The United States, as they saw it, had joined South Africa, Canada, and Australia in the ranks of self-proclaimed white man's nations using immigration bans to stay that way.[42]

And about time, too, according to the New Yorker who wrote to congratulate "The American Consul, Kingston" on July 9, 1924 (at a moment when that authority was still literally running back and forth from steamship-line ticket window to *Gleaner* office begging news of whether Jamaica was covered by the new law at all[43]):

Dear Sir:

I have read with much satisfaction that the influx of Negroes from Jamaica has been checked.

The situation here in New York is becoming almost appalling. The white people are being driven from one street to another to find quarters, and so many of the Negroes who come into this country come from the West Indies. When the Negroes take a white apartment house to live in the white tenants are no longer wanted for the reason that Negro tenants pay much larger rents and the landlords do not want the white people to stay. The Negroes come in and keep many lodgers and pay their rent that way in most cases. I do hope they will be kept in the West Indies for *years to come*. Judging from the inroads they have been making here in New York City it looks as if it were only a matter of a few years before they would have the whole island of Manhattan, unless something is done at once.

May the good work go on.[44]

If some white neighbors were happy to see entry halted, some black Americans seemed none too sad, either. While in 1914, when "an attempt was made to exclude people of African extraction along with Asiatics, American negroes like Du Bois and the late Booker Washington protested vigorously and successfully," PROLETARIAT noted that this time, the silence from black leaders had been deafening. "While American negroes may have taken no active step to have West Indians barred, it is nevertheless my belief that they are not sorry."[45] (PROLETARIAT suspected that black leaders' animosity toward Marcus Garvey had something to do with it.) Du Bois's tepid disavowal of responsibility in December 1924 did little to counter that impression: "The Nordic champions undoubtedly put one over on us in the recent immigration bill. If our West Indian friends had watched more closely and warned us, we might have been able to take some effective step. As it was, by the simple device of discriminating between self-governing and crown colonies in the British Empire, a device whose significance at the time escaped us, immigration to the United States from the West Indies has practically been barred."[46]

This was exclusion achieved through procedural restriction rather than flaunted through explicit bans. Formalities of quota status, preference status, and allocation masked the functioning of power. But the new telegraph codes developed by the State Department for communication about individual cases spoke plainly. REUNION meant the applicant had proven preference status as the spouse or child of a legal resident. FREEDOM meant the applicant was entitled to nonimmigrant status as a temporary tourist or business traveler. IMMOBILE meant the visa application had been denied.[47]

How did paperwork and perceptions translate into the stark goal of IMMOBILIzation? Immigration policy had long relied on shipping lines as gatekeepers, both implicitly (first-class passengers deemed exempt from passport requirements) and actively (ships fined for transporting migrants whose documents officials found inadequate upon landing). Johnson-Reed quadrupled the fines, ramping up the caution that constrained mobility significantly beyond the letter of the law.[48] Replying to a confident request from a Harlem homeowner in 1926 for a temporary visit by his niece, the Kingston consul noted that although U.S. law technically no longer required even passports for British subjects entering the United States in transit or as tourists, in practice, steamship companies refused to carry anyone they suspected might be rejected at Ellis Island. The niece had best acquire a nonimmigrant visa in advance.[49] The demand that consuls, shipping agents, and Ellis Island officials each treat with suspicion claims to temporary-visitor status multiplied the points at which racialized perceptions of need and intent could bar entry.[50] Conversely, with the right mix of appearance, wealth, and connections, "FREEDOM" could be yours. From the earliest reports of the immigration ban in June 1924, the *Gleaner* had been quick to assure that "so far as business men who want to leave for the United States the Act will not, of course, apply."[51]

Amid the swirl of misinformation, this confidence that class privilege would persist proved among the few correct predictions.

What of "REUNION"? Whereas before 1924, patterns of support between British Caribbean siblings and other horizontal kin had corresponded smoothly to U.S. agents' concern for immigrants' economic independence, the new regime's radical privileging of legitimate spouses and children of U.S. citizens—the only kin permitted nonquota status—marked a radical and, for many, insurmountable rupture.[52] Chain migration of siblings and the delegation of child rearing to female kin back home had been fundamental to Caribbean migration northward. Even solidly respectable, well-established married couples relied on extended family to spread reproductive labor across multisited households. After 1924, such patterns could continue only outside the law.

Children and legal spouses of noncitizen U.S. residents were entitled to preference status on the waiting list for quota numbers, but under the draconian allocation, this "preference" was in practice a dead letter. Meanwhile, siblings, nieces, and nephews merited no recognition at all. "I am now in the United States five years and often wish I had one of my Brothers over here as a companion," wrote George Gardner from New York City to the British colonial secretary in Kingston in 1928. "I know that it is a hard job for you to do as I guess there is a lot of applications ahead of him but at the same time anything you do is well done and you alone can grant him a passage for the United States."[53] George was wrong on all counts: the colonial secretary had no say in the matter, and those who did had no interest in brothers. When the U.S. Department of State at its most humanitarian urged consuls to make "the unit of consideration . . . the family rather than the individual," they meant by family "father, mother, and unmarried dependent minor children."[54] That sparse unit looked like no family most British West Indians had ever seen and bore no useful resemblance to the rich branching of affection and support along cognatic lines that made their mobility possible in the first place.

One can make visible the gulf between the new U.S. law and British Caribbeans' moral economy of mobility by noting the gap between what people explained in their letters of inquiry and what one would need to know in order to answer them. "My Wife has a daughter in Labyrinth, Gayle, P.O. St. Mary, Jamaica, B.W.I. who is about 13 years of age. Now I would like to know if I could arrange for her to come to this country?" wrote George Laws in June 1929, explaining that he hoped to finalize arrangements before his wife left for Jamaica in July.[55] His expectation of quick resolution breaks your heart. Five years earlier, it could have been fulfilled. Not now. Had George legally adopted his wife's daughter before January 1, 1924? Had he renounced his British subjecthood and become a U.S. citizen? Unless the answers were yes and yes, none of the other details mattered. Before 1924, the key questions determining British West Indians' ability to enter the United States were: Can you read? Can you work? Will someone help you out? And that was precisely the information people gave when they wrote to officials. Now, although those questions retained nominal relevance, the de facto ban on quota numbers for Britain's black colonies meant that only family reunification actually mattered, and only three ties counted as "family." Were you the legal spouse of a U.S. citizen, the child of a U.S. citizen mother, or the legitimate or retroactively legitimated child of a U.S. citizen father? If yes, a path strewn with documentary hurdles but ultimate hope lay before you. If not, you were going illegally or not at all.

Even birthright citizenship was lost to some. Nothing in Johnson-Reed changed the race-blind *jus soli* conferral of U.S. citizenship on all children born on U.S. soil. Yet for this constitutional entitlement to exist as a substantive right, shipping agents and consuls, the executors of the new mobility-control system, had to believe it existed. In the wake of Johnson-Reed, the Kingston agents of one steamer line wrote to the U.S. consul there to inquire "whether a child born in the United States of America of alien parents is, ipso facto, an American citizen, and if there are any conditions governing this, such as length of time the child remains in the United States after birth. We sometimes have cases of this kind cropping up and have been unable to find anything on the subject in the United States Immigration laws in our possession." The consul replied that he believed (quite incorrectly) that the children came under the nationality of their father "and would require regular visa of their passports if the father is not an American citizen, but I would suggest that you take this matter up with your head office in the United States, and have them to give you the Commissioner of Immigration's decision on same."[56] Given how persistent parents had to be to overcome the steamer lines' presumptive rejection even before Johnson-Reed, how many children found it impossible to reenter the land of their birth as the citizens they were in this new era of viciously effective ambiguity?[57]

Quite apart from these hurdles in law and in practice, the immigration bureaucracy banned those who could not navigate it even if they might have had a nominal claim to do so. In this sense, all the written sources we have are from people within spitting distance of success—those literate, savvy, and confident enough to try to work through the system. A true tally of what quota-control officers labeled "unmet demand"—and a full picture of the range of Caribbean individuals who experienced the exclusionary power of states firsthand in this era and were shaped by that experience—would include not only all the petitioners whom the Barbados consul turned away without even processing their documents for a wait list but also those who wrote to the wrong person, or not at all.[58]

Barriers rose. Lives got harder. But the world did not stand still. In August 1924 press reports described 200,000 would-be immigrants to the United States stranded in Havana, 40,000 of them British West Indians, caught out by Johnson-Reed's new restrictions.[59] Four months later, when asked how many "aliens now in your consular district . . . would proceed immediately to the United States if the quota restrictions were removed," the Havana consul estimated only 14,500 in total, 2,000 of them "Jamaican negroes."[60] Three months later, the Bridgetown consul could hope that his visa backlog would soon disappear entirely "in view of the fact that many of these persons have given up all hopes of getting to the United States and have left for Cuba [or] the Panama Canal Zone" or spent the ticket fare on other things.[61] People dealt with the new reality, whether that meant trying Panama one more time or sending a son north on an older cousin's birth certificate. Through their adaptation, they naturalized the new governmentality, so that it came quickly to seem normal that working-class Caribbeans whose skills were in demand in Harlem must enter illegally or not at all. The radical rupture that was 1924 vis-à-vis the United States, and that was the decade as a whole vis-à-vis the Greater Caribbean, became scarred over, retroactively smoothed, endowed with an aura of inevitability it never had at the time.

POPULATION, POPULISM, AND THE *PUEBLO*: THE RESTRICTIONIST BARGAIN IN THE LATIN AMERICAN REPUBLICS

As late as 1926, it was possible to gaze, appalled, at the still-novel array of practices through which states sought to control movement across borders and hope that "a gradual return to international sanity" might yet be in the offing.[62] "Prejudice against the foreigner" had long been "common enough among the masses," but its current embrace by "men pretending political leadership or intellectual superiority" was unprecedented. "The alien is now almost a pariah," subject to "indignities formerly reserved for condemned criminals," from photographic registry to fingerprinting, and denounced as a Bolshevik for the slightest criticism of the state that abused him. Worst of all, "the effects of this are not confined to our own country" (wrote this U.S.

citizen, resident in the Canal Zone). "The moral influence of the United States is still powerful in other nations." When the United States "stood for lib[ert]y and toleration there was a better chance for those ideals the world over." That day was over.[63]

Racism, of course, was nothing new, and nothing unique to the Colossus to the North. Across nineteenth-century Latin America, elite ideologies valorized European immigrants for their blood and their culture—both of which, elites insisted, were essential to civilize the new nations. Mixing with locals, Europeans would "dilute" or "whiten" African and indigenous "blood"; maintaining their customs, Europeans would counter the barbarity that colonial lassitude had brought. State-subsidized colonization schemes were routinely reserved for immigrants of "good race, for which should be understood European." Typical was the Cuban law of 1906—ultimately unimplemented for lack of funds—which had sought to subsidize immigration from Sweden, Norway, Denmark, and northern Italy.[64] A Venezuelan dissertation penned that same year called for "a good ration of Boer fiber, German muscle, or prolific Italian blood."[65]

But these were not the migrants that Venezuela received. Cuba was the world's sixth-largest recipient of European emigrants in the century leading up to 1930, but no other Greater Caribbean receiving society came anywhere close to matching the millions of Europeans who emigrated to Argentina, Canada, Brazil, and Australia, much less the tens of millions who reached the United States.[66] Even as statesmen in the Spanish-speaking circum-Caribbean waxed poetic about Boers and Swedes, tens of thousands of black islanders had reached their shores to fell forest, load ships, and generally make themselves useful in the export economies. And as we saw in chapter 1, despite ideologues' antiblack musings, in practice foreign-born blacks' labor conditions and civil protections had not been much different from the native-born workers around them.

What shifted in the 1920s were not ideas about blackness or race per se but the place of the "national" masses in national governance. On the one hand, new developments in biology, demography, and medicine suggested that the health and heritage of the masses determined the nation's future, and could be improved, immediately. On the other hand, new structures of politics gave those masses unprecedented weight in deciding who ruled.[67] In rhetoric and in practice, the *pueblo* now mattered as never before. Would-be leaders sought to interpret the "race-mixing" of the past in terms that somehow offered future promise. The emerging mestizo nationalist formula argued that, eugenicists' claims notwithstanding, in *this* nation, the fusion of races had created (or was on the cusp of creating) a people, unified in blood and spirit—a *pueblo*, a *nación*, a *patria*.

Enthusiasm for the *pueblo* went hand in hand with concern for the migratory currents shaping it. Thus, ironically, the same years that brought new acknowledgment of and opportunities for fellow citizens of African ancestry in countries like Cuba, Brazil, and Venezuela also saw the rise of race-based antiblack exclusion at the same sites. "Protection for the worker, let us raise industry and commerce from their ruins, give a gigantic stimulus to education, and favor that immigration that can bring to our shores people robust in body and spirit who can raise up this race of ours that is decaying or stagnating," urged future Venezuelan government minister Alberto Adriani in the 1920s.[68] "We must ban yellow and [South Asian] immigration and restrict black as much as possible, even if at the start those preferences may be costly for us," he reiterated a few years later.[69] Identical plaints sounded in Costa Rica, Cuba, the Dominican Republic, and Panama.[70]

Like Adriani, they increasingly framed the issue as a trade-off between short-term economic benefits (to employers in particular) and the long-range needs of a democratic populace. In Panama, the nationalist press denounced economic arguments in favor of British and French Caribbean immigration as "in addition to being anti-patriotic . . . suicidal if not criminal." The government must turn a deaf ear to claims of "foreign enterprises which are accustomed to contract workers at cheap prices" and instead permit only immigration of "families who will benefit us not only by means of material success but principally by means of morals and race."[71] The Venezuelan minister of interior relations echoed the same logic in 1930, explaining that the nation's latest immigration law placed the state on the side of the people against the powerful. No longer would Venezuela yield to the "demands of those who, on the pretext of the lack of laborers, attempt to inundate our *poblaciones* . . . with inadmissible individuals, brought from certain Antilles to increase the difficulties [*taras*] of our ethnic groupings and complicate the population factor, on which all economic and social processes turn."[72]

Those excluded by it recognized that a profoundly new bargain was being shaped, a bargain that included but went beyond immigration restriction per se. The current moment was one of "universal reconstruction," wrote a British West Indian correspondent from Limón in 1930. "The capitalist is no longer the custodian of the world's economic condition." Instead, governments intervened actively "to create a spirit of mutual good will" between capital and labor. The United States led the way in egalitarian commitment—"from the shoe-shine to the diamond magnate is given constitutional representation at the White House"—and therefore, logically, in official xenophobia as well. America had "found it necessary to legislate and enact laws that would control immigration; of course, this measure came under the fire of criticism from other countries, but here we find the inevitable law of self-preservation, since the slogan that the voice of the people is the voice of the government has become universally accepted."[73]

If the voice of the people was now the voice of the government, foreign workers were in for a rough time. The fact that immigration expanded the labor supply to the detriment of local workers' bargaining power had long been recognized, of course. Common sense dictated that where workers had a real voice in politics, demand for labor would lead to rising wages rather than rising labor supply. Recent research has confirmed the positive correlation between participatory democracy and immigration restriction in the twentieth-century Americas—no secret at the time.[74] As Jamaican observers noted drily in speculating about Cuban leaders' response to calls for the deportation of Haitians, Jamaicans, and Barbadians, "we admit that the temptation to appeal to the masses must be great when one is asking them for their votes."[75] Given Latin American statesmen's continued Europhilia, they were unlikely to heed protests against European immigration. Protests against black immigrants, however, were another story.

Banana disease and volatile sugar prices made the 1920s a decade of frequent contractions in western Caribbean economies. (The 1930s would be even worse.) As times got hard, both anti-immigrant protests and direct intimidation surged. In Honduras, Cuba, and Costa Rica, British Caribbean communities were the targets of "abuse, malignity and violence," reported one correspondent, and as each round of attacks went unpunished, "the perpetrators or their descendants have become more daring and less cautious."[76] In 1926 "gangs" of Panamanians cruised West Indian tenement streets after dark, "banging on doors at midnight and shouting 'afuera chombos!'" and worse.[77] From Venezuela came reports of "banditry by the natives" against British West Indians—cars waylaid along the roads to petroleum camps, Grenadians "trussed up and thrown into an oil hole." Grown men, veteran oil workers, were afraid to walk alone at night. Rumors of riot menaced. "Something is bound to happen there," warned Joseph Williams, heading back to Grenada after years in Curaçao, Aruba, and Maracaibo. "Every Venezuelan, as soon as you have any altercation with him says, 'Alright, you are all going to leave here soon,' which shows that it is a united effort on the part of the people that is forcing the hands of the Government."[78]

Some receiving-society labor leaders pulled against the tide, preaching race-blind class solidarity instead of scapegoating black immigrants. Anarchists and communists consistently hewed to an antiracist, anticapitalist line.[79] A pamphlet distributed in English in Panama's terminal cities by the "Joint Committee of Workers Defense" in 1933 argued: "Race hatred, the worst prejudice that can be imbued into the proletariat, is being instigated by the government in its efforts to divide the working class. . . . That is a wrong way. There is no difference within the working class. We all, Latin Americans and West Indians, belong to the same and unique class: that of the exploited by our common enemy, the bourgeoisie."[80] Such arguments were doomed. State-led mestizo nationalism, promoting cross-class solidarity against the foreign-born, offered national workers powerful allies and ineffective opponents. In contrast, antiracist radicalism, promoting class antagonism and solidarity with dark-skinned outsiders, provoked powerful enemies and brought nearly powerless friends. In the circum-Caribbean as elsewhere, the racialist-nationalist route looked better and better. The mid-1930s saw thousands of workers thronging Panama's plazas for rallies run by the newly formed "Society for National Defense," demanding the expulsion of British West Indians and greeting president Harmodio Arias "with the Fascist salute."[81]

Thus, observed at international scale, the consolidation of the national state as the focus of working-class demands for labor-market protection seems overdetermined by supranational trends. But if we can resist the teleological pull of our knowledge that mobility control ended up in the hands of receiving-society states, we can see that there were multiple contenders at the time. Some thought that the power to protect jobs against outsiders should be lodged in unions themselves. In 1919 the Panama-based West Indian Labor Union (WILU) asked the governor of Jamaica to recognize them as the representatives of British West Indians in Panama, restrict further emigration to Panama, and require all artisans traveling to Panama to acquire in advance a WILU credential.[82] Or, if workers' organizations could not themselves administer mobility control, could they at least have a seat at the table? In 1927 the British West Indian canal employees' union (PCWIEA) announced that they had been lobbying the U.S. secretary of labor to allow British Caribbean Canal Zone residents into the United States as nonquota immigrants. But, PCWIEA's district chairman lamented, due to lack of support from their own rank and file, their plaints had been ignored. If only Negroes from across the hemisphere held annual labor conventions, he suggested, then they could make their demands felt.[83]

It was typical of strivers in Panama's British West Indian press to imagine that sufficient uplift and unity could vanquish racism in all its guises. But this voluntaristic explanation of PCWIEA's failure misses the boat. The emerging international system made states rather than organized labor or civil society the arbiters of mobility control. "Labor Conventions"—or rumors of riot—could indeed bring pressure to bear in this system, as long as the workers involved could use the symbolic leverage of *pueblo*-as-nation and the institutional leverage of electoral politics. Lacking these levers both abroad and at home, British Caribbean working men and women found themselves with no way in to the new bargain between governments and governed.

MOBILITY CONTROL AT THE PERIPHERIES: THE SPREAD OF EXCLUSIONARY LAWS ACROSS THE CIRCUM-CARIBBEAN REPUBLICS

Mobility control had become both a fundamental substantive component of labor and population policy and a symbolic theater of modern state power. Governments crafted their immigration policies for multiple audiences, including national elites, local labor leaders, international experts, and fellow receiving societies. Within this complex array, in the interwar era it was the influence of other restrictionist states that stood out for contemporary observers. "American race prejudice like the virus from a mad dog's bite is infecting the Anglo-Saxon world," warned the editors of the *Barbados Weekly Herald* in 1925, pointing to developments in Australia and Canada, especially the latter's de facto bar on "coloured immigrants" from the British Caribbean.[84] Others had noticed the same. An editorial in Panama's *El Diario* in 1926 demanded that legislators ban black French and British Caribbeans as "undesirable races"—after all, "even the very children in the schools know, that the natives of these islands cannot enter in Australia, Canada or other of the British Dominions."[85] The Colombian minister of government fretted in 1922 over his country's lack of explicit legislation "entitling it to reject all those foreign elements," especially Chinese and blacks, "who because of their ethnic and moral conditions find no home in other civilized countries." Colombia's "*imprevisión*" stood in sorry contrast to the "diligent zeal" of other Latin American states in this "most fundamental matter of self defense."[86] Exclusion had become a matter of national pride on a global stage.

An explicit international frame of reference guided individual nations' pursuit of race-based exclusion.[87] Actual attempts at interstate coordination (like the 1927 Havana Pan-American Eugenics Conference or the international conference on emigration and immigration in that same city a few months later) were the least of it. Circum-Caribbean states of their own initiative surveyed foreign legislation before formulating policy, seeking the "principles put into practice in the matter by the most advanced nations" and evaluating technologies and metrics from consular remote control to quotas.[88] More pervasively, people here read what people there wrote. Foreign newspapers laid bare how your nation's emigrants figured in distant debates. By the mid-1920s, controlling frontiers against foreign workers, rather than just foreign armies, and attending to the eugenic inheritance as well as health and education of future generations had become standard elements of a sovereign state's mission. Placate labor leaders, embrace cosmopolitan science, and impress your aspirational peers all at once? Antiblack bans were irresistible as policy and performance alike.

Across the Americas, a first wave of race-based exclusionary laws in the 1890s had banned immigration or entry by Chinese and subsequently others of "yellow" or "Asiatic" race. Specific North African and central Asian groups—and, everywhere, gypsies—were added over the following two decades.[89] In contrast, laws barring those of "black" or "African" race did not appear until the second half of the 1920s. In less than a decade, antiblack bans were erected across the Americas: in nations with sizable black immigrant populations and those with none at all. In 1925, El Salvador—located on the Pacific coast, with almost no foreign blacks in its populace—outlawed entry by "members of the coloured races," including "Negroes" for the first time.[90] Way down at the other end of the Pacific coastline, Chile did the same in 1930.[91] In such cases, like in the frequent bans on specific southeast European nationalities, the performative element of exclusionary legislation is unmistakable. No one was banning Bulgarians from Central American shores because they constituted a material threat to native employment.

Typically, countries that actually received Afro-Caribbean migrants legislated restriction by steps—first limiting recruitment of black laborers, then demanding differential deposits from black immigrants, and finally banning black entry outright. Thus, Honduras in 1923 barred the "immigration of negroes to work in the banana plantations" and in 1929 added *negros* to the list of "restricted races" obliged to tender a 500-peso deposit to enter the country unless under contract and whom employers had to repatriate immediately upon completion of labor if under contract. In 1934 entry by *negros*, like that of "coolies, gypsies, and Chinese," was outlawed entirely.[92] Similarly,

Guatemala decreed in 1921 that "immigrants of color" must deposit $200 upon entry; in 1931 foreigners of "Negro race" were banned outright "for ethnic reasons."[93]

The typical next step after outright bans were threats of deportation on grounds of supposed illegal entry. Mexico banned foreign black entry in 1926 and showily expelled groups of "negro working men" to British Honduras.[94] Threats of deportation began in Guatemala in 1931—although United Fruit had no trouble retaining those British West Indian employees it actually wanted, according to a nearby observer.[95] In Honduras, where United Fruit operations were shrinking due to declining yield and plant disease, sporadic deportations of dismissed workers proceeded throughout the 1930s.[96] Having banned Chinese immigration along with all its neighbors in 1897, Nicaragua then bucked the trend and included only individual criteria (health, morals, criminality) in the immigration law of 1918. Yet in 1930 Nicaragua realigned with regional standards, banning entry by *negros* alongside Chinese, Turks, Arabs, Syrians, Armenians, Gypsies, and Coolies (those already settled in Nicaragua with "businesses of importance" could reenter if they left).[97]

These examples highlight the diverse class- or labor-based loopholes written into the laws. On the one hand, laws anticipated overlooking race for those who arrived with enough capital in hand, and in most cases when race-specific deportations threatened, owners of real estate or businesses were explicitly exempted.[98] On the other hand, the outsized influence of export-sector multinationals (oil companies in Venezuela, sugar companies in Cuba, United Fruit most everywhere) meant that states generally preserved companies' access to short-term contract labor as long as they could—even though foreign capitalists' "importation" of foreign labor drew the rising populists' showiest denunciations.

The standard solution was to build doublespeak, flexibility, and graft into the system. In Colombia in 1922, rumors that 3,000 Jamaicans would be brought in by U.S. oil companies had triggered state efforts (cited above) to match the "diligent zeal" of other Latin nations. The resultant 1922 law gave the Ministry of Foreign Affairs authority to bar those "whose admittance should be ethnically undesirable by reason of their race being such as would derange the proportion of races forming the Colombian stock." United Fruit had no trouble securing permission for workers in its employ, but independent entry by black working people became ever more difficult.[99] Colombian consuls in Panama in 1924 understood their charge to be to refuse entry permits to all "those of black race and those of yellow race," although accusations of under-the-table improprieties swirled.[100] Three years later, Panama's

British West Indian press warned that Colombian port officials had begun enforcing "an ordinance," formerly a "dead letter," forbidding the entry of "dark-skinned persons . . . in search of employment as laborers."[101] The timing of exclusion often differed from its paper chronology.

Embracing xenophobic populism while keeping exporters happy meant making "dead letters" and open secrets fundamental components of governance. The Dominican Republic from 1912 onward required employers to obtain permits to bring in "laborers of any race except Caucasian." A new decree in 1919 further limited independent entry by nonwhite workers while expanding the exemption for contract workers, who became more subordinate than ever to the specific mill that employed them.[102] Meanwhile, scores of thousands of Haitians (some seasonal cane cutters, others longtime Dominican residents or border-crossing traders) moved to and through the Dominican-Haitian borderlands to the west.[103] A crescendo of antiblack rhetoric under the Trujillo regime culminated in a new law levying a $6 annual tax on foreigners and mandating forced labor for those unable to pay. Pressed by British diplomats in 1933 on how the new laws would impact British West Indians, Dominican officials seemed bemused that any sophisticated observer might think the proclaimed rules would be enforced. Surely it was obvious that this was, in the words of the Dominican minister of foreign affairs, "a law of camouflage"? British Caribbean workers might face "perfunctory arrest" from time to time but no doubt would be released immediately afterward so they could get back to work.[104] That same year, the British minister in Panama rushed to consult Minister of Foreign Affairs J. D. Arosemena in response to President Arias's announcement that 5,000 unemployed British West Indians and their families would be deported in short order. Arosemena marveled that British diplomats had actually taken the idea of mass deportations seriously, and "then [he] said, somewhat sadly, that wholesale repatriation would have a detrimental effect on property owners, on tradesmen, and in fact on the country as a whole."[105] The deportation "plan" had been announced to appease the anti-immigrant wing of Arias's party, but it would not be allowed to get in the way of the business of business.

Acting against foreign-born blacks in nations where Afro-descendants formed a large and acknowledged part of the "native" population posed particular challenges. In this, the United States in 1924 was similar to Cuba and Panama and different from Costa Rica, Guatemala, and Mexico. In Cuba—the American republic where racially inclusive citizenship had been most hard fought and proudly acclaimed—Spanish-language requirements worked to create antiblack outcomes without explicit mention of race, just

as "non-self-governing" colonial status did under Johnson-Reed. The introduction of contract workers (without reference to race) had been forbidden
since 1902 yet was allowed by special permit each year up to the 1929–30
harvest—by which time sugar prices had fallen to less than a third of 1924
levels.[106] Further closing the door to Afro-Caribbean migrants at that point,
a 1931 decree declared that no immigrant "unable to speak Spanish" would
be allowed to land without $200 cash in hand.[107] Meanwhile, laws mandating
deportation of the unemployed made no mention of race but were enforced
against Haitian immigrants primarily, Jamaican immigrants secondarily,
and the far-more-numerous Spanish immigrants not at all.[108] In contrast,
in Panama, where the large Spanish-speaking Afro-Panamanian population
had nothing like the dense tradition of civic activism of Cubans of color, the
criterion of language was used alongside, rather than in substitution for, race.
A 1926 law barred all "Negroes whose native language is not Spanish"; a 1928
law limited access to citizenship for those already resident; and in 1941 a new
constitution took away the ability of black immigrants' children born after
1928 to claim Panamanian nationality.[109]

The fact that many of the lawmakers enacting these measures would not
themselves have been considered white by the northern eugenicists whose
rhetoric they adopted did not go unremarked. Ever "since a majority of colored Panamanians passed a law barring other colored people from entering
the national territory as 'undesirable' and enacted repressive measures against
those already resident in the country," wrote Jamaica-born Sidney Young in
the *Panama American* in 1927, "I have no delusions about the 'brotherhood
of man,' 'liberty, fraternity and equality,' nor in the polite applesauce about 'all
men being created free and equal.' . . . This world was made for white folks
and colored folks are giving it to them on a silver platter."[110]

As always, restriction at one site reverberated elsewhere. New bans set
black sojourners in motion along new routes—for instance, to Port Limón,
known in the British West Indian press by 1930 as the last remaining "free
port for Negroes in these parts."[111] Seeking to ban "coloured persons of any
nationality, who might be drifting from one Central American country to
another, either by sea or over the land frontiers, in search of a livelihood," the
foreign minister in 1934 instructed all Costa Rican consuls abroad to cease
issuing visas "to persons belonging to the Black race, until further notice."
Meanwhile, officials prepared to move from procedural exclusion to explicit
racial ban. By executive decree in 1942, Costa Rica—the last Central American republic to do so—explicitly barred entry by "those of black race."[112]

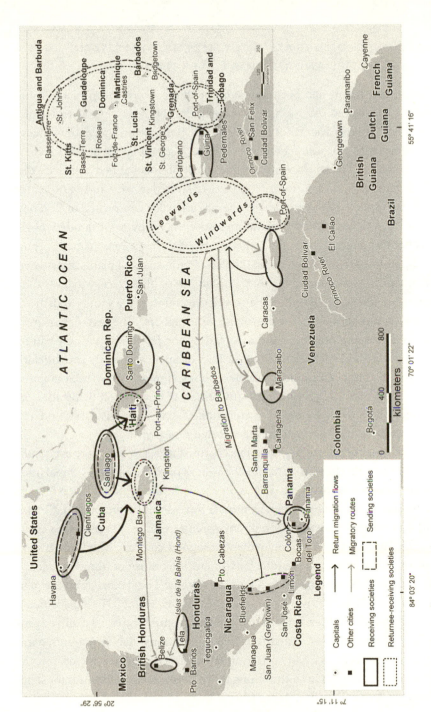

British Caribbean Migration, 1925–1940

Black immigration had been banned, but that did not mean black immigration had ended. As we have seen, extralegality was central to Greater Caribbean polities' systems of border control. Reliance on alternating nonenforcement with periodic action against those "illegally" present was nowhere clearer than in Venezuela. Antillean immigration was banned alongside that of Asians in 1895, and the prohibition was reiterated in 1912 and 1918. Yet the latter laws specifically permitted temporary entry for contract labor.[113] A new law in 1925 tightened entry requirements, yet more migrants flooded in—in part because alternatives in the United States, Cuba, and Panama had become so scarce. In 1926 one Jefe Civil in the Paria Peninsula sent plantation owners a printed circular announcing that "individuals of black race, whatever their origin, are unacceptable when they enter the country in a group to dedicate themselves to agricultural, industrial or other labors." The text, drawn from the 1918 law, was presented and enforced by the Jefe Civil as a new ban on black entry. The Venezuelan consul in Port of Spain fruitlessly sought clarification of what he presumed to be new policy. A terse handwritten notation from the Ministry of Foreign Relations denied all novelty, implicitly allowing the Jefe Civil's freelance crackdown to stand: "Tell [the consul] that the relevant instructions have been communicated repeatedly."[114]

As in other countries, tightened restrictions in Venezuela were eventually followed by outright bans, a step made easier as the contraction of global trade reduced large employers' insistence on access to the regional labor market. By presidential decree in 1929, Venezuela forbade all further "colored" entry and authorized the deportation of any foreign resident of color who could not display certificates of employment and good conduct. The Immigration Law of 1936 formalized the total ban on entry by those of nonwhite race.[115] But enforcement remained capricious—and venal. Local officials on the peninsula of Paria let British West Indians in for a profit.[116] National officials turned a blind eye, then insisted that the illegal entry erased all claim to procedural protections.[117] (Similarly, in Cuba, allegations that immigrants' entry or continued residence had been contrary to laws on the books—despite the complicity of officials in contravening those laws—became grounds for stripping civil protections from those whom the state wished to deport.[118])

By the mid-1930s, Venezuela's ambassador in London warned superiors that any further complaints by him about the frequency of "clandestine entry" from the British Caribbean would only "reveal that Venezuela lacks the police

Modelo Nº 4

ESTADOS UNIDOS DE VENEZUELA

REGISTRO DE EXTRANJEROS

CEDULA DE IDENTIDAD

expedida por *el Jefe Civil del Distrito Arismendi,* *del Estado Sucre* el *28* de *octubre* de 19*32*

Nombre y apellido: *Miguel Jorge Wellington*

Nacionalidad: *Inglesa* adquirida originaria *Inglesa*
(si adquirida, indíquese la nacionalidad originaria:)

Sexo: *varón*

Estado civil: *casado*

Lugar y fecha de nacimiento del extranjero *Nació en Trinidad, Anti-* *lla Inglesa, el 29 de setiembre de 1895*

Profesión u oficio: *comerciante*

Fecha de llegada: *llegó en el año 1919*

Lugar o puerto de entrada: *Guanoco*

Número del pasaporte: .... Autoridad que lo expidió: ....

Fecha del último visto bueno: ....

Autoridad que lo otorgó: ....

Estatura: *1 met. 75 cent.*
Color: *negro*
Ojos: *negro*
Pelo: *negro, grueso*
Señas particulares y defectos físicos per-
manentes visibles:

Señas fisonómicas: *cara ovalada, pómulos salientes,* *nariz ancha, labios gruesos*

Firma autógrafa del extranjero *Michael Wellington*

(A la vuelta)

Venezuelan foreigners' registration card, 1934. (Archivo del Estado de Sucre, Cumaná, Venezuela; Gaveta 28, B72) necessary to impede them," an admission of weakness to be avoided at all cost. Better to dissuade migration through "a severe penal sanction" applied to individual migrants.[119] In practice, this meant that local officials seized Grenadian, Vincentian, and Trinidadian residents, set them to forced labor for months on end, and pushed some overboard at gunpoint in waters off Trinidad's shore to swim or drown. (Because these events were directly linked to British Caribbean disputes over island emigrants' right of return, they will be discussed in more detail in chapter 6.)

Before the Great War, one might have thought that freedom of movement and freedom to sell one's labor among employers looking to hire were part of an emerging international liberal consensus. Yet as we have seen, by the late 1920s, centralized states had firmly established their right (if not always their capacity) to make national borders the limit of the first "freedom." What of the second? Responding to Cuba's new "Nationalization of Labor Law" of 1933, which required all enterprises to employ at least 50 percent Cuban citizens, the Foreign Office instructed its representatives in terms that underline both the new consensus over states' right to control borders and the persistence of dispute over noncitizens' rights within them: "Whereas it is fully admitted that any country is justified in protecting its local labour market by prohibiting the admission of foreign labourers, it is quite a different matter to debar persons long resident in the country from continuing the employments they have long followed. Such action is altogether opposed to the principle of respect for vested rights [and therefore] violate[s] the principles of international law."[120]

But the lesson of the 1930s, *pace* this confident rhetoric, was that no state was going to go the mat to make black noncitizens' "vested rights" a substantive reality. On the contrary, barring longtime residents "from continuing the employments they have long followed" was becoming standard practice. Workplace quota laws like Cuba's 1933 *Ley del 50%* were part of a broader process through which certain foreign-born residents found themselves transformed into second-class noncitizens. In Costa Rica, the workplace quota was both employer-specific and explicitly race-based. Congressmen in 1934 attached a "companion law" to the contract granting United Fruit new land concessions, requiring that "Costa Rican workers" comprise 60 percent of the company's workforce and explicitly forbidding employment of "people of colour" in the company's new Pacific coast operations.[121] The company hired Nicaraguans and Guanacastecans instead and got on just fine.[122] But more commonly, workplace quotas were written in terms of nationality rather than race and gave the largest employers the greatest discretion.

Why were workplace quotas so common in the Greater Caribbean when they were apparently so rare in the industrialized North Atlantic states?[123] Although Cuba, Venezuela, Costa Rica, and others attempted to use their consuls abroad to enact selective limits in this era, circum-Caribbean states did not have the overseas staff or resources needed to enact true "remote control" as had the United States.[124] Nor could they turn steamship lines into effective enforcers in this region where small craft and local captains abounded.[125] Finally, and most of all, there were the many thousands of non-citizen black workers (immigrants or the children of immigrants) already present within each country. If "remote control" was the prerogative of states wealthy and large enough to project their borders outwards and police mobility at migrants' points of departure, workplace quotas were the mirror opposite: "indoor gatekeeping" that allowed states too weak to police their frontiers nevertheless to constrain noncitizens' access to the social goods of the populist bargain.

Thus, in the Greater Caribbean, efforts to preserve labor markets for native workers ended up using as the unit of regulation and enforcement not the national territory as a whole but the individual employing enterprise. As unemployment surged in the 1930s, workplace quota laws were put in place in every Greater Caribbean receiving society except the United States. In Panama, a 1926 law demanded that 75 percent of employees of any enterprise be Panamanian nationals; enforcement was inconsistent but highly visible in terminal cities.[126] That same year, Cuba's secretary of public works declared that no more than 15 percent of employees on public roadworks would be "Antillean workers"; he promised to employ "as many Cuban workers as possible or in their defect Spanish and other European laborers." Cuban papers lauded the "patriotic and foresighted gesture."[127] A Jamaican returnee later that year reported that he and a fellow islander had been able to get work only by passing for "Americans." "The first question an employer asks is: What country do you come from? And when he is told Jamaica, the applicant for the job is told 'you are out of luck.'"[128]

By 1932 laws in Guatemala and Honduras reportedly required all "companies (native and foreign) to employ 75% native labour"; enforcement was tight, and yet United Fruit managed to hire extra Jamaicans in Honduras in years when banana exports were good—and dismiss them when they were not.[129] In keeping with regional trends, the Dominican congress passed laws in 1934, 1935, and 1938 demanding that all businesses employ at least 70 percent Dominicans; equally in keeping with regional trends, sugar companies got the exemptions they wanted.[130] Venezuela's new *Ley de Trabajo* in 1936 required every company to employ 75 percent Venezuelan workers.[131] Foreign oil companies denied that they were bound by the law, yet they announced a voluntary "policy" of favoring Venezuelan workers, which in practice meant firing British Caribbeans first whenever downsizing seemed useful.[132]

Enforced at employers' discretion or local officials' will, such laws increased migrants' vulnerability to economic cycles and political shifts. Threats of enforcement created de facto surtaxes, extralegal fines levied for the crime of being black and crossing borders. The governor of British Honduras reported in 1932 that recent "activity shown against coloured persons" in Guatemala owed largely "to agitation by officials who, having been recently appointed, were endeavouring by the threat of deportation to collect the customary 'graft.'"[133] When Panama passed its 75 percent law in 1926, United Fruit announced that it might be forced to suspend operations in Bocas del Toro. Two years later, banana exports were humming along just fine, but Jamaican workers who lived on the Costa Rican side and crossed the border daily to work found themselves pulled off trains on paydays by Panamanian officials eager to be asked to look the other way for a price.[134]

Thus circum-Caribbean receiving societies turned British West Indians into second-class noncitizens in lands where some had lived for decades and others had been born. This was accomplished at the lowest possible cost to states on the one hand and employers on the other, via systems that meshed legalities and illegalities, gestured toward remote control but relied on indoor gatekeeping, and pledged populism while preserving the privilege that mattered.

IMMIGRATION RESTRICTION IN THE BRITISH CARIBBEAN: NATIVISM ONLY SKIN DEEP

"Unemployment in Trinidad is growing," warned the *Gleaner* in 1930. "The United States of America, Cuba, Jamaica, and Venezuela have all adopted legislation with a view to checking excessive Immigration, and it is time that the Trinidad Government take the opportunity to improve and to tighten its archaic Immigration laws."[135] Modern and effective polities policed population frontiers, and British West Indians found themselves on the receiving end of exclusionary laws around the region as a result. Could the masses within British colonies demand privileged access to home labor markets in turn? Would the classes come to identify their own destiny with that of this *pueblo*? Could colonial elites enact a restrictionist bargain even if they wanted to? Matters of immigration control touched the most fundamental questions of political membership and sovereignty. Anti-immigrant initiatives within the British colonies made visible the islands' connections to regional currents of political thought. At the same time, they underline the ways in which political parameters in these imperial possessions were fundamentally unlike those in the surrounding republics.

Subsidized South Asian immigration, which champions of Afro-Caribbean workers had long railed against for undercutting wages, had finally halted in 1917—not as a result of any populist bargain but in response to activists in British India, who campaigned against the mistreatment of their people abroad.[136] In the 1920s, from one-fourth to one-fifth of the populations of British Guiana and Trinidad had been born elsewhere—roughly split between Windward Islanders and South Asians—while no other British island had more than 3 percent immigrants within its population.[137] Nevertheless, most had small but highly visible Chinese and Syrian communities, concentrated in retail trade; and as had been true a generation earlier in the Spanish-speaking republics, it was these Asian and Middle Eastern immigrants who became the first targets.

Anti-Asian sentiment among the islands' working classes had its own complexities. Moments of violence punctuated daily patterns that mixed mutual disdain with connection. In 1918 Jamaica's 8,000-strong Chinese community (perhaps a quarter of them immigrants, the rest second or third generation) became the target of riots across the island in response to rumors that an Afro-Jamaican policeman had been killed by his sweetheart's Chinese lover. (The rumor—which turned out to be false—captures both the mobilizing potential of group loyalty and the recognition that intimate relations routinely crossed those lines).[138] Chinese immigration accelerated markedly in the late 1920s and 1930s (see Table 3). Popular demonization of the Chinese followed apace. Among Afro-Jamaicans, it was returnees from Panama and Cuba who came to be identified with the most strident anti-Chinese racism—and with the loudest threats of violence if colonial officials ignored demands for action. In Trinidad, as well, the basic pattern repeated. Antiblack exclusion abroad led to nativist agitation at home, within which anti-Asian posturing seemed the only point on which workingmen's leaders, middle sectors of color, and at least some white elites could agree.[139]

But whereas in the Spanish-speaking republics, such coalitions forged populist bargains, as elites jumped noisily onto the nativist bandwagon (and kept the vagaries of enforcement sub rosa), anti-Asian agitation on the islands stuttered to a halt each time it reached the hands of those with actual power to set policy: imperial administrators. British bureaucrats hustled behind the

TABLE 3 Population of Barbados, Jamaica, and Trinidad and Tobago by Race, 1921–1946

	Census	White	Mixed	Black	East Indian	Chinese	Other
Barbados	1921	10,429	34,216	111,667			
	1946	9,839	33,828	148,923	136[a]		74
Jamaica	1921	14,476	157,223	660,420	18,610	3,696	3,693
	1943	13,809	216,348	965,960	26,507[b]	12,394[c]	2,045[d]
Trinidad and Tobago	1931		268,584[e]		138,960	5,239	
	1946	15,283	78,775[f]	261,485	195,747	5,641	1,013[g]

[a] Includes "East Indian" and "Chinese" population
[b] Includes 5,114 "East Indian Coloured"
[c] Includes 5,515 "Chinese Coloured"
[d] Includes 834 "Syrian" and 171 "Syrian Coloured"
[e] Includes "White," "Mixed," and "Black" population
[f] Includes 8,406 "Indian Creole" and 3,673 "Chinese Creole"
[g] Includes 889 "Syrian and Other Asiatic"

Source: R. R. Kuczynski, *Demographic Survey of the British Colonial Empire*, vol. 3, *West Indian and American Territories* (London: Oxford University Press, 1953), 28–29.

scenes to duck colonial demands and avoid the international consequences of anti-Asian acts within empire.

There were other differences as well. As elsewhere in the Americas, the impact of immigration on "native" employment was much discussed. But restrictionist leaders within the British colonies not only came from but also spoke for the middle classes. With the franchise tightly restricted across the islands, there was no "temptation to appeal to the masses" because one was "asking them for their votes."[140] Johnson-Reed, though, had made itself felt among the ranks of those with some voice in island affairs. "So long as the members of our upper and middle classes could emigrate to the United States freely, we said and did little about the immigration of aliens here," explained the *Gleaner*'s editorial page in October 1924. But no longer: "America, Australia, Canada, New Zealand, protect their nationals against the severe and desperate competition of outsiders, even if some of these happen to be British subjects." It was time for Jamaica to do the same and block Chinese entry.[141]

The editors insisted that their campaign was driven not by racial animus but rather by an admirable collective identity: "It is not that we dislike other people, but that we are bound to love ourselves more than we love the alien, and to do something in protection of ourselves."[142] White and near-white Jamaican elites, for whom the *Gleaner* spoke, avoided explicit race talk even when promoting race-based restriction, and with good reason. In this deeply divided society, talk of race and rights could too quickly slip toward social revolution. No wonder Guy Ewen, a white Legislative Council member, begged his fellow councilors in the 1925 debate over Chinese exclusion to stop talking about racial antagonism. "It was not right that in Jamaica they should be treating such a subject as this with any amount of passion which might later bring race feeling to the disadvantage of the Colony," Ewen cautioned. "It was the easiest thing to set fire, and the easiest of all was race prejudice."[143]

For the moment, though, the masses seemed willing to believe the Chinese were the problem.[144] Council members of color, and those whose electorates included significant numbers of Afro-Jamaicans, drove the 1925 debate forward. Council member Cawley declaimed, "The people were saying emphatically that they wanted no aliens in this country (hear, hear)." Afro-Jamaican councilor Rev. A. A. Barclay repeated that the "alien issue" "had been dealt with in Australia, and Canada, and the United States, and so far as Jamaicans were concerned, this matter was being dealt with in the United States, Cuba, and Central America." If laws now "prevent[ed] Jamaicans from going to those places, and prevent[ed] them from earning a livelihood there . . . then it was only to be expected that Jamaicans would not want these aliens to come here and take positions which would be filled by our sons and daughters."[145]

It is worth noting the neat trick of symbolic substitution here: other nations banned Chinese and Jamaicans; therefore Jamaica should ban Chinese. That Chinese immigration had no impact on job prospects for those (working-class) Jamaicans most harmed by foreign restrictionism went unacknowledged, as did the fact that retaliation against *white* immigrants from the restrictionist countries was off the table.[146] Not surprisingly, then, the *Gleaner* commended the elective members' stand: "Whatever" restrictions "necessary for the safeguarding of Jamaica as a home for Jamaicans must be applied."[147]

The utility of having Asian exclusion stand as the answer to antiblack action abroad was underlined two years later, when the return of a native son ramped up the explicit race talk in public debate. Marcus Garvey returned to Jamaica in 1927, deported from the United States after jail time for mail fraud. Welcomed with "thunderous applause" by a packed crowd only one day after arrival, Garvey staked out a fierce claim to black rights within empire. He also denounced Chinese and Syrian merchants as the heart of Afro-Jamaicans' problems and proclaimed their continuing presence the clearest evidence of the abrogation of Afro-Jamaican rights.

Garvey made it clear for whom he spoke: "I am a black man. I have returned under certain circumstances to my native land, not to lead white people, not to lead coloured people who do not call themselves Negroes, but to lead black people and those who call themselves Negroes towards their destiny." He would not be silenced.

> I know what to say within the Empire and how to say it within the Empire (applause). And in this far-flung outpost of the Empire, where great advantage is being taken of the constitution of the Mother Country, England, I want those who think they can fool Marcus Garvey and fool the Negro peoples of this country . . . to know they are making a great mistake. When I look upon the people of this country, their naked condition—their diseased and dirty condition—do you think that I, so long as there is a God, could keep my mouth closed and my soul steady as a black man, and let the Chinaman, the Syrian sap the wealth of this country while our people die in poverty?[148]

Garvey chose to treat anti-Asian exclusion as the litmus test of legitimate rule. "All the people of Jamaica want to do is to seriously understand and know themselves," he said, "and as British subjects to know that they have rights that the British Government is bound to respect when you intelligently represent those rights to them."[149] Anti-Chinese hostility proved highly effective in mobilizing popular protest. But by making the right to enact race-based exclusion the yardstick of rights within empire, Garvey put his imprimatur on a symbolic bargain that offered Jamaica's black masses all of the xenophobia and none of the populism.

Both Garvey's People's Political Party and the disaffected Garveyites who split to form the Jamaica Native Defenders Committee (JNDC) pushed Asian exclusion.[150] By 1930 the "suffering of the population" due to the "entry of Chinese, Syrians, and Turks" again headed the Legislative Council's agenda and Cawley again demanded action, in response, he said, to pressure from the many workers repatriated from Cuba who thronged his constituency.[151] By 1931 leaders of the JNDC were threatening, like their contemporaries in Panama and Venezuela, to take immigration policy into their own hands: "There is not one man among the Executive that has any sense; and so the people will think about cutting throats, burning down shops and do all sorts of things. . . . We are out to agitate for something, and that is to bid chinese goodbye."[152] The JNDC's links to rimland xenophobia were direct: founder

Leonard Waison was himself a second-generation "returnee"—born in Panama to Jamaican parents—and he explicitly linked the JNDC's anti-Chinese demands to "the feeling amongst Jamaicans returning from Latin America."[153]

Like (white) councilor Ewen five years before, JNDC leaders saw race prejudice as explosive; unlike Ewen, they welcomed the violence that could result. "I would not work for a chinaman, because I would kill him everyday," declared one. "The Government are arch-criminals, and they only crush people. I am not a Bolshevik but I can be any moment I want to be. Bolshevik say the only way a country can reform is to cut throat, and I believe in it."[154] If the masses made anti-Chinese laws the price of avoiding revolution, island elites were happy to comply—while working, as always, to tamp down the risky passions of race. The *Gleaner* editors did their best to articulate a less race-conscious reading of "Native Defense." "We are not actuated by racial feelings," they wrote, "when we ask: Why should Jamaica open her doors wide to Chinese immigration, when but few of her sons and daughters can migrate to nearby countries to enter larger fields of industry?"[155]

Just two years before, a British West Indian commentator had declared from Limón that "the slogan that the voice of the people is the voice of the government has become universally accepted."[156] When the *Gleaner* and Garveyites alike declared "Jamaica for the Jamaicans," one might believe that the voice of the people had triumphed on the islands as well. The Barbados Assembly similarly presented immigration limits as evidence of their commitment to "Barbados for the Barbadian."[157] Barbados's tiny "Democratic League," however, struggling to reform the island's famously restricted franchise, were not convinced: "That instead of decency, health, and comfort we have poverty, nakedness and disease is due to the callous indifference and naked greed of the wealthier classes."[158]

In North Atlantic democracies and even the Spanish American republics, populist coalitions spurred on by organized labor translated notional solidarity into material gains: the eight-hour workday, education spending, public health measures. British Caribbean elites were not willing to pay for a real populist bargain, and the structure of colonial rule ensured they did not have to. Asian immigrants seemed an ideal target for those seeking to proclaim national solidarity at a low practical cost.

But it was not that simple. That same structure of colonial rule that shielded elites from the need to "appeal to the masses . . . when asking for their votes" meant that actual policies were shaped by and for empire. And at the imperial level, the politics of Asian exclusion was quite different.

Those seeking to quash restrictionist proposals in the British Caribbean had long warned that barring certain immigrants would cause diplomatic complications for the "Mother Country."[159] By 1925, with the decade-old Republic of China already torn among warring Nationalist, Communist, and regionalist groups in the wake of Sun Yat-sen's death, the *Gleaner* could dismiss this concern as no longer even "a joke":

> No one here is such a fool as to believe that Eastern countries, torn by internal dissensions, riddled with dishonesty and graft, hopeless preys to designing exploiters, can threaten England with serious pains and penalties if Jamaica closes her doors to alien immigration in protection of her legitimate interests. How is it that these foreign nations have not proceeded to strike at England because of the restrictions placed upon immigration by Canada, Australia, New Zealand and South Africa? Are we to be told that they realise that the self-Governing Dominions are free to do what they please to protect themselves, while colonies like Jamaica may be sacrificed with impunity?[160]

Well, yes. Even as Chiang Kai-shek consolidated control of the Kuomintang, battled regional opponents, and clawed back late imperial concessions to European powers, his Nationalist government tracked the evolution of Asian exclusion abroad—and, yes, in disempowered colored colonies as well as assertive white dominions. The Republic of China, just like receiving societies around the Caribbean, was attuned to the geopolitics of biopolitics. Asserting sovereign power within the emerging international order was a matter of territorial frontiers and trade policy, but it was also a matter of racialized populations and their perceived place in the hierarchy of mankind. As the armies of the Nationalist government encircled the international settlement of Shanghai in 1927, Chinese foreign minister Eugene Chen declared to the foreign press that "a great and impressive fact must be grasped by all: the Chinese question now is not what Great Britain and other powers may wish to grant China to meet 'the legitimate aspirations of the Chinese'; but the question is what China may justly grant to Great Britain and the other powers."[161]

Chen had reason to know well the racial ideologies that shaped Western responses to China. A contemporary of Marcus Garvey, Chen had been born on the island of Trinidad. He grew up speaking English in a Westernized

Chinese household, became a prominent Port of Spain barrister, and married a colored Creole. In 1911, the same year that Garvey left Kingston for Costa Rica, Eugene Chen left Trinidad for China, drawn to join Sun Yat-sen's Nationalist movement. He became Sun's most trusted deputy. He negotiated (with little success) on behalf of China at the Versailles Peace Conference in 1919, and, after Sun's death, he emerged as a key leader of the "Left" Kuomintang. In 1927, negotiating this time from a position of strength as the Nationalist army overran British trade enclaves, Chen would achieve in the Chen-O'Malley Treaty the revocation of British control of key treaty ports. Eugene Chen, who never learned to speak or write Chinese, understood well the uses of state power in the interwar international order.[162]

Colonial Office correspondence lets us see just how carefully the Chinese Nationalist government tracked exclusionary laws abroad, even in this tumultuous era. It was the insult of open racial exclusion that Chinese diplomats sought to prevent rather than the consequences of exclusion for those excluded. When a report by Jamaica's Legislative Council in 1931 announced the intent to halt further entry by "Immigrants of Asiatic origin, viz., Chinese and Syrians," the Chinese chargé d'affaires was at the Foreign Office in London, "copies of cuttings from the Jamaica press" in hand, even before a law to enact the proposals could be drafted.[163] As the Foreign Office explained urgently to the undersecretary of state for the colonies: "Dr. Chen expressed the earnest hope that any legislation contemplated would be expressed in general terms, and would not make special mention of Chinese. He made it clear that this, rather than the practical effect of any such legislation, was the main preoccupation of the Chinese Government."[164]

The proposed law had included text defining the targeted "aliens" as those with one or more parents "of Chinese or Syrian race." The Home Office urged a redefinition that would exclude certain individuals "without discrimination," although acknowledging that this might not "be acceptable in public opinion in Jamaica." At a minimum, if reference to race were left in, the law should be revised to spell out "what evidence is to be regarded as affording *prima facie* evidence of race," given that "race," unlike "nationality," offered no "tangible and (from the point of view of proof) effective test."[165] The Foreign Office pushed back. Racial language was absolutely off-limits: "[T]o single out any particular race or nationality by name . . . is apt to be resented in that country concerned, and to lead to retaliatory measures against British subjects."[166]

This high-level concern over the possibility of future restrictions on "British subjects" who might wish to travel to China stands in stark contrast to the frank inaction of the same office in response to the actually existing restrictions rupturing the lives of British subjects in the Caribbean. The first kind of British subjects—whose whiteness was already implicit in their status as full subjects of empire—could count on proactive imperial attention to their scope of mobility. The latter had to kick and scream even to be acknowledged as a nuisance.

Comparing the actions of Chinese diplomats and the Chinese state to those of British diplomats and the British state, we see that racial identification mattered. When laws made "special mention" of the Chinese as undesirable, Chinese diplomats knew their nation's honor was at stake. When laws described British West Indians as racially "undesirable," British diplomats nodded in agreement, or at least some did. Josiah Crosby, British minister in Panama, was particularly egregious. A typical confidential dispatch in 1932 waxed eloquent about the pain this restrictionist moment was causing—to white Panamanian elites, that is, who had waited too long to ban blacks. "The stable door has unhappily been locked too late," Crosby lamented, "and the harm is already done." A second generation of locally born British West Indians would soon be eligible to demand to vote. Crosby predicted "much contention, and perhaps even bloodshed . . . before Panama fulfills what I conceive to be her doom of becoming one day a second Hayti or Dominican Republic, with a population in which the African strain is uppermost. Such will be the harsh penalty attending her failure in the past to stem the tide of West Indian immigration before it had reached full flood."[167]

Caribbean migrants could not hear what was said behind closed doors, but the results were plain to see. Issues of mobility revealed the race-based gap in British subjects' rights. Moreover, the formalization of migratory control meant that this gap might have to be written out in black and white. When His Majesty's government considered an accord with Haiti for the reciprocal waiver of passports, the British consul in Port-au-Prince first urged "that it should not apply to British West Indian subjects, if such an exception were possible"; he then suggested that no accord was necessary, given that there were "so few British subjects staying in Haiti." On second thought, he corrected this by hand to read "there are so few *other* British subjects staying in Haiti"—other than British West Indians, that is, of whom there were several thousand.[168] His intercalated "other" acknowledged that Caribbeans of color must still be counted as British subjects, even as his "if such an exception were possible" asked just how far the formalization of second-class subjecthood could go.

Confronting the same core dilemma in the geopolitical rather than micropolitical realm, Colonial Office functionaries struggled to craft an immigration law that would be nominally universal but permit Jamaicans to ban "the only aliens who really worry them": Chinese and Syrians. To avoid "friction with the Chinese Government" and not "embarrass the Foreign Office in its negotiations," it was essential that "some . . . non-discriminatory method of restricting Chinese immigration should be adopted."[169] Ultimately, they suggested a kind of modified remote control, with British consuls "instructed either to grant no visas without [consulting with] the Colony, or if it is desired in practice to exercise discrimination in regard to persons of Chinese and Syrian race, to grant no visas . . . to persons appearing to belong to those races" without consulting the colony in advance.[170] So it was done. From 1931 onward, British consuls in Hong Kong ceased granting passports to Chinese for Jamaica, a move that "virtually ended all Chinese entry into Jamaica" even though no explicit anti-Asian exclusion was adopted.[171] In other words, just like the United States in regard to British Caribbeans, the empire used remote control to exclude without enunciating race.

The Chinese Nationalist government was busy around the Caribbean in these years, responding to the wave of exclusionary legislation that had brought new assaults on Chinese as well as black migrants. When Rafael Trujillo was sworn in for a second term in the Dominican Republic in 1934, the Chinese government sent a special envoy to confer on Trujillo its "highest Order" of honors. Foreign diplomats understood this to be "in recognition" of the regime's revision of a proposed immigration law in response to Chinese pressure.[172] China was not the only sending state that was acting. Japan took active steps to ensure that its people did not face the stigma of outright racial bans; this was the root of the "Gentlemen's Agreement" through which Japanese entry to the United States was limited from 1907 forward. Similarly, in negotiating a trade accord with Venezuela in 1913, the Japanese government insisted that language labeling Japanese as less desirable than Europeans be excised from Venezuela laws governing subsidized colonization; as a result, throughout the 1920s and 1930s, while Chinese and Afro-descendants were repeatedly banned, Venezuelan laws listed "those of white race *or islanders of the Northern hemisphere*"—which is to say, Japanese—as the sought-after immigrants.[173] Asia's rising powers knew that laws that barred their peoples as undesirable were part and parcel of other attempts to deny them a seat at the table of sovereign states, and they reacted accordingly, and got results.

In sum, multiple trends collided in conflicts over immigration policies within the British Caribbean in these years. Themselves barred by racist states abroad, working-class British West Indians demanded symbolic privilege at home. The rise of international mobility control had turned nationality into something "tangible" as never before, measured at the border through documents, photos, and fingerprints. Working-class demands for Asian exclusion asked colonial legislatures to make nationality tangible as a criterion for entry into British Caribbean islands. That was not identical to making nationality tangible in the sense of real material commitments. But given British Caribbean migrants' experiences of populist exclusion from Havana to Harlem, it was not crazy to think that creating nationality at the borders and endowing it with social content could be made to go hand in hand.

From the point of view of island elites, the popular lunge toward xenophobic nationalism was a mixed bag. Those invested in maintaining social order never welcomed working-class assertiveness. On the other hand, "Jamaica for the Jamaicans" was far less threatening to island elites than many of the collective identities on offer in this era, including Garvey's own "Race First." "Jamaica for the Jamaicans" gave the island's white and near-white elites something to work with: a collective mission they could conceivably position themselves to lead, rather than one for which they would necessarily be the target. Discrete remote control allowed colonial elites to claim to have defended their islands while also allowing empire to maintain the pretense of race-blind universality before the audience that most concerned it—which at this point meant Asia's rising rulers rather than either Spanish American officials or black subjects abroad.

CONCLUSION

In the interwar era, polities across the Greater Caribbean both restricted entry and placed new limits on foreign-born noncitizens already resident, in each case systematically relying on partial enforcement to meet the demands of multiple constituencies at once. The results were systems in which, on the one hand, supposedly ironclad bars were enforced at officials' discretion (generally to their own profit and to the benefit of employers), while, on the other hand, certain apparently neutral rules in fact functioned as bans against those whose skin was a certain color or eyes a certain shape. This world of unpredictable power and unspoken exclusions was not eternal or natural. It was the world that the combined geopolitics and domestic politics of the interwar era wrought.

To British West Indians—just as to Eugene Chen and Japanese imperial bureaucrats—the symbolism of the law mattered. The implementation of the law mattered, too. Everyone knew they were not one and the same. Where domestic politics or foreign relations demanded exclusion without mention of race, so it was. Where domestic politics and foreign relations favored trumpeting state protection of "la raza," that was done. Either way, the targets of exclusion knew who they were. And employers like United Fruit and Standard Oil proved happy to work with either approach. Discriminatory laws' implementation, riddled by systematic illegalities and often delegated to local officials whose excesses national authorities could disavow, worked to increase worker dependency and employer power.

The preceding comparative and connective analysis reveals the United States to have been both part of and slightly out of step with hemispheric trends. Relying on consuls to stanch immigration at migrants' points of origin, the United States (unlike other circum-Caribbean receiving societies) did not institute a system constraining employment by nativity or race for migrants already across the border—or at least not in the Atlantic Seaboard cities that were the overwhelming destination of British Caribbeans. Yet the system of fluctuating mobility control along the U.S.-Mexico border—with its deference to employer needs and its devolution of enforcement to local rather than national agents—looks a great deal like the systems that created second-class noncitizen status across the circum-Caribbean in these years. From across the Rio Grande, the United States looked, in this sense, less like the "Colossus to the North" and more like yet another banana republic.[174]

Nowhere did laws function exactly as written. But the divergence of government practice from legal rules was patterned rather than haphazard. In areas where state power was institutionalized and effective, paperwork, consuls, and shipping lines achieved borders without bloodshed. In contrast, in areas where central state institutions were weak and employers powerful— eastern Venezuela, northwest Panama, southwest United States—responsibility for gatekeeping was handed off to a shifting constellation of bosses, local officials, and vigilantes. Not coincidentally, all of these were areas where geography worked against bureaucratized control: long land borders or porous coastlines where port bottlenecks could not be used to leverage state power. Where state institutions were weakest, state violence was bloodiest. The massacre of tens of thousands of Haitians and Dominicans of Haitian ancestry by Dominican soldiers in Dajabón in 1937 was in this sense the awful parallel to the violence against British West Indians in eastern Venezuela in that same year. States were staking their claim to border control. If they could not achieve it through the smooth hegemony of documentary demands, they would do it by the blade of a machete.[175]

Think back to the cable codes that encapsulated the U.S. quota system's goals, stripped of obfuscation. If you had the resources to convince officials you were just passing through, FREEDOM. If some official decided to deny entry, IMMOBILE. Except that for real people, that was never the end of the story. People began working around the system as soon as it was built. Few wasted their time continually butting up against it. They went elsewhere, or they went outside the law. Thus, the creation of systematic illegality was part of the creation of governmentality. Subterfuge took the place of outrage, and people got on with their lives. But their ideas about how states might bar the bounds of belonging, and what states should do for their own native sons, had irrevocably shifted.

four   The Transnational Black Press and Questions
of the Collective, 1920s–1930s

Any given day, on any street corner in Port Limón, you could buy a copy of
your local paper and read about your world.

> The situation in the British countries has been growing more and more
> distressing for the colored man who has any pride in himself or any
> self respect. The United States can no longer boast preeminence as the
> land in which the poison of race prejudice and race hatred flourishes.
> In England colored subjects of the Empire are being humiliated solely
> because of the color of their skin. In the colonies the door of opportu-
> nity is closed to them, and the boasted tradition of British fair play has
> become in many instances, only a mockery. No Chatham now thunders
> in Parliament against the nefarious color bar in South Africa, no Wil-
> berforce is willing to give his life for human liberties and the equality
> of man. The natives of Australia are ill-treated, Canada closes her door
> to colored immigrants. In British East Africa the white planters vow to
> maintain supremacy over the natives, and to perpetuate the robbery
> of their lands. All this is leading to a serious unrest. India has already
> broken the bonds, and Lord Irwin, the late viceroy was forced to admit
> that the prestige of the white man is lost forever in India. The tribes in
> Africa are stirring, and black men in the West Indies no longer bend the
> knee to the "massa."[1]

Change was afoot in the world, and people like you—people who still cared
about British fair play, who remembered the moral courage of Wilberforce
and Chatham—were making it happen. Natives of Australia, colored immigrants barred from Canada, East African natives, Indians rising, black men
in the West Indies—you all faced white prejudice and race hatred, and you
would no longer bow down.

As British Caribbean migrants spread outward, they linked local publishing with Atlantic- and empire-wide media circuits to create an internationally
connected black press, newspapers densely woven into community life but
looking out across the globe. That expansive vision meant that when black
subjects found their mobility rights curtailed in the late 1920s, they could

see not only the local but the international and interimperial dimensions of the phenomenon. The forms of civic alliance that the same press made possible meant that those targeted by state racism understood themselves not as individual victims but as a collective many thousands strong whose demands had a right to be heard. The salience of race and security of empire were transformed as a result.

Some pieces of this same process—the initiatives of authors and organizers in New York, London, and Paris in particular—have benefited from sizable scholarship.[2] But this chapter seeks to decenter the story of the origins of interwar black internationalism—to move away from W. E. B. Du Bois, Marcus Garvey, and George Padmore and toward the forgotten editors of port-town papers and the many thousands of men and women who read their pages and debated the merits in rum shops and butcher-store queues around the region. This is a shift of locale and a shift of socioeconomic level, an attempt to understand the transformation of claims making in the modern world as rooted in daily life rather than as reflected in declarations and congresses. Only by observing the grassroots intellectual tumult of the circum-Caribbean do we see how antiblack immigration restrictions in the Americas pushed the shared predicaments of communities of color to the forefront of public discussion.

The emergence of a self-aware, race-conscious, transnational black press provided the optic that made black internationalisms internationalist. The *Pittsburgh Courier* had subscribers in Costa Rica, the *New York Age* and *Chicago Defender* were routinely quoted by the *Panama Tribune*, the *Barbados Weekly Herald* was read in hundreds of Brooklyn households. News of discrimination against people of color in Britain and France—and of anti-imperialist organizing in the same—got prominent coverage, drawing in part on reports from Europe-based, black-run periodicals like the *Africa Times and Orient Review* or *La Depêche Africaine*. Meanwhile, New York and London dailies were perused for information on diplomatic negotiations, labor movements, and imperial wars around the globe. The emerging "colour bar" in South Africa and the demands of Gandhi in India received detailed coverage, as did the British imperial government's responses, or lack thereof. The circum-Caribbean/transatlantic black press piggybacked on the institutions, conventions, and market innovations of the broader Anglo-American periodical culture, but it put them at the service of a radical rethinking of race and empire.

Where were the boundaries of the collective? Who formed part of us? Some writers spoke on behalf of "the Negro race" alone, others "coloured subjects of the empire," still others all "darker peoples" under Yankee domination. Were South Asians and East Asians fellow strugglers or alien competitors? Diagnoses diverged. Romantic racialists rooted unity in shared ancestry; they grounded claims to territorial sovereignty in notions of blood-linked birthright similar to those invoked by prominent white racists of the era. In contrast, other activists placed global black suffering in the context of the international political economy of the moment, deriving a brief for Negro unity that eschewed essentialist claims.

The key questions up for debate were not about race alone but about the intersection of race and rights. The surrounding Spanish American republics showcased a new synergy of nation, state, and popular entitlements. In this modern world, could empire secure similar rights? Here again, diagnoses diverged. Some even held hope that a reenlightened British Empire might become a standard-bearer for race-blind justice. Yet such hopes were hard to sustain. Migrants' experience of the 1920s and 1930s cast the fractures of imperial unity into high relief. In the emerging international order, one role of sovereign states was to defend the mobility rights of their nationals abroad—to ensure that established denizens could come and go; to treat official disrespect for immigrants' race as an insult to the nations from which they came. As we have seen, the Japanese and Chinese governments did just this when migration bans threatened in Venezuela, Jamaica, Trinidad, and the Dominican Republic. But when British West Indians tried to insist that insults to them were insults to Britannia herself, the colonial government demurred. Again and again, the imposition of restrictive legislation exposed British ambivalence over its possession of colored subjects and those subjects' possession of British rights.

For Afro-Caribbean observers—and there were many, and they were watching closely, since for scores of thousands, their (literal) next move depended on the high politics of immigration enforcement—the Crown's acquiescence as British subjects of African and Asian ancestry were stripped of the right of entry by nation after nation laid bare the pretense of race-blind belonging. In the emerging international order of racialized nation-states, did "Our People" need a state of our own? For a decade and a half, Marcus Garvey had sought to create such a state in Africa. Other black internationalists anchored aspirations for sovereign space closer to home, linking the exclusions they now faced in North America and the Spanish-speaking republics to demands for a more effective franchise on the islands, or to hopes for a West Indian federation that might, through the strength of unity, offer expatriates a more effective ally.

Louise Little, the mother of Malcolm X, did not just make sure her children could read; she made sure they read what mattered. "Every day when we came home from school" in Lansing, Michigan, in the 1930s, recalled Malcolm's older brother,

> my mother would sit us down and have us read aloud passages from Marryshow's paper *The West Indian*. Marryshow was her country-man and someone she boasted about all the time. He and Garvey were her two idols. Marryshow, a Black Grenadian, could write the English language with more polish and, at the same time, tell you more about the world situation than all those white reporters writing the Detroit papers put together. . . . By reading Garvey's paper and Marryshow's paper, we got an education in international affairs and learned what Black people were doing for their own betterment all over the world.[3]

The international circulation of black-run periodicals, and their integration in communal discussion at multiple sites, generated a transnational black public. It shared the characteristics of a "counterpublic" in the sense that scholars have developed: it created a space for those marginalized by the dominant public to debate the boundaries of their common interests, formulate political goals, and speak out against hegemonic discourses that demeaned them.[4] But this public sphere did not sit within a single polity. Furthermore, members of this public had few mechanisms for political voice within any of the multiple states that governed them, be it the imperial state of their societies of origin or the republican states where many currently resided. Therefore, for reasons of both territorial disjuncture and political marginalization, this transnational black public had no chance of political efficacy, one of the key functions of the "bourgeois public sphere" as originally described.[5]

Yet their lack of efficacy did not dissuade participants. It drove them. They recognized it, they talked about it at length, they proposed solutions. Indeed, it was the lack of access to effective citizenship that spurred the transnationalness of this circum-Caribbean/transatlantic black counterpublic. Lacking avenues for political participation at home or abroad, participants in this public sphere sought to create alliances and build structures that could translate their numbers and consciousness into collective action. Their marginalization elevated the importance of the print sphere in contributors' eyes. The black press had a mission to fulfill. Local papers were so much more than local papers: they were the means of entry into a dialogue that was the only venue for political voice open.

The circum-Caribbean/transatlantic black press was indispensable to the interwar surge of black internationalisms. This print-based public sphere generated potential leaders, and it generated potential followers. The first point has been well established by scholarship on specific people and places, Harlem most of all. The pattern is so universal that we take it for granted. It is simply impossible to find an influential Caribbean activist or intellectual in this era who did not found a newspaper, edit a newspaper, or earn a living writing for newspapers for at least part of his or her life. Think of Garvey, Claude McKay, W. A. Domingo, Hubert Harrison, Cyril Briggs, and Richard B. Moore in Harlem; George Padmore, Harold Moody, and C. L. R. James in London; and—though the press was male dominated, to be sure— women like Amy Jacques Garvey, Amy Ashwood Garvey, Una Marson, and Claudia Jones.[6]

But the circum-Caribbean/transatlantic black press was equally or more important in creating followers. The international network of local papers generated a space within which regular people could and did interpellate themselves as part of something they identified as "Our People," a Negro World—a social collective with a knowable past and a redeemable future. Think of Benedict Anderson's evocative image of the reader of a daily paper of national circulation "well aware that the ceremony he performs is being replicated simultaneously by thousands (or millions) of others of whose existence he is confident, yet of whose identity he has not the slightest notion."[7] In this case, as readers in Port Limón read commentaries from the *Depêche Africaine* alongside denunciations of Jim Crow from the *Pittsburgh Courier* alongside exhortations to unity from the *Panama Tribune*, they may not have known the identities of their fellow readers, but they knew full well that those fellow readers were black, under attack by racist states, and seeking change now.

English was the lingua franca of the print-based public sphere, even though many of the papers that sustained it (including the *Negro World*, the *Panama Tribune*, and the *Limón Searchlight*) published articles or even sections in Spanish. Furthermore, it is clear that every paper had at least some writers on staff who read French and Spanish and followed regional dailies and key international publications in those languages. Articles from all of the preceding were referenced or excerpted in translation on a regular basis.

Meanwhile, especially in the eastern Caribbean, many of the writers writing and readers reading in English spoke another language at home, be it patois, Portuguese, or Hindi.

I will begin by describing the functioning of that circum-Caribbean/transatlantic black press, detailing the mechanisms of publication and circulation that made it possible and the practices of readership that gave it meaning. I will trace the importance of self-identified "Negro" papers, especially common in the western Caribbean (Kingston, Panama, Limón) and its northernmost outpost (Harlem). But I will also show that periodicals that denounced class oppression and imperial abuse *without* adopting a racialized voice—especially common in the eastern Caribbean—were part of the same dialogue. Meanwhile, I will show how closely linked British Caribbeans abroad came to be to the U.S. Afro-American press. Caribbean readership, excerpts, and letters turned U.S.-based black papers into international spaces in ways that may not have been clear to the publishers of the *Courier*, the *Defender*, or the *New York Age* at the time (and have not always been clear to historians of the Afro–North American media since).[8]

What made it possible? First of all, literacy. Working-class but self-selected, British West Indians abroad may have been the most highly literate group of colonial subjects anywhere in the interwar world. Their levels of literacy far surpassed those of the Spanish-speaking populations around them, as well as those on the islands from which they hailed. In fact, migrants' literacy rates approached those of Boston, New York, and other metropoles of the Anglophone world.[9] In 1927, 81 percent of the 10,000 black men and 82 percent of the 7,500 black women living in Limón province could read. In contrast, among Spanish-speaking adults in Costa Rica as a whole, only 66 percent of men and 61 percent of women could read.[10] In Panama overall in 1930, literacy was even lower: 41 percent among men and 39 percent among women, although in Panama's cosmopolitan and merchant-heavy national capital, literacy was twice as high (79 percent for men and 78 percent for women).[11] Yet even Panama City's numbers pale in comparison to British West Indian literacy in the Canal Zone. Already in 1920, 90 percent of "Negro" boys and men and 92 percent of "Negro" girls and women there could read and write. Roughly one-third of the Canal Zone's "Negros" were Barbadian (or locally born children of Bajan parents), one-third were Jamaican, one-sixth were other British West Indian, and one-sixth were French West Indian.[12] Literacy among British West Indian immigrants in Costa Rica and Panama, then, was significantly higher than literacy either in the receiving societies around them or in the sending islands from which they came (52 percent for Jamaica as a whole; 51 percent for Barbados).[13]

The same pattern held in the eastern Caribbean, although migrants there were less different from the folks back home. In Venezuela's Sucre State, only 60 percent of the *negros* of "English nationality" whom authorities registered for *cédulas de extranjeros* in 1932–34 were able to sign their names.[14] Nevertheless, this rough proxy for literacy still compared favorably both to literacy rates among local Spanish speakers (43 percent among Venezuelan men and 37 percent among women in 1936) and literacy rates on the immigrants' islands of origin: Trinidad (47 percent in 1921), Grenada (52 percent), St. Vincent (55 percent), Dominica (42 percent), and St. Lucia (35 percent).[15] Meanwhile, essentially *all* British West Indian immigrants in the United States were literate, since literacy requirements for entry predated Johnson-Reed and continued after it.[16]

Which newspapers made up what I am referring to as the circum-Caribbean black press—and which publications did they connect to in North America and Europe to make this a transatlantic black press? The first decades of the twentieth century saw an emergence within the British Caribbean of not sharply delimited "black" and "white" presses but rather a range of publications that stood in different degrees of opposition to, or alignment with, colonial officials and local plantocracies and that, separately, varied in their degree of explicit racial identification. In Jamaica, from the late nineteenth century forward, a succession of periodicals published by men of the black middle classes raised issues of racism and race-based solidarity explicitly. Dr. Robert Love, originally of the Bahamas, reached Jamaica in 1895 after service in Haiti; his *Jamaica Advocate* (1895–1905) propounded black-led moral uplift and island-wide social reform.[17] S. A. G. Cox, a black politician who sought to broaden the franchise, published *Our Own* from 1910 to 1911, making the internationalist argument that "the coloured and black people in Jamaica can only hope to better their condition by uniting with the coloured and black people of the United States of America and with those of other West Indian islands, and indeed with all Negroes in all parts of the world."[18]

In contrast, the eastern Caribbean, and Trinidad especially, had a tradition of opposition papers that drew support from creole and colored merchants and denounced the power of the plantocracy, but whose editors, authors, and correspondents did not define themselves in print as being of color, and in some cases were not. The significance of the not race-blind, but rather race-open, space this opposition press created was highlighted in Trinidad in 1904 in the wake of fierce debates following the 1903 Water Riots. The West India Committee, the voice of planter interests in England, had called for new legislation to squelch "offences committed by the Press, which in Trinidad is largely under the control of men of colour, unqualified for the profession of journalism."[19] The editors of the *Port of Spain Daily Mirror* wrote a stirring defense of the common mission of opposition journalists across the region. The West India Committee chair's words were an

> insult to the many journalists of colour who have ably voiced public opinion in other colonies as well as in this. He would have those who read believe that "men of colour" are *ipso facto* "unqualified for the profession of journalism." This is an unwarrantable presumption which all the facts belie. We could name papers in St. Kitts, Antigua, Dominica, Barbadoes, St. Vincent, Grenada and Jamaica, all of which have been and are highly respected, and which have won the confidence of the public and stood the infallible test of time in those islands by virtue of their ability, independence, and last but not least, their honour. All those papers are edited by men of color whom we, with our English descent, birth, training, and experience, are proud to have as fellow-labourers in the thorny field of West Indian journalism.[20]

The eastern Caribbean press thus had room for the denunciation of racism and the recognition of nonwhite authorship and readership. Furthermore, the papers linked these to Pan-Africanist initiatives. When "one man of colour, Dr. Abdurrahman, a Mohammedan, who is a graduate of Edinburgh and is a very able man," was elected to the Cape Town Municipality, the *Daily Mirror* both quoted at length the *London Times*'s coverage of this "first instance of the return of a man of colour to a European representative body in South Africa" and added their own local gloss at the end: "Dr. Abdurrahman, our readers will perhaps remember, was associated with Mr. Sylvestre [*sic*] Williams in a recent movement for the better education of the natives of South Africa."[21] That "recent movement" was, of course, the Trinidadian Henry Sylvester Williams's Pan-African Association. Founded at a meeting in London in 1900 that drew representatives from the United States, the Caribbean, Europe, and Africa, it inspired chapters in Trinidad, Jamaica, and elsewhere before dissolving a few years later.[22]

As British Caribbeans moved to the western Caribbean rimlands in massive numbers from 1903 onward, their press traditions moved with them. By the second decade of the twentieth century, there were British West

Indian–owned weekly papers in Bocas del Toro, Port Limón, Bluefields, and the Colombian island of San Andrés (off the coast of Nicaragua).[23] In the eastern Caribbean, in contrast, there is no record of British Caribbean–run papers in El Callao, Ciudad Bolivar, or the peninsula of Paria. But perhaps that should not surprise us. The bulk of early Caribbean migrants to Venezuela were monolingual patois speakers from islands with relatively low rates of literacy. Meanwhile, for the literate English-speaking traders and tradesmen among migrants, Port of Spain papers surely served as the local press; after all, it took less time to travel to Port of Spain from Güiria by boat than it did to reach Port of Spain from some of Trinidad's northeast or southern villages by road. There also seem to have been no specifically British West Indian newspapers published in Cuba, although Havana had multiple English-language dailies that migrants read, and sometimes used as a forum for letters to the editor.[24] Moreover, the UNIA's *Negro World* had already begun publication by the time mass migration to Cuba began, and it became something like a local paper for sojourners there. *Negro World* correspondents from Cuba not only shared news of events ranging from police outrages to weddings among local Jamaicans but also used the New York–based weekly to advertise upcoming events, like an excursion to be held on a United Fruit plantation in April 1923: "Seating capacity is limited, get your tickets at once."[25]

By contrast, in Limón, not only were there locally printed British Caribbean-run papers; there were enough for feuds to develop between them. So it was that a very young Marcus Garvey, arriving in Limón in 1910 with printer's experience from Jamaica, began editing a paper called the *Nation*. Within weeks, he had launched a series of polemical disputes with the editors and correspondents of the *Limón Times* over nonorthodox revivals (of which Garvey disapproved), schoolteachers of rural origin (whom he insulted), and the local celebration of George V's coronation (which he sought to lead).[26] Within months, the *Nation*'s printing press had been repossessed by creditors; Garvey beat a quick departure for Panama, then on to London, then back to Jamaica, and two years later to the United States. The UNIA's *Negro World*, published in Harlem from 1918 to 1933, would become one of the most widely read periodicals of the Caribbean, with a worldwide circulation topping 50,000.[27]

But the *Negro World* was not alone. Had it been, it would not have found the reception it did. Its spread and influence were magnified by the preexisting network of periodical press in the hands of British Caribbeans of color. The *Central American Express* was founded in Bocas del Toro by Jamaican J. A. Shaw Davis in 1905; its early typesetters included men from Cartagena and Jamaica, and it published in both Spanish and English. By 1913 the paper had formal "Agents of the Express" in twenty-six towns along the Bocas lines, in Nicaragua, and in London; by 1917 it claimed a weekly circulation of 1,200.[28] In the same years, the *Panama Workman* was published by H. N. Walrond, whose Guiana-born nephew (and star teen reporter) Eric would go on to edit the *Negro World* in New York.[29] Further up the Central American coast was the *Belize Independent*, edited by black radical and avowed Garveyite Herbert Hill Cain circa 1919.[30] In keeping with past patterns, radical class-identified papers flourished in the eastern Caribbean in this era, demanding labor protections, broader franchise, and responsible government. These included the race-conscious *Argos* (1919–20) and the Trinidad Workingmen's Association's *Labour Leader* (1922) in Trinidad; T. A. Marryshow's *West Indian* (1915–75) in Grenada; and the *Weekly Herald* in Barbados (1919–30), founded by Clement Inniss and edited by Clennell Wickham.[31]

By the 1920s, British Caribbean–run periodicals whose editorials and articles explicitly presumed that all writers and readers were Afro-descended had become the norm in the western Caribbean. This was true of the *Panama Star and Herald*'s West Indian News Section by 1920; the *Panama American*'s West Indian Section, edited by Jamaica-born Sidney Young from 1926 to 1927; the *Panama Tribune*, founded by Young in 1928; the *Limón Searchlight* (1929–31); and the *Atlantic Voice* (Limón, 1934–46). Why did periodicals speaking from an explicitly raced position become so common here? Unlike on the islands, there was no white or near-white elite claiming presumptive civic leadership. "The classes" in Panama and Costa Rica were pharmacists trained in Jamaica, clerks who had served in the British West Indies Regiment, schoolmasters from Guiana—all of them people of color. Here, too, Jim Crow segregation in the Canal Zone and the United Fruit plantations' "white zones" built explicit racial divides into everyday life. The presumption that these periodicals spoke to and for a public of color was so firm that blackness could function as an unmarked category, as when the "Expert Demonstrators and Teachers . . . especially sent by the Mme. C. J. Walker Manufacturing Company" announced in the West Indian News Section of the *Panama Star and Herald* their 1920 arrival "to teach this marvelous discovery to the ladies of Panama."[32] That the salient "ladies of Panama" were women of African ancestry went entirely without saying.

A black-identified press flowered in the metropoles as well, as those reading the rimland papers could plainly see. The *Amsterdam News* and *Boston Chronicle* were known for the strong West Indian presence in their subscribers, contributors, and coverage.[33] The *Chicago Defender* and the *Pittsburgh*

Courier, in contrast, had few Caribbean immigrants in their hometowns. But each was frequently quoted in the circum-Caribbean black press and had loyal subscribers in the region as well. The NAACP's *The Crisis*, founded by W. E. B. Du Bois in 1910 and with a monthly circulation topping 60,000 by the 1920s, was likewise quoted regularly around the region, as was the Urban League's *Opportunity*, founded in 1923.

Meanwhile, British Caribbean migrants were extraordinarily active in founding politically radical, race-conscious publications in interwar Harlem. Virgin Island–born Hubert Harrison founded *The Voice* in 1917, edited the *New Negro* in 1919, and became editor of the *Negro World* in 1920. St. Kitts–born Cyril Briggs founded the *Crusader* (1918–22) in conjunction with the fraternal/radical group the African Blood Brotherhood. Jamaica-born W. A. Domingo moved from editing the *Negro World* to writing for the *Messenger* and then founded the *Emancipator* (1920) with Barbados-born Richard B. Moore, who had been a vital early contributor to the *Crusader*.[34] In the same era, Trinidad-born Sam Manning and Jamaica-born Amy Ashwood Garvey (the former Mrs. Marcus Garvey) published the *West Indian Times and Review*, "a weekly circulated in New York, the West Indies and Panama."[35]

London and Paris, too, housed influential publications in these years, although their circulations were not even a fraction of that of the major U.S. black papers. In London, Dusé Mohammed Ali's *African Times and Orient Review* (which had briefly employed the young Marcus Garvey during his post-Limón travels) appeared sporadically from 1912 to 1920, proclaiming itself "a Pan-Oriental Pan-African journal at the seat of the British Empire which would lay the aims, desires and intentions of the Black, Brown, and Yellow Races—within and without Empire—at the throne of Caesar."[36] The *African Times and Orient Review* had agents in West Africa, the United States, the Canal Zone, Cape Town, and Jamaica. The *African Telegraph* (the organ of the Society for People of African Origin) was edited in London by Venezuela-born, Trinidad-raised F. E. M. Hercules and circulated in Trinidad and beyond circa 1919.[37] In the late 1920s, these would be joined by the Paris-based *Depêche Africaine* (1928–32), in which Jane and Paulette Nardal of Martinique played key roles.[38] The circum-Caribbean black press republished articles from all of the above, while also drawing on the must-read international dailies (the *London Times*, the *New York Times*, the *Panama Star and Herald*, and Havana's *Diario de la Marina*) for coverage of vital themes: the travails of the British Empire; U.S. expansionism and Jim Crow; political unrest in Cuba, Venezuela, and other receiving societies; and the colonial partition of Africa.

The whole was greater than the sum of its parts. Each new paper added more than just eight pages once a week; it connected its community to a network of debate that spanned the Atlantic and cut across boundaries of empire, language, even race. In 1917 the office of the *Central American Express* in Bocas del Toro also offered for sale "weekly at 20 cts The Star and Herald of Panama, the Daily Gleaner, and the Daily Chronicle of Jamaica, [and] New York papers."[39] In 1930 the *Limón Searchlight* reminded readers that "all advices or Births, deaths, marriages, etc, as well as other publications to 'the *Daily Gleaner*' can be sent in to THE SEARCHLIGHT for transmission to Jamaica."[40] The *Searchlight*'s agents sold the *Gleaner* as well, while in the *Searchlight*'s pages, agents for other papers (like Marcus Garvey's Kingston-based *Black Man*) could advertise their offerings.[41] Meanwhile, quotation from papers of distant origin was made possible by the custom of gratis subscription exchange between papers; thus, the *Searchlight* published with fanfare a letter received from H. G. St. Clair, business manager of the *Negro World*, in 1930: "We are today placing you on our exchange list, as we greatly admire the way your paper is made up."[42]

Through such practices of quotation, advertising, exchange, and distribution, the circum-Caribbean press made possible a much broader readership for the U.S. black prints than could otherwise have been the case. So it was that the *Pittsburgh Courier*'s column of astrological advice could field lovelorn queries from subscribers like W. T. D., who begged a published response: "Please don't fail to answer this question because I live in Costa Rica."[43] And a girl like Thelma Anderson, growing up in San José, Costa Rica, could follow each installment of George Schuyler's Negro-chauvinist-antihero Dr. Belsidus in the pages of the *Courier* and write in with a mix of bloodlust, race pride, and piety: "Tell me the truth about Dr. Belsidus. I wish it could be true that he has whipped every Italian as Joe Louis has whipped every white boy. We here in Costa Rica are praying for Joe Louis. Praying that God is on his side and will give him double strength. Joe must pray too and ask God to be his help."[44] Harold Benjamin Plank, born in Panama in 1918 and brought to Cuba by his Jamaican parents in 1921, grew up in Havana reading the *Defender*, the *Courier*, and the *Amsterdam News*. "People were proud of the achievements of black people that they read in the papers."[45] To have a local newspaper as an entrée into this international dialogue meant something special. The *Limón Searchlight* described itself as "the mouthpiece of

Panama Tribune *founder Sidney Young, ca. 1930. (George Westerman Collection, Schomburg Center for Research in Black Culture, New York Public Library)*

particularly the coloured people and the only up to date English journal in Costa Rica." Readers agreed: it was a "privilege to [have] our own paper."[46] This was not just a collective—it was a collective very aware of the medium that made it possible.

Celebrating the first anniversary of the *Panama American*'s West Indian Section at the end of 1926, Sidney Young explained that page's reason for being: "To refute the charges that we are a backward people here, that we are shiftless and incompetent, and that we are a charge on the Government of the Republic. We will prove that we are a valuable asset to the country, that we have added to its material wealth, economic progress and cultural advancement. . . . [W]e will realize our own vast achievements and power."[47] To defend against the new state racism, to clarify the past, to build the future—all this the press could do, it seemed.

All that was needed was more: more writers, more readers, more race pride. A letter printed alongside Young's anniversary peroration called for "More Journalists for the Race": "Good journalists are great assets to their people and country . . . more useful to his country than even the General of an army." With easy familiarity, the author cited examples for "our youths" to emulate, sketching out the print sphere he inhabited as he did so: "T. Thomas Fortune, now editor of the *Negro World*, D. T. Wint of the *Jamaica Critic*, Marcus Garvey, and men who have passed into the great beyond, such as John E. Bruce of America, Dr. Love of Jamaica, and others too numerous to mention."[48] The black press had become both medium and mission. Sidney Young's example echoed, just as Young hoped it would. "Looking upon the size of the Panama Tribune, and the literary food it contains, and the literary Great guns that contribute to it, one feels proud to sit down and jot down a few lines, to help keep ours going," wrote a frequent contributor in the *Limón Searchlight* in 1931. "May all petty differences be removed from our path, and as Negroes, help one another in whatever capacity we can, and may the 'Searchlight' increase its pages, grace, and subscriptions."[49]

Sidney Young and many of his columnists were veterans of the British West Indies Regiment (BWIR), as was Clennell Wickham of the *Barbados Weekly Herald*, as were many of those whose denunciations of British racism lit up the pages of the *Belize Independent*.[50] These young Caribbean men had been roused to volunteer by appeals to patriotism and exhortations to prove the valor of Britannia's Negro subjects. The firsthand experience of second-class status that followed, as BWIR battalions were kept out of combat, forced to dig latrines and carry kitchen slops for white soldiers, and given worse housing than Italian prisoners of war, radicalized a generation. Returnees led strikes and riots in Port of Spain and Belize City in 1919. In response, officials sought to ban the *Negro World* and other papers seen as "exciting racial animosities," including the *Port of Spain Argos*, Cyril Briggs's *Crusader*, and F. E. M. Hercules's *African Telegraph*.[51]

Not only were such bans ineffective—the *Negro World* continued circulating in the hands of seamen, and rimland papers reprinted articles from it on a regular basis—but they also rather missed the point. A generation had returned from war imbued with a sense of civic duty and annealed by imperial racism. They reinvigorated the local tradition of antiracist press radicalism. And they read and reprinted articles from the black-identified papers of New York, Chicago, and London. The Seditious Publications Acts presumed that the popular challenges Caribbean elites faced in the aftermath of the Great War came from new publications. But in reality, they came from a new public.

The whole was greater than the sum of its parts—and the parts that least worried officials still added to a whole that would shake the colonial order. British diplomats praised H. N. Walrond's *Panama Workman* for its wartime service in "keeping West Indians strictly loyal to the Allied Cause" and lauded Shaw Davis's *Central American Express* for its "All British All the Time" verve.[52] Meanwhile, the United Fruit Company was describing Shaw Davis as "one of the most troublesome Jamaicans and labor agitators in this District."[53] Neither bureaucrats nor company spies were wrong. In the years immediately after the Great War, the circum-Caribbean black prints were indeed fiercely loyal and also potentially radical. Taken together, the papers generated a transnational black public possessed of an international optic that showed the global dimensions of local injustice.

THE CONTINUUM FROM IMMEDIATE TO IMAGINED COMMUNITY

We detailed above some of the formal means through which physical papers or their quoted words circulated far and wide in this era. Less visible are the informal practices through which the words were read aloud or passed along. Novels offer glimpses of island streets where a shopkeeper might pass the time "reading a two-days-old newspaper and talking politics with anyone who might drop in for a chat."[54] A letter to the *Searchlight* offers a rare window onto that paper's integration into transnational personal networks and underlines just how dispersed was the community who turned to this paper for news of its members. "It is my habit, 'good or bad,' to send a weekly copy of your Invaluable Weekly to Trinidad, so that my relatives may see what is what in Limón. Again, I send a weekly copy to Colón to a girl friend, who passes it around to her girlfriends, and comment about the doings of Limón. Now and then I would send a copy to Jamaica, to my school friends. And I also keep a weekly copy for my further reference." Indeed, if only "the mass of negroes in Costa Rica, who are always shouting, revivalistic like, would guarantee you their cooperation, by buying at least one copy of your weekly each week," the author insisted, all of the paper's financial problems would be solved.[55]

The communicative space generated by the circum-Caribbean black press was at once very intimate and very international. Every week in the local paper, obituaries traced the webs of connections that travelers wove. When Harold Boyd died in Cartagena, Colombia, in 1920, his loss was noted on the "West Indian News" page of the *Panama Star and Herald*, for "the deceased was well known on the Isthmus, especially in Panama City."[56] "Miss Drayton is a relative of Dr. Reginald Forde, dentist of Colón, and has a number of friends on the isthmus who will regret to learn of her death," wrote the *Panama Tribune* in 1929, describing the funeral in Grenada.[57] When Mildred

Johnson died in New York in 1925, it was through the *Barbados Weekly Herald* that her children reached out to offer thanks "for the many letters, cards, and other expressions of sympathy sent them, in their recent bereavement."[58]

The fact that these papers traveled made them the right venue for communicating among people who traveled. Their pages carried notices disavowing responsibility for disappeared spouses' future debts or seeking news of kin long gone from home: "MISSING: Nina V. Dove, age about 26, coloured, short and stout, worked as a domestic servant. When last heard from in June 1929 was in Havana.... Mother in Kingston anxious for news." And another: "Pollock, Mathilda (Mrs.). Coloured, native of Jamaica. Left Jamaica February 1912 for Cristobal, Canal Zone. Last heard from in 1915. Anyone knowing of her whereabouts, please communicate with Captain Moffett, the Salvation Army, Headquarters, Kingston, Jamaica."[59] Some 10,000 copies of the Kingston-based Salvationist paper that carried these particular notices were sold each month in ports from eastern Guatemala to the Leeward Islands. Wherever Miss Dove and Mrs. Pollock had traveled within the Greater Caribbean migratory sphere, there was some chance they would be found.

The intimate scale of what counted as news made it possible to stay in touch long after departures. In 1931 members of Limón's Alpha Literary Club bid farewell to their comrade Cleveland Clarke, who was sailing to Panama "to seek vaster fields, for intellectual and social developments": "At 1:30 A.M. every body bade their friend a Bon Voyage, and expressed their hopes that his achievements shall grace the pages of every newspaper in Panama." This was not unlikely—after all, we know of this fond farewell because it made the pages of the *Searchlight* the following day.[60]

Since men like Cleveland Clarke regularly read the Panama papers from Limón, he would have known full well that a plethora of literary clubs like the Alpha—and fraternal orders, and youth brigades, and debating societies—awaited his energies at his destination. Like local prints elsewhere, in Yiddish or Italian or English, the circum-Caribbean papers worked in symbiosis with a flowering of civic life.[61]

Indeed, British Caribbean participation in transnational civic associations preceded and aided the formation of black-internationalist ones. The lodges and orders provided templates for officeholding, for finances, for communicating with chapters abroad. They provided skill-building experience, so regular folks knew how to run a meeting and get things done. But most of all, they provided a belief in the efficacy of supranational collectives. Consider your experience as a Salvationist, or simply as a curious observer, buying the *West Indies War Cry* from a street-corner boomer in Port Antonio or Port

Limón. You would read updates on the "brave Leaguers" in the West Indies Regiment, Jamaican soldiers leading Salvationist prayer meetings among the natives while stationed in Sierra Leone. You would follow missionary efforts in Lapland and East London and study the nattily uniformed Sergeant Ellen Corey, who had left St. Kitts to work as a "domestic" in Toronto, where she also led "splendid services" and brought "new souls to the Mercy Seat" weekly.[62]

The world needed saving; only collective effort could save it; every person mattered. It was your duty to learn, and dream, and donate what you could. Show up, keep faith. This was the message that the Salvation Army laid out on the pages of the *West Indies War Cry*, but it was also the message of the Boy Scouts and friendly societies and fraternal lodges. Most rimland friendly societies were chapters of island-specific mutual organizations, while the lodges were affiliates of either English or U.S. Afro-American fraternal orders. None of these were necessarily black-internationalist, and some were white-run at the top, but almost all of the enthusiasts founding new troops or leading local meetings were Afro-Caribbean.[63] And if race-blind full membership rights were not forthcoming, then something had to change—as when the colored members of the Seventh-Day Adventists "voted unanimously to withdraw from the General Conference and to re-organize independently of white control."[64]

Other organizations had been black-run from the start and wore their race lightly and proudly. This was true of fraternal orders from the Improved Benevolent and Protective Order of Elks of the World (the "Coloured Elks," who had chapters in the Bahamas, Cuba, Puerto Rico, Trinidad, Honduras, Panama, British Guiana, Jamaica, and Haiti), to the Grand United Order of Odd Fellows (who carefully sent annual reports to the Sub-Committee of Management in Philadelphia from lodges in Colón, Bocas, Bluefields, Limón, and beyond).[65] In 1911 Port Limón representatives of the Mosaic Templars of America exhorted local readers to "join the people's fraternity. No discrimination because of your color, no privileges debarred. A Templar in Costa Rica is welcomed in the U.S. or elsewhere. A Policy by a member here is paid equally as in the U.S. We aim at the protection of our race and people as members of one family."[66] The group, founded in Little Rock, Arkansas, in 1882, had tens of thousands of members worldwide by the 1920s. Note that Marcus Garvey was still a timekeeper on a Limón banana plantation when this advertisement was published. Not only in its fraternal society structure but also in its international race consciousness, the UNIA followed a route opened up by the transnationalization of working-class black life that came with the turn-of-the-century expansion of the circum-Caribbean migratory sphere.

The circulation of media was a key part of that transnationalization, and although we have focused on print media, radio and films contributed as well. Their role in circulating music and dance moves will be discussed in the next chapter. But they also intensified other kinds of international connection, sports fandom first and foremost. And no star mattered more in the circum-Caribbean migratory sphere than boxer Joe Louis. In a world in which sports heroes stood for nations of origin, Joe Louis stood for his people: Our People, the Negro Race. Thelma Anderson was not alone in praying for Joe Louis to whip every white boy. Trinidad's carnival rang with calypsos in his honor, "blasts of racial pride" according to one traveler who learned them from men liming in a St. Vincent barber shop, its "walls well pasted with pictures of Joe Louis and the Royal Family."[67] The calypsos circulated in vinyl as well. The Lion and Attila composed "Louis-Schmeling Fight" in the wake of the Brown Bomber's 1936 upset loss and recorded it in New York a few months later.

"Schmeling wouldn't like to meet him again," boasted the calypso's final line. Following every step of Louis's comeback in newsreels and headlines, the Caribbean awaited the rematch. (It was at this moment that Thelma Anderson wrote to the *Courier* that "we here in Costa Rica" were praying for God to give Joe double strength.) Another traveler described the scene around a radio in a Canal Zone hotel when the rematch with Schmeling finally came in 1938: "All the coloured bell-boys and porters gathered in the hotel lounge to listen to that inglorious defeat of the German champion. It was all over in a few minutes. The coloured porters were jubilant. They collected dollar notes with a grin from the pallid American travelers. Then swiftly they disappeared to celebrate in riotous fashion among their own kind in Silver Town."[68]

Folks in Limón had considered Louis their champion for years. Back in 1935, one Leonard Dobson had even invited the boxer to a "grand reception" to be hosted by the "colored community" of Limón after his next Havana match. Addressed to Louis through the *Pittsburgh Courier* Readers' Page, the letter captured the author's sense of ownership of both the discursive space of the black press and the transcendent hero that was Joe Louis. It began:

To the Editor
The *Pittsburgh Courier*
Please print the following letter to Joe Louis:
    Dear Joe:
    Please accept the best congratulations from the colored young people of Costa Rica. We are very proud of your improvements and recent victories in the pugilistic world.[69]

Nominally addressing Joe Louis, Dobson really addressed the transnational black public itself. Moreover, he was heard. Three weeks later, a letter from one Dewey Fox of West Virginia occupied the same space: "In my opinion, one of the most interesting sections of your good paper is dedicated to 'What the People Think.' I found in a recent issue the following headlines: 'Higher Purchasing Power Will Bring Benefits to Race,' 'Suggest U.N.I.A. to Aid Ethiopia,' 'Congratulates Joe Louis—Invites Him to Costa Rica.' These are timely topics, well discussed and very commendable." The *Courier*'s pages had captured the international spread of black internationalism, and Fox aimed to cycle that awareness into action. Lauding the contributors' page as a "clearing house for its readers" that could channel "suggestions for racial development and advancement," Fox posed a series of questions about self-definition and goals of "the Negro reading public," culminating in: "Can anyone suggest a movement broad enough and liberal enough to encompass all our interests—religious, economic, social, educational, political, fraternal?"[70]

Leonard Dobson of Limón, Costa Rica, and Dewey Fox of Morgantown, West Virginia—two men who had never met and would never meet—were in dialogue through the medium of the *Pittsburgh Courier*. And Dewey saw in this new possibilities for "racial development and advancement" and used the same medium to call others to join in. There could be no clearer illustration of the process through which the circum-Caribbean/transatlantic black press made possible the creation of a self-aware, transnational black public.

This public sphere was used for the continuous evaluation of both what it meant to be a race and what it meant to confront racism. The papers reported in detail on the demands of Gandhi in India; the labor conditions and land loss being imposed in East Africa; the intensifying "colour bar" in South Africa; the vicious ignorance of U.S. politicians about Haiti; and the violence against black residents in Britain's ports. This coverage sat beside reports of oil-field fires in Trinidad, land-settlement schemes in Jamaica, out-of-work cane cutters in Cuba, and feuds in the UNIA—and alongside news of marriages and deaths, welcomes and farewells, lodge meetings and school pageants.

Just like the *Pittsburgh Courier*'s Readers' Page, such coverage and juxtaposition built collective identities. "Panama Folks in New York" were our concern—and imperial rule in Kenya was our concern, too. The "we" made up of people whom readers knew personally was a part of a larger "we" comprised of black people around the world, striving to triumph in spite of the common racism all faced. In this space, in this moment, how could one distinguish the personal from the political? That the political harmed the collective made it personal; that the personal could be spoken to the collective made it political.

In the modern world everything, good and bad, could be read as a matter of race. A resident of a tiny town twenty-eight miles up the rail line from Port Limón lauded local schoolchildren's performances: "The entire Negro race should be proud of them."[71] A bicycle race in 1931 Limón provoked multiple racial frames. A "Turk" battling a "black boy" for first place ran into a young woman and then "accused her of having run into his way, so that her 'Countryman could win.'" A municipal employee—himself Afro-Jamaican—not only sided with the "Turk" against the young woman but also called her "Nigger girl" before a crowd. Livid, a stalwart of the Limón press called on "the best of our men with genuine *Negro blood* to voice their indignation." The collective of race must trump all other divides: "Now is the age of racial love and unity, when every one of the race should be affected, if any of its members should suffer any injustice whatsoever."[72]

The love that was needed was "racial," the unity required was "racial," the progress to come would be "racial." As Sidney Young summed up the "New Awakening" of his era: "Pride of race is said to be the keystone of racial progress. . . . Today the nations of the world revel not only in their own individual history but in the reflected glory of the race to which they belong." Therefore, "for the negro to succeed he must fall back on his race."[73] The salience of race had come to seem self-evident, that much is clear. But what exactly was this race of which they spoke? Did it depend on "genuine Negro blood," or was something other than biological inheritance at its core? Might a "Turk," or an Asian, or an East Indian be considered fellow members of a broader colored collective?[74]

The same word, "race," signaling the same category, people of African ancestry worldwide, could carry profoundly different analyses of that collective's origins, trajectory, and future. Some black-internationalist proposals, including many of Marcus Garvey's speeches and writings, hewed to the essentialist ethos of other *volk* nationalisms of the era.[75] Other speakers presented the same key terms, "race" and "people," as reflections of history rather than biology. Writers like Sidney Young and many of his interlocutors understood racehood and peoplehood as outcomes of oppression and struggle rather than inborn or God-given essentials. They understood destinies as naturally collective—it was "nations" or "races" that rose and fell—but rejected biologizing claims: "The question of which men shall survive depends upon the conditions under which he shall struggle for survival. There is no law of nature here. It is a law of common sense and good government."[76]

Calisthenics at school on a United Fruit Company plantation, Costa Rica division, 1924. (United Fruit Company Photograph Collection, Box 76, #600; Baker Library Historical Collections, Harvard Business School)

Meanwhile, calls for racial unity routinely led to calls for other kinds of unity and denunciation of other kinds of division. A typical 1935 letter complained of the "Negro Weakness in Collective Propensities." When news of international cricket matches reached Limón, "How unusual it is to hear a Trinidadian give merit to a Jamaican and vice versa."[77] Note that there are three collectives here that are so self-evident they are not even acknowledged as such: Trinidadian, Jamaican, and "Negro"—the very collective accused of failures of collective propensities. What is explicitly under question, instead, is pan–British West Indian loyalty. Similarly, in the pages of the *Panama Tribune*, correspondents tallied the "Perils That Confront Our Race" and concluded that of the "damaging forces now operating to keep our people in this Republic from racial solidarity . . . INSULARITY [is] at the head of the list." Rather than follow the "bigoted" logic that reasoned "'Grenadians are monopolizing the lodge, let us get out and start a social for our countrymen only,'" wrote the author, "let us cultivate the tendency to devise plans for the Universal Coloured Brotherhood."[78]

Of course, Garvey's Universal Negro Improvement Association had begun life as just that—a benevolent organization like the island-specific benevolent associations, but one that could provide a common home for Jamaicans and Barbadians in Costa Rica, or British West Indians and African Americans in New York. In this, the UNIA succeeded and continued to do so, even as other elements of Garvey's plans for Negro progress (steamship line, Liberian colony) foundered. What lessons were to be drawn from Garvey's "Magnificent Failure"?

Sidney Young was among the West Indian community leaders who met with Garvey when the latter stopped in Panama on his way to Jamaica after deportation in 1927. Intending to remain "detached," Young found himself pulled in.

> As the set speeches gave way to free conversation, although Garvey did most of the talking, I became an animated participant in the discussion. I needed nothing to convert me to the doctrine that the Negro must look to himself for his own salvation, that he has his destinies in his hands, that he was given the common heritage of mankind and all the attributes, that so long as racial barriers are erected, it is the duty of black men to maintain their racial integrity and strive for racial independence. This is not a doctrine, it is a formula of life. Garvey has failed in everything except in preaching this formula so that the simplest and least educated black man can understand it. In this his success has been transcendent.[79]

Garvey had spread race consciousness to the masses, an achievement that Young hailed. But a worldview or "formula of life" is not a plan for action. What institutional form should striving for "racial independence" take?

To Sidney Young, West Indian federation seemed the only route forward. Federation was the strategy he urged on British Caribbean immigrants in Panama, whose disparate associations Young attempted in 1926 to federate into a single "Central Organization" to "be composed of representatives from each and every denomination, fraternity or club operating on the Isthmus," creating a united front to ensure "SELF-PRESERVATION" in the face of Panamanian hostility.[80] The same logic applied to the British Caribbean colonies. Like many activists abroad in this era, Young sought self-government for the British West Indies. This must, he and others presumed, go hand in hand with a federation to create a sustainable independence—within empire, still, but with full dominion status.[81] The *Tribune* covered the First West Indies Conference in Barbados in 1929 in enthusiastic detail, insisting that "the eventual political federation and social unity of the West Indies is written into the sky."[82] Or so Young hoped. For if there was one fact the interwar years were driving home, it was that in the absence of institutional change, the passionate embrace of peoplehood could take you only so far.

A STATE OF OUR OWN: THE INTERNATIONAL STRIPPING OF RIGHTS, AND WHAT WAS TO BE DONE

"Negro race, look around and see and listen of what is taking place in other countries with us," wrote T. L. N. Gayle to his fellow *Searchlight* readers in January 1930. "For instance, in Cuba, Panama, and even here in Costa Rica and many other. Who build them up to civilization? We the Negroes, and today we are barred from going to and fro. Is it justice? Men and women, open your eyes."[83] On the same page, a correspondent excerpted an article from the latest *Negro World*, urging the *Searchlight* editor "to publish for the benefit of the friends of the race, a speech delivered at the New York Liberty Hall, by judge Nicholas Klein of Cincinnati, a white American who feels kindly towards the Garvey movement of 'Africa for Africans.'" Readers in Limón thus read in their local paper words spoken weeks earlier by a white ally to a black-internationalist crowd in Manhattan—and the message was the same. Just like T. L. N. Gayle, Judge Klein saw the plight of men and women of the race as a matter of state politics and state power. But Klein stressed the global rather than the regional context. "If the Russians, the Japanese, the Chinese have a homeland, what is the matter with four hundred million Negroes?" Klein asked. "Organize! organize! and stick together; for the time is not far distant when you shall have what is yours, if peace is wanted by the world."[84]

Even before the enactment of Johnson-Reed closed U.S. borders to British Caribbeans, voices within the circum-Caribbean print-based public sphere warned of the looming crisis over mobility rights. They also underlined the crucial role that sending states played in either supporting emigrants or abandoning them to the whims of the new state racism. Writing in June 1924, Clennell Wickham pointed out that the treatment accorded West Indians and Japanese in the United States varied not because of racial difference, nor because of differential racism, but because of differences in sending-state backing. Each was denigrated as "a coloured race," but only the West Indians faced open abuse. "A damned Nigger, America is not for him. Such an attitude of course succeeds with a homeless (relatively) people like West Indians, who are forced to put up with any kind of treatment because there is no redress. Not so the Japanese. A citizen of a mighty empire he can laugh to scorn the frothy nonsense of the upholders of Nordic supremacy. The Japanese with the knowledge that other people hate him but dare not handle him roughly, goes about his business in a quiet way. . . . He knows on which side real superiority lies."[85]

Wickham called out the willingness of some to side with restrictionists when Asians were the target. "We are gravely told by West Indians who would see hell in America that it is because the Japanese are non-assimilable and not because they are coloured that America keeps them out."[86] West Indians needed to realize that restrictionism was driven by *racism*, not by racial or cultural difference. For Wickham, the worldwide exclusionist moment demanded not tit-for-tat nativism but broad colored solidarity. He decried the foolishness of those who insisted on the "right" to "slam the doors of our countries against a man not because he is a thief, not because he is a wastrel, but because he is yellow."[87]

Wickham laid out a realpolitik case for imperial support of race-blind mobility rights, warning of Japanese reaction if Australian and Canadian anti-Asian bans were allowed to stand. But in the end, he framed free mobility as a moral crusade, one linked explicitly to the last great transnational crusade against racial injustice: the fight against Atlantic slavery. "In the readjustment of population which has become necessary," he concluded, "the question will have to be answered 'Is a man a man and a brother?' Then the world will have to decide that no man who is willing to work for his living should be penalised by law. He must not be kept out, and he must have a square deal. We have an abundance of religion. Is this too much to ask?"[88]

Invoking the Christian universalist slogan of antislavery demanded that England live up to moral crusades of the past (as did the reference to Chatham and Wilberforce in the editorial at the start of this chapter). "Am I not a man and a brother?" was the legend above the image of a chained black man on the 1787 seal designed by the Society for Effecting the Abolition of the Slave Trade. That image, however, was designed by white activists to provoke white sympathy. The enslaved supplicant knelt, mute but for the plea abolitionists chose to assign him. Citing this phrase a century and a half later, Clennell Wickham located the international assault on the mobility rights of the world's people of color as parallel to the crisis of slavery: a collision of Christian humanism and racist injustice. But this time, Wickham, asking, "Is a man a man and a brother?," was a man of color writing to a public largely of color—readers who, like him, were the targets of the injustice he denounced. That he chose not to speak in the voice of "the Negro race" but rather in the unraced voice of the Anglo-American crusading-journalism tradition made his invocation of the question all the more radical. Both the framing and the content insisted manhood and brotherhood must be universal and race blind.

"What will Britain do?" was a real rather than rhetorical question in 1925. Observers within the circum-Caribbean migratory sphere still held hope that empire could be the best bulwark against racism in the modern world. Again and again, commentators harked back to Rome as the model of an empire that flourished when it gave rights to all citizens and floundered when internal hierarchies hardened. In 1850 Lord Palmerston had insisted that the core question was "whether, as the Roman . . . held himself free from indignity, when he could say *Civis Romanus sum*; so also a British subject, in whatever land he may be, shall feel confident that the watchful eye and the strong arm of England, will protect him against injustice and wrong."[89] In the second half of the nineteenth century, as empire's architects sought to expand her sphere of influence in the Greater Caribbean as around the world, Great Britain had insisted on the duty to protect subjects of the Crown whatever their color, wherever they were. Could Britain be made to live up to this promise as the threats faced abroad became ever more frequent?

Some thought it was time for some tough love. Writing in the *Panama American*'s West Indian Section in 1927, S. L. insisted on the right, even the duty, of patriotic Jamaicans to criticize the empire they had so loyally served during the Great War. "We are British at heart, British in culture . . . we stand for all that British tradition holds dear": "the courage of our convictions," respect for foes, impartial justice for family and strangers alike. These British traditions now demanded urgent action against racist injustice, the scope of which was visible in the papers that S. L. and his neighbors read every day.

> Intelligent West Indians do not forget their duty to the Empire . . . but they have also not forgotten that they are a colored people. They cannot forget the immigration laws of Canada and Australia. They cannot forget the labor laws of South Africa. They remember the political controversies of the Kenya colony where the natives are mistreated and expropriated. They will ever remember the post war treatment of Negro ex-soldiers in England. Ah! there's the rub. . . . If we are loyal to the Empire we must be first loyal to ourselves.[90]

By the end of the decade, hopes that Britannia would have the "moral courage" to listen to subjects of color who insisted that they "stood for all that Britain h[eld] dear" were dimming. The *Searchlight* surveyed the regional panorama in 1930: "West Indian labourers working at Maracaibo Venezuela going across from Trinidad into the oilfields and States of Venezuela are being gradually dismissed and once they return to Trinidad they are not permitted to reenter that Republic. The same thing is being done in Honduras, where the U.F.Co. is laying off a considerable quantity of coloured labour at the request of the government, which has made laws prohibiting the entry of coloured people."[91]

Race now trumped empire not in far-off Australia but right here next door, and empire seemed to have nothing to say about it. "Panama legislated against the Negro race some time ago, so that today no one can enter Panama"; the *Searchlight* continued, "and yet the British Crown gave no prominent pronouncements of influence on the matter that would bear pressure on Panama in favour of her Negro subjects. The same conditions obtains now in Nicaragua, because while a white English man can enter Nicaraguan territory by showing a hundred dollars in his possession yet the Negro Britisher is so legislated against for under no condition will he be permitted to land."[92] Meanwhile, Central Americans no more virtuous (and not much lighter) than they faced no barriers to entry or employment: "There are hundreds upon hundreds of Nicaraguan and other subjects being contracted into Puerto Armuelles [Panama], whereas no West Indian British Negro is permitted to embark."[93]

The contrast between an (old) international theory of imperial rights and the (new) international practice of race-based restriction had become egregiously visible. British Caribbeans caught in this moment responded with the contradictory politics that a contradictory moment demanded: they insisted on their loyalty to an undying empire and they decried the perfidy of an empire whose days were numbered.

The drumbeat of demands for self-government grew louder, now discussed openly even by those not yet ready to join the chorus themselves. One 1930 editorial reviewed the litany of antiblack laws imposed around the region—in Nicaragua, Colombia, Costa Rica, Panama, Cuba—and concluded, "On account of all these insults and indignities [is] why we find Captain Cipriani of Trinidad in his discourses in London before the Labour Conferences, striking out in no uncertain tones for 'Self Government' in the Colonies."[94] The call for British action again had both realpolitik and moral dimensions. But according to this author, the threat to be avoided was rebellion by black subjects within, rather than retaliation by Asian empires without.

Indeed, if you did not know better, you might think these very respectable middle-class editors were starting to make threats.

> If Britain thinks that because she has and is dominating a quarter of this earth's surface she is destined to go on doing so forever; she had better be at once undeceived, by remembering what Rome was in the ancient days, and what Spain was, only yesterday. Will she remember that what brought on the warfare which caused the downfall of the Roman Empire was colour Prejudice? . . . Let Britain watch well the threat of the Tyrant Hertzog in South Africa to break loose from the Empire so as to enslave the Negroes of Africa more than he now has them. . . . Again we warn, protect these people in times of peace who have been of great help to you in times of war or when war does come, you may find them pitted against you.[95]

These editors read Caribbean events as part of empire-wide trends and framed Caribbean demands on an empire-wide stage. They rhetorically addressed their warning to "you"—Britain, though there is no indication that Britain was listening, and surely the authors did not expect it. For implicitly it was instead the transnational black public being addressed. While the explicit question posed was "what will Britain do?," the implicit question was "what will *we* do?"

At this moment as never before, for British Caribbeans abroad the stakes of state representation were not only high in the abstract but felt in the flesh. The weight of state power was clear as men and women faced deportation, found themselves unable to reunite with family, discovered that years of service could be nullified with the stroke of a politician's pen. If men and women of African ancestry across the globe were to be treated not as people but as "a people" in the emerging nation-state regime, then surely they needed a state of their own to speak on their behalf. The mid-nineteenth-century logic of imperial competition had encouraged empires to treat all subjects as meriting imperial defense. The early twentieth-century logic of nation-state competition meant that republics were at least nominally committed to the welfare of their peoples. Great Britain's colonial subjects were falling through the cracks of a hybrid international regime.

No longer were British representatives abroad insisting, as the chargé d'affaires in Caracas had in 1849, that the descendants of Caribbean slaves had "a perfect right to due protection from their Government" abroad, which their "color" or "the meagerness of their resources and condition" in no way lessened.[96] Migrants' firsthand experiences of Pan-American state racism and imperial inaction led directly to demands to chuck empire altogether.

> Formerly a British Passport demanded from the inhabitants of every Country that the proud holder be allowed to travel *free without let or hindrance and be afforded every assistance in his travels*, under Security of the dominant British Flag, but now he dare not go to certain countries, even though he was instrumental in making that country with his Brawn, his Brain, and his Blood. . . . Is it any wonder that the Indian, the Egyptians, and negroes would like to shake off British dominance and see their own destinies?[97]

Where once the race-blind character of imperial belonging had been hailed on the floor of Parliament and the streets of rimland ports alike, now white Britishers shunned any identification with their coimperials of color. "Formerly it was the greatest pride of any British subject to be able to claim fellowship under the British flag," wrote the editors of the *Searchlight*. "Boastingly you could hear on every side 'I am a British subject' on equal magnanimity that the Romans used the proud phrase 'Romanus sum ego' when Rome was in her glory." But today, "English, Irish, and Scotchmen" in the Spanish American republics "would rather dodge under the Stars and Stripes." Meanwhile, "as for the coloured man, he is indeed, as was said by one of our most popular coloured men in this country some twenty years ago 'a British object,' an object of derision in the eyes of even less cultured peoples; he is legislated against by nearly every country, and yet such legislation is not protested against by the British Consular Offices."[98]

Like Clennell Wickham in Barbados five years before, the *Searchlight* editors insisted it was not simply a matter of race but a matter of the intersection of race and empire—and, more specifically, of the ways the lack of political voice within empire allowed race to become the arbiter of rights abroad. Men of the same skin color but of Latin American citizenship were not "(relatively) homeless" like British West Indians. To belong to the most powerful empire in the world brought no power, if one belonged in the sense that an object belongs to its owner rather than in the sense that a citizen belongs to his state. Indeed, "the coloured man" would have more rights as "a Costa Rica" rather than "a Britisher," for as a Costa Rican, "he has free intercourse in all Latin America, and the world; but as a Britisher, he is only allowed to go to

Jamaica, Barbadoes or Trinidad; he can't go to Australia or Canada or South Africa and hardly to England." Discontent, the editors warned, would "continue to grow until 'Albion' changes her tactics to these what she calls inferior races which in reality are only inferior in 'opportunities' or finds herself stripped of her belongings."[99] Even Rome had not been eternal.

CONCLUSION

The circum-Caribbean/transatlantic black press, together with the black-led civic associations, created a public sphere—"a set of physical or mediated spaces where people can gather and share information, debate opinions, and tease out their political interests and social needs with other participants."[100] The notion of a public sphere allows us to recognize the vital functioning-as-a-whole of distant, linked spaces. Together, the UNIA halls and Oddfellows lodges and *Weekly Herald* editorials and letters to the *Searchlight* allowed shared problems to be debated over time. Discussion began in one of these spaces, carried over into another, morphed into a third. Participants spurred each other to action and then debated the consequences faced. This cohesive public sphere encompassed physical and mediated spaces around the Greater Caribbean from Harlem to Panama to Guiana and linked to other publics generated from London, Paris, and beyond. Not all of these spaces were run by individuals identifying as "Negro," and not all debates within them were about race. But the public invoked by orators, editors, and commentators in these spaces—with conviction so commonsensical it could go without saying—was a public of color in a white-dominated world.

Listening in on conversations in that sphere has underlined the impact of international politics in shaping black-internationalist thought. These decades saw the consolidation of the nation-state as the modal geopolitical unit. The people whose voices we have heard were as concerned about what it meant to have (or not have) a state as about what it meant to be (or not be) a nation. The latter related to ideologies of race and territorial entitlement, but the former remitted to the pragmatics of power and territorial access.

Across the Greater Caribbean, colonial subjects of color watched closely as states asserted the authority to deny entry and employment based on birthplace, citizenship, language, and color. Mobility had gone from being a presumed entitlement to a highly contingent right. Up until this time, the possibility of employment abroad had been an effective counterweight to British Caribbeans' rightlessness at home. But as border control and internal gatekeeping became effective components of other states' sovereignty, opportunity abroad was no longer an antidote to disempowerment at home. Rather, rights of passage became another realm in which the lack of effective political membership at home translated into concrete disadvantage.

Colonial subjects of color observed Britannia's silence as race was made the arbiter of their rights as Britishers by country after country, and in the unwillingness of empire's agents to stand against barriers of race, they foretold the end of empire. Who would speak for *them* in the congress of nations? Multiple geopolitical imaginaries coexisted in this moment of promise and peril. Might there be a Negro colony in Africa with Marcus Garvey as president? Could a federation of the British West Indies provide a strong voice for the united many? Against this backdrop, the failure of the League of Nations to defend Ethiopia against Italian invasion in 1935 would be read as a parable for the present and a lesson for the future. Once again, a system that promised race-blind rights looked the other way as the rights of some people—black people—were violated.

By the 1930s, the men and women of the circum-Caribbean migratory sphere had burning questions to ask. Just as important, they had a place to ask them. Nancy Fraser has defined a "public sphere" as "a theater in modern societies in which political participation is enacted through the medium of talk."[101] The members of the transnational black public made possible by the circum-Caribbean/transatlantic black press did indeed enact their political participation through the medium of words. They had indeed created an "institutionalized arena of discursive interaction," and they used it to the hilt. They saw the results of "citizens['] deliberation" in the lands where they sojourned, and they recognized the weight of their own exclusion from that dialogue. The nominal protections of British subjecthood, long a believable fiction if not a reliable shield, offered no compensation. Caribbean men and women had summoned into existence a new "we," had redefined Trinidadians and St. Elizabeth's parishioners and Chicagoans as forming a single Negro Race. But without structures for representative government that could link their deliberations to state power, in the modern world, their race—as any race—was doomed. Events near and far made that all too clear.

five   The Weekly Regge

Cosmopolitan Music and Race-Conscious Moves in a
"World a Jazz," 1910s–1930s

At Port Limón's "weekly regge" in 1930, Caribbean teens danced the Black Bottom, shimmy, mento, fox-trot, and tango to the music of Limón's home-grown "hot jazz" sextets: the Central American Black Stars, the Merrymakers, and the Red Hot Six. On the streets of this once-prosperous banana port, in a marginalized province of a primly white-identified Central American nation and at the height of mobility restriction, young black men and women mixed music and moves with cosmopolitan panache. Week after week, they shim-mied and tangoed as if they were at the very center of the modern "world a jazz." Their elders grimly worried about race, rights, and empire. But the youth had other things on their minds.

In the previous chapter, I argued that the circulation of black-run peri-odicals and their integration in communal discussion at multiple sites had generated by the 1920s a supranational black public sphere. The creation and circulation of black-identified music and dance in the Jazz Age circum-Caribbean similarly generated both physical and mediated spaces for consid-ering commonality, building cohesion, and wrangling with external prejudice. But it did so not through printed words, but rather through embodied per-formance and irresistible sound.

Sidney Young described the scene at a dance hall in a British Caribbean neighborhood of Panama City in 1926, where music from cornet, saxophone, piano, banjo, and musical saw was punctuated by the "hoarse laughter and indecorous yells" of participant performance: "The bodies of our future mothers become suddenly and wondrously supple, they are bent in bewil-dering convolutions." Moves were for peers as well as partners. "Standing in groups are our young blades. There is a clapping of hands, clap-ap-clap, clap-ap-clap, some acrobatic idiot is demonstrating a new, agile and intricate step to the admiring gaze of his silly companions [who] will all attempt the dextrous contortions in the next dance."[1] Even through the distorting prism of Young's disdain we see the joy of communal motion. This was a space for proud expertise, raucous in-jokes, the exhilaration of youth and the new. I will refer to the broader social phenomenon of which Young's "young blades" knew they formed a part as the supranational black performative realm.

153

Within it, dancers on the floor and musicians on the stage together created the cultural explosion that was jazz.[2]

Paul Gilroy has pointed to the "ubiquity of antiphonal, social forms that underpin and enclose the plurality of black cultures in the western hemisphere," arguing that expressive forms based in call-and-response, storytelling, and music making serve to create "an alternative public sphere" within which specific styles of self-presentation are "formed and circulated as an integral component of insubordinate racial countercultures."[3] While for Gilroy this is "the most enduring Africanism of all," other scholars suggest that similar constellations are generated in response to modern regimes of dominance in general, rather than by particular cultural legacies. Michael Warner labels as "counterpublics" those collectives not only generated *by* subordinated groups, but generated through *means* that defy surrounding norms of public discourse. Reacting to a dominant culture that stigmatizes them and their cultural practices, suggests Warner, subordinated groups may reject "the hierarchy of faculties that elevates rational-critical reflection as the self-image of humanity" and instead use "embodied sociability, affect, and play" to create commonality and demand recognition.[4]

Both Gilroy's and Warner's models are useful in pointing out the serious politics of style. Yet between the print-based public sphere and "alternative public sphere" or "counterpublic" of the Jazz Age circum-Caribbean, we see not fixed opposition but mutual shaping. The black press—following the norms of bourgeois public discourse to perfection—and the black performative realm—rejecting those norms with gleeful abandon—worked simultaneously *in opposition to* and *in alliance with* each other. Readers and writers in the former and musicians, fans, and entrepreneurs in the latter all engaged in the "subjunctive-creative project" of creating publics: summoning a collective into existence by acting as if it were already there. Editors and readers and performers and fans built distinct webs of black-internationalist connections, sometimes by denouncing the others' failings, sometimes by leaning on their strengths.[5] Indeed, at times, international black performers and the international black press worked in tandem, as when Afro-American touring troupes announced their Cuban triumphs on the pages of the *Pittsburgh Courier* and published messages to fans in Panama and Kingston through the same. Meanwhile, the world of the black press and the world of black performance each framed itself in opposition to the racism of the dominant national and imperial publics of their era—yet they also borrowed substance and styles from those antiblack publics on a regular basis.[6]

So on the one hand, the story of Limón's "weekly regge" is further fodder for reconsidering the black internationalism of the interwar years, encouraging us to look even more broadly beyond iconic intellectuals than we already have. On the other hand, the case carries lessons for Caribbean historiography as well. One might frame this as a philological detective tale, in which we find the roots of the term "reggae" where no one thought to look: in Costa Rica, rather than in Jamaica itself or any of the islands usually discussed alongside Jamaica under the rubric of Caribbean music.

What have scholars established about the origins of reggae? It is clear (and nothing that follows will dispute this) that the musical genre today known as reggae emerged in Kingston in the late 1960s, as the ska music that had developed a decade earlier slowed into the form known as rock steady and continued to gain rhythmic and topical complexity from its engagement with Revival and Rastafarian drumming and worship traditions. The origins of the term "reggae" are less clear. The first recorded use of the term in the context of the musical genre was in the title of a 1968 hit by Toots and the Maytals entitled "Do the Reggay" (note that the term here denotes a dance style rather than the accompanying music per se).[7] Interviewed years later, Toots Hibbert reported that "it was just a word you hear on the streets. I don't remember why I apply it to the music. . . . At first reggae sort of mean untidy or scruffy. But then it start to mean like coming from the people."[8] Other protagonists of the West Kingston musical scene offered similarly vague testimonies. Hux Brown suggested, "It's just a fun, joke kinda word that means the ragged rhythm and the body feelin'. If it's got a greater meanin', it doesn't matter."[9] A contrasting derivation, from *reyes* or the related Latin *rex regis*, king of kings, seems to have been commonly asserted in the 1970s, especially by Rastafarians.[10] Timothy White reports that "Bob Marley claimed the word was Spanish in origin, meaning 'the king's music.'"[11]

Most serious lexicographers concur in linking "reggae" to "rege-rege," defined by Cassidy and LePage in 1967 (that is, prior to the Maytals' use of the term) as "1. Rags, ragged clothing" and "2. A quarrel, a row."[12] Allsopp, in his 1996 *Dictionary of Caribbean English Usage*, gives as possible origins the Yoruba "rege-rege," meaning "rough, in a rough manner," and cites also Tobago, "rege-rege," meaning "rough, uncultured," and the occasional use of the same term in Guyana for "a person playing a rattle for, or an older person participating in, an open-air dance."[13] As I will suggest below, the idea that a creole term of Yoruba origin reinforced the borrowing of the North Atlantic musical term "raggy" to label vernacular jazz dance among British

Caribbean youth in Limón is persuasive. But for the moment, I want to point out that the most erudite scholars of Caribbean culture have no qualms about citing usage in Tobago to illuminate coinage in Kingston, 1,174 miles distant. Port Limón was about half as far from Kingston, and you could travel back and forth twice a week by steamer if you wanted. Limón in 1930 was as tightly linked to Kingston as was Colón, Bocas del Toro, Santiago de Cuba, or Havana—which is to say, far more tightly linked than Kingston was to any port in any British Caribbean territory.

By the early 1940s, a cumulative total of 13,000 Jamaicans had returned to Jamaica from Costa Rica, 87,000 from Panama, 113,000 from Cuba, and 36,000 from the United States. A sizeable second generation came "back" as well. At the time of the 1943 census, Jamaicans in Jamaica included 6,713 born in Cuba, 3,417 in Panama, 681 in Costa Rica, and 562 elsewhere in Central America.[14] These were young people like Tommy McCook, born in Havana in 1927, who "returned" to Jamaica in 1933; Roland Alphonso, born in Havana in 1931, who "returned" alongside his Jamaican mother in 1933; Laurel Aitken, born to a Cuban mother in Cuba in 1927, who "returned" to his father's Jamaica in 1938; and Carlos Malcolm, born in Panama in 1935, who spent his formative years traveling between family in Kingston and family on the isthmus. As it happens, Aitken, McCook, Alphonso, and Malcolm would all became major figures in Jamaican ska in the 1950s and 1960s.[15] To search the migratory circuits of the western Caribbean for clues to the history of Jamaican music and dance may not be so crazy after all.

Finally, this chapter is also an effort to contribute to internationalizing the history of jazz. Common myth enshrines jazz as the classic "American" creation. The standard narrative holds that jazz was born in U.S. territory, nourished by Afro-Americans' heritage of rhythms and resistance, and exported outward from there.[16] Recent scholars have amplified this picture by linking New Orleans and the U.S. South to the cultural world of the Caribbean, some stressing the common Afro-descended substrate, others harking to nineteenth-century population movements.[17] Others have noted the impact of musicians from the Spanish- and English-speaking Caribbean on evolving idioms of jazz in mid-twentieth-century New York City.[18]

Such research has generally remained focused on musicians as the creators of music and on U.S. spaces as the sites of creation.[19] My goal is to offer a more thoroughly decentered account of where jazz was made and who made it. I will trace the multidirectional circulation of artists, recordings, and knowledge in the first decades of the twentieth century, focusing on a few places for which we have an unusually rich set of sources: Harlem, Kingston, Panama, and Port Limón. (While the occasional Trinidadian or Barbadian makes an appearance, I make no pretense to reconstruct here the history of music and dance in the migratory eastern Caribbean.[20]) Artists toured across the region, learning from and responding to the reactions of the audiences they sought to entertain. Gramophone recordings and then films circulated widely, their music and moves adopted or adapted into vernacular dance based both on novelty (the latest craze!) and resonance with local expertise (something we can dance to!). A few professional musicians born in Caribbean homes ended up on U.S. stages. But more important, far larger cohorts of sometimes-paid players and dance-loving fans brought musical repertoires with them as they traveled from island to island or shore to shore.

Furthermore, some U.S. places were themselves circum-Caribbean places in this era. The Caribbean space on U.S. soil par excellence was Harlem, of course, where at least a quarter of the population in 1930 was British Caribbean by birth or parentage. Against that backdrop, it is frankly the relative paucity of British Caribbeans among Harlem musicians and performers that is striking, rather than their occasional presence. But who sat onstage was one thing; who danced on the floor below, and who owned the stage and the floor, was another. Relatively rare in the ranks of musicians and composers, British Caribbeans flourished as entertainment entrepreneurs, founding venues, booking bands, and crafting formats. The manager of the Savoy Ballroom across its three-decade heyday was Barbadian; the founders of the Renaissance Casino and its famous floor shows were from Antigua, Montserrat, and St. Kitts; the bandleader of the Alhambra and Renaissance Ballrooms' house bands over the 1920s and 1930s was born in Panama to Jamaican parents. It is not surprising that one of the original "Lindy Hoppers" performing at the Savoy had Bajan parents, for the broader Harlem public attending Battles of the Bands or booking venues for weeknight club socials had a strong islander presence. If we take musicians of the era at their word when they describe the importance of response from the floor in shaping the music they played, we must conclude that the dancing masses of Caribbean origin had a major impact on the swing music of Harlem.

In sum, this chapter will argue that western Caribbean ports were not recipients of the musical fruit of some distant, metropolitan Jazz Age: they were part of the culturally contiguous space within which the Jazz Age and its deeply cosmopolitan music and dance were created. And this music and dance had serious stakes. It is no coincidence that black internationalisms surged within the transatlantic print and performative realms simultaneously. Observing the generation of each at fine-grained scale and at multiple sites will lead us to conclude that the two kinds of black internationalisms were driven by some of the same geopolitical developments—and spurred each other on (at times by duking it out) as well.

MUSIC AND MOVEMENT IN THE WESTERN CARIBBEAN AT THE DAWN OF THE TWENTIETH CENTURY

What were the spaces and steps of popular dance in the anglophone western Caribbean at the start of the twentieth century? Who played what music? How did people move? And how did the moves and spaces of vernacular dance fit into the island's hierarchies of color and class? Writing in 1910, Anglo-Jamaican newspaperman Herbert G. de Lisser described the favored entertainments of working-class Kingston. "They call them 'practice dances.' The theory is that these dances are for learners. But those who attend them are for the most part experts. Yet no one would speak of them as dances pure and simple, for that would be some reflection on one's social life," that is, would imply expenses to which working-class hosts could not aspire. "A dance must be given in a house; dancers must be properly dressed; there must be refreshments." In contrast, "A 'practice dance' may be given in a yard, takes place every week, and you may go to it in your working clothes. You are formally invited, of course. 'Ladies 3d., Gentlemen 6d.' is an intimation that you cannot enjoy the privilege of attending the dance without paying."[21]

Thus, the "practice dance" was a dance held weekly, in an informal space, for profit. Other sources capture the popularity of practice dances as well, though they generally only made the papers when things got louder than usual. One Kingstonian in 1900 called "the attention of the police to a nuisance which occurs nightly at Luke Lane where a practice dance is being carried on to the annoyance of the respectable inhabitants of that locality and where the most abominable language and fighting goes on."[22] In 1917 a "a girl who was very disorderly at a practice dance in Text Lane was fined 5/ or 7 days. . . . District constable Goldson said that this particular form of amusement was very disagreeable to the neighbourhood."[23]

While practice dances were run as fund-raisers for working-class proprietors, other dances were held as fund-raisers for working-class civic associations. "Flaring placards," wrote de Lisser, "inform you that 'A Grand Unique Star of the West Picnic will take place at Wildman Penn on Thursday, King's Birthday: Mr. Johnny's Band in attendance. Admission: Males 1s., Females 6d.'" Visitors recalled seeing up to 2,000 attendees "dancing on the sward and in the shade of the trees."[24] Australian expat Winifred James was following local custom when she organized a bazaar with music among British Caribbean United Fruit laborers in Bocas del Toro in 1916 to raise funds for British ambulance supplies: "Every evening the gay paper lanterns and the noise of the gramophones brought a crowd of jostling niggers and a few Chinamen."[25]

What exactly did folks dance at these dances? De Lisser reported that waltzes and quadrilles dominated most working-class practice dances. But he also fretted over a particular vernacular dance, "a sublimated West African phallic dance" known locally as the "shay-shay" or "mento" that "consists of slow movements of the body, and the point of perfection is reached when, as in Hayti, the dancer never allows the upper part of her body to move as she writhes and shuffles over the ground." Unlike the group sets of lancers and quadrilles, the shay-shay was danced "with your partner alone," and intensely so. "If you are refined, your motions may be a trifle suggestive—hardly even that. If you are not refined, they may be coarsely, brutally, blatantly vulgar."[26]

The huffing over Haiti's moral menace may be boilerplate, but de Lisser's depiction of the shay-shay's gestural contours—dynamism without displacement—is confirmed by innumerable sources.[27] However, according to de Lisser, the Afro-descended, locally generated mentos were losing ground to steps drawn from the respectable British repertoire. "They are by no means the staple of any respectable dance-party given by the working classes now," he wrote in 1910. "They are popular, but, even so, at your open-air 'practice dance' you will have two-steps and waltzes and lancers in plenty. The lascivious dances of West Africa have taken second place."[28]

Either this report of the impending demise of mento and its cousins was wishful thinking on the white newsman's part, or it was a trend on the verge of reversal. Travels and technology had begun to bring the rhythms of New Orleans, Jamaica, Harlem, and Cuba into an ongoing musical commerce in which British Caribbean sojourners would be both producers and consumers. The terms "jazz" and "calypso" became iconic labels for the recordings that resulted, each linked to particular places (New Orleans, Chicago, and New York for jazz; Trinidad for calypso). But in fact, musicians and audiences around the Caribbean participated in the extraordinary creativity of this moment, contributing elements of musical vocabulary always already both mixed and local.[29] Panama-raised writer Eric Walrond described the international rhythms of Colón's red-light district at the height of Panama Canal construction: "Argentine Tango, merengue, 'shimmy-shawbbie,' the 'passion glide'—it was the most cosmopolitan café in the district."[30] The soundscapes of workers' neighborhoods were no less cosmopolitan than this bordello, though with a stronger island-and-rimland cant. Diverse traditions crossed nightly on the verandas of Colón, where "dark, bright-skirted, flame-lipped girls . . . danced in squares, holding up the tips of their flimsy dresses, to the *coombia* of creole island places," and "Jamaica girls, fired by an inextinguishable warmth, danced, whirling, wheeling, rolling, rubbing, spinning their posteriors and their hips, in circles, their breasts like rosettes of flame, quivering to the rhythm of the *mento*."[31]

THE NORTHERN FRONTIER OF THE GREATER CARIBBEAN: WEST INDIAN HARLEM AND "AMERICAN" JAZZ

Even as Jamaican girls' rhythmic mento raised blood pressures in Colón, syncopated dance music was coming into its own in the nearby port of New Orleans. The first published uses of the term "jazz" date from late 1915. An article from the *Chicago Tribune* proposed to explain the new fad to the uninitiated, interviewing a pianist who defined jazz as a matter of "blue notes"—that is, "harmonic discord" added through improvisation, which he attributed to Afro-American musical practice. "They started in the South half a century ago and are the interpolations of darkies originally. The trade name for them is 'jazz.'" Now these notes had become a "craze" sweeping northern cities. Connections between the new music, new steps, and new claims to bodily pleasure stood front and center. The article began with an imagined dialogue between a cosmopolitan couple: "'Ortus,' she murmured, looking into his tired eyes, 'If you don't fox trot with me shortly, I shall bring suit for divorce.'"[32]

Over the following decade, jazz music would come to define a generation and a historical moment, with its appeal both rooted in and contentious because of its twin associations with black people and embodied pleasure. From the start, this put commentators from "the classes" of color on the spot. Was jazz ours, by virtue of race, or not ours, by virtue of class? And if it was ours, was that good or bad? Jamaica-born J. A. Rogers tried to argue all of the options at once: "JAZZ is a marvel of paradox: too fundamentally human, at least as modern humanity goes, to be typically racial, too international to be characteristically national, too much abroad in the world to have a special home. And yet jazz in spite of it all is one part American and three parts American Negro, and was originally the nobody's child of the levee and the city slum."[33] It was in Harlem that that "nobody's child" pulled on a new pair of shoes and started to boogie.

As we know, some 40,000 British Caribbeans and tens of thousands of their locally born children called Jazz Age Harlem home. Fully a quarter of the heads of household of the Harlem block where pioneering bandleader James Reese Europe lived in 1915 were British Caribbean by birth.[34] How did this shape the cultural ecology within which jazz music and jazz dance developed together into a golden age? Evidence suggests immigrants were underrepresented in the ranks of professional musicians (and indeed, twenty-seven of the twenty-nine professional musicians on Europe's block were native born). Yet they necessarily made up a significant portion of the audience whose musical taste and rhythmic vocabulary shaped Harlem dance scenes, from ballrooms to rent parties. And if British Caribbean immigrants were underrepresented among musicians, the opposite was true among the businessmen who shaped Harlem's self-directed entertainment world.

Kingston-born Dan Kildare, cofounder in 1910 of James Reese Europe's Clef Club, a booking agency and social club for black musicians, presaged this music-and-management role. The ragtime, fox-trot, and maxixe played by Kildare's New York–based "coloured orchestra" (or "Ragtime dances and loud singing by a nigger troupe," as London police complained) took London's high society by storm in 1915.[35] A decade later, Amy Ashwood—who had been born in Jamaica in 1897, lived in Panama as a youth, helped found the UNIA in Kingston, and married Marcus Garvey in 1919—produced musical revues and ran jazz clubs alongside her political endeavors in New York and London. She did so in partnership with the hugely influential Sam Manning, born in Trinidad circa 1899, who moved to New York after service in the British West Indies Regiment in France and North Africa. Manning recorded in both Okeh's "Race" and "West Indian" series in the mid-1920s and as a performer, investor, and manager decisively shaped the international presence of Trinidad's calypso complex.[36]

Ashwood's and Manning's ongoing ties to island music and politics have kept them firmly within the "Caribbean" slot in music history. But other innovators of big-band jazz who are now remembered as African American emerged from the British Caribbean dispersion as well. Luis Russell was born in 1902 in Panama and studied piano, organ, violin, and guitar there before immigrating in 1919 with his family to New Orleans, where he founded his own "Hot Six." Moving to Chicago in 1925, he played with King Oliver for two years before founding the New York–based Luis Russell Orchestra in 1927; after seven years of touring and recording, Russell's group became the (anonymous) backup band for Louis Armstrong until 1943.[37] Born, like Russell, in Panama in 1902, Vernon Andrade learned to play violin and bass on the isthmus before moving to New York in the early 1920s. His orchestra became the house band for the Renaissance Casino, as well as for the famed

Sunday matinees at the Alhambra Ballroom, where young fanatics pushed the boundaries of acrobatic dance. (It was to Andrade's orchestra at the Alhambra that the teenage Frankie Manning, an original member of Whitey's Lindy Hoppers, first learned to dance.)[38]

North Carolina–born trombonist Clyde Bernhardt played with Andrade's orchestra at the Renaissance Casino in the midthirties, the years in which a teenage Ella Fitzgerald—"just out of the orphan home"—came up to 138th Street to sing with Andrade's band two or three nights a week. He recalls:

> Half of Andrade's band was West Indian. Since I worked in a few West Indian bands myself, a lot of guys thought I was West Indian too.
>
> They used to tease me, tell me I was passing for colored. "You really one of us," they laugh.
>
> Even Andrade, who was from Panama but his people came from the islands, teased me. "Barnhardt," he say, "What part of Barbados you from?"[39]

It was the musicians' daily experience of the commonalities and cross-cutting hierarchies of Harlem's entertainment world that made the joke funny. But the hierarchies could burn, too, as heard in Bernhardt's uncle's response to Andrade's hiring demands: "That West Indian think he owns a band of nigger slaves— . . . [t]he hell with that damn monkey-chaser!"[40]

The ubiquity of immigrants among the entrepreneurs who shaped the venues and genres of social dance in Jazz Age Harlem stands out in retrospect yet was so consistent with surrounding patterns as to be unremarkable at the time. After all, the bulk of real estate business in Harlem was in the hands of men like Charles Buchanan, born in Barbados in 1898 and raised in New York from the age of six. By 1926 Buchanan's real estate interests led him to the Savoy Ballroom, which he ran for the next three decades as the Savoy, with its swing-mad dancers and "Battles of the Bands," launched Count Basie, Duke Ellington, Jimmie Lunceford, and many others into stardom.[41] Three blocks south and one block over stood the Renaissance Casino and Ballroom, where Panama-born Vernon Andrade played. The "Renny" was founded around 1915 by three business partners, two of Antiguan birth and the other from Montserrat.[42] During band breaks here in the 1920s, patrons cheered on the Harlem Rens, a pioneering black basketball team-cum-floorshow founded and managed by St. Kitts–born Bob Douglas.[43] Musicians playing the Renny in the 1920s and 1930s included Louis Armstrong, Elmer Snowden, Fletcher Henderson, and Jimmie Lunceford. Less prominent than these headliners, yet typical of the audience they served, was young John Isaacs, the Rens' "Boy Wonder" of the 1930s, who had been born in Panama in 1915 to a Jamaican father and Panamanian mother and grew up speaking English and Spanish in Harlem.[44]

The Savoy and the Renny reflected the society around them, a society pervasively Caribbean. As one musician reminisced, "Private organizations gave regular affairs and receptions at the Renaissance—mixed black and white political clubs, leading West Indian and Panamanian social groups, and high-powered colored associations. Andrade played for them all."[45] The Renaissance Casino was four blocks south but worlds away from the Cotton Club, where Duke Ellington played for an all-white clientele. Unlike white-oriented nightclubs that filled their spaces with all comers, or all comers of the right color, the Renny was anchored in the clubs and loyalties of the Caribbean migratory sphere. The Renny hosted events for island benevolent societies, West Indies–wide reform groups, and race-based organizations, like the Brotherhood of Sleeping Car Porters, that counted both Afro-Americans and Afro-Caribbeans among their members.[46] British Caribbean migrants in interwar New York routinely belonged to organizations across all these categories: and the Renny was their place. Events included a mass rally in support of the jailed Marcus Garvey in 1923; a "monster mass meeting" of the West Indian Reform Association in 1924 to commemorate the ninetieth anniversary of (West Indian) emancipation and discuss "vital issues affecting the islands"; and an invitation-only 1930 gala to welcome a Jamaican cricket team brought north "to improve the game in New York."[47] (Due to complications of the kind travelers of color by then confronted around the region, the cricketers ended up in quarantine on Ellis Island, but they were sprung in time for the dance.)

Ironically, the tight integration of the Renny and other West Indian–owned, black-oriented venues into Harlem's civic fabric likely made their role *less* visible to the white aficionados who shaped written memory of Jazz Age Harlem. Andrade's band played club meetings and private parties at the Renny "seven nights a week, plus maybe two or three matinees. Bob Douglas often turned down social parties because the band was booked solid."[48] Clyde Bernhardt recalled that when he was playing with Andrade, "important white writers and fans couldn't get uptown to hear me, because Renaissance dances was usually private. Kept meeting people during this time that thought I'd died."[49]

The spaces of vernacular dance outside the big ballrooms were even less visible to outsiders. Alma Miller met her future husband on the dance floor at

Coronation Pageant and Ball

Under the Distinguished Patronage of the British Consulate in N.Y.C.

¶ You and Your friends are most cordially invited by the
Officers and Members of

St. Ambrose Parish
New York City
to attend their

Grand Coronation Pageant & Ball

WHICH WILL TAKE PLACE AT

ROCKLAND PALACE, 155th St. and 8th Ave.

New York City

On Wednesday Evening, May 12th, 1937

(The same day as the Coronation in England)

VERNON ANDRADE
and his Popular Orchestra will play

Subscription Tickets 3s. 1½d.

Boxes, 12s. 6d.   ::   Loges, 8s. 4d.

Invited by ....

Flyer for Coronation Pageant featuring Vernon Andrade's orchestra, 1937. (From
Ira de A. Reid, The Negro Immigrant [New York: Columbia University Press,
1939])

the weekly "Sons and Daughters of Barbados" dance at 135th and 5th in 1917, two years after she had left Bridgetown. Widowed at nineteen, Alma then supported her daughters with rent parties at which guests paid twenty-five cents for "pigs feet, peas and rice, and jump steady" (whiskey) and an evening of dancing from Charleston to "new jazz."[50] A 1939 "picnic" held by the Trinidad Carnival Committee on Lennox Avenue entered the print record only because a Decca music scout took a *New Yorker* reporter along on a lark. The crowd was made up of beauticians, domestics, elevator operators, "musicians, and a few professional people"; "good hot" music came from the Krazy Kats and calypsonian Wilmoth Houdini, and by midnight "the hall was seething with Suzi-Q and Lindy-hop dancers."[51] (As befitted a Trini event, "patties and paylou," rather than Alma Miller's Bajan trotters and souse, were on the menu here.)

Social dance to hot music permeated the communal spaces that British Caribbeans created for themselves in Harlem, and public demand tied these informal spaces to formal venues and the music evolving in them. Bandleaders' success depended on pleasing the hall. Vernon Andrade kept his spot at the Renny for twenty-seven years because he "knew his business . . . he knew how to call a set; usually four songs, different tempos, maybe a waltz, then a sweet number, a calypso, and then a hot number. . . . Just like King Oliver, he spot a crowd and know exactly what the people wanted to dance to."[52] Scholars confirm the point. Jacqui Malone highlights "the extremely rich cross-fertilization of African American vernacular dance, jazz, and singing in the twenties, thirties, and forties," pointing specifically to the Savoy Ballroom, where (Bajan-born) "Charles Buchanan . . . called the best bands the ones that kept the floor filled. Night after night, the dancers and musicians at the Savoy spurred one another on to greater heights and earthier depths."[53] An unknowable but significant portion of the dancers whose desires spurred the development of jazz and swing were Caribbean-born, just like the man who hired the bands.

Occasionally, they made the papers. A 1931 St Thomas Tennis Club affair at the Renny had a "picnic" theme, including "old fashioned home-made West Indian ginger beer." "But the fun of the whole evening," reported the *Pittsburgh Courier*, "was the grand West Indian and Cuban music that Vernon Andrade's Orchestra played. Those good old-timers, 'Sly Mongoose' and 'Sting No More,' by which your papas swung your mamas, and the latest West Indian tunes and Cuban 'Peanut Vender,' to which their children do a wicked bit of stepping."[54]

We begin to glimpse the breadth of musical heritage that shaped the quotidian rhythms and tastes of British Caribbean Harlem. Walter Bishop was born in Kingston in 1905. The son of an ice cream vendor, he played in church the violin his sister had brought on a visit home from Cuba and made a name for himself singing songs like "Take Me to the Land of Jazz," "St. Louis Blues," and "Memphis Blues" at grammar school events. His father's death in 1921 sent Walter to live with an older brother in Harlem. Lodging with the Glester Hinds family plunged him into a world of black civic activism and cutting-edge music, with James P. Johnson, Fats Waller, and others coming by

Savoy dancers (Whitey's Lindy Hoppers) perform outside at New York World's Fair, 1939. (Manuscripts and Archives Division, New York Public Library, Lenox and Tilden Foundations)

the house parties to "tickle those keys."[55] Bishop became a composer and a songwriter, and his son Walter Jr. would be a pioneering pianist of the bebop era. But more than Bishop's contribution to music, I want to underline the mundane musical cosmopolitanism of both his childhood in Kingston and his adulthood in Harlem. The same is revealed in the testimony of Leonard Gaskin, born in New York in 1920 to Trinidadian parents. "Most of the Caribbean houses in Brooklyn had pianos in their homes, and it was mandatory that most of us take piano lessons." Arriving from Trinidad, Leonard's aunt bought "Strauss waltzes and the light classics" for their wind-up Victrola. But raggier music snuck in as well: "My earliest recollection of hearing syncopated music is through piano rolls—Eubie Blake, Luckey Roberts, Willie the Lion Smith."[56]

Barbadian Alma Miller's daughter Norma Charlestoned as a toddler at her mother's rent parties; spent summer nights on the fire escape with her sister listening to music from the Savoy below; learned to Black Bottom, shimmy, and Pick Cherries from movie musicals; danced the Lindy at Vernon Andrade's Sunday matinees; and became one the Savoy's own "Lindy Hoppers," touring Europe and performing at the 1939 World's Fair. Two years later, Norma, Frankie Manning, and six others from the troupe would perform on a Hollywood soundstage the moves they had perfected, generating the immortal swing-dance scene in the film *Hellzapoppin'*.[57] The stories of Bishop, Gaskin, and Miller underline that any account of music's circulation between the United States and points Caribbean is incomplete without understanding that the people dancing to that music at all of those sites were themselves on the move—already cosmopolitan in their tastes and knowledge, and hungry for more.

MUSIC IN MOTION: FILMS, GRAMOPHONES, AND THE UNSTEADY LOCATION OF THE LOCAL

Walter Bishop could sing "Take Me to the Land of Jazz," "St. Louis Blues," and "Memphis Blues" at Kingston school events in the late 1910s because sheet music, songs, and films flowed along the intensifying commercial routes of the Greater Caribbean. He could play alongside his cousin in church because his sister's earnings from Cuba paid for a violin. A region-wide music marketplace was emerging, and with earnings from abroad, more and more people had money to spend within it. "The classes" were quick to embrace certain elements of modern music from afar. Jamaican newspapers carried admiring reports as (white) dancers Vernon and Irene Castle gained fame, teaching the fox-trot and other twisting steps to the syncopated tunes composed for them by (black) Harlemite James Reese Europe. Films like *Fox Trot Finesse* headlined Kingston theaters in 1916, and by 1917 a "Jazz Band" was performing regularly at the Myrtle Beach Hotel in Kingston.[58] Sophisticated Kingstonites could learn the new steps through proper lessons as well as from the Castles' and others' films. In 1917 one Mr. J. Derbyshire, "just returned to the island," offered lessons "on the following dances: Ritz Waltz, One Step, Three Step, Fox Trot, London Taps in classes or privately."[59] Two years later, the enterprising Mr. Derbyshire had added the syncopated fox-trot, the pendulum waltz, maxixe, and the Chinese toddle to his instructional repertoire.[60]

Yet a core contradiction lurked, for if the new moves offered foreign finesse, the new music makers were undeniably black. How could music be modern ... and African ... and *admired* all at once? Commentators twisted to get their heads around it. A New York–based author reprinted by the *Gleaner* in 1925 explained that "the turkey trot and its descendent the fox-trot—in spite of the barnyard flavor of their labels"—were the first "genuine dance of the city," their jerky and dissonant moves summoning up "the ragged noises which we know as jazz." Already straddling the urban and rural, the author layered on more oppositions: Africa versus here, ancient versus now. "Jazz, meant for the jungle of the city, went back for its primal inspiration to the real jungle. It was built up around the banjo, which is the heir of the African tom-tom. But from that point it orchestrated itself with mechanic city discords."[61] So, ugly urban modernity demanded primitive African barbarity—but then surely there could be nothing here to laud?

Yet the metropolitan acclaim was undeniable, as the international press made clear. Kingston read of the Southern Syncopated Orchestra's London stay in 1920: "The animated performances of this band of 'darkie' musicians . . . are the delight of big audiences, and at the same time attract again and again some of the most 'advanced' music lovers."[62] Making matters worse, conductor E. E. Thompson offered a racial essentialist account of his group's rhythms, staking out his people's ownership of the fox-trot, blues, and their syncopated kin. "Negro music originates in a love of dancing and in dance rhythm," Thompson explained. "Our primitive dance called the blues is the amusement at any simple darkie merrymaking, and goes back to prehistoric times. . . . In remote places this music is twanged on a simple home-made sort of guitar or banjo with one string, and the dancers keep on for hours at a stretch. As instruments improved melody was added to the rhythm and the blues has crystallized into the modern fox trot."[63] *Pace* this framing, Thompson's own biography—known full well to *Gleaner* readers!—made mockery of the notion that Africa floated in a distant past, or that black people's music was "simple darkie merrymaking" in which tom-toms led to Kingsway Hall without intention or expertise. Born in Sierra Leone to a prominent black military family, Thompson had studied cornet as a youth in the British West India Regiment Band School in Kingston while his father was posted in Jamaica, and he served as lieutenant bandmaster in the U.S. Army in Paris before joining Will Marion Cook's very international orchestra after the war.[64]

The music gaining notice worldwide was Afro-originated but urban, black-owned yet urbane. The dances developed with it showcased female bodies and provoked male desire, traits island elites had long touted as evidence of the black lower classes' inability to self-govern. How did this local fit into that world, this past into that modern? These questions were being asked from multiple locals at once. Around the Americas, music and dances that developed within Afro-descended communities were in the process of moving across class boundaries, their déclassé cachet often dependent on success in musical markets abroad. By 1920 in the Dominican Republic, the merengue, associated with rural black communities in the Cibao Valley, had joined Spanish *danzón* and the North American fox-trot in the repertoire of upscale *conjuntos* playing elite salon parties.[65] The *plena* took shape among British Caribbean immigrants in a working-class barrio of Ponce, Puerto Rico, and spread across the island, the "indecent dances" appalling local elites before eventually becoming a mainstay of national identity.[66] At the other end of the continent, tango music was experiencing similar upward mobility, moving from its origins in cantinas where European immigrants mixed with Afro-Argentines to become the toast of Paris. The syncopated music and sensual steps that Walrond saw in the bordellos of Colón in 1915—"Argentine Tango, merengue, 'shimmy-shawbbie,' the 'passion glide'"—were part and parcel of these currents.

Caribbean popular culture of the interwar years confounds all attempts to draw bright lines between high and low, foreign and local, autochtonous and commercial. New technologies were speeding the circulation of sounds around the region. The image of an islander returning from labor abroad with "a Victrola wind-up gramophone" for the folks at home had become iconic.[67] Visiting Jamaica in 1930, A. Hyatt Verrill lamented that commercial music and combos had replaced "native" music everywhere but the deep countryside. Local "orchestras" made up of a drum, "a flute, fife, piccolo or similar instrument; a banjo or guitar sometimes a fiddle; a triangle, a rattle-gourd," and "a nutmeg-grater-like affair, rubbed with a stick" were now found only "in the remote villages and among the country folk, for in the larger towns all the noise and music-making instruments of civilization are in use, and even in distant settlements and huts the ubiquitous gramophone is all too common."[68] Verrill's claim that commercial music displaced traditional was belied by Jamaican observers, who, although they disagreed sharply over the value of shay-shay and jazz, coincided in reporting the coexistence and recombination of music and dance from near and far.

But certainly recorded music had become an ever more important component of the circulation of sounds and styles. Not only was Ciudad Bolivar "an inferno of gramophones," reported Orinoco traveler Lady Dorothy Mills in 1931, but gramophones played "all day and all night in all the towns of Venezuela, and even in the isolated hamlets of the bush." "Sometimes the tune is a bit of imported rag-time, sometimes a tango or the restless rhythm of the *joropa*."[69] Newspapers advertising to the British Caribbean populations of Panama, Colón, and Port Limón in the 1920s hawked gramophones, radios, and the latest "hot" jazz. Myrie's Music Shop in Kingston offered dozens of new "RED HOT JAZZ" records each month; in 1927 the "Black Bottom" held sway.[70] Alongside "race" records by Afro-American artists circulated recordings of Caribbean and South American artists (hence the tango and *joropa* disturbing Lady Dorothy's sleep).

Trinidadian, Cuban, Dominican, and Puerto Rican musicians recorded in New York and on the islands alike in these years; "Mama Ines," "The Peanut Vendor," and other Cuban "rumbas" took Kingston by storm just when they did New York.[71] After touring some dozen islands circa 1937, Glanville Smith pronounced Cuba "pre-eminent in supplying the Spanish-speaking West Indies with their popular music; Trinidad plays a like role for most of the others—that is, it shares the responsibility with Tin Pan Alley. In fact I learned more of the calypsos in Jamaica or St. Lucia than in Trinidad itself, and more still in Grenada" (to say nothing of the Joe Louis calypsos he learned in a barbershop in St. Vincent).[72] Radio broadcasts also linked circum-Caribbean sites. As a San José–based radio installer promised the English-speaking public of Limón in 1930, "You may sit in your home and enjoy Concerts, Pugilistic bouts, speeches or any Amusements, broadcasted from the United States, Cuba, Jamaica or Europe."[73]

What did this mean for the practice of popular dance on the islands? Local and imported sounds and moves mixed in the working-class entertainments of 1920s Kingston. One 1922 observer described a "dignity hop" in "a spacious open yard," its structure identical to the practice dances of the previous decade. It "catered for the ordinary working men, labourers and servant girls who for a modest sum of a sixpence or a shilling can go in and enjoy a dance. . . . The fox trots, camel glide, donkey kick and other stunts with peculiar names gave us too no end of fun."[74] In other words, not only was the international aesthetic backdrop shifting, but the culture of the masses was every bit as international as the classes'.

What to do when the metropolitan anchors of local cultural hierarchies seemed to have come unmoored? Should the shay-shay still be shunned for its rhythmic sensuality and African syncopations, or embraced for those very characteristics? Might one just throw up one's hands and dance? In a jocular report on a 1921 Constant Spring Hotel ball, H. G. de Lisser mocked an upper-class bystander who claimed to be scandalized by "Slide, Mongoose"—"a Jamaican shay-shay, a song and air composed by some unknown guitar player of town or village"—who then headed onto the floor to shimmy with the best of them. De Lisser reported the glee the piece inspired among the gathered wealthy and the police inspector's insistence that the song be played one more time before closing. And de Lisser confessed his own hypocrisy, as skewered by the society matron at his side: "You couldn't keep still for a moment, your feet were moving all the time and your whole body was swaying to the tune."[75]

Three days later, the *Gleaner* published an alternative view from a correspondent who found the upward mobility of the aesthetic creations of the Jamaican masses profoundly unacceptable. Previously, he explained, at least the moves proper to "shay-shay dances" were only "indulged in by the lowest of the low." But now, female morals were degenerating and the "complexion" of society was changing. He could tolerate fads with the imprimatur of foreign origin—"The music written by American composers as Fox Trots etc."—but not the "local low class tunes, suggestive both in words and rhythm," for which they seemed to have opened the door. "I read some time ago that Shimmies, Fox Trots etc. were on their last legs. I sincerely hope that this is true."[76]

The *Gleaner's* response the following day was a far cry from de Lisser's 1910 squeamishness about this "sublimated West African phallic dance." Times had changed. Local popular culture was becoming a global requisite of national pride—even when "the people" were black. For as E. E. Thompson knew, African essence was in vogue. Quoting a recent *New Republic* review of a "Negro American Musical," the *Gleaner* editors explained,

> when this American writer speaks of the cadence and melody and wonderful sense of the Negro spirit, he is really giving an explanation of the remarkable but quite natural and legitimate fascination which our native dances, locally known as shay-shays, possess for everyone who can appreciate melody and rhythm. Of their kind they are unequaled. But prejudice and ignorance condemned them to be regarded for years and generations as things beneath the notice of "the better classes."[77]

The international circulation of Afro-identified performance—and of print-culture commentary on the same—had made shay-shays a resource for national pride. "We must," the editors insisted, "have some designation for them that will stamp them as distinctively Jamaican. We owe that to ourselves."

Even as the local gained potential brand allure, the line between local and international culture was anything but clear. The ways that vernacular and traveling professional dancers learned from each other can be seen in the 1936 Kingston visit of a Spanish dancer, Señorita Valencia, who had performed in "scores of cabarets, night clubs and theaters in Europe, Broadway, and all of Latin America. Every country she has visited she tried to weave new ideas into her dancing." The *Gleaner* captured the intentional exchange of expertise between Señorita Valencia and her Jamaican fans, as "one afternoon this week following the announcement that she would be analysing the dancing of our people free of charge, thirty of [our girls] turned up. . . . She tried to teach them her authentic interpretation of the Argentine ballroom tango and thought they did it nicely." Señorita Valencia learned, too. "Valencia has not yet mastered the unadulterated Jamaica Shay Shay and Mento but with her Latin background she assures us that they will be soon to her repertoire."[78]

Nevertheless, others still saw shay-shay and mento as inherently noncosmopolitan: peasant vulgarity rather than exotic seduction. A few days after Valencia declared her admiration for local dances and dancers in 1936, pioneering Afro-Jamaican performers Slim and Sam wrote in to the *Gleaner* to testify. "We the undersigned, claim to know plenty about this Jamaica song affair, because for years we have, been dealing in them, profitlessly." If since the early 1920s some within the Jamaican elite had embraced "native" authenticity as a marker of aesthetic value, Slim and Sam met other reactions. "We find that there is a type of Jamaican who does not seem to like even to hear, much more to sing, whistle, or even hum native songs or tunes. They seem to consider it degrading, or un-couth, indulging in a Jamaica melody. They would not think of dancing a native mento or shay-shay. No, Sir, why? That wouldn't be Londonish or New Yorkish, or foreignish anyhow." Afro-Jamaican music's irresistible drive both pulled dancers in and made organizers fret. "We will admit that very recently a few of our orchestras are trying to bring themselves to play, now and then, a little Jamaica music (special request) but—'Whenever the Jamaica stuff starts coming over, the dancers always get wild; get hot you know.' Why? Because our native tunes carry a lot of kick in them."[79]

Was getting wild good or bad? Geography—Londonishness or New Yorkishness—mattered to listeners' assessment of the moral valence of irresistible sound, just as (as we shall see below) dancers' color mattered to observers' assessment of their vulgarity. But in each case, voices were raised on both sides from all quarters. Caribbean elites did not have a single position about race, music, and modernity but rather an ongoing argument about the same. Their words formed part of the discursive terrain against which Afro-descended performers and partygoers understood their own music and moves, but there is no reason to believe that the self-imaginations of the latter two were obsessively attentive to the former. The next section marshals evidence that black performers and publics saw in Jazz Age music and dance a privileged realm for collective pride—albeit a realm vulnerable, like others, to race-based injustice. Most of all, this realm was *intentionally* international. As they described it (in contrast to the commentators above), the commonalities of "Negro music" resulted not from inborn Africanness but from conscious endeavor, as performers chose models and built networks of mutual support.

TRAVELING PROS AND WANNABE PROS: INTERNATIONAL EXPERIENCE AND RACE-CONSCIOUS FRAMES

The circulation of films and records built local demand for new rhythms and sounds that was then filled by live performers—and vice versa. An examination of touring troupes large and small reveals both pervasive connections to the Afro-American music world and ongoing local innovation. The two were mutually reinforcing. Indeed, it becomes impossible to draw a clear line between local and foreign, whether with regard to the musicians playing or the music played. But if national origins were fuzzy at best, the supranational raced context was clear. Performers perceived and presented themselves as part of an international black performative realm, marked by glamour, urbanity, and alliance across borders. Just like the black publishers and reading public of their era, these performers and their dance-loving public were engaged in an ongoing struggle to navigate racism and claim respect due.

For U.S. performers, being "on the road" did not end at the shore. The biggest names toured Havana as a matter of course; Panama, Kingston, and Port of Spain, although secondary, were also frequent destinations. The New York showbiz weekly *Variety* included Panama alongside U.S. cities on its "Chatter" pages in the 1930s, announcing arrivals and departures from Havana, New Orleans, California, and the British islands and sharing gossip about the showgirls and cabaret stars of Panama City and Colón.[80] Trinidad-born Sam Manning played multiple engagements in Panama in 1929 on a tour that also took his revue to Jamaica, Trinidad, Barbados, and England.[81] Other groups stayed longer. The "Black Bottom Follies," an "all coloured revue" from the United States with a cast of forty that included comedians, singers, dancers, and a jazz orchestra, reached Kingston on the heels of a multiweek engagement in Cuba in May 1928, "scoring a big success," reported the *Pittsburgh Courier*, "en route to Colón, Panama, and New Orleans."[82]

Who were these touring pros? Where did their sojourns take them, and how did their travels matter? As it happens, documentary evidence allows us to build a relatively complete answer in this case. Alabama-born William Benbow, recognized as a "central figure in the ascendancy of Southern vaudeville," was a comedian, performer, and producer whose troupes entertained southern black audiences on the Afro-American vaudeville circuit from the 1900s to 1920s.[83] It was William Benbow in his early minstrel days who carried a young piano player named Jelly Roll Morton from New Orleans out onto the road.[84] Although in most U.S. theater histories, Benbow disappears from view after 1927, he had not stopped performing. On the contrary: already in 1926 he was ensuring that the public that mattered to him knew of his international direction. He wrote to the "Theatrical Editor, the *Pittsburgh Courier*" that his "'Get Happy' Company" was "still going big in Cuba. . . . The tour of next season will include 32 cities and towns on the island of Cuba, thence to Jamaica, B.W.I., Porto Rica, the Panama Zone, the Philippine Islands and Spain."[85]

The troupe may or may not have made it to the latter two spots, but the Caribbean became a second home—indeed for a while, it replaced the first. The Benbow troupe's 1927 tour covered Cuba, Jamaica, and Panama, at least; the following year, they announced through the *Courier* that they had "smash[ed] all attendance records" in one Cuban city and held "contracts for engagements in Jamaica, San Domingo, Hayti, and Porto Rico."[86] This was the "Black Bottom Follies" mentioned above. Jamaican reviews lauded the show's music from "Don Dawley's 9 Jazz Kings," the synchronized moves of the troupe's male dancers, and the female duet against "crashing jazz." (The bit about the mule went over big, too.)[87] The following year, Benbow wrote from Santiago de Cuba announcing similar success with his new "Miami Follies" and touting a "contract for Panama, Colón, Columbia, Honduras, and Spain," concluding: "He may make a long tour of these places."[88]

They did indeed make a long stay, although less than triumphantly. Sidney Young's *Panama Tribune* reminisced a decade later:

Benbow is well known on the isthmus. He came here sometime in 1930–31 with his famous Miami Follies after an unsuccessful tour in Jamaica and Havana, Cuba. He met no better luck here and went to Colombia, where the show became stranded. Several members of the company along with Benbow returned to Panama and other shows were attempted in Panama and Colón and the Canal Zone club-houses but Benbow's luck was as bad as ever and the troupe finally disbanded. He remained here for some time engaging in various activities, returning a few years ago to the United States.[89]

For a while, Benbow ran a dance school in Panama, while his wife performed in local cabarets.[90]

Regrouped Benbow troupes toured the western Caribbean through the early 1930s with varying itinerary, repertoire, and cast. For just as he had picked up Jelly Roll Morton in New Orleans long before, as Benbow traveled the Caribbean, he brought out local talent and carried some of it along. He also left some folks behind. Months after the troupe's departure from Jamaica in 1928, "The Five Dancing Demons/Late of the Benbow Follies" were entertaining Kingston. The Demons' ads promoted their cosmopolitan blackness and virtuoso expertise in equal measure: "Original dancing of the coloured race in America—Spot Dancing. Buck and Wing. Charleston. Black Bottom (slow motion). The fastest things on ten feet."[91] It is unclear whether this was the nucleus of the "Blackstar Dancing Demons" who toured through Limón in 1930. "Some of the more equipped 'Fans' thought that the girls were a bit 'skinny' although their dancing was superb. The music was the best Jazz music heard in Limón for quite a while."[92]

Benbow's travels meant the troupe could offer supposedly authentic performers of the latest exotic fad, whether from "the colored race in America" or the island next door. Arriving in Kingston from "Panama, Colón, Costa Rica, Bocas, Almirante, Cuba, and Mexico" for a month-long stay in 1932, Benbow's (now) Broadway Follies offered a new show, "Rumbaland," with "Olivia Bennet the Cuban Rumba Queen." New songs included "Yo no tengo madre," "Florecita," "Shantytown" (which met cool reception in Kingston until the "snappy dance interpretation" at the end), and "a Cuba dance by Rita Montenegro."[93] The fluidity of vaudeville origin claims being what it was, Olivia and Rita may have hailed from Mobile or Miami as easily as Cuba or Colón, but certainly Benbow did adopt local performers. A farewell show at the end of the following season's Kingston run included "the addition of a large number of attractive Jamaican Chorus girls" and "some of Jamaica's Best Local Talent" (listed by name), amid the classics of Afro-American vaudeville: "Plantation Songs—Buck Dancers—Cake Walkers—American Jubilee Songs."[94]

The Benbow troupe did not just share their stage; they made friends. The *Pittsburgh Courier* reported in 1929 that when Benbow's troupe left Jamaica for Cuba after six weeks' stay, "the company was highly banqueted by Mr. Marcus Garvey and his U.N.I.A. order."[95] Both the fête and Benbow's care to keep *Courier* readers informed underline the showman's active cultivation of black-internationalist networks.

Benbow's international connections endured even after he returned to the United States in the late 1930s. When Benbow was jailed in Cincinnati in 1939 after shooting a man in an argument over a showgirl, both the *Panama*

Tribune and the *Kingston Daily Gleaner* carried the news. Benbow wrote to the *Courier* after his release, thanking them for supportive coverage that had been "read way down in Central and South America. From there I received quite a few letters from friends I had made during my twelve years' stay while there. This goes to show that the *Pittsburgh Courier* is not only bought and read all over the U.S.A., but is also in demand in foreign countries"—which, of course, we already knew. The people Benbow thanked by name for support included individuals in Panama, Havana, Charleston, Pensacola, and Kentucky, as well as the "grandmaster of Florida masons," suggesting yet another set of transnational black networks that Benbow maintained.[96]

A 1929 controversy offers a window onto the range of Jamaican responses to Benbow's revue, in particular the ways in which perceptions of the troupe's blackness complicated their reception. Benbow's 1929 show included a full sampler of the vaudeville acts and Afro-Americas-wide music of the era, including "Elmo Moore and his jazz band"; "the tango dancers Pachecio and Diaz"; "American Crack Dancers"; "soft shoe dancing"; tap dancing; Apachie Dancing; "Gun Powder, that Mean Mule"; and the "Black Bottom by the Miami Follie Girls."[97] The day after the revue opened, Kingston municipal councilor H. A. L. Simpson, as reported by the *Gleaner*, denounced the "vulgar display" by "some foreigners" at Ward Theater. The theater's license should be revoked "because whilst it was said that the world was now a jazz (and there was a good deal of truth in it), there was no reason why the civilization of Jamaica should be reduced to a primitive African village, and he for one deprecated women displaying their nakedness in public merely for a living." Eight years after the *Gleaner*'s editorial page had lauded the "legitimate fascination [of] our native dances" for their "cadence and melody and wonderful sense of the Negro spirit," the alternative frame that linked black moves to African barbarity and sexual degradation was still alive and well.

Other councilors fell over themselves to agree with Simpson—while also bending over backward to deny that they had seen, or, worse, enjoyed the show. Councilor Harrison reported that "the women kicked their legs up and were half naked. . . . Such people should not be permitted to have their jazz in the nude way they were going on in." He displayed an inconvenient familiarity with international modalities of sexual display: "Some years ago there were such plays in Havana and Panama but . . . the men had remained at the doors, and whoever wanted to go in could peep to see these nude people (laughter) but here it was an open show." Harrison had unwittingly taken his wife to Benbow's follies, "and his wife was so ashamed that she had left early in the show, but as he was a man he said he would remain there as he liked to see the girls' legs (laughter) but as a matter of decency a stop should be put to this thing."[98] It was not easy to be a politician when the conventions of masculine prestige demanded sexual appetite and the conventions of class status demanded its repudiation.

But as other commentators chose to make explicit, it was the conventions of race fundamentally at stake here. Councilor Duval insisted Benbow's Follies were no worse than other troupes who performed undisturbed. Councilor Bryant made the point even more plainly: "There is absolutely no difference between this and Clowns & Clatter; only those were white skins and these others are brown skins."[99] A letter to the editor two days later placed these racial politics of reception in the context of the electoral politics of race. Councilor Simpson, aspiring to higher office, had been "apparently espousing the coloured people's cause," but now, "under the guise of morality," he had "shown his true self within by so flagrantly criticizing a coloured troupe, so miserably that a Councillor, a white Englishman, had to" denounce the racist double standard.[100]

In sum, the Follies' fusion of black and sexy brought opprobrium from some, half-disavowed desire from others, worldly approval from others—and the color or origin of the viewer did not dictate which it would be. Rejection of modern performance on raced moral grounds was hardly universal: the frequent interjection of "(laughter)" into the *Gleaner*'s account of the council meeting above is written evidence that the gathered public were having none of the councilors' moralistic display (and that the reporter chose to align his viewpoint with the public's deflating mirth and the *Gleaner* editor chose to sign off on the same). Yet to draw audiences by pushing the bounds of what people of your color were supposed to do in public was a risky strategy. Benbow's Follies were banned in Colón the following year for violating "an executive order" written specifically to regulate the Follies' "morals"—this in a city renowned for brothels, nightclubs, drunkenness, and dives. This ban seems to have been the beginning of the stretch of Benbow's "Bad Luck" and suspended tours that the *Panama Tribune* remarked on above.

Around the Caribbean, traveling performers trumpeted the race roots of their repertoires but had to confront the race-ing of their reception. If at times this worked through differential perceptions of "jazz in the nude way" when the skin uncovered was brown, at other times it was a matter of explicit color bars. "JIM CROW CRASHES PANAMA SOCIETY," warned a *Pittsburgh Courier* headline in 1937, reporting that "a group of Panamans of West Indian origin" had been ordered off a dance floor after a (Hispanic) would-be carnival queen complained to her date, a police lieutenant, that there were "so many 'blacks' attending."[101] Note that the aggrieved West Indian Panamans went straight to the local stringer for the Associated Negro Press. Recourse to the international black print-based public sphere had become the automatic response to local injustice. Meanwhile, in the era of expanding state racism and border control, bans might start at the port rather than the *puerta*. In 1931 two "colored American cabaret dancers" resident in Colón left for "an engagement" in Venezuela, only to be refused entry as racial undesirables. Unable to disembark, they went on to Europe with the ship, returning to Colón "richer in experience, but nothing else."[102]

Yet pros still traveled, and not only pros of U.S. origin. Circulation between adjacent islands or rimlands by purveyors of modern music was more common yet. There was a reason that "it was said that the world was now a jazz," as per Councilor Simpson's disgruntled report: this world *was* a jazz. For instance, in 1934 "the Aristocrats of Jazz, Panama's famous dance orchestra, which is managed by West Indians, including quite a few well-known Jamaica boys," spent a six-week "pleasure tour" in Kingston, announcing themselves "glad to receive engagements to play at any place, provided that suitable arrangements are made with their agents in Jamaica."[103] Musicians included trombonist Wilfred Malcolm, a stalwart of British West Indian civic activism in Panama who later became better known as the father of Panama-born, Jamaica-claimed ska pioneer Carlos Malcolm.[104] Before departing for the Isle of Springs, the Aristocrats won the title of "Kings of Jazz" in Colón, winning 187,425 votes in a contest organized by the local Club International, an impressive display of vote buying from the isthmus's jazz-enthusiast public.[105]

The range of repertory that public demanded is captured by an ad for a far more modest "family Orchestra" working out of a second-floor flat in a working-class Panama neighborhood in 1926. The ad promised "all the latest music for Fox Trots, Waltzes, Pasillos, Danzons, and the oldest dances, such as Quadrills, Lancers, Mazurka, Schotties, Polka, to suit the old and young. . . . Prices moderate. SIX MUSICIANS."[106] In other words, to encompass the tastes of West Indian Panama, it was necessary to master both the set-dance standbys of the practice dances and dignity hops of Kingston two decades before and the "latest music" from Anglophone and Hispanophone metropoles. Up the coast in Port Limón, the local boys of the Central American Black Stars Orchestra covered the same cosmopolitan range: "This Orchestra accepts jobs for Dances and Excursions. When you want to dance and hear the very latest in Blues, Foxtrots, Waltzes, Tangos, Danzons, Rumbos etc. just write to The Central American Black Stars - P.O. Box 123."[107]

Later that year of 1930, two entrepreneurs recently arrived in Limón recruited local singers, dancers, and comedians for a homegrown "combination company" along the lines of the touring revues. A photo of the self-described "coloured troupe" shows eleven young women in matching short-skirted outfits and two men in high hats and tails.[108] The local black press crowed with pride. "Limón and Costa Rica in general may well compliment herself in having such a local company," boasted the *Searchlight*. "Organized trained and comprised entirely of Costa Rican born players, it only goes to show what our people are capable of doing under proper training. It is only fair to say that the Benbow troupe would sink into insignificance before this company in time." International-level performance might open national horizons. "They intend of breaking out for San Jose at an early date and if they are properly advertised there is no reason they should not have unbounded successes in all the cities of the interior."[109]

Conflicts over loaned instruments and box-office shares intervened, but six months later the troupe had regrouped and, like Benbow before them, was pushing the envelope of acceptable excitation. "The Rumbo Dances were done to over-perfection in muscular gyrations, that we heard one gentleman express that his emotions were worked up to such a pitch that he could not trust himself along the audience," reported one review, "and left enveloped with Cupid's mantel; it is well to calm down such tendencies."[110] But in the discursive space of Limón's black press, no one claimed that these gyrations were atavistically derived from a "primitive African village." Expertise came from professionalism and practice. When one troupe member left in a tiff, the stage manager used the *Searchlight*'s pages to warn "those of our Artists whom I have trained and who wish to join him not to use any of the pieces which I have taught them such as the dances, drills etc. without first making settlement with me, according to the agreement signed between us so as to avoid litigations."[111]

Such semiprofessional players took gigs when and where they could get them, which often required boarding a boat. One excursion chartered from Cuba to Kingston in 1926 carried "Jamaicans who came to renew acquaintances with their native land and people, and Cubans who came to make acquaintance" with Jamaica. "The band that came with the party played typical Cuban music to the delight of many in the city."[112] Similarly, in 1930 a group of "excursionists" from Colón chartered a motor launch for a week-long visit to kith and kin in Limón: "They also brought up the much appreciated Jazz band of that vicinity which has been giving exhibitions of Jazz music in our midst."[113] Glanville Smith happened upon a local band traveling from Point-à-Pitre to Grand Bourg (Guadeloupe) by schooner circa 1937 with bass horn, saxophones, clarinets, guitars, and drums. Reaching the port's one restaurant, the "jazz band" tucked into fried fish, seasickness forgotten. "Then full and joyous, they snatched up their instruments and fell to tootling. It brought all Grand Bourg pushing in at the doors."[114]

Less visible in the historical record are the countless improvised performances in kitchens or yards across the region, when individuals with good rhythm and long memories got together and jammed. In 1926 Sidney Young published a jocular letter from old friend Charles Moulton, just arrived at a United Fruit Company camp in the "wilds" of Colombia, recounting an evening at the home of Mr. and Mrs. Brown there: "Some bachelor boys, came over with their guitar and harmonica 'Made in Germany' stuff and started to play some familiar Negro airs, including 'my Next-door neighbor,' 'Mangoose,' etc. etc. The thing was so lively that somebody said we ought to have a grater, because two pieces could not suffice." So Moulton jumped in as "Jazz Graterist," alongside new pal "Reginald Smith [on] Base (an empty aguardiente bottle)."[115]

Which music was local and which foreign in this world? The Central American Black Stars Combination Co. was composed of Limón-born children of mainly Jamaican parents, managed and bankrolled by English-speaking black men arrived from Nicaragua. When Panama's Jazz Aristocrats traveled to Jamaica, many were visiting the island of their birth, even as they were "abroad" from the isthmian haunts they usually played. Where should such troupes be considered local *to*? Yet if the labels "local" and "foreign" are difficult to apply to these musicians, the racial collective to which their performance belonged could not have been clearer. Of course Caribbean publics knew that not only black people played jazz: Paul Whiteman's records seem to have outsold all others in Limón, and films gave fans a direct view of their favorite stars' color.[116] But Afro-Caribbean commentators understood the cross-color popularity of jazz through the lens of race-conscious pride.

At a moment in which the Limón press was full of reports of highland Costa Ricans' demands that black immigrants and their descendents be fired en masse or barred from the Central Highlands, it was with explicitly racialized pride that the *Searchlight* reported, "Again San Jose has been invaded by a coloured Troupe." Whether the musicians of this "Black Jazz Orchestra" hailed from New York, Kingston, Colón, or all of the above was not noted, but that they were "coloured" was announced in the title and again in the text. "They were applauded tremendously by the immense crowd that went out to see them. Their songs, dancings and drills were unsurpassable."[117]

Appreciating white respect did not mean self-doubt in the face of white rejection. A Limón editorialist wrote of a Central American Black Stars show in 1931: "The coloured element certainly turned out in hundreds to appreciate the efforts of their own," but "there was a marked absence of the white and would be white community, is this from prejudice or is it an idea of discountenancing any attempt at culture in our own?"[118]

Success was understood as representing the race; audience reaction was read in race-conscious terms. Furthermore, just as the line between readers and authors in the print-centered public sphere was blurred by the ubiquity of letter publication, in the supranational black performative realm, too, listeners became dancers and amateurs sought to be authors. And those putting themselves forward did so presuming an international black community as frame of reference and support. When Cyril Corniffe of Siquirres (Limón), Costa Rica, had a song he thought deserved a hearing, he sent it to a "music agent" who advertised in the Afro-American press. And when he began to suspect he was being conned, he wrote to the *Pittsburgh Courier*'s outspoken music columnist, Porter Roberts, who had under way a very public crusade against such "Song Sharks."[119] When George Campbell of Indiana Branch (Limón), Costa Rica, wanted to learn new dance steps, he turned to the same forum, writing: "Dear Mr. Roberts: I shall be glad to get some information from you. Please inform me where I can buy some lessons on the latest dances, such as: 'The Big Apple,' 'The Susie Q,' 'Pecking,' and 'Truckin.' . . . I would be very glad if you would be so kind as to send me the books C.O.D."[120] Roberts published Campbell's letter with a preface calling the attention of "every Negro dancer in this country" to this reminder that "out of all the dances colored creators have given the world, none of said creators have compiled the dances in book form and sold them!" Hence Roberts had no recourse but to reply: "Dear Mr. Campbell, as much as I regret it, I must refer you to ARTHUR MURRAY's dancing school, New York City, N.Y. (white) for your information. Attention, colored dance creators."[121]

Corniffe and Campbell had not chosen just any interlocutor. From his *Courier* perch, Roberts castigated "alleged Negro comedians" for routines that "ridiculed . . . colored people"; he skewered white publications for "contests" that promoted "spent-a-lifetime-copying-colored-musicians white bands" and excluded the huge stars of "the colored band world."[122] As Roberts summed up in 1938: "I have complained about propaganda against Negroes that comes our way via Hollywood and Radio. I have criticized some of our greatest artists, when I thought some particular public action on their part would reflect unfavorably upon the whole Negro race. . . . I have followed the course white writers always follow as to colored writers: They ignore negro writers, so I have scoffed at their various selections (swing bands, best musicians, best dancers, etc.) as a matter of policy."[123] In sum, Porter Roberts understood the entertainment world as a space for intentional and collective black endeavor and a key front in the fight against racism. Letter writers Corniffe and Campbell and William Benbow and the Central American Black Stars and their fans across the western Caribbean agreed. As they reached forward to new horizons and outwards for support, they turned the "colored band world" into an international realm.

THE CHALLENGE OF UPLIFT IN A "WORLD A JAZZ": THE RIMLAND BLACK PRESS CONFRONTS OUR YOUTH'S ADDICTION

Sometimes, then, black performers and the black press worked in tandem to build transnational ties. Yet some respectable black internationalists insisted that the world of letters and the world of moves were far apart—and that the struggle for political rights and economic advance for Our Race was imperiled by black youths' love of jazz. For all the *Searchlight*'s pride in the Black Stars' polished routines, the intracommunal politics of black performance in the western Caribbean were not simple.

Part of the problem was sex. A 1922 article from the *Clarion* of British Honduras denounced the "modern jazz dance" and the new standards of bodily contact it fostered. "It has come to be a common thing for a young man to meet a young lady, in good society," the *Clarion* complained, "invite her to dance, step immediately on the ballroom floor, clasp her in a tight embrace, place his cheek against her and begin a series of gyrations . . . which a few years ago would have brought the blush of shame to a hardened sinner and would have caused the arrest of both if seen by a policeman." A menace to young women's virtue was a menace to the future of society itself: "Cool, hard-headed men who are not reformers have said that the modern jazz dance is doing more harm to our youth and to our country than the saloons ever did. It leads our girls by easy and logical steps to joy rides, drinking, smoking profanity and the indulgence in stories which were supposed to be confined to men's smoking rooms."[124]

Concerns about young people's sexual mores sounded across the Jazz Age Americas but had particular resonance in the circum-Caribbean, where in these same years receiving-society politicians fanned the flames of antiblack xenophobia by emphasizing the threat that black migrants' children posed to national loyalties, bloodlines, and jobs. They were unassimilable, degenerate, and rude, ideologues warned, and might one day be able to vote.[125] In response, the black press of Costa Rica and Panama worked overtime to improve the young. Frivolity and vulgarity in *our* youth were no mere generational failings but threats to the race as a whole, as well as fodder for local enemies. "Close Ranks!" cried one editorial. "The seriousness of the day demands it." Yet Panama's young West Indians—in this editorialist's summation, "an hilarious array of frantic youths addicted to vainglorious jazz and promiscuous joyriding"—seemed intent on ignoring the danger.[126]

As with matters of race and empire, so too in regard to popular culture, Sidney Young gazed out on the world, identified regional trends, and sought to galvanize local action. "Within recent months agitation has been worldwide against the modern dance," he reported in 1927. "The unrestricted freedom of bodily movement has been proclaimed a social menace."[127] As always, Young's primary concern was the welfare and future of West Indians on the isthmus. Things did not look good. In local dance halls, "young gallants and sheiks" dressed in "the latest balloon trousers and crazy coat" paraded themselves alongside "outrageously dressed girls."[128] Attire, stance, contact, steps, noise: it was all wrong.

> The music starts, and, sinuous arms surround in a violent embrace the waists of the eager girls, which by the dictates of the modern dance has descended to the regions of the hips. . . . The dancers pull and tug in a confusion of motion. No harmony, no rhythm, no grace. Sweating couples bump and jostle each other, hoarse laughter and indecorous yells add an infernal obligato to the blaring cornet, the moaning saxophone, the jangling piano, the thrumming of the banjo and the schreeching of the musical saw. . . . The bacchanalia is repeated until everybody is tired.[129]

Surely such joyous release was the opposite of civilized advance. As J. A. Rogers had written in the *Survey Graphic* one year before, "No one can sensibly condone [jazz's] excesses or minimize its social danger if uncontrolled; all culture is built upon inhibitions and control."[130]

Distant authors and moralizing editors were not the only ones who linked jazz and sex. The association between modern dance and the erotic was so strong that the verb "to jazz" seems to have become a euphemism for sex. In a 1933 letter preserved in a judicial case from Bocas del Toro, fifteen-year-old Rose Christie (who had been born in Port Limón, Costa Rica, to

Jamaican parents) wrote to thirty-two-year-old Colón-born Carlos Thomas that his jealousy was unfounded. "I really have only one sweetheart and that is you[,] no man is my sweetheart unless he jazz me if he sleeps with me then I can call him my sweetheart[.] But as I sit down this morning God bears witness is only Carlos sleep with me from I was born till now I am fifteen years of age."[131] Was this where the sweaty jostling of modern music led, breaking down inhibitions and control? Rose evinced few inhibitions, yet she embraced Victorian sentiment and Christian piety wholeheartedly, and she seemed to value control just as much as Rogers. "And now dear," she concluded, "I cut out going to the Zone and make up my mind to stick to you alone and no one. I am praying to God to strengthen the cord that binds us in love and let us be not of one body but also of one mind and heart, and I ask him also to guard me against any evil temptation that may beset me and whatsoever would harm me to turn it into everlasting joy."[132]

What kinds of entertainment did Rose forgo when she "cut out going to the Zone"? According to Sidney Young, if "the modern dance" brought vulgar excess to "better affairs" like the one described above, as one moved down the social spectrum, things only got worse. Most dangerous of all were "those abominations known as 'Twenty-five cents brams,'" at which "obscenity, indecency and sensuality are the dominant notes."[133] The brams seem to have been similar to the practice dances and dignity hops of Kingston and rent parties of Harlem—semiformal working-class entertainments with a low admission price. A young man might pay the entry fee for a young woman, and just what degree of access this entitled was apparently up for negotiation. "Take a walk to the various dance halls and there our girls of tender age are found bending their tiny bodies from side to side," wrote Mrs. Bertie Callender in 1926. "Ask those same girls about work. They think work is a disgrace but not to go down into the depths of sin for a quarter or a half dollar to enjoy a frivolous dance that will bring them to shame and disgrace."[134]

The letters that filled the pages Young edited are as striking for the dance fever they record as for the opprobrium they heap upon it. One author denounced "Our Degenerate Youth": "The young men are ambitious to be known as 'Jazz Kings, Sheiks, or by any other sobriquet,' and would rather hear a eulogy on their ability to dance the 'Charleston' or some other snake dance than to be known as persons possessing the knowledge necessary to earn a livelihood" in a way that would be a credit "to West Indians generally and . . . to the community in which they reside."[135] Another described quotidian scenes. "Day after day as one passes along the streets, one frequently comes across some adult, teaching a child to dance the Charleston or tamborito or to sing some late jazz song," wrote B. J. Waterman in 1926.[136] Rather than wasting time with jazz steps and tunes, Waterman argued, adults should "try to foster in the minds of the children something that will benefit them in later years and be of value both to themselves and the community in which they may reside."[137] Another letter denounced the custom of hiring bands to accompany funeral processions to the cemetery, which would then break into syncopated stylings for the "returning procession": "The very band that played 'Nearer my God to Thee' half an hour before, is now playing a dance piece, headed by a group of hooligans followed by an actually dancing crowd."[138] Local tradition in Panama, in other words, echoed precisely the famed New Orleans jazz funeral, right down to the specific iconic hymn and the improvised second line. But the isthmian author saw this not as colorful folklore (as a *Gleaner* editor might have already by the 1920s) but as egregious frivolity in the midst of crisis: "Things of the kind is unbecoming to a people who are striving for existence."[139]

Dancing on the streets was no way to climb "the stair of upliftment."[140] That was the role of literature instead. Indeed, Sidney Young's explicit goal in creating a "West Indian Section" for the (white North American–owned) *Panama American* was to demonstrate his community's capacity through "literary endeavor": poetry, philosophy, and civic debate. The "literary renaissance" that flowered in response, he explained, put on display the "degree of culture and intelligence of the West Indians on the Isthmus."[141] When the *Panama American* closed the section and pushed Young out the door after only two years, Young republished dozens of the contributions in a book that he dedicated "to the unity, welfare, and progress of the West Indian community in the Republic of Panama, and to the advancement of colored people throughout the world."[142] The pages include photographs of contributors, carefully posed portraits of men in suits and women with hats, which emphasized both the modern propriety and the dark skin of the authors. Racist attacks in the Panamanian press accused black immigrants of a lack of spiritual ideals and civilization; Young countered with spirit, ideals, and civilization. Poetry and prosody were weapons against racism from without, as were communal solidarity, education, and frugality. Slick dance steps and jazz funerals were not.

Some commentators had more sympathy for the popular culture centered on music and moves. G. E. W. looked back in January over the "single stretch of celebrations" that had occupied Limón since October's annual carnival, confessing to what "we" had done rather than accusing some external "them." There had been "parading and parandas"; "circuses and carousels"; "picnic trains and Garden dances" and (Benbow's) Miami Follies. "Every dancing hall and club room" had been booked solid, and "some of us sandwiched a 'petit carnaval' right in between the big one." But now January was here, and it was time to face the harsh economic facts—UFCo layoffs and unemployment—that all had been trying to forget. "It's now time that we leave off jazzing a bit . . . and at least commence to think seriously of the march of life."[143]

Even Sidney Young argued for some middle ground. For all the "obscenity, indecency, and sensuality" of the brams, "only under such disgusting conditions is there any general social contact between our young people." What was needed was to "eliminate the most objectionable features" of "the modern dance" yet still draw young people together through the universal human passion for dance. "This is being done by all communities in nearly every civilized country and we may well follow suit before the threatening danger of social degeneracy engulf our impressionable and heedless youths."[144]

Some of those youths shared his view. In the late 1920s and early 1930s in Panama and Limón, race-conscious young men and women sought community progress through civic association. Club life was the opposite of street life, they explained; youths should join "Literary Associations" rather than spend their evenings on street corners, "wiping the paints from the lampposts."[145] Typical was 1931's "University Club," whose founding goals were to promote "educational pursuits" through "lectures and debates," "secure text books . . . for the use of its members," and push them "to aspire towards . . . an honorable and distinguished career; for service to their respective community." Most immediately, founders explained, the club would offer an alternative to Limón's only current social events, those weekly dances so "indecent in their conduct that it is more than reproachable at times even to watch them."[146]

Two months later, members of the new club, now renamed "the Alpha," reported that they had hosted a successful dance. "The chief aim . . . was to cater to that class of our young ladies who do not appreciate 'Brams' and in this we are glad to say they succeeded in all respects."[147] But what exactly was going on at these "weekly dances" that apparently drew so many young people in Port Limón? And could the Alpha be so different from the brams—and still offer dances worth dancing?

THE "WEEKLY REGGE," PORT LIMÓN, COSTA RICA, 1930–1932

In June 1930 the Salvation Army mission in Limón organized an "excursion train" to the nearby town of Guápiles. The chartered train would be "leaving

Limón at 6.45 am round trip fare ¢3.00; children of other denominations 1/2 rate. Refreshments for Sale along the way. The Black Stars (Merry Makers) Band will Pilot us merrily to the ground. A day's outing will disperse the gloominess of the hard times."[148] This picture of cheery churchgoers taking solace in good, clean fun would soon be challenged by a different reading of that day's events. The ensuing controversy captured in print the common usage of the term "regge dance" in Port Limón and illustrated the controversies over youth morals and racial uplift that swirled around such dances.

"These Excursion Picnics Affect the Community," denounced an editorial in the *Searchlight* a week after the fact. Rather than seeing the Salvationists' excursion as part of the needed uplift through clubs and churches, the editors saw it as yet another vulgar dance, one that the community could ill afford. "Today we see men going to & fro seeking work and unable to find it & yet we see the preachers of religion encouraging their people to be frivolous and careless," raising funds through "picnics, excursions, Reggee Dances and the like; with a view that the young girls and boys must beg or steal from their parents and friends so as to be able to go to these degrading amusements."[149] The rhythms of modern music and the mores of modern youth were equally appalling, and each had been on shameless display that day. "How do our leaders and spiritual educators feel when they look on and see the vulgar scenes," the *Searchlight* asked, "in these blackbottoming, chimeying and mentoing dances as well as hearing the obscene language caused by the carrying of a pint of rum in each youngster's pocket at these festivities, all encouraged by them for the purpose of making a profit of a couple hundreds of colones for church purposes; again, let us ask, how do they feel when they gaze at these degrading scenes?"[150]

The actual social practices visible through this diatribe are utterly familiar, echoing Kingston's picnics held as civic fund-raisers or practice dances held weekly for profit. Limón's "regge dances" were privately organized events where participants paid to dance to live music from across the Jazz Age Americas: mento, Black Bottom, shimmy, tango, fox-trot. It is worth noting that mento is mentioned twice in this article; of all of genres named, mento is the only one that was not being recorded and marketed internationally, yet clearly it was an integral part of the repertory of musicians and dancing public in Limón.[151] And yet, if the social practice and sounds here are quite familiar, the term "regge dance" seems to appear out of nowhere.[152]

What echoes did these syllables elicit in the context of circum-Caribbean music and dance? If there was, as some linguists assert, an eastern Caribbean "rege-rege" of Yoruba origin, referring to roughness, it would have resonated with an Anglo-American term—raggy—which had come to mean the same thing with particular reference to modern music. The "rag" in "rag-time" referenced its ragged rhythm, and "raggy" as a label for syncopated music overlapped with the prior and ongoing meaning of raggy and ragged as uneven, informal, downscale.[153] The term thus denoted genre, style, and an edge of dissolution all together, as in a 1911 report of Chicago police action to stamp out the "turkey trot" and other suggestive new dances: "Where the 'raggy' music held sway after midnight plain clothes detectives are on guard to see that the dances are not on the program."[154] Oral historical sources suggest that both "raggy" and the variant "raddy" were particularly common in New Orleans creole slang. Lizzie Miles, born in New Orleans in 1895, explained: "Jazz is just one of the names that was given to ole American ragtime music mostly played by ear, instead of reading music. . . . We called it 'raddy music', and nowhere have I heard raddy music like they played in New Orleans in the twenties and thirties, believe me!"[155]

In the same years that a young Lizzie Miles was singing "that ragtime 'raddy' music" with King Oliver in New Orleans and Louis Armstrong in Chicago, the term "raggy" became a common musical descriptor in the Jamaican press. An ad for player piano rolls in Kingston in 1913 offered "the finest pieces by Liszt, Chopin, etc., or the finest raggy dance music."[156] An arch note the same year reported "our local musicians of the ninth-night type" had composed a "ballad" in honor of an inept local dogcatcher "to the setting of a very raggy air."[157] The choruses at a Young Ladies Social Club benefit in Kingston in 1922 were "particularly bright and raggy"; "a pretty catchy, raggy song" at a YMCA benefit earned praise the following year; and a concert in Falmouth Baptist schoolroom in 1928 included two "Raggy Duets" and several "Rag Choruses" before culminating with a "Song and Charleston Dance."[158] Meanwhile, in the U.S. entertainment world, "raggy" and cognates continued to signal syncopation, informality, and bravado. In 1934 Paul Whiteman was quoted in the *Courier* as dismissing "Negro bands" for their "loud, raggy, brassy" style—"he turns it off with a laugh, 'nothing to fear from them', he says."[159]

For English-speaking black folks in 1930s Limón, then, "raggy" would have meant informal, rough, and linked to syncopated modern music. It seems utterly plausible that this Jazz Age "raggy" was adopted in Limón to denote young dancers' semioppositional gatherings, and that this Limón usage of "regge" became part of the linguistic repertoire of returnees and their neighbors in West Kingston, whose children (like their aunts and uncles a generation earlier) grew up to seize public space for brash weekly dances where the latest imported and local rhythms fused—and they called what they did "reggay." This proposed genealogy helps make sense of the disparate associations attested by protagonists of that latter era, including Toots Hibbert's "it was just a word you hear on the streets. . . . Sort of mean untidy or scruffy"; Hux Brown's "joke kinda word that means the ragged rhythm and the body feelin'"; and Bob Marley's claim that the term had Spanish roots.

As the above Jamaican citations underline, by the 1920s "raggy" airs, "the latest American music," "Jazz orchestras," and even Charleston dance had become standard draws for church fund-raisers in Jamaica. How far could this go? Could really raddy music and dance be part of communal uplift in a threatening world? Precisely this debate would rage in Limón. According to the *Searchlight*'s editors, the fact that the particular "reggee dance" inciting comment in 1930 had been organized by a church group did not make it acceptable: it made it appalling. Church leaders should stand up against modern youth culture. This kind of event must be replaced with educational excursions so that "our young people . . . will not be looked on as an inferior degenerate race whose only aim is to follow the fox, the tango, the chimmey, the blackbottom, the mento, interspersed by dialogues of obscene language which can only be met with among a race whose highest aspirations are such frivolities."[160] Like Sidney Young's, above, the *Searchlight* editors' plans for moral uplift had room for dance: ballroom genres and traditional set dances, that is, "garden parties at which only your Waltzes, Quadrilles, Steps, Chotisches, Foxes etc. will be encouraged." Acceptable styles offered vertical rectitude, emotional reserve, and space between partners—not syncopated blue notes, full-body enthusiasm, or passionate contact. Anything linked to Africa or sex was out. We must not be "looked upon as a people only aiming toward Tantgoism, Voodoism, obscenism."[161]

Not all community members agreed. Mr. Charles Ambrose wrote to rebuke the editors: "It is evident you realize that the present economic situation is a trite one, and that serious thought should be given to the future welfare of our people; I glean that much from your editorial, but I fail to see how the low morals of young people affects the economic situation." Most parents and children were already embracing church and community. "The majority of coloured people in Limón are clean-minded and are thinking seriously for the future of their children and striving hard to raise their standard of living." Ambrose defended the morality (and *au courant* bonafides) of Limón's dancers, too. "Even at the degrading dances you referred to there isn't such a lot of immorality as you will have your readers believe. I have looked on at quite a few of those dances and have never seen a youth with a pint of rum in his pocket: and furthermore, they don't dance the shimmy nor the mento anymore. The new dance is the OUT O TIME, in this the dancers hold hands and go through some gyrations that are not at all vulgar, but rather amusing."[162] In response, the editors reiterated that organizers must work to prevent "immoral scenes" on excursions: "refus[e] to sell Tickets to known leud characters, insist on a *dry* train," and "instruct your musicians not to play any pieces which may be a temptation to those spectacular copulative gyrations to which Mr. Ambrose refers."[163] Apparently, the difference between "amusing" and spectacularly copulative gyrations was in the eye of the beholder.

Debates over the propriety of church excursion trains continued for months in the *Searchlight*.[164] Then, in early 1931, the role of "regge dances" in youth culture again came to the fore. "The Night Hawk," a regular contributor, wrote an extended analysis of threats to youth morals in Limón. The "most destructive" "enticements" luring girls to ruin were "the Jazz Band, the glare of the night life, our parents' propensities in not showing very edifying examples, the apparent indifference of our spiritual leaders," and "our apparently decent young men's" cynical seductions.[165] While others had touted racial uplift through clubs, the Night Hawk claimed that existing clubs merely made matters worse through their sponsorship of "'The weekly rege' . . . where the worst sort can hide and perpetrate their rascally deeds. What is the use of all these clubs, when one has to stoop to the lowest depth to collect funds, to pay more rentals, and more taxes, so that a few can stand and preach improvement, when there is no improvement to show the public? . . . Whose ideas for upliftment rest upon 'the end justifies the means'[?]"[166] The regge dances had become such an affront to public order, Night Hawk claimed, that the Costa Rican authorities had them in their sights, "about to make a war on these 'Régés' and the number of street urchins, who are pests in the atmosphere of good society."[167]

Others agreed with the Night Hawk's censure of regge dances but held that clubs could still be part of the solution. "BAS BLEU" urged support for a new young men's literary club, an alternative to the streets and the dance: "The money that [youths] take to enrich the proprietors of the weekly 'rejes' and dances they would keep them, buy books, assemble, read and exchange thoughts; there is much to learn in that manner. . . . Since we see and know that knowledge is power, and without it we the negroes are nobody, we should always endeavor to get as much as we can."[168] This call for racial uplift through literature and against dance resonated with at least some young aspirers. Dolores Joseph wrote the next month to report that a dozen young men had founded a "University Club" (described above): "We have all promised to do our very best to boost this club, as we feel ashamed that our only solace has been in associating with the 'REGE' class."[169]

Two months later, this club, renamed "Alpha and Omega," was touting the "wonderful change" that had come over Limón and planning a social event to crown it off and combat "the spirit of depravity" that still lurked in "this little town of ours." Perhaps defensively, aware of criticism of previous uplifters who raised funds through public dance, Joseph put deportment and morality front and center. The Alpha's dance would serve as shining counterexample to the vulgarity of the regge. Alpha's aims were "first to collect funds to provide us with chairs, books, indoor games, etc., and secondly to cultivate that spirit of social equality, where our young men will meet the best of our young women, and will be compelled to acquit themselves gentlemanly. We know they possess that germ of refinement, that they are unable to manifest at a picnic dance or a Rege."[170]

Yet for all of Joseph's efforts, the distinction between the Alpha's uplifting events and the degrading "weekly regge" refused to stand firm. "Miles Militante" criticized the new clubs' reliance on paid dances for funds; responding, Joseph let slip the terminological distinction on which he had insisted and denounced "my friend 'Militante'" for "casting remarks at our Rege Dances. He ought to know that that is the greatest means of revenue for those who make them. 'Rege dances are a necessity.'" Indeed, even "our Improvement Associations make them to help pay lights and rents."[171] This in turn prompted an officer of the local UNIA chapter to denounce Joseph for having said "that the 'Rege dances are the greatest means of revenue to such Association[,] for we are aiming at a Nationhood that he cannot go to.'"[172]

Finding his black-internationalist bona fides thus maligned, Joseph fired back. It was the older generation—and the local UNIA in particular—that had failed to uphold the dual mantle of upliftment and Pan-Africanism. "I have seen my brother youths idling away their time under street lamps at nights, just because there is no where interesting, other than the movies, to go," he insisted. "I have seen, after quiet U.N.I.A. meetings, the officers and members standing in the streets, quarreling, and but for the early arrival of the cop, would have come to fists; and I have heard it said repeated by my youthful companions, sons of these officers and members. THESE GARVEY PEOPLE ARE ALL THE WHILE FIGHTING."[173]

It was this abdication of communal leadership by the local UNIA, their betrayal of Garvey's true vision, that opened youth to ruin, wrote Joseph. "Then, I have seen how gladly these youthful companions welcome the strains of Jazz Bands, telling of the glad tidings of a REGE DANCE TONIGHT; and how quickly tickets are being sold to prostitutes from the RITZ, to mingle with the sons of these decent mothers and fathers, under the canopy of the great hall of Negro Liberty. . . . Our young men, who should have been the backbone of such a noble organization," are thus lost; and the UNIA, "unadulterated with all the sound philosophy of that Great Negro the Hon. Marcus Garvey, is today the tool of shylock looking officers and members, whose only aim is Dead Fund and Sick Relief."[174] No wonder the youth these days just wanted to dance.

To invoke Garvey in debate over public dances and uplift was particularly apropos. After his return to Jamaica in 1927, Garvey founded a paper (the *Blackman*) and an entertainment venue (Edelweiss Park), thus reestablishing himself in both the print and performative realms. Edelweiss Park boasted its own band, the Universal Jazz Hounds, and its own troupe, "the Follies," whose director, Gerardo Leon, had worked in show business in New York, Cuba, Belize, and Paris. (In later years, he would write hugely successful mentos and calypsos for his brother Rupert, "Lord Fly"—another veteran of New York and Cuban sojourns).[175] The goal was to draw working-class Kingston to "Social Uplift Parties" that combined music, dancing, and oratory, Garvey's oratory in particular. A report published in the *New York Age* in 1932 sneered at the sight: Garvey "lighted the grounds with bright and coloured lights and placed signs at the gate which invited the public to come in and be 'socially uplifted' at a quarter per head. And so nightly a motley crowd of laborers and domestics shuffled around on that bit of concrete to the syncopated strains of a jazz band and later sat on the benches and enjoyed a concert program of doubtful quality."[176] How distant was Garvey's twenty-five-cent-a-head social uplift from the Alpha's weekly regge—and how far from the twenty-five-cent brams that so exercised Sidney Young? Some commentators sought to be rid of the lot of them. But others, Garvey among them at this moment, saw in the popular passion for jazz music and dance a key lever for racial advance.

Raising funds for the Salvation Army and the UNIA; sounding the jazz that could lead young girls to ruin or allow a "coloured troupe" to conquer the capital; showcasing gyrations either innocently amusing or spectacularly copulative—regge dances in Port Limón were both a mainstay of youth culture and a multivalent symbol within communal dispute. Were regge dances a resource for respectable clubs seeking funds in straitened times or a raunchy domain no parents should let their daughters near? Were they a route to communal decency or the depths of collective slackness? There is no answer, of course. Rather, regge dances were a flashpoint for debate over how British

Caribbeans could make their way forward in an era marked by new mobility and new barriers, dreams of progress and accusations of moral decay.

CONCLUSION

It is telling that the *New York Age*'s biting account of Garvey's "Social Uplift Parties," above, was penned by Vere Johns. Of an age with Sidney Young, the Jamaica-born Johns shared all the experiences that shaped Young's cohort of anti-imperialist, antiracist, always-respectable activists: BWIR service, Lads and Scouts, lodge leadership, sports and Shakespeare. Like Young, Johns sought new horizons abroad after the Great War, and, like Young, he poured his seemingly boundless energy into the print-based transnational black public sphere. His articles for the *New York Age* exposed discrimination against black actors and advocated boycotts against employers who refused to hire people of color. At the same time, as the quote above makes clear, Johns was bitingly anti-Garvey and none too keen on housemaids dancing jazz. Yet in later decades, Johns, through his "Opportunity Knocks Talent Show," would play a key role in opening doors for the downtown Kingston musicians who created ska, rock-steady, and reggae.[177] Johns's intervention in debates over public dance and uplift in the 1930s reminds us that positions vis-à-vis popular culture were never simple or fixed, especially across the tumult of decolonization and nation building.[178]

In the first three decades of the twentieth century, music and movement in the western Caribbean reflected intense intercultural contact that spanned English- and Spanish-speaking communities, knit together islands and rimlands, and tied all of them tightly to New Orleans and Harlem. Against this panorama, the "regge dances" of Port Limón look simultaneously very local (with their small-town spats and home-coined label) and very cosmopolitan (with their broad swathe of styles and cutting-edge steps). Denounced as vulgar, degrading, and dangerous by some, regge dances were defended by others as a way for young people to forge a common mission in difficult times. In debating on these terms, the young men and women of Port Limón were part of a broader debate within the supranational black public sphere, visible in both print-based and performative realms. Could irresistible rhythms and the kinetic pleasures they inspired be part of the "New Awakening" of black internationalism that Sidney Young and his cohort espoused? Could musical achievement, like literary endeavor, gird the race against insult and ignorance? The answer was genuinely not clear, and different people reached different conclusions over time.

Examining the world of migrants and music has reiterated just how connected the interwar Caribbean was to metropolitan circuits, in ways that should disrupt some facile assumptions. One widely read account of the dawn of reggae declares, "Isolated for centuries, Jamaica rejoiced [in the 1950s] to find itself linked, however tenuously, to the rest of the music world."[179] Well, no. Another suggests that "big bands" and jazz were only accessible to the island's elites.[180] Sidney Young's diatribes against the "Charlestoning fools and illiterate sheiks" of Panama and Colón, and the *Searchlight*'s denunciations of youths of "the 'REGE' class" for their addiction to "Jazz," should put paid to this notion.[181] The empirical evidence is clear and confirmed from every available source. The presumption that "the classes" embraced modern, metropolitan culture while the masses lived out an instinctive legacy of African rhythms was, as we have seen, a commonplace of elite discourse in the interwar Caribbean. It was not an accurate description of cultural patterns at the time. Just how integrated rural hinterlands were to the transnational black performative realm that spanned ports across the region is less clear. But given the prevalence of outmigration from and return migration to rural households by the 1920s, and the many spaces where returning emigrants and internal migrants collided in the 1930s (West Kingston most prominently), the idea that Caribbean rural soundscapes made it through the Jazz Age in splendid autochthony seems unlikely to be right.

More serious scholars recognize the importance of early twentieth-century migration in shaping Jamaican music. Garth White has argued that "the Cuban, Costa Rican and Panamanian sojourn of the workers helps explain why the music of Cuba, in particular, and to a lesser extent that of the Dominican Republic–Haiti, held some sway in the late forties and fifties. Returned workers fattened the demand for Latin music to the extent that Cuban combos would come and play at night-clubs here."[182] Similarly, Clinton Hutton suggests "the migration of Jamaicans to Panama, Costa Rica and Cuba in the late 19th century and early 20th century, paved the way for music traditions from these former Spanish colonies to influence Jamaica through returning residents from these countries."[183]

Clearly this is true. What may be less visible in retrospect is that places like Colón, Limón, and Santiago de Cuba were not only located within Spanish-speaking republics; they were located within a supranational black public sphere, within which Afro–North Americans and Afro-Caribbeans spoke to each other literally and figuratively, read the same papers, and danced to overlapping arrays of musical styles. The tens of thousands of Jamaicans returning to Jamaica from Cuba, Costa Rica, Panama, and beyond in the 1920s and

1930s were coming back from musical environments saturated with multiple varieties of ragtime and swing as well as multiple varieties of *son*. This is not a claim that Jamaicans in Limón were influenced by black North American music; it is a claim that labels like "black North American music" mask more than they reveal.

To scope the contours of the Greater Caribbean Jazz Age, one need only consider the travels of the Sly Mongoose. A Jamaican mento from the turn of the century (protagonized by a chicken-stealing mongoose whose fame spreads to foreign: "Sly Mongoose, yuh name gone abroad"), we have heard it luring Herbert de Lisser's society peers onto the floor at the Constant Springs Hotel in 1921; performed by "Jazz Graterist" Charles Moulton on a Colombian banana camp in 1926; and animating the St. Thomas Tennis Club's affair at the Harlem Renny in 1931. The mongoose traveled by vinyl as well. Sam Manning recorded "Sly Mongoose" as a calypso in 1925. The melody was picked up by Ghanaian highlife musicians in the late 1920s and recorded in West Africa under multiple titles. Charlie Parker recorded a bebop version in New York in 1951; north-coast tourists in Jamaica grooved to mento renditions in the same years.[184]

The travels of this very sly mongoose challenge us to understand Jazz Age music as created simultaneously in, and ricocheting between, sites geographically distant and socially diverse—not just formal venues like the Renaissance Casino and Constant Spring Ballroom, but the upper rooms of a Guachipali tenement and an excursion train heading out of Port Limón. Each rendition drew difference from its performers and context—new rhythms and instrumentation, new lyrics, new take. Yet the sameness mattered, too. Surely there was an experiential dimension to diasporic consciousness, one that involved reencountering the familiar in unfamiliar sites: hearing a childhood melody strummed by another black musician's hands; dancing in a glamorous casino to "those good old-timers . . . by which your papas swung your mamas"; finding a spot in Harlem where the air was thick with the accent of home and the Sons of Barbados knew how to lead what the Daughters of Barbados knew how to follow.[185] It is far easier to trace the history of the print-centered public sphere and its particular black internationalisms; but the international consciousness generated by the black performative realm may have mattered more, and mattered to many more.

Six The Politics of Return and Fractures of Rule in the British Caribbean, 1930–1940

Sacred music still sounded in the circum-Caribbean migratory sphere in the 1930s—Sankey hymns, Pukumina drums, Salvationist cornets. But now voices raised in song, whether spiritual or secular, were often demanding radical change. In Trinidad, meetings of the Workingmen's Association ended with the international socialist anthem "The Red Flag." The (Marxist) Negro Welfare Cultural and Social Association ended their meetings singing "The Internationale." And Tubal Uriah "Buzz" Butler ended meetings among oil workers with a hymn, "From Greenland's Icy Mountains," in keeping with Butler's day job as a Spiritual Baptist preacher.[1] On the streets of Kingston, Leonard Howell led crowds in hymn while he held up a photo of Ethiopian monarch Haile Selassie, calling on Jamaicans to acknowledge "their King, Ras Tafari, king of kings, lord of lords, conquering lion of Juda, elect of God, and messiah of love."[2] And in 1938, with Kingston paralyzed by strikes and police attacking unarmed protestors, hundreds marched from West Kingston into the center of town "playing drums and singing 'Onward Christian Soldiers.'"[3]

The 1930s were years of crisis and transformation across the British Caribbean. Not only were island economies facing the same global market collapse as the rest of the world, but emigration outlets were barred. Remittances dried up as British Caribbeans abroad were made to bear the worst of employment crises in those lands. And many who had left the islands decades earlier were forced by hostility or hunger to return home. Prices rose, but with so many desperate hands seeking employ, wages stagnated or fell. Hunger was a daily reality in hundreds of thousands of homes. T. U. B. Butler led "Hunger marches" of laid-off workers northward from Trinidad's southern oil fields. Marches of the unemployed in Kingston carried banners: "Starvation, Nakedness, Shelterless."[4] The end of the decade saw a wave of strikes and riots across the British colonies: British Honduras in 1934; St. Kitts, St. Vincent, St. Lucia, and British Guiana in 1935; Barbados and Trinidad in 1937; Jamaica in 1938.

These events did not take place in a vacuum. Across all the lands that migrants had made part of the British Caribbean world, colliding trends shook the foundations of rule. As the export profits that had bolstered traditional elites plummeted, popular mobilizing accelerated. A communist-led strike immobilized United Fruit's Costa Rican plantations in 1934. In the Guatemalan and Honduran banana zones, labor organizing provoked a wave of repression in 1931 and 1932.[5] In Panama, a 1931 coup by nationalist reformers led the election of Harmodio Arias, with enthusiastic support from the West Indian community. Arias pledged land reform, education spending, wage hikes, and tenants' rights but met rent strikers' demands with violence in 1932. His brother Arnulfo followed him into power in 1940, shoring up support through a xenophobic populism that had crowds of thousands chanting "Panama for the Panamanians."[6]

In Cuba, a general strike in 1933 toppled Gerardo Machado after nine years in power. As the new regime, an unwieldy coalition of radical and nationalist groups, passed a flurry of progressive legislation—including female suffrage, labor protections, security for rural tenants, and the "Nationalization of Labor Law" (the 50 percent workplace quota law)—revolution gripped the countryside. Sugar workers formed soviets and seized mills. Roundups of Haitian migrants began: some 8,000 would be deported by July 1934. British Caribbean sugar workers joined actively in the mill takeovers, then faced backlash from restored managers and Cuban workers alike after Sergeant Fulgencio Batista sidelined the reformers (with U.S. encouragement) in early 1934 and began building a decade-long dominance.[7]

Even as Cuban workers of many colors were demanding the "nationalization of labor," in Harlem, Sufi Abdul Hamid was leading street protests and boycotts demanding "Jobs for Negroes." As "acute misery" and "appalling" poverty worsened, in 1935 a rumor that a child had been killed sparked a riot that destroyed 200 businesses and caused $2 million in damages.[8] In Venezuela, dictator Juan Vicente Gómez's death in 1935 sparked a similar popular explosion, most violent near the oil fields whose profits had sustained his brutal rule. Pressured by mobilized workers, the Venezuelan congress in 1936 passed the most progressive Labor Code Latin America had yet seen. A mass strike on the Maracaibo oil fields in February 1937 placed the law's promises on trial.[9] Across the region, working people pursued old demands with new action. Their struggles shifted the baseline of state commitment in the regimes that resulted, whether these were authoritarian and enduring or democratic and at risk. No one watching could have thought change came easy.

That migrants returning from Cuba, Panama, and beyond catalyzed labor movements and political protest in the British Caribbean in the 1930s was clear to observers at the time.[10] It was even clear in advance. A Colonial Office minute in 1931 warned that "any large number of discontents returning from

Panama or the Central American Republics to Barbados" might spur "riotous outbreaks."[11] They did. The importance of the circum-Caribbean migratory sphere to island events in the 1930s, then, is well known. This chapter will go further to argue that detailed reconstruction of the politics of return reveals previously unacknowledged events and sheds light on dilemmas to come.

First, the era saw the boundaries of belonging within the British Caribbean under dispute. The anti-Asian agitation that we detailed in chapter 3 was one manifestation of this. As restrictionists in the Spanish American republics moved from banning Afro-Caribbean entry to threatening to deport Afro-Caribbeans already there, additional lines were drawn. It was no longer just a question of which "aliens" would be allowed into the British colonies, but of which "natives" would be allowed back. Immigrant communities in Panama, Costa Rica, Cuba, and Venezuela included people who had traveled in multiple stages from birthplaces long ago and far away, alongside others who were the second generation of their family to be born outside of British territory. Where could these men, women, and children be kicked out *to*?

As we shall see, internal Venezuelan government documents reveal that it was precisely the refusal by colonial bureaucrats and Trinidadian authorities to accept responsibility for non-Trinidadian British Caribbeans—even to allow small-island deportees off the boat in Port of Spain—that caused Venezuelan authorities to use forced labor and physical abuse as deterrents to migration. This unheralded Venezuelan chapter in the history of Caribbean migration casts in vivid relief the erosion of migrants' civil rights as restrictive regimes gained international purchase. Contrasted with the patterns traced in chapter 1, these events illustrate in stark terms just how far the position of black colonial subjects vis-à-vis imperial ambitions had deteriorated in a few short decades.

Second, social protest in the era of return was not limited to labor unrest. It included intense religious revivals and unorthodox millenialist cults, like Leonard Howell's street preaching, above. The "Ras Tafarian" faith he founded embraced a Manichaean theology of race, significantly similar to that of the Nation of Islam, its North American contemporary. Just as we saw in the previous chapter that the black performative realm was, despite apparent opposition, tightly tied to the print-based public sphere, Rastafarianism—although apparently a total rejection of the respectable and the Western—in fact subsumed much material from the international print circuits of its era, including both black-internationalist and white-supremacist publications.

Finally, we will look at labor organizing itself to assess the interplay of off-island experience and interisland alliance among Caribbean working people in these crucial years. Migrants played key roles—not just returnees (in Jamaica, from Cuba and Panama, especially), but intercolonial immigrants (in Trinidad and Guiana, from Barbados and the other Windwards, especially). Around the Caribbean, working people on the move had learned from the Latin American labor movements whose demands had helped push them out the door. Now, with nowhere left to go, returnees and their island-bound peers forcibly pushed their own demands to the forefront of island debate. Might political and social citizenship be achievable for colonials of color? And if not, could colonialism endure? With British warships as back-stops, these regimes did not fall in the 1930s as did those in Panama or Cuba. But change was under way. Over the 1940s and 1950s, the role of the state in social provision and the voice of the people in government would be renegotiated here as well. The endgame of empire had begun.

AT RISK OF RETURN: THE DEMOGRAPHIC PANORAMA

By the early 1930s, the long-standing British Caribbean communities in the Central American republics included large numbers of locally born individuals already reaching adulthood. The multigenerational British Caribbean community in the Canal Zone and the Republic of Panama combined was estimated at over 50,000 in 1932. The 1930 Panamanian census counted some 23,000 *negros* of British-island birth spread across Panama City, Colón, and Bocas del Toro, while the Canal Zone in 1930 tallied 11,000 British island–born adults and 5,000 of their locally born children.[12] Limón, Costa Rica, was home in 1927 to 10,000 men and women born in the British Caribbean and 7,000 children and adults born locally to British Caribbean parents or grand-parents.[13] Circa 1930, 4,500 British Caribbeans lived in Honduras, 1,500 in Nicaragua, and perhaps 800 in Guatemala.[14]

Migration to the Greater Antilles had been of shorter duration but larger scale. Many arrivals had been seasonal cane cutters who left after each sugar harvest, but some women found long-term employ as domestics or dress-makers in Havana, and the other British Caribbeans settled on sugar mill house plots or in nearby towns, growing food in the "dead season" to get by.[15] In the mid-1920s, British representatives had estimated that nearly 80,000 British West Indians worked in Cuba, but in the dead season of 1931, Cuban census takers tallied only 28,000 British island–born (alongside 77,000 Haitians); British authorities the following year estimated British West Indians on the island at 40,000 to 50,000.[16] The Dominican Republic in 1935 reported some 9,000 British Caribbean residents; Haiti, in the same era, tallied 3,000 to

4,000.[17] Far to the south, Venezuela's British Caribbean population included perhaps 10,000 immigrants divided among the petroleum camps in Zulia and Monagas, Caracas's service sector, the on-again-off-again gold diggings around El Callao, and the cacao farms of Paria.[18]

Meanwhile, in 1931 Trinidad's cities, towns, and oil fields housed some 46,000 Afro-Caribbeans born elsewhere (Barbados, Grenada, and St. Vincent most prominently), while Guiana had some 7,500.[19] Unlike British Caribbeans in the Latin American republics, British Caribbeans within the British Caribbean were never threatened with mass deportation; but whether more small islanders could follow them to Trinidad, and whether they themselves would be allowed back if they left, were, as we shall see, matters of dispute. Likewise, the 72,000 Caribbean immigrants in the United States in 1930 faced no threat of mass deportation (although radical organizing could get individuals expelled).[20] Nevertheless, they found transnational family networks truncated and mobility radically constrained.[21]

The above tallies treated "British Caribbean immigrants" as a single collective, and certainly that is how they were seen by the mestizo populists doing their best to kick them out. Nevertheless, island divisions loomed large in the eyes of British Caribbeans abroad—indeed, more so than for those who stayed home. Montego Bay farmers and sophisticated Kingston tradesmen discovered their shared Jamaicanness only in contrast to the patois-speaking small islanders and boastfully "South American" Guianese they encountered in Panama.[22] Immigrants looked after their own, and those sharing an island of birth were understood to be "own" in a particularly binding way. Island-specific civic associations abounded in every receiving community, as did island-specific stereotypes. "We have lived together for twenty years," lamented Sidney Young in 1927, "and in that time we should realize that Barbadians are no greater liars than Trinidadians or that Jamaicans are no slicker thieves than Demerareans, or that Antiguans are no bigger fools than Montserrateans."[23] The "petty and insignificant customs and idiosyncracies of the particular groups" loomed large.[24]

Yet boardinghouses, docksides, and dance halls from Baraguá to Brooklyn brought islanders of every origin together. Within such communities, insular identities and a broader "West Indian" (by which was presumed *British* West Indian) collective were forged simultaneously.[25] Indeed, they were complements rather than alternatives. The fierce island loyalties of lodge membership and cricket fandom and the boisterous rivalries of rumshop debate tied British Caribbeans together and further marked their difference from the Afro-Americans or Panamanians or Cubans around them. However, as external hostility intensified over the 1920s, island divides seemed to some an unaffordable luxury. Voices from Panama in particular urged unity among "our people, West Indians."[26] On the pages edited by Sidney Young, racial allegiance and "West Indian" alliance were often treated as interchangeable. (Where this left British Caribbeans of South Asian, East Asian, or Middle Eastern ancestry remained, for the moment, unaddressed.) "We ignore the example of other races as to race unity," inveighed one columnist in 1926.

> If we were united and able to hold our own would we be treated thus? There is Mr Reed, merchant jeweller, Main Street, Guachipali, exclaiming that he is proud that he is a Demararan and not a Jamaican; here is the writer, a Jamaican, looking down with contempt on a Barbadian, and there is Mr Small of Red Tank, a Barbadian, regarding a St Lucian as inferior. We have forgotten, or failed to observe, that we are all regarded as One People.[27]

The need for unity was driven not only by receiving-society hostility, according to this author, but by colonial disenfranchisement. It was "useless" to seek support from "our respective [island] governments," he concluded, "for they are under the control of the Secretary of State for the Colonies at Downing Street and they do not, in all instances express the feelings of our people."[28]

Thus, calls in the rimland black press for spiritual unity among the Negro Race worldwide went hand in hand with calls for more immediate organizational unity among British Caribbeans. "In the appalling situation facing the community we cannot afford to remember sects, factions or denominations," insisted Sidney Young again and again. "We are not Barbadians, Jamaicans, Grenadians, Trinidadians, Guianese, St Lucians or Vincentians but WEST INDIANS."[29]

Yet when push came to shove, that aspirational "West Indian" collective turned out to count for nothing, at least in the eyes of those who controlled the purse strings and the ports. Island elites were not eager to welcome *any* indigent emigrants back to colonies where jobs were scarce and the masses restive. Specific island origin turned out to be the one ground for right of entry they did not attempt to deny. In other words, of the plethora of territories that might have been understood as the unit of the right of abode—some smaller, like parish of origin, and some larger, like the British Empire—the consensus unit of belonging turned out to be the island of one's own or one's parents' birth. There was no Caribbean-wide right of return.[30]

"LIQUIDATE THE BRITISH ELEMENT": DEFINING SUBJECTHOOD DOWNWARD; NARROWING NATIVE CLAIMS

Sidney Young looked to the West Indies Conference, to be held in January 1929, for joint action on the mobility rights of Caribbeans of color. For this reason, as for many others, federation among the islands was a crucial goal. "As a united and federated group," the British colonies might have enough "political importance in the great commonwealth of nations" to demand "greater respect by the governments of the world for native West Indians forced to travel abroad."[31]

Progressive island opinion agreed in the abstract that something must be done for poor emigrants—done by British consuls abroad, that is, or the Foreign Office, or the Colonial Office in its coordinating role. Looking ahead to the same conference, the editors of the *Barbados Advocate* declared: "The fact that the majority of the immigrants are poor is no reason for not providing them with protection. West Indian opinion needs awakening to the peril of the situation and steps should be taken to afford adequate protection to West Indians who are forced to emigrate to foreign countries to seek a livelihood. The question is one of West Indian importance and should be dealt with by the West Indies as a whole."[32]

But in fact the only coordinated response that would come out of the 1929 conference in regard to emigrants' troubles was a Colonial Office effort to push island legislatures to require a deposit of emigrants before departure, so that the cost of their eventual repatriation would be covered if necessary.[33] This was the system that Jamaica had used to fund a "Protector of Emigrants" in Cuba, a system that by the late 1920s was providing destitute Jamaicans with passage home on a regular basis. Set the deposit high enough and the system would even turn a profit.[34] Let us pause to notice just how far this response was from the kind of unified and *identified* pressure on behalf of "native West Indians forced to travel abroad" that Sidney Young and others were calling for and that sending states like China routinely provided. Rather than choosing to treat an insult to British West Indians as an insult to the British Empire and bringing diplomatic pressure to bear, the Colonial Office and island governments were defining action against Caribbean migrants as migrants' individual problem and requiring them to cover the ensuing costs out of pocket, and up front.

As hostility toward Afro-Caribbeans rose in Spanish American receiving societies and large-scale return threatened, both imperial bureaucrats and island elites sought ways to disavow responsibility for the welfare of British subjects of color abroad, all the while pointing fingers at each other as the responsible parties. One way they did so was by cleaving to the letter of British doctrine regarding the transmittal of British nationality through *jus sanguinis* to children born abroad to British subjects. By metropolitan tradition, nationality was transmitted by male British subjects to their legitimate children. Yet in the British Caribbean, between two-thirds and three-quarters of all births were to unmarried mothers, many of them in long-term coresidential unions identical to "common law" marriages elsewhere, and others in more short-term pairings.[35] Given the many dislocations that migration involved, and the difficulties of legalizing unions in a foreign land, what is amazing is that *only* 70 percent of second-generation British West Indians in Panama were born to unmarried parents.[36]

That translated to some 16,000 young people in Panama alone for whom British officials could deny all responsibility, a fact that British minister Josiah Crosby underlined with unseemly glee. "These persons are not entitled to an asylum in British territory," Crosby reminded his superiors, "and I derive some satisfaction from making the point clear to my Panamanian acquaintances. I am at pains to impress upon them that by no means every black face seen in Panama today belongs to one of His Majesty's subjects, and that in a few years the great majority of negroes in the republic is likely to be composed of Panamanian citizens."[37]

Not if Panama could help it. The 1928 Panamanian constitution stripped *jus soli* citizenship from all persons born within Panamanian territory to parents of "undesirable alien" stock. Across the 1930s, confusion reigned, as Panamanian and British officials each insisted these youths had no claims on them, and British West Indians worried that mass statelessness might ensue. Questions of nationality law were anything but academic. The Panamanian government threatened to deport out-of-work noncitizens, and the Cuban government in fact deported some British Caribbeans alongside the thousands of Haitians forcibly expelled.

But where would they be deported *to*?

The Colonial Office, at Crosby's urging, wrote to all of the colonies that had émigrés in Panama, describing the potential crisis and asking that British diplomats in Panama be authorized proactively to extend travel documents without having to consult island authorities in advance about every longtime resident of Panama who said they belonged on a given island. From each island the responses streamed back, staking out stringent parameters in no uncertain terms. Only those deportees who could prove they had been born on *this* island, their legitimate children, and (as a gesture of compassion) illegitimate children aged sixteen or younger would be allowed in.[38] According to colonial officials, it was the island elites represented on privy councils and executive committees who were most insistent on defining the right of return as narrowly as possible. The (almost exclusively white) elites governing Barbados through that island's elected assembly had the worst reputation for hostility. Even on the extraordinary occasion when they had voted for a symbolic sum to be sent to Cuba to assist Barbadians left homeless by a hurricane, it was on the condition that none of the funds be used to buy tickets home.[39] The "Unofficials" in the Leewards were likewise steadfast in refusing to extend any assistance to emigrants whose wish to return would "add to the unemployment difficulties at home." Colonial Office functionaries were not even certain the Leewards elites could "be induced to accept" island natives deported at Panamanian expense, although "in the last event," the officials planned to insist.[40] Jamaica, in contrast, routinely repatriated needy Jamaicans—who, after all, had paid for their own return passages in advance—but steadfastly refused responsibility for any who could not prove their Jamaican origin, even in cases where rimland consuls saw "no reasonable doubt."[41]

These were the same years in which Jamaican elites found it expedient to echo the Jamaica Native Defenders Committee's slogan, "Jamaica for the Jamaicans." Did the narrow right of return reflect island elites' heartfelt love of their own? The idea is hard to reconcile with the alacrity with which they excluded the teenage children of "their own" who happened not to have married. The documentary record captures little elite sympathy for working-class migrants of any origin. Yet there was clear consensus that island birth conveyed a lifelong right of abode "in the last event"—and, conversely, that entry by "destitutes who might hail from other parts of the British West Indies could not be countenanced."[42]

Even as imperial officials clucked over island elites' lack of sympathy for emigrants, the Foreign Office was just as eager to shed obligations. Ever candid, Josiah Crosby pronounced himself "anxious to see th[e] liquidation of the British element [in Panama] accelerated" by the loss of subject status to Panama-born youth.[43] Other officials were more willing to construe rules in favor of British Caribbeans abroad—and found themselves reprimanded as a result. A 1929 Foreign Office inspection discovered that consuls in "Puerto Cortes, Truxillo, Bluefields and Port Limón" had been issuing "British passports to Jamaicans unable to produce evidence of British nationality." Such profligacy must stop. Henceforth, only "emergency certificates," valid for travel to Jamaica alone, would be issued, so that "there will be less likelihood in the future of illegitimate persons born in Central America obtaining British passports."[44] The same bottom line was clear. In cases of "emergency," those born abroad would be permitted to return to their parents' island of origin. But the Foreign Office would not widen that right to the full mobility rights that possession of a British passport would verify.

In response to Cuban efforts to deport Leeward Islanders on ships carrying Jamaicans back to Jamaica, the Foreign Office enunciated the international consensus on territorial rights as Britain intended it to apply to the Caribbean colonies: "Countries can only be required to accept their own nationals as deportees. Consequently, if the Cuban authorities attempted to deport a Trinidad negro to Kingston, Jamaica, because he sailed from that port to Cuba, or a Haitian negro to Nassau, Bahamas, because he had been previously residing there, the respective colonial authorities would be quite justified in refusing to accept them."[45] The phrasing reveals more than intended. Why illustrate with reference to "a Trinidadian *negro*" and "a Haitian *negro*" when the principle laid out was a supposedly race-neutral affirmation of the precedence of "national" belonging? The reality was that differently colored subjects did have different mobility rights, both within empire and beyond empire's borders.[46]

Note how far the doctrine of imperial subjects' rights had shifted since we first heard them invoked during the 1849 gold rush in El Callao. Now, not only was the Foreign Office not attempting to assert uniform British rights for subjects whatever their color and wherever they were, but it was not even attempting to assert a right of entry for "Trinidad negroes" to Kingston. This was not a matter of shifting racial attitudes but of shifting geopolitics. There had been some racist functionaries then, and there were some antiracist functionaries now.[47] But in the second half of the nineteenth century, British West Indians moving into the rimlands had provided legal justification for a sphere of influence Britain sought to expand. Now, Britain's concerns lay elsewhere. It was time to liquidate.

COLORED PERSONS, BRITISH CITIZENS OF PORT OF SPAIN: THE POTENTIAL AND THE FRAGILITY OF ANTIRACIST ALLIANCE

The class divides over boundary drawing in the era of return are underlined when we compare island elites' efforts to shrink the right of return to the expansive visions of collective identity and mobility rights articulated by workingmen's representatives in 1930s Trinidad. Within a Crown colony governed by a Legislative Council whose majority was governor-appointed, the Port of Spain municipal council was a hard-won anomaly: a wholly elective body, elected by broad franchise. Even though its formal remit was quite limited, it was the most prominent platform within the British Caribbean that included leaders actually elected by the masses, and those leaders routinely demanded to speak their mind on issues that had nothing municipal about them.[48] In 1930 what they were speaking about was mobility, race, and rights. The "Venezuelan Government has summarily prohibited coloured persons—inclusive of burgesses of the City of Port-of-Spain—irregardless of their financial status or moral worth, from entering Venezuela, either for temporary or permanent residence." Yet "Venezuelan citizens, the majority of whom are also themselves coloured, continue to enjoy the privilege of entering Port-of-Spain."[49] Thus: "Be it therefore resolved, that in the opinion of the Council the local Government should make representations to His Majesty's Government for the adjustment of this anomaly—relations between coloured persons, British citizens of Port-of-Spain, and Venezuela should be reciprocal."[50]

The resolution was put forward by Alfred Richards, pharmacist, labor leader, gadfly; founder in 1897 of the Trinidad Workingmen's Association; eventual mayor of Port of Spain; and himself the son of a Chinese father and black Trinidadian mother.[51] His resolution, with its emphasis on "moral worth" and property ownership, may seem class bound or conservative. But its explicit racial identifications made it radical indeed. From its first phrases, openly identifying the "burgesses of the City of Port-of-Spain" with the other Trinidadians *de la raza negra* impacted by the law, to its last line, confidently presuming "coloured persons" of Port of Spain to be "British citizens"—a status not on offer in imperial doctrine at the time—this was a radical departure from the euphemisms by which other governmental bodies in the British Caribbean tiptoed through public discussion of racism and rights in this era.[52]

Richards's outspoken demand for international mobility rights for Britannia's citizens of color found wide support among his fellow City Council members. Indeed, his was not the most radical voice in the room. Others pushed further in pointing out the interlocking geo- and micropolitics of race and borders: "Councillor Achong . . . said they were primarily concerned about evaluating their rights as citizens of the British Empire. Venezuela had every right to protect her citizens. They were not complaining against that, but against the discriminatory methods employed. He thought it would bring home to men that they had no status at all in the British Empire. Venezuela could point out to them that even in a British country—Australia—they would not be admitted."[53]

Citizens of Latin American republics enjoyed mobility guarantees across the Americas regardless of the color of their skin. Colored subjects of empire enjoyed none. Ultimately, argued the Port of Spain councilors, the problem was not Venezuelan exclusion; the problem was imperial subordination. "'We are so accustomed to insults being heaped on our heads in the West Indies,' [Achong] said, 'That when we go to foreign countries—take America for instance—you hear West Indians claiming to be Venezuelans or Colombians. They are ashamed to state that they are West Indians. Why? Some even try to speak Spanish.' It was, Dr. Achong asserted, because Venezuelans were citizens of Venezuela, whether white or black. A West Indian must be a negro with no rights."[54]

Tito Achong spoke from experience when he described how West Indians attempted to evade Jim Crow by "passing" for South Americans. After all, he had done his own medical training in the United States and had been labeled "colored" by Ellis Island officials when he arrived in 1916 on his way to study at Howard University.[55] In speaking from the subject position of a "West Indian" as "negro with no rights," Achong himself was making an intentional move, in some ways the opposite of "passing" and in line with Richards's inclusive use of "coloured persons" as the proper category of political self-assertion. For as it happened, both of Achong's parents were Chinese.[56]

In fact, the Municipal Council's East Indian, Chinese, and Afro-descended members all united in denouncing the Venezuelan ban as evidence not just of foreign racism but of imperial racism. Councilor Maharaj called for the legislature to demand action from London, although in the absence of self-rule, he was pessimistic. "They were governed by the Home Government," he complained. "If they in the West Indies had their own Parliament they would not be so subject to the whims and caprices of other countries."[57] (One is reminded of the Panama-based columnist's sad confidence that "our respective [island] governments" would not "express the feelings of our people.")

The contrast with contemporaneous Jamaican debates covered in chapter 3 is striking. There, light-skinned elites and black politicians converged to define Chinese migrants as the true enemies of "Jamaica for the Jamaicans." In contrast here, black, part-black, Chinese, part-Chinese, and East Indian elected representatives stood together in insisting that the lack of political rights was what made race matter, and that international racism was a dilemma shared by colored colonials—of all colors—together.

This stance, though, was hard to sustain. It existed in tension with other notions of the collective that made African ancestry a proxy for working-class solidarity. And those passions, in the final analysis, were less threatening to the status quo. So when the leading dailies of Jamaica and Trinidad called the attention of "the Trinidad Government" to the new immigration laws of "the United States of America, Cuba, Jamaica, and Venezuela," the lesson they chose to draw was the urgency of limiting the "influx" of Chinese.[58] And when Trinidad's Legislative Council took up debate on proposed responses to the Venezuelan ban five months later, it was not the imperial system but Trinidad's 2,000 Chinese and 200 Syrian residents who found themselves under attack.[59]

Tito Achong landed again at the forefront of debate, but now in his capacity as vice president of the Chinese Association. "The Chinese community to-day consider that this move is primarily aimed at them," he told reporters. "The question of restriction of Venezuelans and other alien immigration is looked upon as a camouflage."[60] Throughout the 1930s, Achong would remain one of the most radical voices on the radical Municipal Council.[61] Yet when threatened with popular xenophobia, even Achong was quick to insist on his community's capitalist docility. "Instead of being a charge to the community, the Chinese are a valuable asset to the Government. . . . There is no foundation to the suggestion of Chinese exporting all their money earned. Most of them have inter-married with West Indians and settled here. . . . As a class they keep away from politics."[62] Suddenly, political inaction was a virtue meriting protection, loyalty a matter of investment rather than colored solidarity.

Ultimately, the new immigration laws enacted by the Legislative Council in 1931 and tightened in 1936 increased entry deposits for all immigrants, but they placed those for immigrants from the Far East at ostentatiously punitive levels. As the governor privately acknowledged, these rates were "much in excess of the cost of passages back to country of origin, but I am advised that any attempt to reduce the amount would be strenuously opposed" by the island public.[63] Those who bore the symbolic brunt of Trinidad's reaction to Venezuelan action against *negros*, then, were the Chinese. But those who would bear the highest physical cost would be other black migrants. They were the casualties of Trinidadian elites' and officials' efforts to embrace nativism without expanding state commitments. To this story we turn.

OVERBOARD: NAVIGATING THE CARIBBEAN WITH NO RIGHT OF RETURN

Claims about race-based or birthplace-based "native" entitlement suffused public rhetoric high and low in the British Caribbean in the 1930s. But which racial and which native divides seemed important, and why, varied enormously by class. Working-class British Caribbeans may have worn insular loyalties with pride in Central America, New York, and Trinidad, but such divides were "more marked by jocular derision than by any form of sustained hostility," as Lloyd Braithwaite would put it two decades later.[64] The readiness with which the (heterogeneous) workforces of Trinidad and Guiana followed labor leaders born elsewhere, as we will see, further confirms that insular identities were just not that salient to the masses in this era. Racial identities, though, were another matter. In contrast, those who held power in the strained 1930s were doing their best to embrace the mantle of nativism at the possible lowest cost to themselves. This might well mean placing migrants from other islands alongside the Chinese as targets for exclusion.

The first draft of the Immigration Ordinance debated in Trinidad's Legislative Council in 1931 called for a £50 deposit from all immigrants, which was needed, the colonial secretary explained, to stanch the flow of newcomers looking for work, in light of oil industry layoffs and rock-bottom cocoa prices. Captain Arthur Cipriani, labor leader and elective member, called foul. Retaliation should certainly be made against countries like Venezuela and South Africa that had "made it clear that they do not want our coloured men there." But Trinidad should not charge "her West Indian brethren" the same high deposit assessed "aliens," least of all "just at the time when West Indian politics are full of federation." The colonial secretary insisted that the draft reflected concern for the laboring classes—"in a time like this our first duty must be to see that the natives of this Colony should be considered before immigrants from another Colony"—but Cipriani refused to agree that support for the workingman required insularity. It came down, he insisted, to whether "the West Indians are a people."[65]

Five years later, with unemployment worse than ever, a new immigration ordinance was proposed. It gave the Executive wide powers to ban not just individuals likely to become paupers but "any member of a class of persons deemed to be undesirable . . . on economic grounds, or on account of standards or habits of life"—widely understood as a coded promise to ban Chinese entry.[66] This time, Cipriani was at the forefront of an explicit attack on "Chinese and Assyrian" immigration. Furthermore, he had abandoned his former defense of other British Caribbeans' rights of entry, saying that immigrants, "no matter from what part of the world," should be barred entirely until unemployment improved. (A fellow legislator noted acidly that Cipriani "proves himself an internationalist and a socialist in theory but as sturdy and economic a nationalist as Herr Hitler himself.")[67]

So if one of the things the bill offered was typical anti-Asian posturing, ultimately more consequential was its detailed discussion of "who shall be deemed to belong to the colony," essentially regulating the right of abode. "A person who belongs to the colony cannot be deported: that is perfectly clear," explained the attorney general. The contours of "belonging" set by the bill will sound familiar: British subjects born in Trinidad, children of parents who belonged to Trinidad, and immigrants (as long as British subjects) after seven years' continuous residence in Trinidad.[68] As with *jus sanguinis* and the legitimate line, the details were anything but academic. In the eastern Caribbean, where small islanders' laboring lives routinely took them to and through Trinidad and onward to Venezuela (or Curaçao, or Panama) and back, "belonging" to Trinidad meant crucial asylum. For the answer to Cipriani's 1931 question was that West Indians were *not* treated as "a people" anywhere in the West Indies in the 1930s—and navigating a regional economy based on seaborne mobility was risky indeed if you had only a highly constrained right of abode.

As Cipriani and his fellows knew, "Venezuela had made it clear that they do not want our coloured men there." For eastern Caribbeans seeking work, this was not a symbolic insult but a personal threat. As layoffs continued on the oilfields of Trinidad, men hoping for better luck in Venezuela traveled by small craft from southern Trinidad to the Venezuelan coast around Pedernales, or from Port of Spain to the coast near Macuro on the peninsula of Paria. Venezuelan authorities stuck the "clandestine" migrants they caught (or the ones who failed to pay bribes?) on ships headed back to Port of Spain. But beginning in 1934, this strategy ran aground. Captains refused to carry deportees not demonstrably of Trinidadian birth, explaining that Port of Spain authorities refused to allow Grenadians or Vincentians to disembark without a £20 deposit and would fine the captains £50 if the men disembarked illegally. The 1931 ordinance was being enforced.

Venezuelan authorities railed in vain. We "are unable to understand why the authorities of Trinidad should refuse free admittance to the island to British subjects of the neighbouring islands," wrote Venezuelan diplomats.[69] The question had British officials equally off balance. Trinidad's new laws, passed with Colonial Office approval, had drawn distinctions between those who "belonged to" the island and other British subjects. Now Colonial Office, Foreign Office, and Trinidadian authorities argued over whether or not Trinidad had "grounds for refusing admission to . . . British subjects" born elsewhere. The Foreign Office judged this position to be "legal by the law of the country but not in international law," while the Colonial Office backed up Trinidad in her refusal to "become a dumping ground."[70] The reply transmitted to Venezuelan authorities by the British minister in Caracas sought to insist on the narrowest right of return. Following "standard international practice," Venezuela must first verify origin claims through the British consulate and then provide deportees with "means" to "return to the British Territory to which they belong."[71]

Since no scheduled shipping connected Venezuela to Grenada, St. Vincent, or the other Windwards, this in practice made small islanders undeportable except at prohibitive expense. Appalled, authorities in Caracas sought confrontation, but the Venezuelan minister in London counseled otherwise. Given the "autonomy" that Trinidadian authorities enjoyed regarding domestic policy, he argued, officials in London could do little. A true resolution to the problem of illegal immigration would come not from international entreaties but from Venezuelan "national measures, independent of the action of other countries"—specifically, "a severe penal sanction . . . applied inexorably in every case" and strong enough to deter future emigrants. His superiors agreed.[72]

Thus, faced with British officials' public insistence (despite private doubt) that they could not force Trinidad to accept islanders born elsewhere, the Venezuelan state developed a border-control system that relied on punitive violence rather than international coordination. The death of dictator Gómez, just months after this correspondence, brought no mercy. Seeking nationalist/populist bona fides, the democratizing successor regime pursued foreign blacks with more violence than ever. British West Indians, some with decades of residence, were seized at gunpoint, sent to labor on road gangs, "beaten with cutlasses" just for protesting, and in two dozen recorded cases, carried by Venezuelan coast guard boat to the seas off the coast of Trinidad and forced at gunpoint overboard.[73]

The systematic nature of the violence was visible to British officials at the time.[74] The Foreign Office instructed the British minister in Caracas to bring as much pressure to bear on behalf of deportees as he could while being careful not to "prejudice wider British interests" (the Anglo-Persian Oil negotiations under way drew particular concern). Faced with such contradictory instructions, one diplomat allowed himself a rare, undiplomatic reply, pointing out "the difficulty of complying with the instructions" as given. When "every case of claim is treated with flippant indifference it is hard to indicate what attitude to adopt without a flagrant disregard of British, if coloured, interest."[75] His protest made no pretense that all British interests were equal. But surely even colored British interests still counted as British—and should not be *flagrantly* disregarded? He received no reply.

Venezuelan authorities insisted that they were defending their territory against recent "incursions," but to judge by the men pushed overboard, any dark-skinned immigrant had become fair game. Joseph Benjamin had been born in Grenada in the 1880s, moved to Trinidad, then left for Venezuela in 1908. He squatted in Monagas and built up a cocoa farm over three decades, "getting married to a Venezuelan lady," and had "5 children alive." Arrested while buying provisions in town in 1938, Benjamin was set to forced labor for nine months before being dumped off the coast of Point Icacos and forced to make for shore. "I am a large landholder at Monagas, paying taxes to the Govt.," he insisted. "I was dragged from my home and family who are now left starving in Venezuela."[76] As awareness of impunity spread, neighbors took advantage of the shifting macropolitics of race to settle personal scores. Sixty-year-old Edwin Richardson had also been in Venezuela since 1908; in the late 1930s, he found himself in a land dispute with a wealthy Venezuelan "who requested the magistrate to expel him as 'an insolent negro' who was illegally in Venezuela." The magistrate did.[77]

Their goods and papers seized by agents of the Venezuela state, these men washed up on the shores of Trinidad as paupers—and destitute refugees born elsewhere were precisely the people for whom British Caribbean authorities refused to open doors in these years. Grenada-born Eldon Cudjoe had left Trinidad for Venezuela in 1927, worked at the pitch lake in Guanoco for two years, and then labored on the Quiriquire oil field for ten. Dumped overboard off the coast after seven months of hard labor, Cudjoe was brought from Icacos to Port of Spain by police. "I am about the streets pennyless and hungry," he said, "and to make matters worst, the Government of Trinidad has ordered me to leave here in 14 days, and I have no where to go."[78] Grenada-born Metan Stafford had worked for almost a decade on different oil fields in Venezuela when he was seized, sent to hard labor, and then pushed overboard. Trinidadian authorities gave him a permit for seven days' stay, but that was small consolation: "I have nowhere else to go. It was Trinidad I sailed from for Venezuela, and all my interests lie in Trinidad, and I ought not to be made to leave the island where I have been domiciled all the years."[79] But had they been seven *continuous* years, as statute now required?

The remaking of border regimes in this crucial era of state formation hit British Caribbean migrants both coming and going: "going" as they were pushed out of Spanish American republics, "coming" as they sought refuge in the British colonies and found themselves restricted to the islands of their own or their parents' birth. Moreover, these developments accelerated each other. Authorities here observed how authorities there treated those who did not "belong," and they adjusted accordingly. Panamanian president Harmodio Arias warned Josiah Crosby that there might be "a serious outbreak of feeling against the coloured population . . . if it became known that British West Indian Governments were denying admission to persons who possessed a moral, if not a legal, claim to their assistance and protection."[80] Knowledge of sending-state disavowal could reverberate at the smallest scale as well as the largest. Grenadian Samuel Sandy, arrested after twelve years in Venezuela, described how the governor of Tucupita, "after reading a *Trinidad Guardian* report of the tale of seven who had returned to Trinidad . . . came to me in my cell and told me and others, your own Government does not want 'you,' so you better spend some time with me still."[81] Hard labor got harder still.

RETURN, IN SPITE OF IT ALL: THE DEMOGRAPHIC PANORAMA

Josiah Crosby wondered aloud in 1931 about what "workless British West Indian subjects" would find if they did return home. "It appears only too likely that to some extent they will be walking out of the frying pan into the fire."[82] The process was under way as he wrote. Over 3,000 Jamaicans returned from Cuba alone each year from 1925 to 1929; that number jumped to nearly 5,000 in 1930 and nearly 10,000 in 1931.[83] The yards and gullies of St. Andrew Parish, around Kingston, grew ever more crowded as it gained a net 15,000 residents due to external migration and another 48,000 internal migrants (people who, in earlier years, would have sought opportunity in foreign instead).[84] In Barbados, returning emigrants increased the island's population by 8 percent in just five years from 1932 to 1937.[85]

In Trinidad, a sending and receiving society at once, the typical family impacted by the reversals of the 1920s and 1930s might look something like that of Mabel Charles. Born in the Panama Canal Zone in 1919 to parents from Montserrat and Antigua, Mabel was denied a visa when her family moved from Panama to New York in the mid-1920s because her birth record could not be found. The child was sent to Montserrat instead. Stuck in Port of Spain from 1936 onward while she petitioned U.S. consuls for a copy of her birth certificate, she met a young man through church, himself the son of a Tobagan mother and Barbadian father. Their second child, Stokely Standiford Churchill Carmichael, born in Port of Spain in 1941, would follow them to the Bronx at age eleven to become a radical civil rights activist and an originator of Black Power.[86]

The first half of this chapter laid out the circumstances that confronted British Caribbeans abroad and at home in the lean years of the 1930s. The rest will look at the social and cultural revolutions they generated in response. Some developments reflected the generative collision of the local and the global, as international news of struggle between races was read by Jamaicans confined to the island, forcibly localized as never before. Rastafarianism, worshipping Ethiopian king Haile Selassie and offering new dreams of African power, was the result. Other social detonations reflected processes not global or local but intraregional—linking islands and rimlands and islands to each other. This was the case for the labor rebellions of 1937–38, the culmination of a half decade of unprecedented mobilization. Here, too, we see the impact of both preceding migrations and current mobility restriction, in this case with Latin American labor movements the key part of islanders' broadened horizons and colonial officials the ones attempting to bar the door.

BACK ON THE ISLANDS: RELIGIOUS RADICALISM

The cosmopolitan ports, economic crises, and xenophobic ultimatums of the late 1920s seem to have acted as a kind of crucible for race-conscious revivals. The highly religious circum-Caribbean migratory sphere got more religious yet. In Port Limón, "tabernacles" founded by "Shepherds" drew hundreds of supporters. They spoke of the power of a "black God," echoing Garvey's exhortation to worship God "through the spectacles of Ethiopia." In Kingston, a new version of Revival dubbed Pocomania spread fast, believers "shouting and singing throughout the night, with children and adults lying upon the earth, night and day, in a 'trance.'"[87] Identical groups arose in Limón, called "pocomia" or "cocomia" in the Costa Rican press, with dancing and trumping of extraordinary intensity leading to prostrate trances that lasted full days.[88]

The *Gleaner* reported a disturbing fusion of old and new. "The old fashioned drum-playing used in Jamaica a hundred years ago" had been resurrected by these new converts to "the old myalism"; "we suspect that these recent drums, however, are of Haitian origin and are intended to stir the passions . . . in the well-understood Haitian manner."[89] Ignore the hype, and the hypothesis is plausible. Between 1930 and 1935, some 27,000 Jamaicans had returned from Cuba, where many had labored side by side with Haitian migrants.[90] Recent research has highlighted religious interaction between Haitians and Cubans on and around the sugar plantations.[91] Given the patterns that we observed in chapter 2, there is every reason to presume that spiritual learning and exchange occurred between Jamaican creole-speaking and Haitian kreyol-speaking migrants in Cuba, as they did between Bajan creole-speaking and St. Lucian patois-speaking migrants in Colón.

Meanwhile, antiblack restrictionism had migrants spiraling back to Kingston from multiple sites of black-internationalist ferment—with both spiritual and secular baggage. Grace Jenkins Garrison and Charles Goodridge founded the Hamatic Church in Kingston in 1925, inspired by the mystical *Holy Piby*, which claimed Marcus Garvey as the apostle of a new "Blackman's" religion. The *Holy Piby* was published in Newark, N.J., in 1924, although Garrison and Goodridge encountered it in Colón, apparently that same year.[92] Joseph Hibbert returned to Kingston in 1931 after twenty years in Limón, where he had belonged to the Ancient Order of Mystic Masons of Ethiopia. In Kingston, he founded an "Ethiopian Coptic Faith" that included classic Science healing, using the apocryphal *Ethiopic Bible of St. Sosimus* alongside de Laurence books and drawing clients from far and wide.[93] Rabbi Ford's followers, Annie and David Harvey of Port Limón, Panama, Harlem, and Addis Ababa, returned to Kingston from Ethiopia around 1930 to found a storefront church, the Israelites. Leonard Howell, whom we last saw working as a healer on 136th Street in New York, reached Kingston in 1932. These travelers drew from sacred and secular texts a milliennialist conclusion: Ethiopian monarch Haile Selassie—known before his coronation as Ras Tafari—was God returned to earth, and his coronation in 1930 began the end of black subjugation worldwide.[94]

Global and regional events had converged to invest Ethiopia with extraordinary significance. As we saw in chapter 2, Ethiopia had long been a symbolic touchstone for black Christians in the Americas. Garveyism had given new prominence to the prophecy that "Ethiopia will stretch forth her hands." Meanwhile, military victories in the late 1920s had made the actual state of Ethiopia an icon of black prestige across the transnational black public sphere. If Britain, France, or Italy could have imposed their will by force, observed the *Pittsburgh Courier*, they would have. "But they couldn't. Abyssinia is united and strong, hence respected. Negroes elsewhere take notice."[95] Jamaica-born journalist J. A. Rogers, the epitome of respectable middle-class black internationalism, covered the coronation of Ras Tafari for the *Courier* in person in 1930.[96] "Powerful Nations" were forced to "Pay Respects" when black people controlled state power, reports underlined.[97] Attempts by white observers to defang the racial lesson by claiming Ethiopia's imperial family were "not Negroes" drew mockery from black writers. Bring "upper class

Abyssinians," Moors, and Hindus to the United States "and let them try to purchase sleeping car berths from Cincinnati to Atlanta"—"Then the questions of what race they belong to would be settled for all time."[98]

Thus Leonard Howell was reworking widely shared ideas about race pride and geopolitics when he began preaching in Kingston that "George the Fifth has sent his third son down to Africa . . . to bow down to our new king Ras Tafair. . . . The negro is now free and the white people will have to bow to the Negro Race."[99] Tried for sedition in 1934, Howell explained that empire had always been temporary, and now the messiah had come. "I told them that our King had come to redeem them home to their Motherland, Africa. That there was a vast amount of people who believed that they were British subjects, but that the British Government were only protecting them until their King came, and when he came, the Crowned Head of England would turn them over to their King."[100]

The movement spoke to other international developments as well. Howell obtained a souvenir photograph of Ras Tafari (likely from the Harveys) and sold copies in the streets as he preached; one rumor held that these were "passports" to enable holders to be repatriated to Africa.[101] The rumor not only treated Garvey's rhetorical "Back to Africa" as an imminent event but also reflected the new weight of mobility-control documents in popular culture. Most of all, though, the photographs were understood as evidence of the existence of a living black God, for Selassie was "Dead stamp, dead stamp of Jesus Christ," one convert recalled.[102] Adherents saw the photographs as "incontrovertible, logical and true, brought all the way from 'foreign,' the great outside world where truth is not surpressed."[103]

Oral history holds that Howell was only allowed to disembark after sending for a copy of his birth certificate from a parish archive, since his Jamaican accent was gone after so many years abroad. Given the strictly delimited right of return in this era, the story may well be accurate. More fundamentally, the claim that "God had made him be born in Jamaica so that he could come back and save us" captures a bigger truth.[104] By 1930 birthplace boundaries fractured access to global knowledge in unprecedented ways. Typed onto the bottom of one card seized by police is the legend "Presented By Leonard Howell. Trave[le]d the World Through"—as Howell in fact had, and as his followers no longer could. From Garrison and Goodridge to Hibbert to the Harveys to Howell, all the leaders of the emerging faith had acquired their spiritual expertise in lands Jamaicans were now forbidden to enter.[105]

The conviction that Selassie was Messiah, Christ, or God became grounds to challenge the authority of the colonial state—all the more so when news

RAS TAFARI
KING of KINGS of ETHIOPIA
A DESCENDANT of KING SOLOMOND AND THE QUEEN of SHEBA

Presented By Leonard Howell

Traved, the World Through

One of the photo cards of Ras Tafari distributed by Leonard Howell in Kingston, 1934. (Courtesy of the Jamaica Archives and Records Department, Spanish Town, Jamaica; Ref. 1B/5/77/283–1934)

of Mussolini's 1935 invasion of Ethiopia rocked Jamaica, as it did the Afro-Americas as a whole. The transnational black public sphere rang with denunciations, not only of Italy's aggression but also of the perfidy of Great Britain in acquiescing to the betrayal of a black ally by a white enemy.[106] Jamaicans mobilized in response. UNIA leaders organized what one scholar describes as "free floating street fraternities" with names like "Ethiopian Allied Defense."[107] In the eyes of some, the barriers between local news and international news, and those between political crisis and eschatological crisis, had dissolved. Howell's followers by 1936 were declaiming on the streets that "Jamaica will have its own war and every negro must come to their colors and fight for their rights! . . . If Britain has taken Africa from them then they must have Jamaica. And the white men must be under them."[108] The movement also spread among cultivators in rural St. Thomas, linking community concerns to race-wide injustice. The *Gleaner* reported in 1934 that followers in St. Thomas refused to pay taxes, insisting "that the land belong to the black people: no longer are they accountable to Government or property owner."[109]

The worship of Ras Tafari thus drew adherents from Kingston's squatter settlements and rural village poor alike. In each case, these were men and women who a decade before would have sought opportunity abroad and now could not. These were the same settings and same groups where new Revival worship emerged in the same years. But although outside observers lumped "pocomanian or Ras tafarian or myalistic or revivalistic meetings" together as dangerous fanaticisms of the "illiterate" masses, the differences between them are striking.[110] Pocomania dug deep into Revival roots, possibly reinforced by Afro-Cuban and Afro-Haitian spiritual practice. The meanings that worshippers—many of them women and children—ascribed to their experiences are inaccessible. It was the *absence* of intelligible words, both in the trumping and then in the prostrate trances, that characterized Pocomania.

In Rastafarianism, in contrast, words were everywhere. All of the disparate groups preaching the divinity of Ras Tafari in the early 1930s were deeply enmeshed in modern print culture. We have already seen the influence of the spiritualist publishing market that produced texts from the de Laurence guides to the *Ethiopic Bible* to the *Holy Piby*. There was, too, the circum-Caribbean/transatlantic black press, which provided race-conscious coverage of Selassie's coronation and the Italian invasion and insisted on their relevance to black people's local politics across the Americas. The *Pittsburgh Courier* took on special significance at the King of Kings Mission, where preacher Robert Hinds had a standing order for two dozen copies; *Courier* articles were read for definitive confirmation of English cannibalism and the leprous origin of white skin.[111] And there was a final key contributor: the international white supremacist press.

Again and again, Rastafarian leaders and followers took the semihysterical screeds typical of interwar white racism and read them as news of black world-historical victory. Indeed, Rastafarian doctrine contains a kind of inverted archive of Western culture at the nadir of antiblack racism. In 1921 Lothrop Stoddard's *Rising Tide of Color against White World Supremacy* had argued that "the frightful weakening of the white world" during the Great War had "opened up revolutionary, even cataclysmic, possibilities."[112] Five years after Stoddard introduced the phrase "white supremacy" into common usage, Reverend Fitz Ballantine Pettersburgh published in Kingston *The Royal Parchment Scroll of Black Supremacy*, a parallel survey (though in the arcane language of Masonic esoterica) of the looming demise of "The Angle Saxon Slave Dynasty . . . called white supremacy" and the triumph of the "ETHIOPIAN DYNASTY . . . called Black Supremacy."[113] Leonard Howell fused passages from the *Royal Parchment Scroll* with the *Holy Piby* to create his own sacred book, the *Promise Key*, published in Kingston in 1935.[114]

Another building block of Rastafarian belief apparently originated as Nazi propaganda, loosely based on an actual East African spiritual tradition that worried colonial administrators in the 1910s and 1920s. The article (dateline Vienna) described an Africa-wide "ominous secret league," called "Nya-Binghi" or "Death to the Whites," which Haile Selassie had agreed at a secret conference in Russia to lead as a "black avalanche" against Europe. White-run Jamaican papers published the report in alarm in 1935 and again in 1937; Rastafarians, too, found it utterly plausible and began to define themselves as local affiliates of Nya-Binghi.[115] George Schuyler's black superhero-cum–mad scientist, Dr. Belsidus, serialized in the *Pittsburgh Courier*, became further fodder once "Dr. Belsidus" was recognized as a code name for Haile Selassie. At the King of Kings Mission, "Hinds had his secretaries transcribe each episode into large log books. . . . The installments were read out at each meeting, like a war news bulletin."[116] One is reminded of Thelma Anderson, begging the *Courier* editors from Limón in 1937 to "tell me the truth about Dr. Belsidus. I wish it could be true that he has whipped every Italian as Joe Louis has whipped every white boy."[117]

Thus Rastafarians read as literal texts intended as parodic and read as encouraging texts intended to sound alarms. They drew together spiritualist, black-internationalist, and white-supremacist prints to create a radical theology of racial vindication. Strikingly, while the proselytizers who brought these texts before the Kingston public were literate and urbane travelers, those who made the religion their own were largely of Jamaica's unlettered masses. Not only did they appropriate international print culture, but they also transformed it into a religion centered on erudite *oral* "reasonings." Over the course of the 1950s and 1960s, the language of Rastafarian debate became ever more arcane, a rejection of the standard English that dominated black internationalism; styles of self-presentation similarly morphed away from the respectable.[118] One could find no better illustration of how, as Michael Warner describes, a "dominated group [that] aspires to re-create itself as a public" can challenge the very "norms that constitute the dominant culture as a public" to create a counterpublic.[119]

Dangerous truths needed to be told, explained Hinds's secretary: "The Government . . . complain in English and tell we: 'Listen, it is not that we feel that unu [you] is so ignorant or illiterate, but we were not expecting unu to carry all these subjects and read it so plain to the public.'" But the King of Kings Mission persisted in reading to the public—and in doing so, created a counterpublic. Another book read aloud explained how, when Africans were brought to the Americas, "their bodies were going in machines and their bones, blood, flesh, brain were mixed with the manure and thrown in the roots of trees."[120] As with rumors of witchcraft a generation earlier, the spiritual realm continued to provide deadly accurate metaphors for sufferers' vulnerability. Appropriately, by the 1930s, stories of global white conspiracy and deadly agrobusiness supplemented stories of village soucouyants.

Thus Rastafarianism was forged from the dual legacy of the extraordinary cosmopolitanism of the 1920s and the forced localization of the 1930s. Rastafari and Jamaica have come to define each other in international iconography, a remarkable result for what remains a small and marginalized religious community on an island none too large itself. Yet, observed at its origins, Rastafarianism would have looked not uniquely Jamaican but like one among multiple movements fusing esoteric knowledge, world religion, and race-conscious self-help in the "economic maelstrom" of the 1930s.[121] That Rastafarianism's birth was part of a supranational trend becomes clear if we pan out to see what was going on at the outer edges of the circum-Caribbean migratory sphere in that same moment. So let us check in, one more time, with Louise Little and her son Malcolm.

As Louise Little struggled to keep the family together after Earl Little's violent death, her children faced a Depression-era Lansing even less secure than the Grenada of Louise's youth. By 1938 Louise talked to herself more and more, responded less and less. State welfare agents institutionalized her and parceled the children out. Grim years passed. As they reached early adulthood, though, Louise's children found hope in a new church: one full of people like themselves, raised in Garveyite homes; one where, as in their father's UNIA meetings, religion, race pride, and politics were fused. Malcolm Little's older siblings visited him in jail in 1950 to share the prophetic word. Give up pork and cigarettes; seek God in prayer; take heart, for "the white man [is] fast losing his power to oppress and exploit the dark world; . . . the dark world [is] starting to rise to rule the world again, as it had before."[122]

The Lost-Found Nation of Islam had emerged in the early 1930s. It drew on prior movements that brought African Americans to identify with Islam while borrowing ritual and theology from an eclectic array of spiritual and spiritualist traditions. The most important precursors were the Moorish Science Temple and the Ahmadiyya Islamic Movement, each with multiple connections to the UNIA. Garvey's introduction to African and Middle Eastern activists had come long before when he worked for the London-based *African Times and Orient Review*, whose publisher, Dusé Mohammed Ali, was a prominent Ahmadiyya. When Ali came to the United States in the early 1920s, UNIA chapters and the *Negro World* helped publicize his tour. In the same years, Moorish Science Temple congregations reached out to potential converts with a race-conscious philosophy directly drawn from UNIA roots.[123] In 1931, just as Garveyites and others in Kingston were suspecting that Ras Tafari might be a Messiah come to announce the end of black subjugation, Garveyites and others in Detroit were flocking to UNIA halls to hear "Prophet" W. D. Fard herald the redemption of his "long lost brethren" from racist ignominy.[124] The theology and rituals of the Nation of Islam in the 1930s and 1940s drew as heavily on arcane esoterica and Christian apocrypha as on orthodox Islam. It reflected a particular moment in Afro-American history marked by race pride, popular Orientalism, and a will to understand black people in the Americas as misplaced natives of elsewhere.

That these same factors echoed in Rastafarianism is no surprise. Indeed, the parallels were clear at the time to those who could travel. At the UNIA convention in Kingston in 1934, Garvey denounced the "prevailing religious fanaticism" that had "very simple and ignorant people . . . founding and organizing new cults." The delegate from Gary, Indiana, seconded him vehemently: "Simple-minded Negroes were turning [into] Moors, Arabs, Abyssinians" in the United States, "growing beards and refusing to cut their hair," even changing their names "to be know as Mohammed Ali or Mohammed Bey or some peculiar Moorish or Mohammedan religious mystical name." A delegate from Kingston jumped in to inform "the American delegates that demonstrations of that kind were not peculiar to America alone, but right in Jamaica there were Negroes claiming to be Abyssinians, who were starting to grow beards as an indication of their religion and had announced that on a certain day they would walk on the sea from Jamaica to Abyssinia."[125]

Rooted in Garveyism and other black internationalisms of the era, both the Lost-Found Nation of Islam and Rastafarianism had pushed beyond where Garveyites were willing to go. Each declared whites not only unjustly privileged but also inherently debased—a bleached-out devil race, said Fard; leprous, wrote Ballantine and Howell.[126] Each moved toward flat rejection of corrupt and racist state authority. That Malcolm Little, a child of the British West Indian diaspora, would emerge as a leader of the Nation of Islam is not happenstance but quite the contrary: it is another episode in the long history of mutual influence and reconvergence of spiritual traditions between Afro–North America and the Greater Caribbean.

And that Malcolm X should make it his mission to turn that worship community into a base for local and national political organizing, and reach out to form anticolonial connections within global Islam, is likewise unsurprising, given where he was coming from. He was a black nationalist and a black internationalist. We can think of Malcolm alongside other grandchildren of the circum-Caribbean migratory sphere—like Stokely Carmichael, born in Port of Spain in 1941 to Panama-born Mabel Charles. Stokely Carmichael (like Richard B. Moore and Claudia Jones before him) found in Marxism a compelling complement to race consciousness and forged a secular black internationalism. Malcolm X (like Leonard Howell and Annie Harvey before him) found in popular faith an alternative but equally compelling complement and forged an equally revolutionary black internationalism.

BACK ON THE ISLANDS: LABOR RADICALISM

If some saw in this moment of crisis the need for a distant messiah to overturn global hierarchies of race, others saw the need for direct action against local hierarchies of privilege. Here, too, migrants and returnees provided crucial leadership. Union experience; Garveyism; contact with international anarchism, socialism, or communism; a willingness to challenge colonial authorities—these were not unique to those who had been to foreign, but they were especially concentrated among them.

The way migration intersected with labor organizing differed between the eastern and western Caribbean—and, as a result, so did the legal rights that labor leaders could or could not claim. In the eastern Caribbean, labor leaders were less often returnees and more often islanders born elsewhere. The pattern was long-standing. Those at the forefront of strikes in Trinidad in 1919–20 had included immigrants from Barbados, Grenada, British Guiana, and Jamaica. White elites denounced them as "anarchists from other islands," "conspirators against the peace and tranquility of Trinidad" who were hatching "diabolical plots . . . saturated with racial animosity."[127] In fact, the leadership was barely more heterogeneous than Trinidad's workforce itself, but certainly it was true that the black-internationalist press, and British West Indies Regiment veterans' anger at white racism, played a role in the strikes. To Trinidad's mobilized workers, solidarities of race and class mattered more than insular divides. However, island birth dictated legal rights. Strike leaders born elsewhere could be deported, and they were.[128]

In the same years, the governor of Jamaica lamented that Jamaica would have to accept Garvey if the United States expelled him: "Unfortunately he is a native, and thus not deportable."[129] And in some ways, Garvey's 1927 return was an early and unusually prominent case of a broader pattern, as Jamaicans with organizing experience abroad found themselves thrust back to the island and there put into practice the organizing lessons they had learned. As we have seen, by the mid-1930s, tens of thousands of returnees from Panama and Cuba filled the ranks of Jamaica's unemployed and semiemployed. They were fully aware that Panamanian and Cuban workers' empowerment had been part of what occasioned their own current straits. "Forceful Labour Unions in this republic of Cuba" had "brought the terror against foreigners," wrote one. But that itself gave incontrovertible evidence of the value of unions. He went on: "I was a member of a Union for many years in this Republic. . . . A Union demands respect and it gives protection from every angle."[130]

"Republican" ideas brought from Cuba and Central America, just like labor activism in those nations, included both jingoist and internationalist strains. Anti-Chinese xenophobia ran strong among returnees, but returnees' experience with the antixenophobic Cuban Communist Party also shaped Jamaican discussions of where workers' priorities should lie. Returnees who became key leaders came from across the ideological spectrum. There was L. E. Barnett, who had been a bread-and-butter union leader in Limón; Cleveland Antonio King, raised in Cuba and a longtime Communist Party member there; Hugh Buchanan, Cuban returnee and pioneering Jamaican communist; St. William Grant, New York returnee and Garveyite street speaker; Robert Rumble, twelve-year resident of Cuba and millenarian peasant organizer; and future prime minister and force of nature Alexander Bustamante.[131] Light-skinned and middle-class, Bustamante had lived in Cuba, Panama, Cuba again, and New York before returning to Jamaica and entering street politics in the late 1930s. His mercurial, labor-based charismatic authoritarianism echoed Latin American authoritarian populists from Panama's Arias brothers to Cuba's Batista to Argentina's Perón.

Fed by the "Starvation, Nakedness, and Shelterlessness" that the immobilization of working-class Jamaica had wrought, marches of the unemployed and work stoppages in 1936 and 1937 intensified into strikes and riots that shook the island between April and June 1938. Strikers were beaten, bayoneted, and shot by police or by the "special constables" deputized from among the "light complexioned members of the upper and middle classes" as the emergency spread.[132] Bustamante emerged with "the rank of deity among the masses," noted other organizers in wonder.[133] An anonymous special correspondent to the *Pittsburgh Courier* judged the root causes to be "years of ruthless British exploitation and official indifference," aggravated by hunger as workers were "forced home" from Spanish American republics, adding up to "labor unrest . . . increasing racialism (growing hatred of the white oppressors) and a loud agitation for self-government."[134] Meanwhile, racialism that targeted Chinese merchants rather than "white oppressors" had not been absent: Chinese businesses bore the brunt of rioters' anger in many towns.[135]

Writing from London to the Royal Commission inquiring into the riots' cause, Marcus Garvey doubled down on xenophobic populism. Returnees driven home by hostility abroad had found Jamaica "being dominated by Chinese, Assyrians, and in some respects Indians, and [could] find no opportunity for work, employment, or business, in the land of their nativity."[136] The category of nativity was fundamental to Garvey's analysis. It was the West Indian islands' destiny to be peopled by "natives," the "Negro race," who needed aid in their struggle against economically powerful and emphatically nonnative "Asiatic races."[137]

But not everyone saw things this way. As the *Courier* correspondent's reference to "agitation for self-government" made clear, the lesson some were drawing from regional trends was not that alien races threatened natives' rights, but that without political rights, nativity was worth nothing. As Alfred Richards's and Tito Achong's identification as "Coloured Citizens of Port of Spain" at the start of the 1930s suggested, in Trinidad a strong current of local thought embraced anticolonial antiracism rather than anti-Chinese racism when challenging the status quo. Labor organizers in 1930s Trinidad built cross-ethnic alliances even despite the island's occupational segregation. East Indian lawyer Adrian Cola Rienzi and Grenada-born former oil worker T. U. B. Butler together organized workers and cultivators in the southern oil region. Meanwhile, in Port of Spain, the Negro Welfare Cultural and Social Association (NWCSA) espoused class-based rather than race-based solidarity, despite its title. It was linked to the Communist International's International Trade Union Committee of Negro Workers (itself initiated by Trinidad-born, Europe-based George Padmore) and reached out to the East Indian sugar workforce from the early 1930s onward. NWCSA leaders included St. Vincent–born Elma François, a domestic, and Jim Headley, a former ship's cook who had been active in the Young Communist League in the United States.[138] As the examples of Butler and François suggest, migrants from other islands played an outsized role as organizers in the 1930s, as they had in 1919–20.[139]

As unrest roiled, the colonial state again relied on the narrow definition of domicile that made some labor leaders deportable. Clement Payne, ally of T. U. B. Butler and leader in the NWCSA, arrived in Barbados from Trinidad in late March 1937 and connected immediately with local Garveyites and activists. His speeches brought news of unrest on other islands and the invasion of Ethiopia and promoted trade unionism and Garveyism. In other words, the civic institutions, communications networks, and shared symbols that circum-Caribbean migration had wrought enabled Payne to build a mass following in a few brief months. He himself was a product of the migratory sphere and its multiple eddies: he had been born in Trinidad to Barbadian parents, then raised in Barbados before heading back to Trinidad to work as a young man. It was precisely the fact that Payne had mistakenly declared his birthplace to be Barbados upon disembarking in 1937 that gave authorities justification for deporting him from Barbados four months after arrival— and it was news of his deportation that would spark a four-day uprising that left cars overturned, windows shattered, fourteen black Barbadians dead, and over 500 arrested.[140]

"Religion, political and industrial factors are intricately jumbled in Negro life and the indiscriminate mix-up is not only appalling, but also paralyzing to Negro progress," wrote Claude McKay of 1930s Harlem.[141] As the sounds we heard at the start of this chapter suggest, religion, politics, and labor activism were jumbled on the islands as well, and the combination was anything but paralyzing. For Jamaica, the significance of Ethiopianism (including Rastafarianism) and Garveyism in shaping the terrain on which the Labour Rebellions would occur has long been recognized.[142] For the case of Trinidad, we know more about the importance of international allies (Marxists, socialists, and trade unionists) in shaping labor action in this era than we do about the possible role of spiritual practice. But in fact the "mix-up" may have been significant. T. U. B. Butler was not only a BWIR veteran and former oil worker but also a Spiritual Baptist preacher. Butler's public meetings included symbolic references to then-banned "Shouter" worship, and his rhetoric drew from Scriptures, Marx, and Garvey alike.[143] It is possible that if we had the kind of historiography for the Spiritual Baptists in 1920s and 1930s Trinidad that we do for Rastafarianism in 1930s Jamaica, we would see faith and worship intricately jumbled with working-class mobilization in Trinidad as well.

Butler's local following was inherently international. Trinidad was that kind of place. When authorities finally managed to capture and try him for sedition—after an unsuccessful arrest attempt in 1937 triggered riots that left fourteen dead and fifty-nine wounded—support poured in.[144] Money came from "Barbados, St Vincent, Grenada, Carriacou, and even neighbouring Venezuela"; and from "Joe Louis, heavyweight boxing champion of the world," remembers one local historian.[145] There seems no documentary record of Louis's role, although one cannot rule it out. But that people *thought* Joe had helped makes perfect sense, because they understood themselves to be part of a larger black international whose champion Joe Louis was. Again, it was the print-based public sphere that had made it so. We see traces of the process in a 1936 letter from "the Trinidad Negroes" to Joe Louis via the "Editor of the Pittsburgh Courier"—the same means that "the colored young people of Costa Rica" had used to write to Joe the year before. In 1936 condolences were in order: "We the Negro people of Trinidad and the British West Indies" consoled "our sensational Negro heavyweight contender, that the Negro populace here are extremely grieved with sorrowful hearts to learn of his defeat at the hands of the German."[146] Joe must persevere. As The Lion and Attila's 1937 calypso insisted, he had been "defeated but not disgraced."[147] And in 1938 Louis did indeed bounce back to defeat Schmeling, as Caribbeans everywhere cheered. So why wouldn't a grateful Joe have sent money when the people's Chief Servant, Buzz Butler, was in need? They were one people, after all, fighting distinct phases of the same battle.

CONCLUSION: DILEMMAS DELEGATED TO FUTURE NATION-STATES

In the wake of the uprisings, the kinds of substantive state commitments that organized workers had gained in populist pacts in the Spanish American republics and the United States over preceding decades finally made it onto the negotiating table in the British Caribbean: housing and education, the rights to organize and strike, a mediating role for the state between labor and capital. Middle-class Caribbeans of color, who had long demanded greater political rights, and the working men and women of the islands, who were no longer able to seek sustenance abroad, made common cause. Expanding citizenship, both political and social, might come to Britain's black colonies as it had to the surrounding republics in which black colonials had sojourned.

But just who would count as full members of these societies was unclear. Within Britain's Caribbean colonies, the restrictionist era saw access and belonging constrained in line with different criteria for different people: by island of birth, if you were a black British subject; by supposed standard of living, if you were Chinese; by legitimacy (which in practice meant by class), if your mother had borne you abroad. In each case, we have suggested, this reflected strategic maneuvering by elites and officials who sought to claim the mantle of nativism on the cheap, while limiting the numbers of people who could make claims on the governments they ran. Elites made sure that the costs of antiblack restrictionism would be shouldered by individual migrants rather than by the societies that migrants' remittances had sustained over the preceding generation. (The pattern was most obvious, and the personal costs highest, in the case of Venezuelan arrestees, beaten in labor camps because the Colonial Office would not bite the bullet and tell Trinidadian authorities that they could not refuse entry to fellow British Caribbean subjects.)

Thus, differences of birthplace loomed large in diplomatic correspondence in the 1930s, in the same years in which differences of race loomed large in popular complaint in the Spanish American republics and British islands alike. You might think this was a reflection of the masses' "insularity" and racial chauvinism. But when we examine the dynamics at a micro level on a region-wide stage, we see that matters of class—in particular, the efforts by the islands' white and near-white minorities to maintain their extraordinary privileges in a democratizing world—were fundamental in pushing criteria of birthplace and race to the forefront of public debate.

Among working-class Caribbeans, in contrast, the politics of race and belonging were complex. Men and women committed to racial solidarity protagonized the 1930s upheavals that set the British Caribbean on the road to decolonization. But racial solidarity meant different things to different people, and which Caribbean subjects could claim its embrace was up for debate. Likewise, disparate notions of territorial belonging were on display in the 1930s. Indeed, key dilemmas of the independent Caribbean were fore-shadowed in the era of return.

The first set of dilemmas had to do with external frontiers. For all that British West Indians abroad cherished home-island identities, the most ardent support for federation came from these same places. Activists as ideo-logically distinct as Sidney A. Young, Richard B. Moore, and C. L. R. James exemplify the point.[148] Few of those agitating for self-government in the late 1930s imagined that it would come in the form of independent microstates alone against the world. It is beyond the scope of this book to trace the process through which alliance into a Federation of the West Indies was painstakingly hammered out as decolonization was negotiated in the 1940s and 1950s—and then collapsed within four years of inauguration in 1958. But disputes over the scope of the right of abode in the 1930s do shed some light on that failure.

Supposed popular chauvinism and Alexander Bustamante's personal ambitions have been prominent in explanations for federation's demise. The processes we have observed in the 1930s should make us question explanations that foreground the (sometimes noisy) identifications of the masses and ignore the (sometimes silent) calculus of the privileged. The two groups most insistent to keep island belonging as the boundary of social and political entitlement in the 1930s were white elites and colonial officials. The pattern suggests divisory forces not at the level of popular culture or demagogues' egos, but in the realm of state and obligation. By the middle of the twentieth century, political belonging carried some claim to social citizenship. Ruling over masses was not as cheap as it once was. Continuing the pattern of interislander alliance we saw in the 1930s mobilizations, organized labor was among the most enthusiastic supporters of federation through the 1940s and 1950s. The dissolution of federation in 1962 left united workers without a unitary stage.[149]

The second set of dilemmas had to do with internal frontiers: of wealth and mobility; of popular culture and class; of race. The role of religion in marking social divides is particularly clear. The very practices through which some marginalized Jamaicans created a counterpublic and a political critique marked them as unfit for political participation in the eyes of some other Jamaicans, from Garveyites on out. As middle-class nationalists positioned themselves to lead soon-to-be independent nations, "religious fanaticism" provided a nominally nonracist, nonclassist grounds for placing some potential citizens outside the bounds of political and civil rights.[150]

Meanwhile, the color/culture/ancestry nexus called "race" seemed poised to bar others from full belonging. If "Our People, West Indians," were the same as "Our People, the Negro Race," where did that leave East Indian or Chinese Caribbeans? Did their multigenerational rootedness count for nothing, just like those of British Caribbean ancestry found in Panama or Limón? Garvey's assertion of the precedence owed "natives" looks painfully hypocritical in an era in which nativism was so often turned against Afro-Caribbeans. But this was complicated, too. Those Caribbeans who could claim "native" standing on the grounds of African race were often precisely the ones being marginalized by all the other criteria at work in this era (wealth, education, respectability). Should we wonder that some of the masses held tight to the one political logic available that made them central rather than marginal to their homelands' futures? Not only did race-based nationalism echo the nativist populism that across the hemisphere had proved the most reliable route for working classes to claim social citizenship; but Caribbeans facing a political system in flux might well believe it was all they had.

Conclusion

The preceding pages have argued that the black-internationalist and anti-colonial movements that would shake the twentieth century were rooted in the experiences of ordinary men and women—not only on the cosmopolitan streets of Harlem and Paris but also in the banana ports and dance halls of the tropical circum-Caribbean. When we widen our optic—as the lives of men and women like Louise Little of Grenada, Montreal, Omaha, and Lansing and Sidney Young of the Kingston Boy Scouts, the BWIR, and the *Panama Tribune* have persuaded us to do—we find that multiple subfields of twentieth-century history are in fact part of a single story. It is the story of how low culture and high politics, racist laws and radical religions, dockworkers and diplomats interacted to remake the modern world.

Attention to the lives of people on the move has revealed multiple organic connections between Afro-American, Caribbean, and Latin American history. Afro-American historiography has been anything but insular in recent years. A wealth of research has shown how U.S.-based black activists reached outward: toward West Africa in the first generations after emancipation; through the Pan-African Congresses in the early twentieth century; toward North and West Africa as part of the radicalization of the civil rights movement.[1] Activists like black Marxist Claudia Jones (of Trinidad, Harlem, and London) and AFL-CIO organizer Maida Springer (of Panama, Harlem, Tanganyika, and Pittsburgh) have drawn overdue attention as well.[2]

One goal of this book has been to show that, just as Jones and Springer did not begin their travels from within the United States, black internationalism did not move outward from a U.S. origin point. The fact that so many foundational black-internationalist leaders had intercontinental origins is one component of that argument, but it is not the central component. Tracing supranational circuits, we have found that Caribbean creations played a role at the roots of "U.S." jazz and radical activism, and that Afro-American creations played a role in the birth of "regge" dance and decolonization. We have also found that none of these can be understood without attention to time spent in Panama, Venezuela, Cuba, and Costa Rica and to the changes afoot in each of those lands. All of this becomes visible when we discard national or imperial boundaries as the limiting frame for observing social and cultural processes.

But we have also tried to think outside of another kind of box in this book. We have tried to set aside the presumption that certain kinds of things— like popular culture and social movements—are generated by "local" actors, while other kinds of things—like export economies and regimes of state power—are dictated by "global" forces or "international actors."[3] Were the British bureaucrats scrambling to set policy or the senators wrangling over laws more "international" than the men and women whose demands and travels set off the need for those policies or those laws? The bureaucrats and politicians in Whitehall and Washington were doubtless better fed. They had more years of formal schooling and more secure employment. And even after the new laws went into force, the bureaucrats and politicians—like wealthy people everywhere—did not need to worry that they might end up on the opposite side of a border from loved ones and be forced to make a permanent choice.

And nevertheless, center-state officials and elites and employers no more made history as they pleased than did the sojourners of the circum-Caribbean or the "native workers" of Havana or Detroit. As the international mobility-control system consolidated, ordinary people navigated a world of rules set by employers and bureaucrats. But employers and bureaucrats had to navigate a world in which workers demanding protection, subjects demanding representation, and citizens demanding rights at multiple different sites could listen to and learn from each other.

The "isms" of interwar history—nativism and populism, state racism and black internationalism, nationalism and anticolonialism—were not disembodied global forces somehow hanging in the ether and making things happen. Rather, such terms are our shorthand for common and connected results—the outcomes, on the one hand, of similar processes operating at different sites for similar reasons and, on the other hand, of a moment in history in which awareness across distance was more widespread than ever before. Panamanian labor leaders read Australian protectionist legislation, and Barbadians followed the disenfranchisement of the Cape Town Coloureds. People borrowed strategies, adopted slogans and self-identifications. Each of those "isms" summarizes the patterned results of myriad interactions.

Thus we have not only found unexpected and multidirectional connections among British Caribbean history, Latin American history, and U.S. history; we have found that the remaking of national and international political systems, from the high diplomacy of imperial assertion to the minutiae of border control, was enmeshed in the story of tropical labor and popular culture at the peripheries.

I hope that this volume serves as one piece of a collective effort to explore transnational history "from the bottom up." Academic historians in many parts of the world are thinking through a "transnational turn." Faced with evidence of the impact of connections across borders in the present, we are looking for the same in the past. It is hardly news that powerful states and corporations have long acted internationally, with international consequences. But now we are noticing connections at multiple levels of society and assessing their consequences as well.[4]

Ultimately, though, if we confine our mission to uncovering the existence of connections in the past, we will be hard-pressed to build a case for how they matter. If connections are constant, how can they explain historical change? We need to move beyond establishing the historical fact of connections and move toward *historicizing* connection. What moved, when, and in what volumes? How many people, from where to where when? What kinds of information? Which sounds in which forms? Many of these questions are only answerable with the tools of social history: demography, prosopography, quantitative analysis of commerce and employment, the steady accumulation of records to be read against the grain. These can make possible the bottom-up reconstruction of lives of the forgotten many rather than the vocal few.

Furthermore, we need to begin historicizing barriers as well as connections. If mobility mattered to the course of history, it must be that the lack of mobility mattered too. Who was prevented from moving where when? When were ideas, publications, ideologies, and cultural products *less* likely to travel? I hope to have demonstrated here that not just the existence of barriers but their precise timing mattered. British Caribbeans who volunteered for military service in the Great War found their treatment by the Mother Country a travesty of the proud British subjecthood they had been promised. It mattered that members of their generation came back to islands with little room for their energies and were forced to seek work farther afield, in Panama, Cuba, or Brooklyn. These travels, atop their wartime internationalization, put BWIR veterans at the forefront of writing and reading an expansive Negro People into existence. But it also mattered that a mere decade after the Great War's end, these proud veterans would find their rights of passage blocked at all of those destinations and would be reduced to the narrowest right of return—to the island of each one's own birth.

The confinements imposed by international borders should be as central to transnational scholarship as the travels of ideas and activists across those borders. By the 1940s and 1950s, the great majority of people of color were barred from seeking employment in foreign even as the words of Mahatma Gandhi and the sounds of calypso and rhumba resonated across metropolitan space. In order to have explanatory power, our stories of connection and influence must map disconnection and exclusion as well.

INTERWAR BLACK INTERNATIONALISM AND IDEAS OF THE AFRICAN DIASPORA

"I didn't know it till I reach the States," explained a Barbadian returnee to an uncomprehending childhood friend in George Lamming's *Castle of My Skin*. "'My people,' he said again, 'or better, my race. 'Twus in the States I find it, an' I'm gonner keep it till they kingdom come.'"[5]

What exactly is the "African diaspora"? The label is used in both academic and everyday discussion to designate the set made up of people of African ancestry across the globe. Interest in the African diaspora has surged over the last generation in locales from Montevideo to Liverpool. Questions of definition necessarily come to the fore. Are we talking about a population? A process? A people? Nineteenth-century commentators never doubted that groups defined by ancestry should be the subjects of history. Groups that shared a linked inheritance of blood and culture—called "races," "nations," or "peoples"—were the core units of human destiny, and shifts among them were the motor of global change. Now that academia has abandoned such biological essentialism, we are healthily forced to make explicit our goals in defining a "diaspora" as an object of study and to explain the criteria by which we delimit it and the presumptions we make about commonalities and divergences within it.[6] A key question (here as always in social science) is the degree to which we make actors' self-understandings part of the parameters of study.

Thus, a major subfield within recent research in the history of the African diaspora has been research into conceptions of that collective generated within it. The present inquiry into the black internationalisms of the interwar Greater Caribbean contributes to that larger project. As we have seen, claims about the common origins and destiny of people of African ancestry living in distant lands became a mainstay of public debate in and around the Greater Caribbean in this era. As we have also seen, the question of just where to draw the boundaries of this collective—whether to include dark-skinned Panamanian policemen who insisted that no *negros antillanos* be allowed to share the dance floor with "their" women, or "Coolies" of South Asian ancestry who shared island birthplaces and common disenfranchisement but claimed different traditions and pasts—was continually contested.

Scholars noting the surge of black internationalisms in the interwar era have offered multiple explanations, including the intensification of international racism, the radicalizing experience of Great War military service, and the spread of movements promoting radical global analysis, including anarchism, socialism, and communism.[7] I would like to suggest as a supplementary hypothesis, based on the present "bottom-up" history, that mass migration of postslavery populations, triggered by world-historical shifts in the early twentieth century, were a turning point in the imagining of the African diaspora.

PATTERNS IN WORLD MIGRATION AND THE "MAKING" OF THE AFRICAN DIASPORA

From the beginnings of the Atlantic slave trade, there were secondary migrations within the New World on an individual and small-group level. Ports of arrival like Cartagena and Havana were nodes in wide networks of reexport. The acceleration of internal slave trades in the wake of the abolition of the transatlantic trade has long been recognized by scholars of Brazil and the United States as having brought crucial results.

Mass migration under conditions of freedom, however, was a twentieth-century phenomenon. To be sure, the right to mobility was one of the least fictitious rights promised to freedmen and freedwomen with the end of formal slavery. Nevertheless, in the immediate aftermath of the emancipations that rolled across the Americas in the nineteenth century, mobility was largely a matter of short relocations—usually off the plantations and into nearby towns or hills where unclaimed land might be turned to own-account farming.

But by the end of the nineteenth century and most intensely in the first three decades of the twentieth, the particular histories of communities of African origin in the Americas intersected with a process of accelerating mobility worldwide. Scholars of global migration have drawn attention to the unprecedented mass migrations of the years 1840 to 1940, which went far beyond the movement of Europeans to North America. Recent research underlines that up until the 1880s, Asian migrants were reaching the Americas and Africa as well as Southeast and Northeast Asia in massive numbers. (These included the scores of thousands of Chinese contracted by Cuban sugar planters over the era of gradual emancipation and the hundreds of thousands of South Asians brought under indenture to Trinidad, Guiana, and beyond.) The anti-Asian bans of the 1880s, 1890s, and 1900s in the Greater Caribbean were local components of a much broader phenomenon. It was precisely as the movement of Asians to the Americas was barred and diverted that the movement of Afro-descended Americans within the Americas began accelerating rapidly.[8]

The mass mobility of the era reflected multiple shifts: the acceleration of the international economy, with new mechanisms for direct foreign investment that sped the relocation of capital and therefore of labor demand; a transportation and communications revolution that made it both cheaper to travel and easier to hear about why one might want to; changing sociopolitical systems that freed people to exit their homelands in search of a better life elsewhere; and the rise of new cities as nodes for transportation, industry, political influence, and financial services, leading to large-scale internal migration. For each of the sending societies that scholars have studied, it has become clear that social networks linking those who left home to one another, as well as to those back home, had a crucial multiplier effect within the mix, spreading knowledge and resources and reducing the risks of leaving home.[9]

The exact timing and conditions under which different sending societies and receiving locales were integrated into transoceanic and transcontinental circuits differed importantly. For the moment, what I want to emphasize is that along with other communities across the Americas and across the world, Afro-descended communities felt the impact of these macro-level shifts and were active participants in similar responses: they started to move. Viewed from this vantage point, the making of the circum-Caribbean migratory sphere traced in this book; the Great Migration of southern Afro-Americans to northern cities; the mass migrations within Africa toward new mining enterprises in the south; and the movement of rural Afro-Brazilians into São Paulo, Rio de Janeiro, and other cities were all small pieces of the same bigger story.

These migrations brought individuals from disparate communities of African ancestry into direct contact with others of the same, making both their divergences and their commonalities visible in stark new ways. We have seen multiple examples of the recognition of the commonalities of black subordination from place to place. We have also seen the recognition of commonalities in the realm of quotidian cultural practice, as when Vincentians in Panama and Trinidad found themselves in demand as obeah practitioners because the specialized knowledge they possessed was recognized by locals as knowledge worth having.

But resemblance is not identity. Rather, people found enough common-ality for mutual comprehension and enough difference to demonstrate the importance of innovation and local pasts. As noted in chapter 2, scholars' models for explaining Afro-diasporic cultures have tended to emphasize either shared cultural heritage (roots), intradiasporic connection (routes), or the common experience of racist oppression. The history I have recounted suggests the answer is not either-or, but all-because. The genuine resonance between traditions made reencounter generative. Outside racism encouraged collective identification; cultural content re/generated together meant that collective identification drew on more that just common oppression. Think back to the Brooklyn fête where domestics and elevator operators from across the Caribbean ate patties and paylou and danced to Wilmoth Houdini; or to the British Caribbean migrant glimpsed on the streets of Colón, teaching an English-speaking child to dance the Afro-Panamanian *tamborito*; or to Joe Louis fans from Costa Rica and West Virginia encountering each other in the pages of the *Pittsburgh Courier*.

In primary accounts of that era by participants from all shores of the Greater Caribbean, both similarities and differences, commonality and cre-ativity are noted. It is all the more striking, then, that scholarship by outsiders from that era forward—such as the writings of Melville Herskovits, who com-pleted his dissertation at Columbia three years before the *tamborito* vignette and published *Life in a Haitian Valley* two years before Houdini entertained Brooklyn—has tended to stress only one or the other: common ancestry or creativity, African survivals or American creolization.[10]

Furthermore, alongside their recognition of commonalities and differ-ences of culture, black people on the move also recognized commonalities and differences in their social and political situations. Volumes could be written about the assessments of the comparative politics of race written by people of color in the interwar era. Recent scholars have written several and still only scratched the surface.[11] Tito Achong was engaged in just this kind of comparative political analysis when he informed his fellow Port of Spain councilors that "Venezuelans were citizens of Venezuela, whether white or black. A West Indian must be a negro with no rights."[12] And he was simply one among countless many whose comparisons entered the written record, and one among scores of thousands making such comparisons in the course of daily debate. The comparative moment echoed through the circum-Caribbean press, as we have seen at length. "Negro race, look around and see and listen of what is taking place in other countries with us," wrote T. L. N. Gayle in the *Searchlight* in 1930. "Men and women, open your eyes."[13]

In sum, secondary migrations accelerated across the African diaspora in the first decades of the twentieth century, as the descendants of freedpeople moved into economic spaces that Asian migrants were now banned from entering. As reencounter in distant lands made possible the recognition of commonality and difference, this moment gave rise to a surge of thinking about the oneness of people of African ancestry. Vernacular analyses of the comparative politics of race were a key part of that process. This book has looked at imaginings of the African diaspora that emerged from one subsystem within a world on the move. Others may have been similar, or very different. Conceptions of "Negro" universality emerged from multiple particular histories that we have only begun to explore.

POPULAR CULTURE IN THE MAKING
OF THE AFRICAN DIASPORA

The account above suggests that periodic moments of intentional "diasporization" (to use Frank Guridy's term) rest on substrate of popular culture, within which the quotidian practices, cosmologies, and self-concepts of Afro-descended people from distant lands turn out to have a family resemblance that makes possible both recognition and reworking. But that popular cultural substrate is not in any simple sense the holdover of a common African past. Rather, it is the evolving outcome of repeated reencounter and creation, the latter sometimes the work of anonymous thousands and sometimes of one individual touched by God or genius. Moreover, that substrate has been shaped not only by periods of intense interchange but also by eras of isolation or marginalization. The geography of connection has changed over time; and indeed, some places in some times have been frankly disconnected, and for knowable historical reasons. The history of black peoples in the Western Hemisphere has been a history of dislocation but also a history of location, and sometimes forced localization. Barriers as much as border crossings have sparked the cultural creativity of ordinary people in challenging times.

We see this exemplified in the history of Rastafarianism, a product of extremes of international travel and insular isolation. Rastafarianism would not have been created as it was had Arthur Ford not gone from Barbados to Harlem to meet the son of a Falashan Jew and Nevisian mother and become a Commandment Keeper; had David and Annie Harvey not followed Rabbi Ford to Addis Ababa; had Fitz Ballantine Pettersburgh not heard the ideas of Lothrop Stoddard in Panama or New York and agreed that "white supremacy" was menaced by "black supremacy" rising. But Rastafarianism also would not have evolved as it did had the rise of restrictionism not sent thousands of sufferers back to Kingston from Cuba, or had the hostility of colonial elites not sent Leonard Howell's core followers back into the hills, where the faith grew among peasants whose possible routes to foreign were blocked.

Or consider the ebbs and flows of music in the Greater Caribbean. We watched as jazz, *son*, and mento reverberated between Harlem, Havana, and Colón in the interwar years. Two decades later, the reencounter between Jamaican popular music and U.S. rhythm and blues created ska. A new generation of Caribbean youth carving space from a disapproving society would dance to ska at the same kinds of weekly dances known as regge dances in Costa Rica a generation before. Moving through a Kingston soundscape infused by the kumina drumming that Rastafarianism had revitalized, in the hands of Bob Marley and others whom Rastafarian ideology had shaped, ska was transformed into the explicitly black-internationalist music now known as roots reggae. Recordings in turn carried reggae outward to sites of diasporic reencounter, from East London to Maranhão to Soweto. These were profoundly cosmopolitan peripheries whose popular cultures reflected the syncopated alternation of mobility and immobilization. With good reason, reggae was recognizable.

The descendants of enslaved Africans in the Americas have broadly shared experiences of both displacement and placement, as imposed by European expansion and then by the transition of empires, by the growth of modern states and then the growth of social citizenship within them—all processes that people of African ancestry have been both systematically engaged with and systematically excluded from. From stories of wealthy Caribbeans stealing poor people's children to use their body fat to ensure racing success, to stories of black bodies ground up to make manure for twentieth-century agrobusiness, popular beliefs have provided ongoing commentary on the evolving world system. Showing how personal destinies entwine with international political economy, such rumors wrote global history from below *avant la lettre*.[14] Religion, music, and rumors stand alongside vernacular analyses of the comparative politics of race as components of interwar black internationalism. If we have seen claims of race-based solidarity constantly complicated by divisions of class, we have also seen the mutual dependence of respectable and popular cultures of black internationalism: Garvey defining his own proper Christianity in opposition to "religions that howl," sons of Barbadian Brooklyn turning piano lessons into funky jazz, the King of Kings Mission reading the *Pittsburgh Courier* aloud for hidden truths.

Abstract nouns like "retention," "acculturation," and "transculturation" can obscure the role of self-aware culture creators in fusing elements they understood to be from different roots into new practices. Similarly, to talk in terms of middle-class "appropriation" of popular culture, or to contrast "assimilation" to "resistance," risks obscuring the role of intentional actors on all sides. In the Caribbean, at least, the cultures of the respectable middle classes and the cultures of the less-literate masses developed in tandem—at times borrowing from each other, at times condemning each other, and at times even celebrating each other. The debates over difference and sameness that scholars now see as central to the generation of African diasporaness occurred across borders of birthplace, language, and citizenship.[15] But they also occurred across borders of class: between youths of the "regge class" and their respectable elders; between those who believed their children menaced by witches and those who questioned such convictions in court. Interwar black internationalisms responded to racism from without. But they also responded to the sometimes conflictive, sometimes collaborative class-bound politics of culture.

A final story. I visited El Callao in the summer of 2010, driven south from Ciudad Bolivar by a Venezuelan man named Chete, one of this world's great storytellers. Chete's grandmother was a black woman from the island of Margarita who ran her Lebanese paramour's store in Guasipati with unerring tally marks. Chete's other grandfather was a Corsican merchant who married a shy young Venezuelan and made the most of every opportunity that the Orinoco offered. In El Callao, we found Father Adams Delgado, the local Anglican priest and the great-grandson of Martinican and Trinidadian immigrants. The two men had never met but got on famously. At one point, I asked Father Adams about Marcus Garvey and the UNIA. "It wasn't some kind of fight between races," he hurried to explain (we were speaking Spanish). "It was to maintain the culture, the language." He turned to Chete. "You should have heard those old men who met over there at the 'Black Star Light.' Why, they could tell you exactly where in Africa you came from, just by looking at the shape of your nose!" "No!" said Chete, impressed, and the two went off in gales of laughter.

There are many different ways of thinking about roots, and routes, and race. These days, North American academics find it useful to describe race as a social construct. The idea of race as a physical inheritance smacks of the biological essentialism used to justify the worst violence of the twentieth century. College professors these days do not look at people's noses and tell them where in Africa they came from. But really, who are we to say? The Caribbean immigrants who founded a UNIA chapter in El Callao in the early 1920s took Garvey's message of personal pride in African heritage and used it in a way that made sense to them. Today, Chete, son of the Corsican, Lebanese, and African diasporas, thinks of himself as "one hundred per cent Venezuelan," and Father Adams, grandson of the circum-Caribbean migratory sphere, thinks of himself as no less so. Their mutual delight in the "Black Star Light" experts confounds every analytic frame I have to offer—which is as it should be.

Notes

INTRODUCTION

1. Marable, *Life of Malcolm X*, 16, 20–32; Carew, *Ghosts in Our Blood*, 121–33. Louise had one more child after Earl's death.

2. Adi and Sherwood, *Pan-African History*.

3. Ottley, *New World*, 103–4. Emphasis in original. Similarly, see discussion of nationalism and "Pan-Nationalism" in Allen, "New Negro."

4. E.g., Hubert Harrison, "Wanted: A Colored International," *Negro World*, 1921, rpt. in Perry, *Hubert Harrison*, 223–28; Kelley, "Black History's Global Vision"; Kelley

and Patterson, "Unfinished Migrations"; Dawahare, *Nationalism, Marxism, and African American Literature*; Stephens, *Black Empire*; and West and Martin, "Contours of the Black International."

5. Recent syntheses that provide the bases for such analyses include Andrews, *Afro-Latin America*, and Manning, *African Diaspora*.

6. Anderson, *Imagined Communities*, 6.

7. Important discussions of the term and its usage include Drake, "Diaspora Studies and Pan-Africanism," and Moses, "Introduction."

8. James, *Holding Aloft*; Edwards, *Practice of Diaspora*; Pennybacker, *From Scottsboro to Munich*; Makalani, *Cause of Freedom*.

9. I am grateful to Oyebade Dosunmu for insisting on this point. Recent works that center on nonmetropolitan subfields of this phenomenon include Seigel, *Uneven Encounters*; Guridy, *Forging Diaspora*; Prais, "Imperial Travelers"; and James, "Culture, Labor, and Race."

10. Carnegie, "Reaching for the Border," v–ix.

11. Marshall, *Citizenship and Social Class*. See elaborations in Bosniak, *Citizen and the Alien*, and Fahrmeir, *Citizenship*.

12. See among many Bergquist, *Labor in Latin America*; Collier and Collier, *Shaping the Political Arena*; Moore, *Nationalizing Blackness*; de la Fuente, *Nation for All*; Appelbaum, Macpherson, and Rosemblatt, *Race and Nation*; Bronfman, *Measures of Equality*; Andrews, *Afro-Latin America*; and Alberto, *Terms of Inclusion*. For nuanced discussions of the complexity and diversity of populism, see Skurski, "Ambiguities of Authenticity," and McGillivray, *Blazing Cane*.

13. Vallenilla Lanz, "Disgregación e Integración," 325, 326. On the contradictions of scientific racism in interwar Latin America, see Stepan, *Hour of Eugenics*.

14. Critical thinking about how to define the "African diaspora" and how the history of that continuously remade "place" and/or "people" might be written has been a precocious and rich subset of that broader disciplinary effort. Important elaborations include Palmer, "Defining and Studying"; Kelley, "'But a Local Phase'"; Kelley and Patterson, "Unfinished Migrations"; Bennett, "Subject in the Plot"; and Manning, "Africa and the African Diaspora." See also Putnam, "To Study the Fragments/Whole."

15. Similarly, see discussions in Fink, *Workers across the Americas*; and Kramer, "Power and Connection," esp. 1353.

16. Prior to my findings from the English-language press of 1930 Port Limón, the earliest print trace of the term "reggae" or "reggay" in reference to popular music or dance that scholars had found dated from Jamaica in 1968. I make no claim that the musical genre known as reggae had its roots in Port Limón. But I do argue below that my findings offer a plausible new hypothesis for the etymology of the term itself.

17. Gilroy, *Black Atlantic*; Edwards, *Practice of Diaspora*; Stephens, *Black Empire*; Luis-Brown, *Waves of Decolonization*.

18. Turner and Turner, *Richard B. Moore*; James, *Holding Aloft*; Taylor, *Veiled Garvey*; Lee, *First Rasta*; Schwarz, *West Indian Intellectuals*; Turner, *Caribbean Crusaders*; Davies, *Left of Karl Marx*; Pennybacker, *From Scottsboro to Munich*; Chude-Sokei, *The Last "Darky"*; Parascandola, *Look for Me*; Chude Sokei, "Foreign Negro Flash Agents"; and, more broadly, West, Martin, and Wilkins, *Toussaint to Tupac*.

19. See Kelley, "Afric's Sons"; Lewis, *W. E. B. Du Bois*; Adi, "Negro Question"; Makalani, *Cause of Freedom*; and McDuffie, *Sojourning for Freedom*.

20. E.g., W. E. B. Du Bois, "A Lunatic or a Traitor," *The Crisis* 28, no. 1 (May 1924): 8–9; Perry, *Hubert Harrison*, 194–99; McKay, *Harlem*, 143–80; Moore, "Critics and Opponents."

21. Key titles include Martin, *Race First*; Lewis and Bryan, *Garvey*; Lewis, *Marcus Garvey*; and Vincent, *Black Power and the Garvey Movement*. Works that approached Garvey from a less politically engaged perspective include Cronon, *Black Moses*, and Stein, *World of Marcus Garvey*.

22. E.g., Rolinson, *Grassroots Garveyism*; Giovannetti and Roman, "Garveyism in the Hispanic Caribbean"; West, "Seeds Are Sown"; Macpherson, "Colonial Matriarchs"; Dalrymple, "In the Shadow of Garvey"; Shakes, *76 King Street*; Sullivan, "No Surrender."

23. Calculated from Martin, *Race First*, 15–16. On Trinidad as a receiving society, see chapter 1.

24. Hill, *Garvey and UNIA Papers*, vol. 11, lxii.

25. Ibid., lxxxix.

26. Ibid., lxxxvi.

27. Proudfoot, *Population Movements*; Roberts, *Population of Jamaica*. Early contributions also included histories written "from within" by second-generation community leaders to educate Spanish-speaking fellow citizens: Westerman, *Inmigrantes antillanos*, and Duncan, "Negro antillano." Subsequent region-wide overviews include Thomas-Hope, "Establishment of a Migration Tradition"; Marshall, "History of West Indian Migrations"; Petras, *Jamaican Labor Migration*; Richardson, "Caribbean Migrations"; and Richardson, "Migration Experience."

28. Newton, *Silver Men*; Richardson, *Panama Money*; Bourgois, *Ethnicity at Work*; Greene, *Canal Builders*; O'Reggio, *Between Alienation and Citizenship*; Corinealdi, "Redefining Home."

29. Palmer, "*What Happen*"; Chomsky, *West Indian Workers*; Harpelle, *West Indians of Costa Rica*; Putnam, *Company They Kept*.

30. Gordon, *Disparate Diasporas*; Opie, *Black Labor Migration*; Chambers, *Race, Nation, and West Indian Immigration*; Colby, *Business of Empire*.

31. See the as-yet-unpublished dissertations of Cadence Wynter, Marc McLeod, Jorge Giovannetti, Audrey Charlton, and Frances Peace Sullivan; see also Maughan, "Some Aspects of Barbadian Emigration," and Carr, "Identity, Class, and Nation." Further research on Cuba and other circum-Caribbean destinations appears in preliminary or excerpted form in various publications organized by Annette Insanally of the UWI Latin American-Caribbean Centre, Mona, Jamaica.

32. Watkins-Owens, *Blood Relations*; James, *Holding Aloft*.

33. Caribbean immigration is covered in the context of the oil boom in Tinker Salas, *Enduring Legacy*, and is discussed at several points in Wright, *Café con leche*. Nineteenth-century migration from Trinidad to Venezuela is the subject of Michael Toussaint's unpublished Ph.D. dissertation (University of the West Indies at St. Augustine). See also Molina Duarte, "Impacto cultural y socioeconómico," and Ferreira, "History and Future of Patuá."

34. Chamberlain, *Caribbean Migration*; Puri, *Marginal Migrations*; Carnegie and Martinez, "Crossing Borders of Language and Culture"; quote in Carnegie, "Reaching for the Border," vi.

35. Brubaker, "Immigration, Citizenship"; Wimmer and Schiller, "Methodological Nationalism"; Torpey, *Invention of the Passport*; Ngai, *Impossible Subjects*; Zolberg, *Nation by Design*. Among recent work, see especially Erman, "Puerto Rico and the Promise of United States Citizenship."

36. Tabili, *"We Ask for British Justice"*; Gilroy, *Ain't No Black*; Paul, *Whitewashing Britain*; Lake and Reynolds, *Global Colour Line*; Brown, *Dropping Anchor, Setting Sail*.

37. Fahrmeir, Faron, and Weil, *Migration Control*; again, Lake and Reynolds, *Global Colour Line*; McKeown, *Melancholy Order*; Fahrmeir, *Citizenship*; Ueda, "State Development and International Migration"; Cook-Martín and FitzGerald, "Liberalism and the Limits"; Hoerder and Gabaccia, *Connecting Seas*.

38. Hammar, *European Immigration Policy*; Hahamovitch, *Fruits of Their Labor*; Hahamovitch, *No Man's Land*.

39. McKay, "Mattie and Her Sweetman," in *Gingertown*, 63–64.

CHAPTER ONE

1. Barry, *Venezuela*, 10–11; Verrill, *Book of the West Indies*, 144, 130 (quote).

2. Wickham, *Rough Notes*, 22.

3. Brereton, *History of Modern Trinidad*, 32–51; Toussaint, "George Numa Dessources"; Tinker Salas, *Enduring Legacy*, 109–10; Dalton, *Venezuela*, 189; André, *Naturalist in the Guianas*, 34, 40–44, 61, 64–67, 75; "Güiria Opened to Trade," *Port of Spain Commercial Review* 1, no. 3 (February 1904): 3.

4. Dalton, *Venezuela*, 216–17; André, *Naturalist in the Guianas*, 50–53; "The Gold Mines of Venezuela," *Engineering and Mining Journal* 38 (July-December 1884): 380; Great Britain, Foreign Office, "Report for 1886 on . . . the Mines of Yuruary," 14; Great Britain, West India Royal Commission, *Report of the West India Royal Commission*, 50; Roberts, *Population of Jamaica*, 331.

5. CO 295/423, Correspondence with Foreign Office, etc., on matters relating to Trinidad: Venezuelan Claims: Confidential, Letter from G. Craven, El Callao, to FO, June 22, 1903; letter, Aug. 3, 1903; CO 295/443, Correspondence with Foreign Office, etc., Report from C. H. de Lemos, British consul, Caracas, Mar. 30, 1907.

6. CO 295/423, Correspondence with Foreign Office, etc., on matters relating to Trinidad: Venezuelan Claims: Confidential, Aug. 12, 1903, Section 1; Sept. 22, 1903, Section 4; Oct. 8, 1903, Section 1; Sept. 24, 1903, Section 6. Author's analysis, AHS, Gaveta 28, B72: Cédulas de Identidad, Registros de Extranjeros; Gaveta 23, B37: Cédulas de Identidad, Registro de Extranjeros (1932); Gaveta 22, B32: Cédulas de Extranjeros (1932), including full sets for *distritos* Arismendi, Mejías, Benítez, Rivero, Mariño.

7. Thomas-Hope, "Establishment of a Migration Tradition"; Petras, *Jamaican Labor Migration*; Richardson, "Caribbean Migrations"; Putnam, "Eventually Alien."

8. Richardson, *Panama Money*; Newton, *Silver Men*.

9. Maughan, "Some Aspects of Barbadian Emigration"; Richardson, *Panama Money*, 101; Brereton, *History of Modern Trinidad*, 97; Barbados, *Report on the Census, 1911–1921*, 23.

10. "Intercolonial Passenger Traffic," *Port of Spain Daily Mirror*, Nov. 7, 1904, 7; Brereton, *History of Modern Trinidad*, 97.

11. Ford and Cundall, *Handbook of Jamaica*, 432.

12. Adams, *Conquest of the Tropics*, 69–97; "Caribbean Markets for American Goods," *Panama Times*, Apr. 10, 1926.

13. Roberts, *Population of Jamaica*, 139; Eisner, *Jamaica, 1830–1930*, 150–51.

14. Giovannetti, "Black British Caribbean Migrants"; Giovannetti, "Caribbean Migration"; Charlton, "Cat Born in Oven"; *The Canal Record*, Oct. 28, 1914, 91.

15. Calculated from Cuba, *Informe y movimiento de pasajeros*, 1916 and 1917.

16. Proudfoot, *Population Movements*, 79; Charlton, "Cat Born in Oven," 31–33 et passim; McLeod, "Undesirable Aliens," 80–86; Casey, "Haitian Migrants in Cuba."

17. James, *Holding Aloft*, 356–57; "Jamaicans in Cuba," *Kingston Daily Gleaner*, Aug. 20, 1919, 13.

18. Marshall, *Triangular Road*, 52–66; Marshall, *Brown Girl, Brownstones*; U.S. Census 1930, Brooklyn Borough, Enumeration District 24-109, Sheet 11B.

19. Barbados, *Report of the Census of Barbados*, 13.

20. See table 1.

21. Roberts, *Population of Jamaica*, 131; Kuczynski, *Demographic Survey*, 341.

22. Kuczynski, *Demographic Survey*, 341, 156.

23. Dalton, *Venezuela*, 216–17; Molina, "Impacto Cultural"; CO 318/406/1, Immigration of British West Indians in Central and South America (1932); CO 318/417/6, Treatment of British West Indians in Venezuela: Claims for Compensation (1935).

24. "The Asphalt Lake in Venezuela," *New York Times*, Feb. 17, 1901, 14; Tinker Salas, *Enduring Legacy*, 41–43, 110–13, 131–33.

25. U.S. Bureau of the Census, *Census of the United States, 1930*, vol. 2, 231, 33. These numbers exclude immigrants from Cuba and Puerto Rico but include other Spanish- and French-speaking islands.

26. U.S. Bureau of the Census, *Census of the United States, 1930*, vol. 2, 33, 70-71, 250.

27. Data on island origin here and below is drawn from the electronic databases for the 1920 and 1930 censuses at Ancestry.com, but this data—although unique of its kind and therefore invaluable—needs to be treated with caution. Census takers sometimes wrote down specific islands of origin, but often they simply used collective labels (most often "British West Indian"). Patterns in this tendency to "lump" may have varied by island of origin and/or changed over time. Kuczynski, *Colonial Population*, 19.

28. "A Postal Matter," *Barbados Weekly Herald*, Apr. 11, 1925, 5.

29. See table 1.

30. Author's analysis of 1930 census database via Ancestry.com. See methodological caveats in note 27 of this chapter.

31. Domingo, "Tropics in New York," 648.

32. AHS, Gaveta 3, A 14: (1916) Various: "Asunto de los súbditos ingleses Pedro y Lazaro Marin, trabajadores en la explotación del mangle en la isla Turuépano."

33. Archivo Histórico de Guayana, Documentos 1928, 6.1.3.6: Correspondencia al Secretario General del Gobierno, 1928.

34. McKay, *Gingertown*, 172, 200, 222, 233.

35. "Six Weeks in Trinidad," *Port of Spain Daily Mirror*, Nov. 22, 1904, 11.

36. Richardson, *Panama Money*, 142.

37. Walrond, "Consulate," orig. pub. *The Spectator*, 1936, in Parascandola, *Winds Can Wake Up the Dead*, 306.

38. Fletcher, "Friendly Societies"; Fletcher, "Decline of Friendly Societies"; "J.B.S.S. Supreme Council Hold Convention," *Kingston Daily Gleaner*, Mar. 15, 1937, 23.

39. Putnam, "'Nothing Matters but Color'"; Giovannetti, "Elusive Organization of 'Identity'"; Sullivan, "No Surrender"; Charlton, "Cat Born in Oven," 341–58.

40. Martin, *Race First*, 16; Hill, *Garvey and UNIA Papers*, vol. 7, 997–1000; ibid., vol. 1, 74.

41. "Memos of the Month," *All the World*, October 1918, 459; "Memos of the Month," *All the World*, September 1918, 413; "The Territorial Commander in Cuba: Enthusiastic Welcome," *West Indies War Cry*, April 1919, 3.

42. "Cuba: A Small Beginning in a Great Island," *All the World*, July-August-September 1922, 361.

43. "News from San Domingo," *All the World*, November 1928, 456; "Splendid Opening of Republic of San Domingo: General Secretary Dedicates New Corps," *West Indies War Cry*, September 1928, 4.

44. Tinker Salas, *Enduring Legacy*, 113–15; Putnam, "Work, Sex, and Power"; Putnam, *Company They Kept*.

45. Putnam, "Contact Zones"; Putnam, "Undone by Desire."

46. Bryan, *Jamaican People*; Chamberlain, *Family Love*; Putnam, "Work, Sex, and Power."

47. LJca, vol. Portland, Respondent 33Pfc Grange Hill, "This Day They Say Is Modern Day," 2.

48. LJca, vol. St. Catherine, Respondent 49StcFb Orangefield, "Aunt Dore," 3, 10–11.

49. RG84Jca, Entry 2821, Box 2: Correspondence, American Consulate, Kingston, 1936. Letter from Charles Mundy, New Orleans, La., Jan. 9, 1936.

50. Ibid.

51. Putnam, "Eventually Alien," 284–88.

52. AGNJust, Tomo CCCXCVI (1849), no. 14, "Una nota irrespetuosa del cónsul británico hacia el Gobernador de Guayana," folios 70–74.

53. "The Venezuelan Brief," *New York Times*, July 21, 1896, 1.

54. AGNJust, Tomo CDXXVII (1850), no. 18, "Como consecuencia de la afluencia de extrangeros en el cantón de Upata, ocasionado por el descubrimiento de una mina de oro en Yuruari, el Gobernador de la provincia de Guayana establece un Juzgado parroquial en Tupuquén. Ciudad Bolívar, 8 de julio de 1850," folio 122.

55. See Palmerston's handwritten notes, accessed via http://www.broadlands archives.com/palmerston-papers-of-a-prime-minister-and-foreign-secretary/.

56. Great Britain, Parliament, *Hansard* CXII [3d Ser.], 380–444: "Palmerston's speech on affairs in Greece (25 June 1850)." Accessed via http://www.historyhome .co.uk/polspeech/foreign.htm.

57. Ibid.

58. Brown, *Palmerston*, 12.

59. "Note of protest from Her Majesty's chargé d'affairs in Venezuela . . . to the Secretary of State for Foreign Affairs . . . Caracas, Aug. 14, 1850," transcribed in Spanish in Arreaza Arana and Blanco, "Relaciones Diplomáticas," 59. My translation into English.

60. E.g., AGNJust, Tomo DCCCLXXIX, no. 18, "Datos sin firma para el ministro del Interior y Justicia. Sobre algunas observaciones para la realización de un plan referente a la civilización de las tribus de indígenas en el Estado Guayana. Caracas, 3 de febrero de 1874," folios 96–97. On similar dynamics in the frontier region between Costa Rica and Panama, see Boza and Solórzano, "Estado nacional"; for the (Anglophone Caribbean) Colombian island of San Andrés, see Crawford, "Under the Colombian Flag."

61. "The Venezuelan Brief."

62. Ibid.

63. Barry, *Venezuela*, 56.

64. Ibid., 72.

65. "The Venezuela Boundary Question," *Kingston Daily Gleaner*, Mar. 10, 1888, 6.

66. AGNJust, Tomo MCI (1884), no. 4, "Documento que refiere asesinato de súbditos ingleses en Venezuela," folio 108. Translation of article from *Port of Spain Gazette*, May 17, 1884. My retranslation.

67. Barry, *Venezuela*, 118.

68. "The Venezuela Boundary Question."

69. Barry, *Venezuela*, 56.

70. CO 295/423, Correspondence with Foreign Office, etc., on matters relating to Trinidad: Venezuelan Claims: Confidential: Letter from Herbert Harrison, British Mixed Commission representative, Caracas, to FO, May 26, 1903; RelExtAA vol. 128 (Gran Bretaña), "Gestiones y Reclamaciones de Gran Bretana 1904–1906," folios 49–96: "La misma [legación] se queja en favor de ingleses a causa del mal tratamiento de la Compañía minera El Callao Gold Mining Company."

71. Seymour, *Ups and Downs*, 218.

72. Dalton, *Venezuela*, 217.

73. RelExtAA, vol. 129 (Gran Bretaña), "Gestiones y Reclamaciones de Gran Bretana 1906–1908," folios 49–96: "La misma [legación] se queja en favor de ingleses a causa del mal tratamiento de la Compañía minera El Callao Gold Mining Company." The workers made multiple references to the fact that the passports they had received with the governor's signature before departure bore language entitling them to the full protection of Great Britain abroad.

74. RelExtAA, vol. 129 (Gran Bretaña), "Gestiones y Reclamaciones de Gran Bretana 1906–1908," folios 49–96: Letter from Bax-Ironsides, British Minister, to

Ministro de Relaciones Exteriores, Nov. 26, 1906. He also urged "mining authorities" to repatriate the particular workers who claimed deceptive contracting.

75. RelExtAA, vol. 129 (Gran Bretaña), "Gestiones y Reclamaciones de Gran Bretana 1906–1908," folios 49–96: Copy of letter from Murray, Stapleton, and others to Clifford, Sept. 29, 1906.

76. CO 295/443, Correspondence with Foreign Office, etc., on matters relating to Trinidad: Letter from FO to Bax Ironside, British Minister Caracas, Mar. 25, 1907.

77. CO 295/443, Correspondence with Foreign Office, etc., on matters relating to Trinidad: Report from C. H. de Lemos, Consul at Ciudad Bolívar, Mar. 30, 1907.

78. CO 295/443, Correspondence with Foreign Office, etc., on matters relating to Trinidad: Letter from C. H. de Lemos, Consul at Ciudad Bolívar, Jan. 4, 1907. See also RelExtAA, vol. 129 (Gran Bretaña), "Gestiones y Reclamaciones de Gran Bretana 1906–1908," folios 49–96: Letter from Gobernador del Territorio Federal Yurari to Ministro de Relaciones Exteriores, Dec. 3, 1906.

79. CO 295/423, Correspondence with Foreign Office, etc., on matters relating to Trinidad: Venezuelan Claims: Confidential: Aug. 3, 1903, Section 4. Letter from Mellor, Caracas, to FO, July 9, 1903.

80. CO 295/423, Correspondence with Foreign Office, etc., on matters relating to Trinidad: Venezuelan Claims: Confidential: Sept. 24, 1903, Section 2. Letter from Bax Ironside, British Minister, Caracas, to Venezuelan government, Aug. 28, 1903.

81. Ibid. See also RelExtAA, vol. 127 (Gran Bretaña), "Gestiones y Reclamaciones de Gran Bretana 1902–1903," "Gestiones de la Legación en pro de súbditos ingleses," folios 143–208; and "La Legación hace observaciones respeto del Decreto del 17 de abril sobre extranjeros residentes en Venezuela," folios 209–31.

82. CO 323/634, Correspondence from Foreign Office to Colonial Office, 1914: Letter from Frederic Harford, Caracas, to FO, Apr. 7, 1914. The consul at Cumaná instructed British subjects of whom registry had been demanded "on no account to sign the declaration, or to offer a certificate of good conduct." The Foreign Office instructed the governors of all the British insular colonies to warn intending emigrants that they must carry proofs of identity to enter Venezuela, but that they should not cede to demands for certificates of good conduct and should sign no declarations ceding their right to British protection. CO 323/634, Correspondence from Foreign Office to Colonial Office, 1914, "Venezuelan Law on Foreigners," May 28, 1914.

83. RelextAA, vol. 129 (Gran Bretaña), "Gestiones y Reclamaciones de Gran Bretana 1906–1908," "La misma [legación] se queja en favor de ingleses a causa del mal tratamiento de la Compañía minera El Callao Gold Mining Company," folio 68.

84. E.g., "24th MAY," *Limón Searchlight*, May 31, 1930, 1; Giovannetti, unpublished ms.; Charlton, "Cat Born in Oven," 328.

85. Gómez, *Poder andino*, 128.

86. CO 318/442/8, Treatment of British West Indians in Venezuela—Compensation Claims: Hand-written report by doctor F. H. Leekam, Dec. 16, 1939, re: examination of Joseph Mitchell, age 49, on Dec. 13, 1939.

87. AHS, Gaveta 3, A12: Various, 1915, "Reclamaciones de varios súbditos británicos." My translation.

CHAPTER TWO

1. Chevannes, *Rastafari*, 91.

2. "Shouters' Meeting," *Port of Spain Weekly Guardian*, Mar. 20, 1920, 7.

3. James, *Mulberry Tree*, 277; Adams, *Conquest of the Tropics*, 192; Bury, *Bishop amongst Bananas*, 110.

4. Bury, *Bishop amongst Bananas*, 44–45.

5. Letter to the editor signed by Marcus M. Garvey, *Times*, Mar. 17, 1911. See Hill, *Garvey and UNIA Papers*, vol. 11, 9–24. Garvey described U.S. evangelist Charles Taze Russell as "unlike the Bedward of Jamaica, possess[ing] sufficient intelligence as to cause serious tro[uble] among the people who hap[pen] to come in contact with his [dis]gusting disciples." (The intercalation of "[not]" in the *Garvey and UNIA Papers* transcription of this sentence is incorrect.)

6. "All you Barbadians always want to put more interpretations upon the Scriptures and that's why those prophets live down there in that way." "Religion in Woodbrook," *Port of Spain Weekly Guardian*, July 31, 1920, 12.

7. For instance, Marcus Garvey in an anodyne 1914 publication praised the Jamaican churches as "the living voices of the classes as well as the masses." Marcus Garvey, "The Evolution of Latter Day Slaves," *The Tourist*, 1914, rpt. in Hill, *Garvey and UNIA Papers*, vol. 1, 43. In a more radical day, he said of Jesus that "when the masses indicated they would follow Him, the classes who always rule said that He was a disturber of the peace." "Christ the Greatest Reformer," speech delivered at Liberty Hall, New York, Dec. 1922, rpt. in Garvey, *Philosophy and Opinions*, 28, 29. A commentator in 1930 Limón lauded a recent UNIA event as reminiscent of the "good old days when the associates of the Organization were men & women of the classes not the masses of the Negro race." "A Reception Banquet, and an Evening at Home," *Limón Searchlight*, June 7, 1930, 3. No doubt the "men and women of the classes" who formed the UNIA aristocracy of Port Limón would have been soundly snubbed by "the classes" of Kingston. "The classes" and "the masses" are vernacular labels that capture perceived relational status rather than objective position.

8. "Tobago: Scarborough Police Court: The Mount Marie Obeah Case," *Port of Spain Daily Mirror*, Nov. 2, 1904, 13.

9. Butler, Wacker, and Balmer, *Religion in American Life*, 39; Latimer, "Foundations of Religious Education," 91–98.

10. Hunte, "Protestantism and Slavery," 102–15; Da Costa, *Crowns of Glory, Tears of Blood*; Turner, *Slaves and Missionaries*.

11. Brereton, *History of Modern Trinidad*, 67–68.

12. Stewart, *Religion and Society*, xvii.

13. Ibid., 107–52; *West Indian Census of 1946*, 42; Schuler, *Alas, Alas, Kongo*.

14. Trotman, "Yoruba and Orisha Worship"; Houk, *Spirits, Blood, and Drums*, 47–70; Henry, *Reclaiming African Religions*, 1–29.

15. Stewart, *Religion and Society*, 139.

16. Austin-Broos, *Jamaica Genesis*, 51–92; Moore and Johnson, *Neither Led nor Driven*, 51–95; Chevannes, *Rastafari*, 17–37.

17. Henry, *Reclaiming African Religions*, 30–48.

18. Underhill, *West Indies*, 47; Hunte, "Protestantism and Slavery," 111.

19. Houk, *Spirits, Blood, and Drums*, 73–74; Henry, *Reclaiming African Religions*, 32–33.

20. "Police Court: Larceny of a Petticoat," *Port of Spain Daily Mirror*, Nov. 3, 1904, 15; "Shouters' Meeting," *Port of Spain Weekly Guardian*, Aug. 7, 1920, 12; "Shouters' Meeting," *Port of Spain Weekly Guardian*, Mar. 20, 1920, 7.

21. *West Indian Census of 1946*, 36–39.

22. Bury, *Bishop amongst Bananas*, 36 et passim, 167–81; Thompson, *Into All Lands*, 516–17.

23. Thompson, *Into All Lands*, 526–27.

24. Personal collection of Father Adams Delgado, El Callao, Venezuela, and personal interview, July 30, 2010.

25. Grubb, *Religion in Central America*, 39, 86, 112–13.

26. And yet even they could run into trouble. "The Salvation Army," *Port of Spain Daily Mirror*, Oct. 20, 1904, 10.

27. E.g., Col. F. W. Pearce, "The Isles of the Sea: The Army's Work in the West Indies," *All the World*, January 1913, 42; and "Jamaica and the Isthmus Zone," *All the World*, June 1913, 367–70. For similar patterns among Adventists, see *Caribbean Watchman*, vol. 1, no. 1, June 1903.

28. "Cuba: A Small Beginning in a Great Island," *All the World*, July-August-September 1922, 361; "News from San Domingo," *All the World*, November 1928, 456; "Splendid Opening of Republic of San Domingo," *West Indies War Cry*, September 1928, 4. Similarly, see Charlton, "Cat Born in Oven," 240–42, 291, 360–61, 366–67.

29. Austin-Broos, *Jamaica Genesis*, 93–116; Richardson, *Panama Money*, 97; Beckles, *History of Barbados*, 153–54.

30. Henry J. Randall's unpublished memoir, "Banks of the Mighty Orinoco," as quoted in Lewis, *Orinoco!*, 65.

31. "The Preaching Craze," *Port of Spain Weekly Guardian*, Jan. 31, 1920, 9.

32. ANCR, Limón Juzgado Civil 103 (separación de bienes, 1902).

33. Cited in Moore and Johnson, *Neither Led nor Driven*, 83.

34. Cited in Austin-Broos, *Jamaica Genesis*, 86.

35. Craine, *Cruise of Port Kingston*, 91–101 (quote on 93); Beckwith, *Black Roadways*, 168–71. See also Brooks, *History of Bedwardism*; Burton, *Afro-Creole*, 116–19; and Moore and Johnson, *Neither Led nor Driven*, 79–86. Note that here, too, an Afro–North American immigrant had played a role: a charismatic prophet called "Shakespeare" led a revival near Kingston in the 1880s and anointed Bedward his successor.

36. "A Disgraceful Meeting," *Limón Times*, Mar. 16, 1911.

37. The dialectical evolution of Myal and Obeah and their supposed West African roots were laid out in detail in the pages of the *Limón Times* later that year. The excerpted essay concluded: "Those who go to obeahmen in these days do so mainly for charms to make them lucky, or that a ghost may be 'taken off' them. For though there are few who will put a ghost on, there are not a few rather willing to think that ghosts have been put upon them. These sometimes resort to the obeahman, who has thus become the healer as well as the ill-doer whereas he was once an ill-doer

entirely, with the myalman as his professional enemy." "Tracing the origin of obea-hism," *Times*, Nov. 4 and 5, 1911. This article, with its detailed discussion of the West African research of Mary Kingsley and Sir A. B. Ellis, should push us to consider the role of print culture in shaping obeah—and perhaps in transmitting African practice. See Palmié, "Afterword."

38. Eric Walrond, "The Wharf Rats," in Parascandola, *Winds Can Wake Up the Dead*, 211.

39. Herskovits, *Myth of Negro Past*; Mintz and Price, *Anthropological Approach*. Helpful overviews include Yelvington, "Introduction" and "Invention of Africa"; Mintz, "Introduction" and "Melville J. Herskovits"; Price and Price, *Root of Roots*.

40. AC, vol. 26, no. 3, "Autobiografía de ST" (interview conducted in Spanish), 197–98. This subsection draws on some material published earlier in Putnam, "Rites of Power," reprinted by permission of Duke University Press.

41. Marshall, *Brown Girl, Brownstones*, 72.

42. Pollak-Eltz and Isturiz, *Folklore y cultura*, 146.

43. Interview with Padre Adams Delgado, El Callao, July 30, 2010.

44. Pollak-Eltz and Isturiz, *Folklore y cultura*, 166; personal communication, Blandine Wetohoussou and Karen Sandí, Sabanilla, Costa Rica, May 1999.

45. E.g., "Varieties," *Port of Spain Mascot*, Feb. 19, 1898; Elkins, "William Lauron DeLaurence."

46. "Tobago: The Obeah Case," *Port of Spain Daily Mirror*, Nov. 16, 1904, 13.

47. Kingsley, *At Last*, 338. Campbell reports "an instance during the early twenties when many citizens from the United States of America traveled to Guyana to make contact with a well-known obeahwoman." Campbell, *Obeah Yes or No?*, 4.

48. ANCR, Limón Juzgado del Crimen 218 (homicidio, 1911).

49. Putnam, "Rites of Power," 251–52; Forde, "Moral Economy of Spiritual Work."

50. "The Coroner's Court at Tunapuna," *Port of Spain Daily Mirror*, Sept. 30, 1904, 11.

51. Eric Walrond, "The Godless City," in Parascandola, *Winds Can Wake Up the Dead*, 164.

52. Eric Walrond, "The Wharf Rats," in Parascandola, *Winds Can Wake Up the Dead*, 211.

53. ANCR, Limón Juzgado del Crimen 309 (lesiones, 1903).

54. "The Home Circuit Court," *Kingston Daily Gleaner*, Jan. 14, 1921, 3.

55. "Obeah Worker Trapped," *Port of Spain Weekly Guardian*, Feb. 21, 1920, 6.

56. "West Indian Rhythm: Trinidad Calypsos on World and Local Events Featur-ing the Censored Recordings, 1938–1940," Bear Family Records, BCD 16623.

57. FO 288/200, Consulate, Panama: General Correspondence (31 Dec. 1918–31 July 1919): Letter from Yallah's Bay, Jamaica, May 22, 1919, folios 382–87.

58. ANCR, Policia 3276 (causa, 1894).

59. AC, vol. 26, no. 1, "Autobiografía de MGL."

60. AC, vol. 26, no. 1, "Autobiografía de RGC," 19.

61. AC, vol. 26, no. 3, "Autobiografía de L. Campesino," 126–27.

62. Bronfman, *Measures of Equality*; Roman, *Governing Spirits*.

63. See Putnam, "Rites of Power."

64. "Begging in Bridgetown," *Port of Spain Daily Mirror*, Aug. 30, 1904, 10; "What Is Obeah?," *Kingston Daily Gleaner*, Oct. 14, 1904, 8.

65. See, e.g., "Obeahmen Pay Penalty with Lives," *Limón Weekly News*, Dec. 31, 1904; and Eric Walrond, "The Godless City," in Parascandola, *Winds Can Wake Up the Dead*, 164.

66. Further examples of the menace of blood-sucking soucouyants come from everywhere from contemporary Güiria, Venezuela (interview with Rosa Bosch, Aug. 4, 2010), to 1905 Grenada, where believers included Portuguese immigrants and "Negro bakers" alike (Mendes, *Autobiography*, 21, 24–25), to early twentieth-century Bocas del Toro, where "obeah people . . . could fly and suck young children's blood" (Reid, *Light in Dark Places*, 150).

67. "Tunapuna: The Mysterious Death of a Child," *Port of Spain Daily Mirror*, Sept. 12, 1904, 7.

68. "The Santa Cruz Inquest," *Port of Spain Daily Mirror*, Oct. 13, 1904, 11.

69. Ibid.

70. "The Coroner's Court at Tunapuna," *Port of Spain Daily Mirror*, Sept. 30, 1904, 11.

71. Ibid.

72. "The News Condensed," *New York Times*, Nov. 1, 1899, 1.

73. "Confession of a Murderer," *Kingston Daily Gleaner*, Nov. 6, 1905, 11, reprinting coverage from *St. Lucia Voice*.

74. "The St. Lucia Murder Case," *Port of Spain Daily Mirror*, Nov. 1, 1904, 13.

75. Kingsley, *At Last*, 290–91.

76. "Tobago: Inquest," *Port of Spain Daily Mirror*, Nov. 7, 1904, 2; "San Fernando: Inquests," *Port of Spain Daily Mirror*, Nov. 19, 1904, 13.

77. "The St Lucia Murder Case: The Evidence," *Port of Spain Daily Mirror*, Oct. 26, 1904, 12–15.

78. "The Coroner's Court at Tunapuna," *Port of Spain Daily Mirror*, Sept. 30, 1904, 11.

79. "A Missing Child," *Port of Spain Daily Mirror*, Aug. 22, 1904, 8.

80. "Superstition Still Is Rife in Haiti: Latest, 'Death Car.' Humble Classes Are Panic-Stricken at Rumour of Kidnapping at Night by 'Voodoo' Workers," *Kingston Daily Gleaner*, May 11, 1932, 21.

81. Alejandra Bronfman, "The Technology of Torture in U.S.-Occupied Haiti," paper presented at the 42nd Annual Meeting of the Association of Caribbean Historians, Cave Hill, Barbados, May 10–14, 2010.

82. "Superstition Still Is Rife in Haiti." Note the similarity to contemporaneous vampire tales in colonial Africa, in which official cars (firemen, police) captured Africans for their blood. White, *Speaking with Vampires*.

83. For an example from Venezuela, see Tinker-Salas, *Enduring Legacy*, 133–34 (footnote 279); for Costa Rica, see Putnam, *Company They Kept*, 179.

84. "Jamaican Murdered by Cuban Mob in a Town Near Havana," *Kingston Daily Gleaner*, July 10, 1919, 6. See discussion in Palmié, *Wizards and Scientists*, 241–42; and Roman, *Governing Spirits*, 82–106.

85. Carew, *Ghosts*, 120–30 (quote), 49.

86. Domingo, "Tropics in New York."

87. Richards, *Conversations with Maida Springer*, 38–39. As Watkins-Owens notes, West Indians' degree of participation in Harlem's storefront churches is unknowable. But the prevalence of memories like Springer's suggests that the high-church predominance was an accepted truth at the time—even if, perhaps, only partially accurate. Watkins-Owens, *Blood Relations*, 195 (footnote 8).

88. Watkins-Owens, *Blood Relations*, 58.

89. Reid, *Negro Immigrant*, 124–25.

90. Ottley, *New World*, 47.

91. Jones, *James K. Humphrey*; "Adventists Dispute," *Limón Searchlight*, Jan. 11, 1930, 4.

92. *New York Amsterdam News*, Jan. 26, 1928, quoted in Watkins-Owens, *Blood Relations*, 59.

93. Makonnen, *Pan-Africanism*, 47–48. Griffith played a key role in the International African Service Bureau and successors in Britain, under the name T. Ras Makkonen.

94. Reid, *Negro Immigrant*, 124; David R. Bains, "George Alexander McGuire," in Gates and Higginbotham, *Harlem Renaissance*, 342.

95. X and Haley, *Autobiography*, 7–9; DeCaro, *On the Side of My People*, 38–58.

96. X and Haley, *Autobiography*, 9; Martin, *Race First*, 67–80.

97. Carew, *Ghosts in Our Blood*, 89.

98. Fredrickson, *Black Liberation*, 61–91; Chevannes, *Rastafari*, 33–42.

99. George Alexander McGuire, *Universal Negro Catechism*, 1921, quoted in Hill, *Garvey and UNIA Papers*, vol. 3, 307.

100. Gordon, "Garvey and Black Liberation Theology," 136–39 (quote on 137).

101. Ottley, *New World*, 143–48 (quote on 145); Hill, *Garvey and UNIA Papers*, vol. 7, 451–52.

102. Hill, *Dread History*, 27–28; Lee, *First Rasta*, 56–59.

103. McKay, *Harlem*, 45.

104. Ibid., 83.

105. Ottley, *New World*, 86–87.

106. McKay, *Harlem*, 75. Reid, too, suggested that Caribbean immigrants "maintained numerous suspicions and beliefs which are to some degree overtly practiced or worshipped . . . even if under the guise of some esoteric cult." Reid, *Negro Immigrant*, 136–37.

107. Hurston, "Hoodoo in America." On bundles and bottles in conjure, see "Concerning Negro Sorcery."

108. Ottley, *New World*, 86–87.

109. McKay describes Fu Futtam's "charming" face and "tiny, svelte form," so "pleasing" as to exert "seductive fascination"; he also reports on her aspirations, opinions, and reaction to her husband's death. Clearly he knew her well, so his claim that she "was born in Panama" must have some kind of basis. McKay, *Harlem*, 79–81. However, LaShawn Harris has located Fu Futtam's U.S. naturalization petition (under her full married name, Dorothy Matthews Hamid), in which Matthews gives her birthplace

as Black River, Jamaica. See also Harris, "Dream Books." I am grateful to LaShawn Harris for sharing her research in progress.

110. Eric Walrond, "The Godless City," in Parascandola, *Winds Can Wake Up the Dead*, 164.

111. McKay, *Harlem*, 185.

112. Ibid., 181–213.

113. Hill, *Dread History*, 22–23; Lee, *First Rasta*, 32–36.

114. Marshall, *Brown Girl, Brownstones*, 71, 75, 81.

115. McKay, *Harlem*, 83.

116. Ibid., 73–74.

117. McKay, *Banjo*, 200. See Magloire and Yelvington, "Haiti and the Anthropological Imagination"; and James, "Culture, Labor, and Race," 452–57.

118. Diana Paton, "The Truth about Obeah: Perspectives from Inside and Outside the Caribbean," paper presented at the annual conference of the Association of Caribbean Historians, Cartagena, Colombia, May 9–13, 2005; Forde and Paton, "Introduction." J. J. Thomas's *Froudacity* is an early exemplar of this genre. See Smith, *Creole Recitations*. Du Bois informed the reading public that *Home to Harlem*, McKay's 1928 novelized homage to black popular culture, made him feel "distinctly like taking a bath." Lewis, *When Harlem Was in Vogue*, 225 et passim.

119. Sidney A. Young, "Superstition and Our People," in Young, *Isthmian Echoes*, 165–66.

120. Ibid.

121. Quoted in Ottley, *New World*, 102–3.

122. Ibid., 101–2.

123. Eric Walrond, "The Godless City," in Parascandola, *Winds Can Wake Up the Dead*, 164–65; J. A. Rogers, "Book Review," in *Pittsburgh Courier*, Mar. 5, 1927, SM8.

124. "Address by Marcus Garvey," Aug. 26, 1915, rpt. in Hill, *Garvey and UNIA Papers*, vol. 1, 134.

125. Editorials from *New Jamaican*, quoted in Hill, *Dread History*, 24. See also Lee, *First Rasta*, 47.

126. Pioneering socialist Hubert Harrison was particularly antireligious. See Perry, *Hubert Harrison*.

127. Turner, "Richard B. Moore," 39–40; Turner, *Caribbean Crusaders*, 69–70 (quote, from unpublished ms. by Brown, on 70). Campbell was born in Georgia to a Jamaican father.

128. Turner, "Richard B. Moore," 20–22, 34–35; Turner, *Caribbean Crusaders*, 165–67 (quotes 166, 167, 166); Makalani, *Cause of Freedom*, 153.

129. Chevannes, *Rastafari*, 91.

130. Makalani, *Cause of Freedom*; Turner, *Caribbean Crusaders*; Pennybacker, *From Scottsboro to Munich*; Zumoff, "American Communist Party."

CHAPTER THREE

1. Census of 1920, Borough of Manhattan, Enumeration District 1414, Sheet No. 1855; Jackson, "Ottley."

2. W. A. Domingo, "Immigration Restriction in U.S.," in *Kingston Daily Gleaner*, Nov. 24, 1924, 12, reprinting article from *New Amsterdam News*; statistics in James, *Holding Aloft*, 355.

3. Tilly, "Citizenship, Identity and Social History"; Wimmer and Glick Schiller, "Methodological Nationalism"; Fahrmeir, *Citizenship*.

4. Marshall, *Citizenship and Social Class*.

5. *Actas de la Primera Conferencia Panamericana*. See discussion in Stepan, *Hour of Eugenics*, 174–88; Putnam, "Eventually Alien."

6. AHS, Gaveta 4, A17; Gaveta 4, A18.

7. McKeown, *Melancholy Order*; Zolberg, *Nation by Design*; Daniels, *Guarding the Golden Door*.

8. Daniels, *Guarding the Golden Door*, 27–48; Zolberg, *Nation by Design*, 251–54.

9. Letter from Latham, U.S. Consul, Kingston, to Bryan, Colonial Secretary, *Kingston Daily Gleaner*, Oct. 30, 1920, 20; "Jamaicans Who Intend Going to United States," *Kingston Daily Gleaner*, July 16, 1923.

10. RG84Bdos, vol. 201, 1923, vol. 2, various; RG84Jca vol. 321, 1923, Part 5, various.

11. See Putnam, "Ties Allowed to Bind."

12. RG84Jca, vol. 323, 1923, Part 7: Letters from consul, Kingston, July 31, 1923, and July 28, 1923.

13. RG84Bdos, vol. 208, 1925, vol. 3: Transcript, Board of Special Inquiry, Ellis Island, Apr. 8, 1925: ALLEYNE, Ada.

14. RG84Jca, vol. 321, 1923, Part 5: Letter from Theodora Richards. "Captable" spelled as in original.

15. RG84Jca, vol. 321, 1923, Part 5: U.S. Consul, Kingston, to Colonial Secretary, Kingston, July 1923.

16. "Jamaicans Who Intend Going to United States."

17. Statistics recalculated from Reid, *Negro Immigrant*, 235; see also James, *Holding Aloft*, 355. On the impact of U.S. quotas from 1922 to 1924, see Zolberg, "Matters of State," 74–75.

18. Domingo, "Tropics in New York." Domingo's apparently precise figures differ somewhat from those for 1920 reported by the 1930 census: U.S. Bureau of the Census, *Census of the United States, 1930*, vol. 2, 70. Meanwhile, the 1930 census reported 39,833 foreign-born "Negroes" in Manhattan, 11,266 in Brooklyn, and 3,655 in the other boroughs. Ibid.

19. U.S. Census 1930, New York, Manhattan Assembly District 21, Enumeration District 31-997, Sheet No. 19B.

20. Stoddard, *Rising Tide of Color*, 253.

21. Foerster, "Racial Problems," 304 et passim.

22. RG84Jca, vol. 323, 1923, Part 7: Letter from "Commonwealth Club of California" to consul, Nov. 14, 1923. See Ngai, "Architecture of Race," 76; and Stern, *Eugenic Nation*, 88–92.

23. RG84Bods, vol. 201, 1923, vol. 2: Letter from consul, Jan. 2 1923.

24. Davie, *Constructive Immigration Policy*, 33, 6–7. Consulted via http://pds.lib.harvard.edu/pds/view/4666248.

25. Zolberg, *Nation by Design*, 254–64; Stern, *Eugenic Nation*, 57–81; Ngai, *Impossible Subjects*, 50–55.

26. King, *Making Americans*, 153–59.

27. RG84Bdos, vol. 205, 1924, vol. 4: Circular from Department of State, July 1, 1924. See Daniels, *Guarding the Golden Door*, 49–58; and Ngai, *Impossible Subjects*, 21–55.

28. "Emigration of Jamaicans to U.S. Stopped," *Kingston Daily Gleaner*, June 14, 1924, 1. Details emerged in bits and pieces: "Jamaica Negro Influx Is Checked," *The World* (New York, Joseph Pulitzer), July 7, 1924; "Some Confusion," *Kingston Daily Gleaner*, July 30, 1924; "Jamaica Falls in U.K. Quota, Says Washington Report," *Kingston Daily Gleaner*, Aug. 2, 1924; "Immigration Visas along the Colonies," *Kingston Daily Gleaner*, Sept. 4, 1924, 3. See Putnam, "Unspoken Exclusions."

29. RG84Bdos, vol. 205, 1924, vol. 4: Letter from J. Sydney de Bourg, "For Publication," reprinting article "New Alien Bar Goes Up" from *The World*, dateline Washington, July 1, 1924.

30. RG84Jca, vol. 329, 1924, Part 8: Letter from consul, Kingston, to Department of State, Aug. 5, 1924.

31. RG84Jca, vol. 329, 1924, Part 8: Letter from consul, Kingston, to consul, London, Aug. 5, 1924.

32. RG84Jca, vol. 329, 1924, Part 8: Telegram from consul, London, Sept. 2, 1924.

33. RG84Jca, vol. 329, 1924, Part 8: Letter from consul, Kingston, to consul, London, Sept. 4, 1924.

34. RG84Jca, vol. 329, 1924, Part 8: Sept. 22, 1924.

35. RG84Bdos, vol. 205, 1924, vol. 4: Letter to consul from Colonial Secretary, Barbados, Nov. 19, 1924; reply from consul, Bridgetown, Nov. 21, 1924. The allocation first announced had been a mere ten quota numbers annually. "Barbados Quota," *Kingston Daily Gleaner*, Aug. 27, 1924.

36. RG84Bdos, vol. 208, 1925, vol. 3: Letter from consul to Department of State, July 6, 1925.

37. "Big Reduction in Quota to U.S.," *Panama American*, July 1, 1927.

38. United States, *Annual Report of the Commissioner General of Immigration*, 62, 151. This total includes British Guiana, British Honduras, and the British Islands.

39. E.g., RG84Jca, vol. 331, 1924, Part 14: Open letter from consul, Honecker, to Editor, *Gleaner*, June 14, 1924.

40. Not only did consuls and their superiors never discuss, as far as I can tell, the impact of Johnson-Reed in terms of race, but they almost never made reference to the race of specific petitioners. (One U.S. consul in Antilla, Cuba, did indeed routinely label British West Indian applicants as "colored" in his correspondence about their cases; this stands out by its divergence from his fellow consuls' standard practice.) In contrast, consular correspondence contains frequent discussion of the legal consequences of the racial status of other groups: Chinese (deportable to Spanish American republics, or not?); Mexicans (white or nonwhite?); South Asians (barred on racial grounds if born in Trinidad and hence outside the barred zone, or not?). When employers or local elites wrote letters to consuls on behalf of applicants, they

too routinely described the petitioner's race: "my negro cook," "a respectable girl, black," etc. It seems they presumed race was among the issues relevant to the consuls' response. Yet in all the letters I have reviewed, no British Caribbean applicant makes mention of his or her own color or that of the family member for whom he or she is writing. (Mentions of literacy, legitimacy, employment, and reputation, in contrast, are common, even in informal letters of inquiry that did not require such information.)

41. "The American Immigration Law," letter to the Editor from PROLETARIAT, New York City, July 25, 1924, *Kingston Daily Gleaner*, Aug. 6, 1924, 10. See also "American Ban on Emigration," *Kingston Daily Gleaner*, Aug. 18, 1924, 12; and "The Immigration Restriction in U.S.: Writer Says U.S. Limitation Act Has Achieved Object of Its Framers," *Kingston Daily Gleaner*, Nov. 24, 1924, 12, reprinting article by W. A. Domingo from *New York Amsterdam News* of Oct. 15, 1924.

42. "The Colour Bar: An Incident and Some Thoughts," *Barbados Weekly Herald*, Feb. 24, 1925, 4; "Bill to Repeal Super Tax Passes Committee," *Kingston Daily Gleaner*, May 15, 1925, 7, 8, 9; see Lake and Reynolds, *Global Colour Line*.

43. RG84Jca, vol. 329, 1924, Part 8: Letter from consul to Department of State, Aug. 5, 1924.

44. RG84Jca, vol. 331, 1924, Part 14: Letter from J. N. Wright to consul, July 9, 1924.

45. "The American Immigration Law."

46. W. E. B. Du Bois, "Opinion . . . West Indian Immigration," in *The Crisis* 29, no. 2 (December 1924): 57. For upbeat predictions of the benefits of the 1924 law for African Americans, and no mention of black immigrants, see "Get Ready to Work," *Pittsburgh Courier*, May 16, 1925, 16.

47. RG84Jca, vol. 329, 1924, Part 8, 811.11: Diplomatic Serial No. 318, from Department of State, Washington, Dec. 6, 1924.

48. RG84Jca, vol. 331, 1924, Part 14: Copy of cable (translated) from UFCo New York to UFCo Kingston office, June 10, 1924. See Zolberg, "Archaeology of 'Remote Control.'"

49. RG84Jca, vol. 352, 1926, Correspondence 811.11, Visas for Foreign Passports.

50. On importance of assessing the "bona fide" intentions of those claiming tourist status, see RG84Jca, vol. 321, 1923, Part 5: Copy of letter from Secretary of Labor to Secretary of State, Oct. 8, 1923; RG84Bdos, vol. 205, 1924, vol. 4: Circular, Nov. 19, 1924, re: Temporary Visits of Aliens.

51. "Emigration of Jamaicans to U.S. Stopped," *Kingston Daily Gleaner*, June 14, 1924, 1.

52. Putnam, "Ties Allowed to Bind." On the related "mismatch between theory and practice" with relation to current family/citizenship law, see Bhabha, "'Mere Fortuity of Birth'?"

53. JNA, 1B/5/77/24: Emigration to USA (Individual Enquiries), 1928–1948.

54. U.S. Department of State, *Admission of Aliens*, 96–100; RG84Bdos, vol. 205, 1924, vol. 4: Circular from Department of State, Dec. 15, 1924.

55. JNA, 1B/5/77/24: Emigration to USA (Individual Enquiries), 1928–1948.

56. RG84Jca, vol. 331, 1924, Part 14: Letter to consul from Jamaica Fruit & Shipping Co., Aug. 15, 1924; reply from consul, Aug. 26, 1924.

57. See, for instance, RG84Jca, vol. 321, 1923, Part 5, Letter from Joseph Henry Morgan and Daisy Thelwell Morgan to American Consul, Kingston, Mar. 8, 1923, and associated correspondence.

58. For rejections by the U.S. consul of even those applicants who should have been accorded preference status, see RG84Bdos, vol. 208, 1925, vol. 3; RG84Bdos, vol. 209, 1925, vol. 5. In theory, it was the length of each consulate's waiting list that served the London-based quota control officer as evidence of "active demand" and thus determined the allocation of quota numbers among consulates. See U.S. Department of State, *Admission of Aliens*, 104, 192.

59. "Today's News: Foreign," *Kingston Daily Gleaner*, Aug. 11, 1924, 10.

60. RG84Havana, vol. 523, Part 21, 1924, Classes 851-861.3: Cable from Department of State and reply from consul, both Dec. 15, 1924.

61. RG84Bdos, vol. 209, Correspondence, American Consulate, Barbados, 1925, vol. 5: Report from consul, Mar. 27, 1925.

62. "The Passport Nuisance," *Panama American*, Feb. 27, 1926; see also "News of the World: Coming Back to Pre War days," *Limón Searchlight*, Feb. 15, 1930, 1.

63. Editorial, "The Undesirable Alien," *Panama American*, Oct. 10, 1925, 2.

64. CO 318/413/1, Immigration of British West Indians into Central America: Report by Rogelio Pino, June 1934, translation enclosed in Letter from British Legation to FO, Aug. 8, 1934.

65. Gómez, *Contribución al estudio de la inmigración*, 9. See also Hernández González, "Raza, inmigración e identidad nacional."

66. Moya, *Cousins and Strangers*, 46, 423. Nearly 800,000 Spaniards entered Cuba between 1902 and 1931, and though many returned home after a few years' work, some stayed: 1931 found over 250,000 Spanish-born on the island. Ferenczi and Willcox, *International Migrations*, vol. 1, *Statistics*, 525–27; de la Fuente, *Nation for All*, 101.

67. Stepan, *Hour of Eugenics*; Fahrmeir, *Citizenship*; Cook-Martín and FitzGerald, "Liberalism and the Limits of Inclusion."

68. Uslar Pietri, "Introducción a la Primera Edición," 4, 12 et passim. On growing Afro-Latin incorporation in this era, see Andrews, *Afro-Latin America*, 153–69.

69. Adriani, "Venezuela y los problemas de la inmigración," 150; see Tinker Salas, *Enduring Legacy*, 133–35.

70. Chomsky, "West Indian Workers"; Soto Quirós, "Inmigración e identidad nacional"; Harpelle, "Racism and Nationalism"; McLeod, "Undesirable Aliens"; O'Reggio, *Between Alienation and Citizenship*.

71. "Panama's Immigration Need Is Discussed by 'El Diario,'" *Panama American*, Dec. 29, 1926. On the role of U.S. employers' policies in provoking anti-immigrant nationalism, see Bourgois, *Ethnicity at Work*; Tinker Salas, *Enduring Legacy*; and Colby, *Business of Empire*.

72. Venezuela, Ministerio de Relaciones Interiores, *Memoria 1929*, xvi.

73. "Consolidated Cooperation Only Solution to Negro Problem," *Limón Searchlight*, Sept. 20, 1930, 8.

74. Cook-Martín and FitzGerald, "Liberalism and the Limits of Inclusion."

75. Editorial, "Their Policy," *Kingston Daily Gleaner*, Aug. 18, 1924, 12.

76. "West Indian Labourers in the Republics," *Kingston Daily Gleaner*, Sept. 5, 1924, 3.

77. Sidney A. Young, "Sid Says: Within the Law," *Panama American*, Oct. 27, 1926. "Chombos" was a derogative term for foreign blacks.

78. "West Indians Are Not Wanted in Venezuela," *Kingston Daily Gleaner*, Sept. 18, 1930, 5. See Pellegrino, *Historia*, 158–60; and Tinker Salas, *Enduring Legacy*, 107–42.

79. E.g., Chomsky, "West Indian Workers"; Chomsky, "Barbados or Canada?"; Carr, "Identity, Class, and Nation"; Bergquist, *Labor in Latin America*, 223.

80. CO 318/408/3, Immigration of British West Indians to Central and South America, 1932: Transcribed pamphlet, signed Francisco Nieto, June 26, 1933, enclosed by Crosby.

81. CO 318/408/4, Immigration of British West Indians to Central and South America, 1933: Letter from British Legation Panama, Aug. 10, 1933.

82. FO 288/200, Consulate, Panama: General Correspondence (31 Dec. 1918–31 July 1919): Petition to Governor, Jamaica, from West Indian Labour Union, Guachipali, Panama, n.d.

83. "Urge Members to Turn out at Meetings," *Panama American*, Aug. 11, 1927.

84. "The Colour Bar," *Barbados Weekly Herald*, Feb. 24, 1925, 4. See Winks, *Blacks in Canada*, 298–313; and Calliste, "Race, Gender, and Canadian Immigration Policy," esp. 138–39.

85. "Panama's Immigration Need Is Discussed by 'El Diario': Says Bar Exists in Dominions," *Panama American*, Dec. 29, 1926.

86. Archivo del Congreso (Bogotá, Colombia), Leyes Autógrafas 1922, tomo XII, folios 373–76. I am grateful to Sharika Crawford for sharing this document with me.

87. See Cook-Martín and FitzGerald, "Liberalism and the Limits of Inclusion"; Shanahan, "Scripted Debate," 67–96; Lake and Reynolds, *Global Colour Line*; and McGraw, "Neither Slaves nor Tyrants," 416–22.

88. CO 318/413/1, Immigration of British West Indians into Central America: Report by Rogelio Pino, June 1934, translation enclosed in Letter from British Legation to FO, Aug. 8, 1934.

89. Lee, "'Yellow Peril' and Asian Exclusion"; Putnam, "Eventually Alien." Note that colonization, immigration, and entry were three separate categories—the first denoted state-supported landed settlement schemes; the second, entry with intention of permanent residence; the last, border crossing, whatever the goal or intended length of stay. Thus, for instance, an 1862 Costa Rican law frequently cited as having banned black immigration in fact only outlawed colonization schemes using black settlers. Ley de Bases y Colonización, no. 24, Noviembre 3, 1862, in Costa Rica, *Leyes y Decretos*. See also Berglund, "Bases sociales y económicas," 954.

90. "Salvador Passes Law Barring All Coloured Immigration," *Panama Star and Herald*, May 4, 1925, 1; El Salvador, *Ley y reglamento de migración*, 18.

91. CO 318/406/1, Immigration of British West Indians in Central and South America: Letter to FO from British Embassy, Santiago, Chile, Feb. 24, 1932.

92. "Honduras Bars Negroes," *New York Times*, Feb. 13, 1923, 32; Euraque, "Banana Enclave," 152; and Honduras, *Reglamento para la Ley de inmigración, 1929*, 7–9.

93. Those already in the country were permitted to stay, but they could not reenter if they left for any reason. Guatemala, Decreto Número 1735 de la Asamblea Legislativa de la República de Guatemala del 30 de mayo de 1931, artículo 2; cited in Zorraquín Becu, *Problema del extranjero*, 55–56. See Mosquera Aguilar, "Regulación jurídica de la migración en Guatemala," accessed via http://www.angelfire.com/mo/squera/derecho.html.

94. "Mexico Forbids Negroes to Enter," *New York Times*, Oct. 31, 1926, 17. Research in progress by Elisabeth Cunin will illuminate the legal and extralegal measures involved in barring Mexico's southern border to black immigrants in this era.

95. CO 318/406/1, Immigration of British West Indians in Central and South America: Letter from Governor of British Honduras, Apr. 14, 1932.

96. Chambers, *Race, Nation, and West Indian Immigration*, 115–35.

97. Nicaragua, Decreto legislativo, 9 de Octubre de 1897; Decreto sobre la entrada y admisión de extranjeros en el territorio de la república, 16 de Abril de 1918; Ley de Inmigración, 25 de Abril de 1930, accessed via http://legislacion.asamblea.gob.ni/Normaweb.nsf/.

98. E.g., "Exclusion Bill Passed Again, Few Changes," *Panama American*, Oct. 21, 1926; and "Modification of Immigration Ban to Venezuela," *Kingston Daily Gleaner*, Nov. 17, 1930, 17.

99. CO 318/406/1, Immigration of British West Indians in Central and South America: Reply to FO from British Legation, Bogota, Mar. 29, 1932. See also Flores Bolívar, "Beyond the White Republic," 20–21; and McGraw, "Neither Slaves nor Tyrants," 422–29.

100. Archivo del Ministerio de Relaciones Exteriores (Bogotá, Colombia), Legación de Colombia en Panama, Caja 673, Transferencia 8, folios 329–31: letter from consul of Colombia in Panama, Oct. 24, 1924. I am grateful to Sharika Crawford for sharing this document with me.

101. "Colombia Imposes Law against Dark-Skinned Immigrants," *Panama American*, June 10, 1927.

102. Bryan, "Question of Labor in the Sugar Industry"; del Castillo, *Inmigración de braceros azucareros*, 45–58; Baud, "Sugar and Unfree Labour," esp. 314–18; Martínez Vergne, *Nation and Citizen*, 88 et passim.

103. Derby, "Haitians, Magic, and Money"; Turits, "A World Destroyed."

104. CO 318/408/3, Immigration of British West Indians to Central and South America, 1932: Letter to FO from British Legation, Santo Domingo, June 1, 1933.

105. CO 318/408/3, Immigration of British West Indians to Central and South America, 1932: Letter from British Legation, Panama, to FO, June 27, 1933.

106. CO 318/406/1, Immigration of British West Indians in Central and South America: Letter from British Legation Havana, Apr. 4, 1932; Pollitt, "Cuban Sugar Economy." For debates within Cuba on the racial politics of immigration, see de la Fuente, *Nation for All*, 51–53.

107. "News From Abroad: Immigrants to Cuba," *Limón Searchlight*, July 18, 1931, 3.

108. See Decree No. 1601, July 28, 1925, enclosed in CO 318/394/3, Immigration of British West Indians: Letter from British Legation, Havana, Apr. 25, 1929; McLeod, "Undesirable Aliens"; and de la Fuente, *Nation for All*, 100–105. The report of Cuban

special investigator Rogelio Pino in 1934 urged immediate decrees to prohibit the entry of "Negroes and Mongolians in general." See report included in translation in CO 318/413/1, Immigration of British West Indians into Central America: Letter to FO from British Legation Havana, Aug. 8, 1934.

109. Conniff, *Black Labor on a White Canal*, 65–66, 80–84, 98–106, 127–30. The retroactive denationalization was reversed in 1945. See Westerman, *Inmigrantes antillanos*, 95–101.

110. Sidney A. Young, "Being a Philosopher," in Young, *Isthmian Echoes*, 238–39.

111. "Undesirables," *Limón Searchlight*, Apr. 12, 1930, 3.

112. Costa Rica, *Colección de leyes y decretos*, Decreto no. 4 del 26 de abril de 1942; Soto Quirós, "Inmigración e identidad nacional," 216–49.

113. Berglund, "Bases sociales," 954.

114. RelExtDPI 164 (Gran Bretaña, 1926), Inmigración de raza negra: Letter from vice-consul of Venezuela, Port of Spain, Oct. 21, 1926.

115. "Venezuelan Act Rouses West Indies," *New York Times*, Nov. 2, 1929, 20. "Coloured Immigration into Venezuela," *London Times*, Nov. 2, 1929, 11; Tinker Salas, *Enduring Legacy*, 136–37; Berglund, "Bases sociales," 955.

116. E.g., CO 318/417/6, Treatment of British West Indians in Venezuela, Claims for Compensation: Letter from Lloyd, British vice-consul, Yrapa, Apr. 6, 1935; AHS, Gaveta 31, B88: Varios, 1935, "Rafael Hernandez denuncia el desembarco de tres ingleses en Caño Braval por Jose Sanchez." Four-fifths of the British West Indians registered by Sucre state authorities in the early 1930s had entered without documentation. Author's analysis, AHS, Gaveta 28, B72: Cédulas de Identidad, Registros de Extranjeros; Gaveta 23, B37: Cédulas de Identidad, Registro de Extranjeros (1932); Gaveta 22, B32: Cédulas de Extranjeros (1932), including full sets for *distritos* Arismendi, Mejías, Benítez, Rivero, and Mariño.

117. E.g., RelExtDPI 164 (Gran Bretaña, 1926), Inmigración de raza negra; RelExtDPI 298 (Gran Bretaña, 1934), Sobre la entrada clandestina a Venezuela de los extranjeros provenientes de Trinidad.

118. CO 318/413/1, Immigration of British West Indians into Central America: Translation into English of report by Rogelio Pino, forwarded to FO by British Legation, Havana, Aug. 8 1934. On the emergence of "illegal alien" as status in the United States in the same period, see Ngai, *Impossible Subjects*, 56–90.

119. RelExtDPI 569 (Gran Bretaña, 1936), Memoria de labores de la Legación en 1935.

120. CO 318/413/1, Immigration of British West Indians into Central America: Telegram from FO to Watson, Havana, Jan. 3, 1934. On the Cuban law itself, see McLeod, "Undesirable Aliens," 604–5; and de la Fuente, *Nation for All*, 104–5.

121. Harpelle, "Racism and Nationalism," 48–49; Harpelle, *West Indians*, 71–73, 86–87, 133; Colby, *Business of Empire*, 184–91.

122. Costa Rican national mythology so effectively identified Costa Rican-ness with whiteness that the prohibition on Pacific employment made no mention of citizenship as a criteria at all: self-evidently, "people of color" must refer to foreigners. The British West Indian press of Limón mocked this perception. "Is this not ridiculous? (to say the least of it) when we find that 2/3 of the population of Puntarenas

are people of coloured origin, being a mixed breed of Negroes and Indians. . . . And what of the thousands of people of colour, Costa Ricans by naturalization or birth, who vote?" "The Costa Rican Negro's Place in Costa Rica?," *Atlantic Voice*, Nov. 3, 1934.

123. Differentiated access to labor markets for noncitizens is commonly managed today through the issuance of work permits ("green cards," etc.) specific to the worker, rather than through quotas specific to the workplace.

124. See Records of the Department of State Relating to Internal Affairs of Venezuela, 1910–1929, Micro F 265, Reel 13, slide 0174: Report, American Legation, Caracas, Feb. 5, 1927; JNA, 1B/5/77/179, Cuba, Prohibition against entry of women and families (1929); El Salvador, *Ley y reglamento de migración*, 21–23; and Honduras, *Reglamento para la Ley de inmigración, 1929*, 9–10.

125. See Casey, "Haitian Migrants in Cuba"; CO 318/382, West Indies: General, 1925, Item 21, May 1925: "Treatment of B W Indians in Santo Domingo": Letter from Chargé d'Affaires, Santo Domingo, Apr. 24, 1925.

126. CO 318/406/1, Immigration of British West Indians in Central and South America: Letter to FO from Crosby, British Legation Panama, Feb. 24, 1932. A 1927 revision specifically exempted agricultural enterprises that could "prove" insufficient "national" workers were available. "Enforcing New Employment Law," *Panama American*, Jan. 14, 1927; "West Indians to Be Excluded from Provisions of Law on Immigration," *Panama American*, Jan. 19, 1927.

127. "Jamaican Labor to Be Restricted on Cuban Roads," *Panama American*, Feb. 19, 1927, reprinting article from *El Comercio de Cienfuegos* via the *Havana Post*.

128. "Appalling Conditions in Cuba," *Panama American*, July 22, 1927, reprinting article from the *Jamaica Mail*.

129. CO 318/406/1, Immigration of British West Indians in Central and South America: Letter from British Legation, Guatemala, to FO, Apr. 8, 1932.

130. Martinez, *Peripheral Migrants*, 44.

131. Pellegrino, *Historia*, 169.

132. RelExtDPI 592 (Gran Bretaña, 1936), "Supuesto maltrato de los antillanos en los campos petroleros."

133. CO 318/406/1, Immigration of British West Indians in Central and South America: Letter from Governor of British Honduras, Apr. 14, 1932.

134. "Panamanian Law Hits the United Fruit Co," *Kingston Daily Gleaner*, Dec. 9, 1926, 5; "Jamaicans in Bocas del Toro," *Kingston Daily Gleaner*, Feb. 9, 1928, 22.

135. "Unemployment in Trinidad Is Growing," *Kingston Daily Gleaner*, Sept. 11, 1930, 16.

136. Brereton, *History of Modern Trinidad*, 159.

137. Kuczynski, *Demographic Survey*, 155, 341. The population of British Honduras included 15 percent born elsewhere, largely Guatemala, Mexico, and Honduras.

138. Johnson, "Anti-Chinese Riots"; Anshan, "Survival, Adaptation, and Integration," 57; Bouknight-Davis, "Chinese Economic Development," 84; Hu-DeHart, "Indispensable Enemy or Convenient Scapegoat?"

139. Examples from Trinidad are discussed in more detail in chapter 6.

140. Editorial, "Their Policy," *Kingston Daily Gleaner*, Aug. 18, 1924, 12.

141. "The First Question," *Kingston Daily Gleaner*, Oct. 11, 1924, 12. For examples of those previous arguments, see "Parochial Board of St. James," *Kingston Daily Gleaner*, Jan. 7, 1918, 13. On Asian exclusion in the "white settler" colonies and the intraimperial tensions occasioned, see Gorman, *Imperial Citizenship*, 158–71; McKeown, *Melancholy Order*; Lake and Reynolds, *Global Colour Line*; and Mongia, "Race, Nationality, Mobility."

142. Editorial, "Jamaica's Case Stated," *Kingston Daily Gleaner*, Jan. 7, 1925, 10.

143. "Bill to Repeal Super Tax Passes Committee," *Kingston Daily Gleaner*, May 15, 1925, 7. On Guy Ewen, see Carnegie, *Some Aspects of Jamaica's Politics*, 76, 81, 87. On the *Gleaner*'s place in island politics in this era, see ibid., 162–78 et passim.

144. See, e.g., "The Alien Question," *Kingston Daily Gleaner*, May 15, 1925, 8.

145. "Alien Issue in the Legislature," *Kingston Daily Gleaner*, May 15, 1925, 9; Carnegie, *Some Aspects of Jamaica's Politics*, 44, 64, 74.

146. Even the Jamaican Imperial Association, the voice of the wealthiest planters, was happy to urge "vigorous enforcement" of the existing immigration law—"which of course," they clarified, "would not apply to persons from the Mother Country, the self-Governing Dominions and the United States of America." "Points Placed before the New Governor," *Kingston Daily Gleaner*, Oct. 1, 1924, 7.

147. "Explicit Speaking," *Kingston Daily Gleaner*, May 15, 1925, 8.

148. Article in *Kingston Daily Gleaner*, Dec. 12, 1927, rpt. in Hill, *Garvey and UNIA Papers*, vol. 7, 23–24.

149. Ibid.

150. Carnegie, *Some Aspects of Jamaica's Politics*, 111, 119–21; Post, *Arise Ye Starvelings*, 208–12; Stein, *World of Marcus Garvey*, 264.

151. "On Immigration," *Limón Searchlight*, Dec. 13, 1930, 1; "Committee Starts to Deal with the Alien Question," *Kingston Daily Gleaner*, Dec. 30, 1930, 1; Carnegie, *Some Aspects of Jamaica's Politics*, 83, 79. Cawley was member for St. Catherine.

152. "Another Sedition Case," *Limón Searchlight*, June 6, 1931, 2. On anti-Asian agitation among Garveyites and others in the mid-1930s in connection with threats of mass repatriation from Cuba, see Post, *Arise Ye Starvelings*, 208–12.

153. Carnegie, *Some Aspects of Jamaica's Politics*, 101, 121 (quote), 150.

154. "Another Sedition Case," *Limón Searchlight*, June 6, 1931, 2.

155. *Kingston Daily Gleaner*, Sept. 7, 1932, quoted in Bouknight-Davis, "Chinese Economic Development," 88.

156. "Consolidated Cooperation Only Solution to Negro Problem," *Limón Searchlight*, Sept. 20, 1930, 8.

157. "Here and There in the News, by the Speaker," *Kingston Daily Gleaner*, Oct. 27, 1933, 10.

158. "The Democratic League: Its Policy and Creed," *Barbados Weekly Herald*, Mar. 28, 1925, 4; Chamberlain, *Empire and Nation-Building*, 26–50.

159. E.g., speech by Brown in "Parochial Board of St. James," *Kingston Daily Gleaner*, Jan. 7, 1918, 13.

160. "Explicit Speaking," *Kingston Daily Gleaner*, May 15, 1925, 8.

161. "CHINA: Dragon v. Lion," *Time* magazine, Feb. 7, 1927. Accessed via http://www.time.com/time/magazine/article/0,9171,729959,00.html#ixzz1D04aM0c4.

162. Chen, *Return to the Middle Kingdom*. J. A. Rogers gave Chen prominent billing in his 1940s *World's Great Men of Color*, 180.

163. CO 137/794/14, Proposals for restriction of immigration into Jamaica: concerns raised over Syrian and Chinese applicants, 1931: "Report of Committee appointed to enquire into and report upon the question of the Immigration of Aliens into Jamaica," Jan. 30, 1931.

164. CO 137/794/14, Proposals for restriction of immigration into Jamaica: Letter from FO to Under Secretary of State for Colonies, Jan. 29, 1932.

165. CO 137/794/14, Proposals for restriction of immigration into Jamaica: Letter from Home Office to Under Secretary of State for Colonies, Aug. 6, 1932.

166. CO 137/794/14, Proposals for restriction of immigration into Jamaica: Letter from FO to Under Secretary of State for Colonies, Apr. 4, 1932.

167. CO 318/406/2, Immigration of British West Indians to Central and South America, 1932: Letter from J. Crosby, British Legation in Panama, Sept. 8, 1932.

168. CO 318/394/3, Immigration of British West Indians: Letter from British Legation, Port au Prince, Jan. 16, 1929. My emphasis.

169. CO 137/794/14, Proposals for restriction of immigration into Jamaica: Minutes.

170. CO 137/794/14, Proposals for restriction of immigration into Jamaica: Colonial Office draft correspondence.

171. Bouknight-Davis, "Chinese Economic Development," 87. Similarly, see CO 295/596/17, Criticisms by the Chinese Government of the immigration legislation recently enacted by the Government of Trinidad: FO response to Chinese ambassador, June 18, 1937.

172. CO 318/413/1, Immigration of British West Indians into Central America: Letter from consul, Santo Domingo, to FO, Sept. 10, 1934.

173. Tarchov, "Esquema historico." My emphasis. Venezuela, Ministerio del Interior y Justicia, *Memoria 1931*, n.p., xvii; Tinker Salas, *Enduring Legacy*, 136.

174. Particularly relevant here is Zolberg's description of southwest border control as a "success" if judged by its benefits to powerful constituencies rather than by the rhetoric of exclusionary intent. Zolberg, "Matters of State," 71–93. Meanwhile, the U.S. government–run guestworker programs that brought British Caribbean migrants to Atlantic Seaboard farms, by the thousands in the interwar years and by the scores of thousands during and after World War II, form a third modality. These migrants did not have the autonomy of British Caribbeans who had paid their own way to New York City, "show money" in hand, before 1924. However, they had more means to demand accountability from receiving- and sending-state officials than did most *braceros* in the Southwest. Hahahmovitch, *Fruits of Their Labor*; Hahamovitch, *No Man's Land*. See also Ngai, *Impossible Subjects*, 127–66.

175. Turits, *Foundations of Despotism*, 144–80.

CHAPTER FOUR

1. "Halt Race Prejudice," *Limón Searchlight*, July 25, 1931, 1. Quoting from *Panama Tribune*.

2. E.g., Turner and Turner, *Richard B. Moore*; James, *Holding Aloft*; Schwarz, *West Indian Intellectuals*; Turner, *Caribbean Crusaders*; Stephens, *Black Empire*; Edwards, *Practice of Diaspora*; Makalani, *Cause of Freedom*.

3. Carew, *Ghosts in Our Blood*, 117. Louise Little was herself a contributor to the *Negro World*, and Malcolm and his siblings sold copies of the paper. Turner, *Islam*, 177.

4. See Fraser, "Rethinking the Public Sphere"; Warner, "Publics and Counterpublics"; and Squires, "Rethinking the Black Public Sphere."

5. Fraser, "Rethinking the Public Sphere" and "Transnationalizing the Public Sphere."

6. For overviews, see James, *Holding Aloft*; Turner, "Richard B. Moore"; and Macdonald, "The Wisers Who Are Far Away."

7. Anderson, *Imagined Communities*, 35.

8. Important histories of U.S.-based Afro-American media that do not address the papers' international readerships (and writerships) include Dankey and Wiegand, *Print Culture*, and Vogel, *Black Press*. In contrast, Penny Von Eschen highlights the importance of the U.S. black press reaching outward in the late 1930s and 1940s, and Brent Edwards underlines the importance of the "periodical print cultures of black internationalism," which were "robust and extremely diverse on all sides of the Atlantic." Von Eschen, *Race against Empire*, esp. chap. 1; Edwards, *Practice of Diaspora*, 8 (quote).

9. In 1930 literacy was 97 percent in Boston and 95 percent in New York. U.S. Bureau of the Census, *Census of the United States, 1930*, vol. 2, 1275, 1277.

10. Author's analysis of the Censo de 1927 CIHAC database, accessed through http://censos.ccp.ucr.ac.cr/.

11. These figures are doubtless elevated by their inclusion of British West Indians, who made up roughly one-seventh of Panama City's 74,000 inhabitants. Panama, Secretaría de Agricultura y Obras Públicas, Dirección General del Censo, *Censo Demográfico de 1930*, vol. 2, 80–81.

12. U.S. Bureau of the Census, *Fourteenth Census of the United States, 1920*, vol. 3, 1251–52, 1245.

13. Literacy in Kingston was 79 percent in 1921. Roberts, *Population of Jamaica*, 78–79.

14. Author's analysis, AHS, Gaveta 28, B72: Cédulas de Identidad, Registros de Extranjeros; Gaveta 23, B37: Cédulas de Identidad, Registro de Extranjeros (1932); Gaveta 22, B32: Cédulas de Extranjeros (1932), including full sets for *distritos* Arismendi, Mejías, Benítez, Rivero, and Mariño. Over 95 percent were men.

15. Venezuela, Ministerio de Fomento, Dirección de Estadística, *Sexto Censo de Población, 1936*, vol. 3, 40. *West Indian Census of 1946*, Part A, General Report, 44, gives literate adults as a portion of total population in preceding censuses. On Dominica and Trinidad, see *Census of 1921* for each island.

16. The only exception was for the parents of naturalized U.S. citizens. See discussion in James, "Explaining Afro-Caribbean Social Mobility."

17. Hill, *Garvey and UNIA Papers*, vol. 1, 532–33.

18. Quoted in Lewis, *Anti-Colonial Champion*, 44. Hill, *Garvey and UNIA Papers*, vol. 1, lxxi.

19. Editorial, "Misrepresentation," *Port of Spain Daily Mirror*, Aug. 17, 1904, 8.

20. Ibid.

21. "A Precedent," *Port of Spain Daily Mirror*, Nov. 5, 1904, 10.

22. Mathurin, *Henry Sylvester Williams*, 16, 52.

23. On the *San Andrés Searchlight*, see Crawford, "Under the Colombian Flag," 13 et passim.

24. E.g., Charlton, "Cat Born in Oven," 206, 375.

25. Cited in ibid., 376. On Garveyism in Cuba more broadly, see ibid., 371–84; Giovannetti, "Elusive Organization of 'Identity'"; and Sullivan, "No Surrender."

26. See Hill, *Garvey and UNIA Papers*, vol. 11, 9–36.

27. Martin, *Race First*, 4, 106, 16, 93; Hill, *Garvey and UNIA Papers*, vol. 7, 997–1000.

28. ANP, Juzgado Segundo del Circuito de Bocas del Toro, 1908 contra Manuel Valencia por perjurio; Juzgado del Circuito de Bocas del Toro, 1914 (case file includes copy of *Central American Express*, Dec. 20, 1913); Universidad de Panamá, Biblioteca Central Simon Bolívar, Hermeroteca, Microfilm Rollo 13: *Central American Express*, June 23, 1917.

29. Hill, *Garvey and UNIA Papers*, vol. 1, 182; Floyd Calvin, "Eric D. Walrond Leaves 'Opportunity'; To Devote Entire Time to Writing," *Pittsburgh Courier*, Feb. 12, 1927, 2. On these and other papers in Panama, Costa Rica, Cuba, and beyond, see Marshall, *English-Language Press in Latin America*.

30. Bolland, *Politics of Labor*, 197–98. The *Bluefields Weekly* was closely aligned with Moravian missionary perspectives but gave space to British Caribbean and Afro-identified correspondents; e.g., "From Our Detroit Correspondent," *Bluefields Weekly*, June 16, 1928, 2.

31. Bolland, *Politics of Labor*, 199; Brereton, *History of Modern Trinidad*, 161–65; Lent, "Commonwealth Caribbean Mass Media," 44–47; Hoyos, *Common Heritage*, 142–47.

32. "Announcement: The Walker Mission Has Arrived," *Panama Star and Herald*, West Indian News Section, Nov. 27, 1920, 3.

33. Reid, *Negro Immigrant*, 140–41; Watkins-Owens, *Blood Relations*, 158–64.

34. James, *Holding Aloft*, 123–26, 157–63, 270–71; Turner, "Richard B. Moore," 30–34; Wintz and Finkelman, *Encyclopedia of the Harlem Renaissance*, 179–81, 337, 538–39, 655, and overview on the U.S. black press, 133–37; Parascandola, *Look for Me*, 26–30; Ottley, *New World*, 268–88.

35. "News from the West Indies. Garveyites Warn Editor of Times," *Panama Tribune*, Nov. 18, 1928, 10.

36. "Foreword," *African Times and Orient Review* 1 (July 1912): iii, as quoted in Hill, *Garvey and UNIA Papers*, vol. 1, 26.

37. Elkins, "Hercules and the Society of Peoples of African Origin."

38. Boittin, "Black and White"; Edwards, *Practice of Diaspora*.

39. Universidad de Panamá, Biblioteca Central Simon Bolívar, Hermeroteca, Microfilm Rollo 13. *Central American Express*, July 21, 1917, 1.

40. "Notice to Our Readers," *Limón Searchlight*, Aug. 23, 1930, 2.

41. Advertisement, *Limón Searchlight*, Dec. 27, 1930, 6.

42. "An Appreciation," *Limón Searchlight*, Jan. 25, 1930, 2.

43. Abbé Wallace, "In the Shadow of the Stars," *Pittsburgh Courier*, Feb. 15, 1936, A3.

44. "Advises Joe to Pray," *Pittsburgh Courier*, Sept. 4, 1937, 15.

45. Charlton, "Cat Born in Oven," 206.

46. "Wanted," *Limón Searchlight*, July 25, 1931, 7; "Anonymous Letters," *Limón Searchlight*, Mar. 1, 1930, 4.

47. Sidney A. Young, "Sid Says," *Panama American*, Dec. 29, 1926.

48. "Correspondence: More Journalists for the Race," *Panama American*, Dec. 29, 1926.

49. "Render unto Caesar What Is His," *Limón Searchlight*, Feb. 14, 1931, 5.

50. Hoyos, *Common Heritage*, 145; "Jamaican Founder of 'Panama Tribune' Dies," *Kingston Daily Gleaner*, May 29, 1959, 2; Thoywell-Henry, *Who's Who Jamaica*, 657; Putnam, "To Study the Fragments/Whole"; Bolland, *Politics of Labour*, 197–99.

51. See Trinidad and Tobago, *Debates in the Legislative Council*, January-December 1920, debate of Mar. 5, 1920, second debate, Mar. 19, 1920, 77 (quote); Bolland, *Politics of Labour*, 202; Brereton, *History of Trinidad*, 161–65; and James, *Holding Aloft*, 52–66.

52. FO 288/200, Consulate, Panama: General Correspondence (31 Dec. 1918–31 July 1919): Letter from H. N. Walrond to British Minister, Panama, Feb. 18, 1919; ibid., Annual Report, 1918.

53. Letter from manager, United Fruit Company, to Geo. Chittenden, Dec. 6, 1919, rpt. in Hill, *Garvey and UNIA Papers*, vol. 11, 452.

54. De Lisser, *Jane's Career*, 8, 17.

55. "The Firefly Responds," *Limón Searchlight*, Sept. 12, 1931, 4.

56. *Panama Star and Herald*, Dec. 31, 1920, 3.

57. *Panama Tribune*, Jan. 13, 1929, 4.

58. "Acknowledgment," *Barbados Weekly Herald*, Apr. 18, 1925, 4.

59. "Missing," *West Indies War Cry*, November 1929, 8.

60. "Comrades Bid Farewell [*sic*] to Friend," *Limón Searchlight*, July 4, 1931, 3.

61. Putnam, "'Nothing Matters but Color,'" 110–15.

62. E.g., see "Leaguer Comrades," *West Indies War Cry*, January 1906, 2; "The Call for West Africa," *West Indies War Cry*, April 1906, 3; "Zululand, Its History and People," *West Indies War Cry*, August 1906, 3; and "News of a Southerner in the North," *West Indies War Cry*, October 1926, 3.

63. See Reid, *Negro Immigrant*, 156–58; Watkins-Owens, *Blood Relations*, 55–74; and Putnam, "'Nothing Matters but Color.'"

64. "Adventists Dispute," *Limón Searchlight*, Jan. 11, 1930, 4.

65. E.g., "Negroes' Special Service in Abbey," *Limón Searchlight*, June 20, 1931, 6; Louis Launtier, "Elk Ruler Leaves for S. America," *Pittsburgh Courier*, Feb. 20, 1926, 14; and "Grand Exalted Ruler of Colored Elks Arrives," *Panama American*, Mar. 3, 1926.

66. *Limón Times*, June 2, 1911. See Smith, "John E. Bush."

67. Smith, *Many a Green Isle*, 264, 262; Rena Kosersky, liner notes to *Joe Louis, American Hero* (Rounder 82161-1106-2, 2001).

68. Makin, *Caribbean Nights*, 264. For the reaction to the same event in Harlem, see Ottley, *New World*, 186–202. On boxers and popular black internationalism, see Runstedtler, "Visible Men."

69. "Congratulates Joe Louis, Invites Him to Costa Rica," *Pittsburgh Courier*, Dec. 28, 1935, A2.

70. "Wants Readers' Reactions on Vital Questions," *Pittsburgh Courier*, Jan. 18, 1936, A2.

71. "From 28 Miles Waldeck," *Limón Searchlight*, Oct. 18, 1930, 5.

72. "Deplores Lack of Racial Sentiment," *Limón Searchlight*, June 13, 1931.

73. Sidney A. Young, "A New Awakening," in Young, *Isthmian Echoes*, 279.

74. On the use of the label and concept of "colored" to undergird alliance between Asians and Afro-Americans, see Slate, *Colored Cosmopolitanism*.

75. E.g., "Speech by Marcus Garvey," Kingston, Sept. 9, 1929, rpt. in Hill, *Garvey and UNIA Papers*, vol. 7, 335.

76. S. M. Nightengale, "Survival of the Fittest," in Young, *Isthmian Echoes*, 8; similarly, Elijah Hunter, "A Healthy Sign," in Young, *Isthmian Echoes*, 33–34.

77. "Negro Weakness in Cohesive Propensities," *Atlantic Voice*, Apr. 6, 1935, 7.

78. C. G. Whittingham, "Perils That Confront Our Race," *Panama Tribune*, Jan. 13, 1929, 8.

79. Sidney A. Young, "Magnificent Failures," in Young, *Isthmian Echoes*, 254.

80. Sidney A. Young, "The Proposed Central Organization," *Panama American*, Nov. 10, 1926. After a promising start with some 4,000 members affiliated, the Central Organization fractured, to be briefly revived in 1929. See Rachel Gately, "After the Canal: An Analysis of the Lives of West Indians in Panama through the Lens of the Local Press, 1926–1933," Undergraduate Social Sciences Summer Fellowship Research Paper, University of Pittsburgh, Fall 2012.

81. See Proctor, "Development of the Idea of Federation"; Parker, "Capital of the Caribbean"; Duke, "Diasporic Dimensions"; and Chamberlain, *Empire and Nation-Building*, 38–46.

82. "Federation and Unity," *Panama Tribune*, Jan. 13, 1929, 8. See also "The West Indies Seek Salvation by Federation," *Panama American*, Nov. 26, 1926, reprinting article from *Jamaica Critic*.

83. "Better Service," *Limón Searchlight*, Jan. 18, 1930, 2.

84. "Negro Appreciation," *Limón Searchlight*, Jan. 18, 1930, 2. On Nicholas, see Stein, *World of Marcus Garvey*, 236 (footnote 30).

85. Clennell Wickham, "The Yellow Peril (?): Nippon Uber Alles. Who Shall Inherit the Earth?," *Barbados Weekly Herald*, June 14, 1924, 4.

86. Ibid.

87. Ibid.

88. Ibid.

89. "Palmerston's Speech on Affairs in Greece (25 June 1850)," Great Britain, *Hansard* 112 (3rd ser.), 380–444; accessed via http://www.historyhome.co.uk/polspeech/foreign.htm.

90. "Correspondence: The Question of Loyalty and Patriotism," *Panama American*, Jan. 9, 1927.

91. "What Steps Will Britain Take," *Limón Searchlight*, Oct. 4, 1930, 2.

92. Ibid.

93. "James Graham Handed to Cuban Police and British Protection," *Limón Searchlight*, Aug. 9, 1930, 3.

94. "What Steps Will Britain Take."

95. Ibid.

96. "Note of protest from Her Majesty's chargé d'affairs in Venezuela . . . to the Secretary of State for Foreign Affairs . . . Caracas, Aug. 14, 1850," transcribed in Spanish in Arreaza Arana and Blanco, "Relaciones Díplomáticas," 59.

97. "24th MAY," *Limón Searchlight*, May 31, 1930, 1.

98. Ibid.

99. Ibid.

100. Squires, "Rethinking the Black Public Sphere," 448.

101. Fraser, "Rethinking the Public Sphere," 57.

CHAPTER FIVE

1. Sidney A. Young, "The Modern Dance," in Young, *Isthmian Echoes*, 248.

2. For a related but distinct argument, see Corbould, "Streets, Sounds, and Identity."

3. Gilroy, *Black Atlantic*, 200.

4. Warner, "Publics and Counterpublics," 88–89. I am grateful to Matthew Bernius for pointing out the relevance of this article.

5. Ibid., 82 et passim.

6. My understanding of the symbolic freighting of music and dance in the early twentieth-century Americas owes much to rich recent work on race and performance in transnational contexts: Burton, *Afro-Creole*; Wade, *Music, Race, and Nation*; Chude-Sokei, *Last "Darky"*; Hersch, *Subversive Sounds*; Seigel, *Uneven Encounters*.

7. A *Gleaner* article contemporaneous to that release captures the term's multiple resonances at the time: "REGE — Another dialect word at present in popular use is rege (at least this I take to be the spelling), the new term for a new local 'beat' and dance, successor, presumably, to the ska and rock steady. But rege is better known as the nickname for such foods as coconut run-down and fritters. Rege-rege is a different matter. It is probably a form of rag (compare the term raga-raga, for instance) and means ragged clothing. It is sometimes used also for a quarrel or fuss." DeB, "Take My Word," *Kingston Daily Gleaner*, Nov. 23, 1968, 3.

8. Chang and Chen, *Reggae Routes*; Senior, *Encyclopedia of Jamaican Heritage*, 412.

9. White, *Catch a Fire*, 16.

10. Erna Brodber, opening plenary, Global Reggae Conference, UWI-Mona, Feb. 18, 2008.

11. White, *Catch a Fire*, 16.

12. Cassidy and LePage, *Dictionary of Jamaican English*, 380.

13. Allsopp, *Dictionary of Caribbean English*, 471.

14. Proudfoot, *Population Movements*, 77–78, 101.

15. Walker, *Dubwise*, and personal communication.

16. E.g., Shipton, *New History of Jazz*, 261 et passim. In contrast, recent scholarly efforts in ethnomusicology foreground jazz's multi- and transnational strands. Atkins, "Towards a Global History of Jazz," xi–xxvii; and "Conference Report," Jazz Worlds/World Jazz Conference, organized by Goffredo Plastino, Philip Bohlman, and Travis Jackson, University of Chicago, May 25–26, 2006, http://www.bfe.org.uk/conferencearchive.html.

17. Abrahams, "Afro-Caribbean Culture," 97–125; Szwed, "World Views Collide," 193–94; Fiehrer, "From Quadrille to Stomp," 21–38; Washburne, "Clave of Jazz"; Hersch, *Subversive Sounds*, 20, 143–47; Don Rouse, "New Orleans Jazz and Caribbean Music," http://www.prjc.org/roots/nojazzandcarribe.html.

18. Cowley, "West Indies Blues," 187–263; Miller, "Syncopating Rhythms." See, too, the many references to British Caribbean peers in Kelley, *Thelonious Monk*. On jazz in Jamaica, see Porter, "Jazz to Ska Mania."

19. But see Cowley, "'Cultural Fusions'"; Chude-Sokei, *Last "Darky,"* especially chap. 4; Waxer, "Of Mambo Kings."

20. Patterns in the eastern Caribbean were surely distinct, in particular because of the centrality of Trinidad's carnival tradition and associated social institutions and businesses in shaping the musical landscape there. See Cowley, *Carnival, Canboulay and Calypso*; Liverpool, *Rituals of Power and Rebellion*; and Guilbaut, *Governing Sound*; see also Pinckney Jr., "Jazz in Barbados." Meanwhile, the story of what happened to the music and moves of British Caribbeans in Cuba remains opaque in my account. Given that the impact of Cuban-born "returnees" in the development of ska is irrefutable, this absence is a big deal. (See White, "The Evolution of Jamaican Music, Part 1.") The present chapter may be useful to those seeking to reconstruct the off-island roots of 1950s Jamaican music, but it is not itself that account in any sense.

21. De Lisser, *In Jamaica and Cuba*, 108.

22. "Correspondence: A Nuisance," *Kingston Daily Gleaner*, June 11, 1900, 1.

23. "In Metropolitan Tribunals: Petty Sessions Court," *Kingston Daily Gleaner*, Mar. 13, 1917.

24. De Lisser, *In Jamaica and Cuba*, 110.

25. James, *Out of the Shadows*, 215.

26. De Lisser, *In Jamaica and Cuba*, 109. Similarly, see Henderson, *Jamaica*, 58. For an insightful critique of claims about Africanness within Caribbean music, see Neely, "Mento."

27. In 1925 a *Daily Gleaner* wag explicated "Flora" as referring to "that portion of the living kingdom which displays activity, but is permanently stationary, such as a flower, a bunch of bananas when there are no praedial thieves about, or a couple dancing the shay-shay." "The Flora and Fauna of the Island," *Kingston Daily Gleaner*, June 13, 1925, 1.

28. De Lisser, *In Jamaica and Cuba*, 109. See commentary in Neely, "Mento." On set dances, see Szwed with Marks, "Afro-American Transformation," 153–67.

29. Manuel with Bilby and Largey, *Caribbean Currents*; Cowley, "Cultural Fusions."

30. Walrond, "The Godless City," in Parascandola, *Winds Can Wake Up the Dead*, 165.

31. Walrond, "Subjection," in *Tropic Death*, 152.

32. "Blues Is Jazz and Jazz Is Blues," rpt. in *Syracuse Herald*, Jan. 30, 1916, 32.

33. Rogers, "Jazz at Home," 665.

34. Watkins-Owens, *Blood Relations*, 47, 178, 182.

35. Brooks, *Lost Sounds*, 299–319 (quotes on 312).

36. Cowley, "West Indies Blues"; Cowley, "'Cultural Fusions'"; Liverpool, "Researching Steelband," 186 et passim.

37. Yanow, *Swing*, 113.

38. Hurwitt, "Renaissance Casino," 1044; http://www.pbs.org/jazz/biography/artist_id_manning_frankie.htm; Chadbourne, "Vernon Andrade's Biography," All Music Guide, http://www.allmusic.com/artist/vernon-andrade-p552590.

39. Bernhardt, *I Remember*, 118–19.

40. Ibid., 124.

41. "Obituary: Charles Buchanan Is Dead," *New York Times*, Dec. 14, 1984, D19.

42. Hurwitt, "Renaissance Casino," 1043–44; http://www.harlemonestop.com/organization.php?id=564.

43. Wiggins and Miller, *Unlevel Playing Field*, 102; "Robert L. 'Bob' Douglas," Naismith Memorial Basketball Hall of Fame, http://www.hoophall.com/hall-of-famers/tag/robert-l-bob-douglas; Kuska, *Hot Potato*, 88–91.

44. Sonja Steptoe, "Meet an Ageless Wonder," *Sports Illustrated*, Dec. 24, 1990.

45. Bernhardt, *I Remember*, 119.

46. Hurwitt, "Renaissance Casino," 1043–44.

47. "Case against Marcus Garvey in United States," *Kingston Daily Gleaner*, July 9, 1923, 14; "The Labour Act: Leeward Islands," *Kingston Daily Gleaner*, Aug. 18, 1924, 16; "Cricket Crusaders Return Home," *Kingston Daily Gleaner*, Sept. 23, 1930, 9.

48. Bernhardt, *I Remember*, 119.

49. Ibid., 124.

50. Miller with Jensen, *Swingin' at the Savoy*, 11, 20–21, 3.

51. Joseph Mitchell, "A Reporter at Large: Houdini's Picnic," *New Yorker*, May 6, 1939, 61–71 (quotes on 61–64).

52. Bernhardt, *I Remember*, 123–24, 120.

53. Malone, *Steppin' on the Blues*, 110, 102.

54. Edward Perry, "Manhattan Madness," *Pittsburgh Courier*, June 6, 1931, A8.

55. Griffiths, "Walter Bishop Sr.," *Hot Jazz*, 132–38 (quote on 135); Steve Voce, "Obituary: Walter Bishop Jnr," *The Independent*, Jan. 28, 1998, http://www.independent.co.uk/news/obituaries/obituary-walter-bishop-jnr-1141367.html.

56. Stokes, *Growing up with Jazz*, 3. Gaskin became a renowned bassist, playing with Dizzy Gillespie, Charlie Parker, and others.

57. Miller with Jensen, *Swingin' at the Savoy*, 20–21, 25, 37, 136–40, 157–64.

58. The term "Jazz" first appears in the *Daily Gleaner* in December 1917, with reference to "The Jazz Band" (apparently well known because not otherwise identified) playing at the Myrtle Beach Hotel. "A Happy Time for Juveniles," *Kingston Daily Gleaner*, Dec. 20, 1917, 6; Advertisement, *Kingston Daily Gleaner*, Aug. 10, 1916, 4.

59. Advertisement, *Kingston Daily Gleaner*, June 22, 1917, 8.

60. Advertisement, *Kingston Daily Gleaner*, July 18, 1919, 20.

61. Carter Irving, "Jazz Brings First Dance of the City," *Kingston Daily Gleaner*, June 27, 1925, 2, reprinting article from *New York Times*, June 14, 1925, SM9.

62. "Music Which Is Rage in London," *Kingston Daily Gleaner*, Sept. 1, 1920, 4.

63. Ibid.

64. Ibid. and Cowley, "'Cultural Fusions,'" 87.

65. Manuel with Bilby and Largey, *Caribbean Currents*, 101.

66. Amador de Jesus, "*Plena*'s Dissonant Melodies."

67. Senior, *Encyclopedia of Jamaican Heritage*, 413.

68. Verrill, *Jamaica of Today*, 145–46. "As everyone knows they have a predilection for syncopated music or 'jazz' as we call it."

69. Mills, *Country of the Orinoco*, 185–86.

70. *Kingston Daily Gleaner*, Aug. 13, 1927, 4; May 28, 1927, 24; and many more.

71. Advertisement, *Kingston Daily Gleaner*, May 27, 1931, 5. See Cowley, "'Cultural Fusions,'" 92; and Manuel, *Caribbean Currents*, 36.

72. Smith, *Many a Green Isle*, 261. See Cowley, "L'Année Passée," 2–9.

73. "Radio Installation," *Limón Searchlight*, June 21, 1930, 2.

74. "Scenes and Sights in Metropolis by Night," *Kingston Daily Gleaner*, Sept. 22, 1922, 3.

75. H. G. de Lisser, "A Kingston Diary: Run Mongoose Run," *Kingston Daily Gleaner*, July 19, 1921, 6.

76. "Constant Spring Ball: A Correspondent Who Has No Liking for Jazz Dances," *Kingston Daily Gleaner*, July 22, 1921, 6.

77. "So-Called Shay-Shays," *Kingston Daily Gleaner*, July 23, 1921, 10.

78. "Our Girls Are Fine Dancers Says Valencia," *Kingston Daily Gleaner*, Aug. 8, 1936, 10.

79. Letter to the Editor from Slim Beckford and Sam Blackwood, published under title "Jamaica Folks Songs," *Kingston Daily Gleaner*, Aug. 13, 1936, 40. On Slim and Sam, see Chang and Chen, *Reggae Routes*, 15.

80. E.g., notes by Bea Drew, "Panama," in *Variety* (New York), Jan. 28, 1931; Mar. 4, 1931; Feb. 12, 1935.

81. Cowley, "'Cultural Fusions,'" 83.

82. "American Coloured Review Arrives in Island for Season," *Kingston Daily Gleaner*, May 4, 1928, 14; "Stars That Shine," *Pittsburgh Courier*, Mar. 17, 1928, A2.

83. Peterson, *African American Theatre Directory*, 27–28; Evans, *Ramblin' on My Mind*, 80–81; "Happenings at the Local Playhouses," *Pittsburgh Courier*, Dec. 20, 1924, 10.

84. Charters, *Trumpet around the Corner*, 204–5.

85. "A Letter from Cuba," *Pittsburgh Courier*, Jan. 8, 1927, A3.

86. "William Benbow and Gang in Cuba," *Pittsburgh Courier*, Feb. 25, 1928, A2; "Benbow's Follies Impress," *Pittsburgh Courier*, Apr. 14, 1928, A2. See Peterson, *Century of Musicals*, 144, 31.

87. "Performance by Benbow Troupe," *Kingston Daily Gleaner*, May 10, 1928, 8.

88. "'Follies' Score on Islands, Say Howdy," *Pittsburgh Courier*, Mar. 30, 1929, A3.

89. "Showman Known Here Held for Murder in USA," *Kingston Daily Gleaner*, Feb. 7, 1939, 4, reprinting article from *Panama Tribune*.

90. Bea Drew, "Panama," *Variety* (New York), Apr. 29, 1931.

91. Advertisement, "Palace To-Night," *Kingston Daily Gleaner*, May 23, 1928, 4.

92. "Current Items: Blackstar Demons," *Limón Searchlight*, Apr. 5, 1930, 4.

93. "The Broadway Follies Arrived Here Yesterday," *Kingston Daily Gleaner*, Dec. 7, 1932, 11; "Broadway Follies Put on Splendid Show," *Kingston Daily Gleaner*, Dec. 9, 1932, 22.

94. Advertisement, "Ward Theatre," *Kingston Daily Gleaner*, Feb. 28, 1933, 2; "Benbow's Follies Show at Theatre Wednesday Night," *Kingston Daily Gleaner*, Mar. 10, 1933. On the performance of origins within vaudeville, see Chude-Sokei, *Last "Darky."*

95. "Follies Feted," *Pittsburgh Courier*, May 4, 1929, A3.

96. "Benbow's Self Defense Plea Wins His Freedom," *Pittsburgh Courier*, Jan. 28, 1939, 5. See also "Showman Known Here Held for Murder in USA," *Kingston Daily Gleaner*, Feb. 7, 1939, 4, reprinting item from *Panama Tribune*.

97. "Miami Follies Again Entertain Good House," *Kingston Daily Gleaner*, Mar. 26, 1929, 3; Advertisement, "Ward Theatre, To-Night," *Kingston Daily Gleaner*, Mar. 27, 1929, 2.

98. "Councillors Are Censors of Miami Follies," *Kingston Daily Gleaner*, Mar. 26, 1929, 3.

99. Ibid.

100. "The Attack upon Benbow's American Follies," *Kingston Daily Gleaner*, Mar. 28, 1929, 12.

101. "Jim Crow Crashes Panama Society," *Pittsburgh Courier*, Mar. 13, 1937, 6. They explained they "would not have been so peeved if the order had included the entire party, but Lt. Echeona distinctly said that all those of light skin who could 'pass' could remain, but that the darker ones would have to leave."

102. Bea Drew, "Panama," *Variety* (New York), Jan. 28, 1931.

103. "Panama Orchestra to Play at Jamaica Industrial Exhibition," *Kingston Daily Gleaner*, Jan. 6, 1934, 5.

104. E.g., "Mr. N. W. Manley Talks in Panama on Chances of Our Olympic Team," *Kingston Daily Gleaner*, Jan. 13, 1938, 14; http://www.carlosmalcolm.net/; Porter, "Jazz to Ska Mania."

105. "Jazz Aristocrats Take Title of 'Kings of Jazz,'" *Kingston Daily Gleaner*, Jan. 20, 1934, 5. Other premier jazz orchestras of the western Caribbean included Kingston's Kings' Rhythm Aces and Panama's Isthmian Syncopators. Walker, *Dubwise*, 106; Advertisement, *Panama American*, July 25, 1926.

106. Advertisement, *Panama American*, July 22, 1926.

107. Advertisement, *Limón Searchlight*, June 14, 1930, 3.

108. Advertisement, *Limón Searchlight*, May 16, 1931, 5. By then it was the Red Hot Six Orchestra providing the music.

109. "Another Function by the Star Combination Company," *Limón Searchlight*, Jan. 10, 1931, 1.

110. "The Central American Stars and Combination Co.," *Limón Searchlight*, June 6, 1931, 5.

111. "The Stage Manager Explains," *Limón Searchlight*, June 13, 1931, 1.

112. "Excursionists from Santiago de Cuba Sailed Yesterday," *Kingston Daily Gleaner*, Sept. 1, 1926, 3.

113. "The Excursionists from Bocas," *Limón Searchlight*, Nov. 22, 1930, 6.

114. Smith, *Many a Green Isle*, 221.

115. Sidney A. Young, "Sid Says: Charley's Letter," *Panama American*, July 16, 1926.

116. E.g., Advertisement, "New Columbia Records," *Limón Searchlight*, Mar. 22, 1930, 1.

117. "The Coloured Troop in San Jose," *Limón Searchlight*, Mar. 22, 1930, 4. See also "A False Attack," *Limón Searchlight*, Mar. 15, 1930, 4.

118. "The Central American Stars and Combination Co.," *Limón Searchlight*, June 6, 1931, 5.

119. Porter Roberts, "Praise and Criticism," *Pittsburgh Courier*, Sept. 3, 1938, 20; Nov. 26, 1938, 20. The song shark in this instance was Sylvester Cross, whose remarkably profitable business model drew more than one lawsuit. See "U.S. Judge Says Westmore Isn't Guilty of Fraud," *Billboard*, May 19, 1945, 18.

120. Porter Roberts, "Praise and Criticism," *Pittsburgh Courier*, Dec. 10, 1938, 21.

121. Ibid.

122. Ibid.; Porter Roberts, "Praise and Criticism," *Pittsburgh Courier*, Nov. 26, 1938, 20.

123. Porter Roberts, "Praise and Criticism," *Pittsburgh Courier*, Sept. 3, 1938, 20.

124. "Shimmy Dance Condemned by a Newspaper," *Kingston Daily Gleaner*, Feb. 10, 1922, 5, reprinting article from the *Clarion* of British Honduras, Jan. 5, 1922, which addressed itself "for the special benefit of the 'Shimmy' dancers of British Honduras. Directed to all shades of colour and opinion."

125. See discussion of citizenship issues involving the second generation in the chapter 6.

126. C. C. Moulton, "A Review," in Young, *Isthmian Echoes*, 80.

127. Sidney A. Young, "The Modern Dance," in Young, *Isthmian Echoes*, 247.

128. Ibid.

129. Ibid., 248.

130. Rogers, "Jazz at Home," 665.

131. ANP, Sección Justicia, Ramo Criminal, Juzgado Superior de Panamá, Expediente 7113, Cajón 99 (begun Apr. 17, 1933, Juzgado Segundo Circuito de Bocas del Toro), folios 7–8.

132. Ibid.

133. Sidney A. Young, "The Modern Dance," in Young, *Isthmian Echoes*, 248. The term was common in Jamaica as well, as in Ivy Baxter's description of popular dance in 1940s Jamaica: "a little 'shay-shay' and 'bram' on a Saturday night." Baxter, *Arts of an Island*, 297.

134. Mrs. Bertie Callender, "An Appeal to Mothers," in Young, *Isthmian Echoes*, 70.

135. C. S. Elcock, "Our Degenerate Youth," *Panama American*, Mar. 20, 1926.

136. B. J. Waterman, "Education," in Young, *Isthmian Echoes*, 62. The tamborito was a traditional Afro-Panamanian dance.

137. Ibid.

138. S. A. Borrows, "Correspondence: Bands at Funeral Processions," *Panama American*, Oct. 2, 1926.

139. Ibid. On New Orleans, see Southern, *Music of Black Americans*, 341.

140. "Philomela Counsels," *Limón Searchlight*, May 16, 1931, 5.

141. Sidney A. Young, "Preface," in Young, *Isthmian Echoes*, viii.

142. Ibid., v.

143. "Right about Face," *Limón Searchlight*, Jan. 11, 1930, 1.

144. Sidney A. Young, "The Modern Dance," in Young, *Isthmian Echoes*, 248–49.

145. "Function of the University Club," *Limón Searchlight*, July 25, 1931, 3.

146. "The University Club," *Limón Searchlight*, May 2 1931, 1, 6.

147. "A Successful Function," *Limón Searchlight*, July 25, 1931, 6.

148. "Excursion Train," *Limón Searchlight*, June 28, 1930, 1. The Merry Makers or Black Stars Orchestra had evolved from the same core of musicians who performed as part of the Central American Black Stars Combination Company, above.

149. "These Excursion Picnics Affect the Community," *Limón Searchlight*, July 12, 1930, 2. I am grateful to Ileana D'Alolio for the original transcription of this and several other articles from the Limón press.

150. Ibid.

151. Meanwhile, the term "calypso" is absent here and indeed from all of the print record of interwar Limón, suggesting a minimal impact here of the calypso recordings already under way in Port of Spain and New York. The term, however, would soon be adopted in Limón as a label for locally created mento music. Monestel, *Ritmo, canción e identidad*, chap. 1. Most likely, this lexical shift took place in the 1940s, the same years when Jamaican popular musical artists began recording mento pieces under the label "Jamaican calypso."

152. As will be clear from the transcriptions below, the spelling employed for the term shifted constantly, often even within a single article or letter. This was clearly a word from oral rather than print culture—and it would stay that way, apparently, leaving no further print traces over the following three decades. Note that when the term "reggae" as a reference to dance (re)emerged in 1968 Kingston, the spelling "rege" seemed more likely to some: see footnote 7, above.

153. The *Oxford English Dictionary* notes also early twentieth-century British usage meaning "angry, irritated," as in (1900): "He was jolly raggy about us taking his old gee." *Oxford English Dictionary Online*, www.oed.com.

154. "No 'Grizzly Bear' Dance," *Washington Post*, Apr. 30, 1911, 24.

155. "Lizzie Miles," in Griffiths, *Hot Jazz*, 27.

156. Ibid., 20; "In the Stores: The Display of Goods at Messrs. Winkler & Son," *Kingston Daily Gleaner*, Dec. 10, 1913.

157. "A Visit from 'Johnny,'" *Kingston Daily Gleaner*, Mar. 10, 1913, 10.

158. "Variety Concert," *Kingston Daily Gleaner*, Nov. 10, 1922, 5; "Concert at Y.M.C.A.," *Kingston Daily Gleaner*, July 2, 1923, 15; "Fine Concert Was Staged at Stewart Town," *Kingston Daily Gleaner*, July 2, 1928, 18.

159. James E. Bowen, "Noble Sissle and Ethel Waters Steal Spotlight as '34 Radio Sensations but Whites Knock 'Em," *Pittsburgh Courier*, Feb. 3, 1934, A1.

160. "These Excursion Picnics Affect the Community."

161. Ibid.

162. Letter to the Editor, "A Criticism," *Limón Searchlight*, July 19, 1930, 2.

163. Editors' note in response to "Another Critic," *Limón Searchlight*, July 26, 1930, 1. Spelling as in original.

164. "Substantiated," *Limón Searchlight*, July 26, 1930, 4; "To Leaders and Excursion Trains," *Limón Searchlight*, Aug. 2, 1930, 4; "Another Opinion," *Limón Searchlight*, Aug. 9, 1930, 1; "Cyrilo Again," *Limón Searchlight*, Aug. 9, 1930, 2; "A letter from the Crystal Gazer Critic," *Limón Searchlight*, Aug. 9, 1930, 4.

165. "The Night Hawk Talks," *Limón Searchlight*, Mar. 7, 1931, 5.

166. Ibid.

167. Ibid.

168. "Educational Sociology," *Limón Searchlight*, Apr. 11, 1931, 4.

169. Dolores Joseph, "Young Men to Open Club," *Limón Searchlight*, May 16, 1931, 3. Punctuation and capitalization in original. From other letters, it is clear that Dolores was a young man.

170. Dolores Joseph, "Something Again about the Alpha," *Limón Searchlight*, July 18, 1931, 4.

171. Dolores Joseph, "The Alpha's Call a Failure," *Limón Searchlight*, Nov. 21, 1931, 3.

172. Sydney Montague, "In Defense of the U.N.I.A.," *Limón Searchlight*, Nov. 28, 1931, 2.

173. Dolores Joseph, "In Defense of My Philosophy," *Limón Searchlight*, Dec. 5, 1931, 2.

174. Ibid.

175. Hamilton, "Marcus Garvey and Cultural Development," esp. 99, 101. Central America's British West Indian press covered these developments, as they did every move Garvey made. E.g., "An Amusement Co.," *Limón Searchlight*, July 4, 1931, 2. On Lord Fly, see "The King of Calypso: Meet Lord Fly," *Kingston Daily Gleaner*, Sept. 26, 1948.

176. Articles by Vere Johns in the *New York Age*, August-September 1932, rpt. in Hill, *Garvey and UNIA Papers*, vol. 7, 534; see Miller, "Marcus Garvey," 121 et passim.

177. "Vere Johns, Journalist, Dies at 73," *Kingston Daily Gleaner*, Sept. 11, 1966, 1, 2; Editorial, "Vere Johns," *Kingston Daily Gleaner*, Sept. 12, 1966, 10; "Vere Johns Gets Military Burial," *Kingston Daily Gleaner*, Sept. 16, 1966, 5, 18; Bradley, *Bass Culture*, 19–21.

178. On the independence era, see the invaluable Thomas, *Modern Blackness*.

179. White, *Catch a Fire*, 134–35.

180. E.g., Chang and Chen, *Reggae Routes*, 17, 16. Jamaican experts, in contrast, do underline the importance of the jazz training and big-band experience of the pioneers of ska. Hutton and White, "Social and Aesthetic Roots," 91–92.

181. Sidney A. Young, "Sid Says: I Am Peeved," *Panama American*, Mar. 23, 1926.

182. White, "Evolution of Jamaican Music," 11.

183. Hutton, "Cuban Influence," 162. Hutton notes the importance of "swing-jazz" and "Jamaican big bands" in the 1940s (165); my research would confirm this but push the start date back two decades.

184. John Collins, "The Impact of African-American Performance on West Africa from 1800," paper read at 19th International Biennial Conference of the African Studies Association of Germany, University of Hannover, Germany, June 2–5, 2004; Neely, "Mento."

185. Miller with Jensen, *Swingin' at the Savoy*, 13.

CHAPTER SIX

1. Jacobs, *Butler versus the King*.

2. "Leonard Howell, on Trial Says Ras Tafari Is Messiah Returned to Earth," *Kingston Daily Gleaner*, Mar. 15, 1934, 20.

3. Post, *Arise Ye Starvelings*, 280; Hart, *Rise and Organise*, 48–52.

4. Post, *Arise Ye Starvelings*, 244.

5. Chomsky, *West Indian Workers*, 239–53; Echeverri-Gent, "Forgotten Workers," 301–7; Figueroa Ibarra, "Marxismo, sociedad y movimiento sindical."

6. Conniff, *Black Labor on a White Canal*, 81–90, 98–101; Pearcy, "Panama's Generation of '31"; "Cause for Praise and Congratulation," *Panama Tribune*, June 12, 1932, 8.

7. McGillivray, *Blazing Cane*, 204–37; Carr, "Identity, Class, and Nation"; McLeod, "Undesirable Aliens"; CO 318/408/4, Immigration of British West Indians to Central and South America, 1933: Letter, British Legation, Havana, to FO, Oct. 11, 1933; Memo from Bunbury, consul, Oct. 11, 1933. Bunbury predicted: "The part played by [British West Indian labourers] in the recent strike movement will be immediately forgotten by their fellow workers in the industry, though remembered to their disadvantage by the employers."

8. Ottley, *New World*, 115–21, 151–66; McKay, *Harlem*, 181–229 (quote 186–87).

9. Bergquist, *Labor in Latin America*, 226–31; Ewell, *Venezuela*, 72–82. For region-wide overview, see Bolland, "Labor Protests."

10. See, for instance, the testimonies before the West India Royal Commission from observers ranging from an aging Marcus Garvey to a very young W. Arthur Lewis. CO 950/44, Mr. Marcus Garvey (Universal Negro Improvement Association): Memorandum of Evidence; CO 950/56, Mr. W. Arthur Lewis, B Cam.: Memorandum of Evidence. Carnegie, *Some Aspects of Jamaica's Politics*, 144–51; Bolland, *Politics of Labour*, 157–63, 366–67; Chamberlain, *Empire and Nation-Building*.

11. CO 318/404/13, Immigration of British West Indians into Central and South America, Stockdale, Minute of 25.11.31.

12. CO 318/408/3, Immigration of British West Indians to Central and South America, 1932, Enclosure No. 4 in Panama Despatch No. 308 of 6th Dec. 1932: Memorandum regarding the British West Indian population on the Isthmus of Panama; Panamá, Secretaría de Agricultura y Obras Públicas, Dirección General del Censo, *Censo de 1930*, 17; U.S. Bureau of the Census, *Fifteenth Census, Report on Outlying Territories*, 328, 334, 335.

13. *Censo de Población de Costa Rica*, 1927, consulted at http://censos.ccp.ucr.ac.cr/.

14. Honduras, Dirección General de Estadística y Censos, *Censo de 1930*, 32; Nicaragua, Dirección General de Estadística, *Censo General de 1920*, 4; Guatemala, Dirección General de Estadística, *Censo de 1921*, 139.

15. "Cuba, Panama Are Where the Jamaicans Go," *Kingston Daily Gleaner*, Sept. 5, 1924, 3; CO 318/408/4, Immigration of British West Indians to Central and South America, 1933: Memo, Oct. 11, 1933, "Regarding the Position of British West Indian labourers in Cuba, as a Result of the recent labour agitation on the Sugar Mills"; CO 318/394/3, Immigration of British West Indians: Report to British Minister, Havana, from Secretary of Immigration.

16. CO 318/382, West Indies: General, 1925: Letter from British Legation, Havana to Governor, Jamaica, Jan. 23, 1925; Cuba, *Memorias inéditas*, 74; Cuba, *Censo de 1943*, 888–89; CO 318/406/1, Immigration of British West Indians in Central and South America: Report from British Legation, Havana, Cuba, Apr. 4, 1932; McLeod, "Undesirable Aliens."

17. Dominican Republic, Dirección General de Estadística, *Población de la República Dominicana*, 2, 5. In 1929 the chargé d'affairs estimated 10,000 "British subjects of colour in Dominican territory." CO 318/394/3, Immigration of British West Indians: Letter to FO from W. Gallienne, Sept. 16, 1929; CO 318/406/2, Immigration of British West Indians to Central and South America: Summation, "Position of British West Indians in Central and South American Countries."

18. Venezuela, Ministerio de Fomento, Dirección de Estadística, *Sexto Censo de Población*, 1936, 189, 540, reports only 5,261 British "colonials" in total, but the estimate by the British minister in Caracas of 10,000 in the country overall in 1932 is more consistent with provincial documentation I have seen. CO 318/406/2, Immigration of British West Indians to Central and South America, 1932: Summation, "Position of British West Indians in Central and South American Countries."

19. Kuczynski, *Demographic Survey*, vol. 3, 155, 341.

20. Additionally, there were over 60,000 U.S.-born children with at least one Caribbean parent tallied in the same census. U.S. Bureau of the Census, *Census of the United States, 1930*, vol. 2, 231, 33. (These figures exclude immigrants from Cuba and Puerto Rico but include other Spanish- and French-speaking islands.) The Smith Act of 1940 made supporting any organization that "advocate[d] . . . the overthrow of any government" a deportable offense; it was under this act that Trinidad-born communist Claudia Jones, for instance, was deported. See Davies, *Left of Karl Marx*, 147–50. As discussed below, British colonial authorities likewise insisted on their right to deport British Caribbean migrants back to the islands of their birth if they engaged in labor organizing or "seditious" activities.

21. In theory, legal residents could leave and return without a problem; in practice, those attempting to do so risked running afoul of consular suspicions and documentary demands.

22. Makonnen, *Pan-Africanism*, 33–34.

23. Sidney A. Young, "Ranting and Tearing for Unity," *Panama American*, Dec. 8, 1926, 11.

24. Sidney A. Young, "A Deplorable Trend," *Panama American*, Feb. 10, 1927.

25. The term "West Indian" had shifting and ambiguous referents in this era in contexts as varied as U.S. censuses and anti-imperialist poetry (see, e.g., Nicolás Guillén's 1934 *West Indies Ltd.*). Although authors like Claude McKay and Eric Walrond sometimes used the term to encompass French, Dutch, Spanish, and British Caribbeans as a single whole, in quotidian usage in the Anglophone world, "West Indian" meant British West Indian.

26. Herbert Morrice, "Is West Indian Unity a Fact?," *Panama American*, Oct. 28, 1926.

27. Herbert Morrice, "Morricisms: Between Ourselves," *Panama American*, Oct. 4, 1926.

28. Morrice, "Is West Indian Unity a Fact?"

29. Sidney A. Young, "Sid Says: A Practical Plan," *Panama American*, Oct. 26, 1926.

30. I refer here to "island" as the unit of belonging, but more precisely it was the specific colony, which in some cases included two or more islands. Thus, for instance, authorities in the colony of Trinidad and Tobago (unified since 1889) did not dispute Tobagonians' right of return to Trinidad. In the context of the contentious 1930s, though, this did not go without saying: it had to be said. See, e.g., CO 295/586/7, Refusal of Trinidad authorities to admit deportees from Venezuela: Letter from Hollis, Governor Trinidad, to CO, Dec. 21, 1934, insisting that, despite Venezuelan allegations to the contrary, "in no case has a native of Tobago been refused permission to enter Trinidad whether arriving from Venezuela or any other place."

31. Sidney A. Young, "The Federation of the West Indies," *Panama American*, Aug. 23, 1927.

32. "Urge Steps to Protect West Indians Abroad," *Panama American*, July 14, 1927.

33. See extensive correspondence in CO 318/394/3, Immigration of British West Indians.

34. CO 318/390/4, Emigration of Labourers into Cuba etc.: Visit of Mr. H. H. Trusted to Cuba, Santo Domingo, etc.

35. The literature on these family forms in the British Caribbean is vast. For an overview, see Barrow, *Family in the Caribbean*; for statistics and discussion, see Roberts, *Population of Jamaica*, 263–306.

36. CO 318/408/3, Immigration of British West Indians to Central and South America, 1932: Enclosure No. 4 in Panama Despatch No. 308 of 6th Dec. 1932.

37. CO 318/408/3, Immigration of British West Indians to Central and South America, 1932: Despatch from Crosby to CO, Nov. 28, 1932.

38. See extensive correspondence in CO 318/408/3, Immigration of British West Indians to Central and South America, 1932; and CO 318/408/4, Immigration of British West Indians to Central and South America, 1933.

39. CO 318/406/1, Immigration of British West Indians in Central and South America: Minute; CO 318/408/3, Immigration of British West Indians to Central and South America, 1932: Draft of letter from Colonial Secretary, June 1933.

40. CO 318/408/3, Immigration of British West Indians to Central and South America, 1932: Minutes.

41. CO 318/408/4, Immigration of British West Indians to Central and South America, 1933: Reply from Governor of Jamaica to CO, Oct. 16, 1933.

42. CO 318/408/3, Immigration of British West Indians to Central and South America, 1932: Letter from Crosby, July 10, 1933. Crosby attributed the phrase to the governor of Jamaica.

43. CO 318/406/2, Immigration of British West Indians to Central and South America, 1932: Copy of letter from Crosby, Panama, Sept. 8, 1932. Similarly, CO 318/408/3, Immigration of British West Indians to Central and South America, 1932: Letter from Crosby to CO, Dec. 6, 1932.

44. CO 318/394/3, Immigration of British West Indians: Letter from Inspector General of Consular Establishments to FO, May 27, 1929. A U.S. diplomat in 1930 Costa Rica reported that it was "practically understood by British consular representatives that they are to do nothing by way of protecting the rights and interests of West Indian negroes." Quoted in Colby, *Business of Empire*, 179.

45. CO 318/394/3, Immigration of British West Indians: Response from FO to Chancery, British Legation, Havana, June 4, 1929.

46. See Mongia, "Race, Nationality, Mobility"; and Lake and Reynolds, *Global Color Line*.

47. E.g., "British Protection," *Limón Searchlight*, Feb. 1, 1930, 2.

48. Magid, *Urban Nationalism*, 197–206; Brereton, *History of Modern Trinidad*, 152–53, 165–69.

49. "Trinidad Protests against Venezuela Ban on West Indians," *Kingston Daily Gleaner*, Oct. 14, 1930, 10.

50. Ibid.

51. See Chien Wei-Hong, "Our Trinidad Chinese," in Chien Chiao, *The Chinese in Trinidad*, December 1944, excerpted in Look Lai, *Chinese in the West Indies*, 238–40.

52. Neither "British citizenship" nor "imperial citizenship" existed as a legal category at the time. Rather, the populaces of the United Kingdom, the dominions, and the dependant colonies were British Subjects (the nonwhite among them sometimes specified as "non-European British Subjects"), while those of the empire's other territories were British Protected Persons. Attempts to create such a status foundered on the question of the intercolonial mobility of rights. If colonial subjects of color shared a formal citizenship status with white Britons and white colonials, on what grounds could Chinese, South Asian, or black British subjects be banned from Canada and Australia (whose leaders refused to budge on this issue)? See Gorman, *Imperial Citizenship*, 19–24; Lake and Reynolds, *Global Colour Line*, 120–22, 144–45, 186–87, et passim; Mongia, "Race, Nationality, Mobility"; and Killingray, "Good West Indian."

53. "Trinidad Protests against Venezuela Ban on West Indians."

54. Ibid.

55. Passenger record for Tito Princelliano Achong, arr. Sept. 24, 1916, Passenger manifest, S.S. *Terence*, from Santos, Brazil, via Trinidad, 1916, http://www.ellisisland.org.

56. Wei-Hong, "Our Trinidad Chinese," 240.

57. "Trinidad Protests against Venezuela Ban on West Indians."

58. "Unemployment in Trinidad Is Growing," *Kingston Daily Gleaner*, Sept. 11, 1930, 16.

59. RelExtDPI 249 (Gran Bretaña, 1929), Prohibición entrada a negro indease-ables, folios 16 a 19, includes clippings of Trinidadian press responses advocating Chinese exclusion. Kuczynski, *Colonial Population*, 26.

60. "Chinese and Syrians Fight Trinidad Bill," *Kingston Daily Gleaner*, Mar. 31, 1931, 18.

61. See Neptune, *Caliban and the Yankees*, 70, 76, 97.

62. "Chinese and Syrians Fight Trinidad Bill."

63. CO 295/596/17, Criticisms by the Chinese Government of the immigration legislation recently enacted by the Government of Trinidad: Letter from Governor, Trinidad, to CO, Mar. 4, 1937. Note that once again, Chinese diplomats had intervened in London, seeking to have discriminatory language removed.

64. Braithwaite, "Social Stratification," 9.

65. Debate of May 29, 1931, in Trinidad and Tobago, *Debates in the Legislative Council, January-December 1931*, 423–29.

66. Debate of Apr. 3, 1936, in Trinidad and Tobago, *Debates in the Legislative Council, January-December 1936*, 115.

67. Ibid., quotes on 119, 118, 120, 121. Those labeled "Assyrian" in Trinidad included immigrants from what is now Lebanon as well as current Syria; they were Arab Christians, associated here as across Latin America with dry goods and peddling.

68. Ibid., quotes on 115, 135.

69. RelExtDPI 298 (Gran Bretaña, 1934), Sobre la entrada clandestina a Venezuela de los extranjeros provenientes de Trinidad: Letter from Venezuelan Minister, London, to FO, Oct. 23, 1934. Letter as translated and received appears in CO 295/586/7, Admittance of undesirable deportees from Venezuela.

70. RelExtDPI 298 (Gran Bretaña, 1934), Sobre la entrada clandestina a Venezuela de los extranjeros provenientes de Trinidad: British Minister, Caracas, to Ministerio de Relaciones Interiores, Caracas, June 1935; CO 295/586/7, Admittance of undesirable deportees from Venezuela: Minutes; Letter from Governor, Trinidad, to CO, May 27, 1935.

71. CO 295/586/7, Admittance of undesirable deportees from Venezuela: Telegram from FO to British Minister, Caracas, May 16, 1935.

72. RelExtDPI 298 (Gran Bretaña, 1934), Reply from Venezuelan Minister, London, to Cancillería, Caracas, May 24, 1935. See also RelExtDPI 569 (Gran Bretaña, 1936), Memoria de labores de la Legación en 1935, 6–7; and AHS, Gaveta 28, B 72: "Relacionado con el arribo clandestino a las costas de Venezuela de extranjeros, procedentes de Trinidad, sin documentos requeridos y dificultades de capitanes de buques para el reembarco de expresados elementos." Given that Trinidad was a Crown colony, colonial officials could in theory impose the legislation they wanted. But the Venezuelan ambassador's perception of island "autonomy" matches the tone of Colonial Office internal correspondence, which treats Trinidadian leaders' opinion as a near ironclad constraint. (Similarly, see CO minutes regarding Leewards Unofficials, above.)

73. CO 318/436/10, Venezuelan Affairs, Deportation of Foreigners: Letter from British Minister, Caracas to FO, Aug. 10, 1939; CO 318/436/15, Treatment of British

West Indians in Venezuela: Compensation Claims. Quote from CO 318/417/6, Treatment of British West Indians in Venezuela, Claims for Compensation: Letter from John Baptist Edward Laronde to Governor, Leeward Islands, 1935. Those deported in 1938 reported that at least another fifty British West Indians were being held at the labor camp for immigration violations. The "creation of a labor camp for inadmissible and pernicious foreigners" is described in Venezuela, Ministerio de Relaciones Interiores, *Memoria [respecto al año 1937]*, 883. Other British Caribbean migrants were put over the border into British Guiana in the same years; see CO 318/436/10, Venezuelan Affairs, Deportation of Foreigners.

74. E.g., CO 318/417/6, Treatment of British West Indians in Venezuela, Claims for Compensation: Letter from Lloyd, British Vice-consul, Yrapa, Apr. 6, 1935.

75. CO 318/436/15, Treatment of British West Indians in Venezuela: Compensation Claims: Telegram from FO to Gye British Legation, Caracas, Oct. 7, 1938; Letter from Gye, British Legation, Caracas to FO, Sept 5, 1938. On Anglo-Persian negotiations, see CO 295/586/7, Admittance of undesirable deportees from Venezuela.

76. CO 318/436/15, Treatment of British West Indians in Venezuela: Compensation Claims: Statement of Joseph Benjamin, July 8, 1939.

77. CO 318/442/8, Treatment of British West Indians in Venezuela: Compensation Claims: Testimony of Edwin Alexander Richardson.

78. CO 318/436/15, Treatment of British West Indians in Venezuela: Compensation Claims: Statement of Eldon Cudjoe, July 8, 1939.

79. Ibid.: Statement of Metan Stafford, July 8, 1939.

80. CO 318/408/3, Immigration of British West Indians to Central and South America, 1932: Copy of letter from Josiah Crosby, British Minister, Panama, June 15, 1933.

81. CO 318/436/15, Treatment of British West Indians in Venezuela: Compensation Claims: Statement of Samuel Sandy, July 8, 1939. See also testimony of Samuel Dean in same file.

82. CO 318/406/1, Immigration of British West Indians in Central and South America: Letter from Josiah Crosby, British Minister, Panama, to CO, Sept. 21, 1931.

83. Proudfoot, *Population Movements*, 77–78.

84. Roberts, *Population of Jamaica*, 141, 147, 148 (discussion on 152–64).

85. Chamberlain, *Empire and Nation-Building*, 2. A rough indication of the relative weights of return streams are the birthplaces of British West Indians tallied in the various colonies by the 1946 census. Barbados's 1946 population included 1,000 people born in Trinidad, 1,000 born in Guiana, and another 1,500 divided equally between Panama and the United States. Jamaicans tallied in the 1943 Jamaican census included 6,700 born in Cuba, 3,400 born in Panama, 1,400 born in the United States, and 1,000 born in the eastern Caribbean. Of these foreign-born Jamaicans, 6,700 had "returned" to the island between 1921 and 1930, and 5,600 "returned" between 1931 and 1935 alone. Proudfoot, *Population Movements*, 94–99, 101, 102. The preceding numbers tally only foreign-born children who "returned." As is clear from the statistics at footnote 83, above, the numbers of actual returnees—that is, islanders returning to the islands of their birth—were far higher.

86. Carmichael, *Ready for Revolution*, 14–21.

87. "Smith Village Assn. and Council of the K & S.A. Corporation," *Kingston Daily Gleaner*, Dec. 9, 1935, 23. Scholars link Pocomania to the Pukumina tradition that had emerged in those regions of nineteenth-century Jamaica where postemancipation African immigrants settled. Alleyne, *Roots of Jamaican Culture*, 96–102; Besson, "Religion as Resistance."

88. "Pocomaya," *Limón Searchlight*, May 17, 1930, 3; "Los sacerdotes del diabólico culto de la cocomia, invaden la zona del Atlántico," *Diario de Costa Rica*, Sept. 20, 1936, 5, 8. See Harpelle, *West Indians*, 108–19; Duncan, "Negro antillano," 121.

89. "A Public Danger," *Kingston Daily Gleaner*, Mar. 18, 1938, 12.

90. "Hon. H. E. Allan Exhorts the Citizens of Eastern Kingston," *Kingston Daily Gleaner*, Dec. 9, 1935, 23.

91. Casey, "Haitian Migrants in Cuba."

92. Hill, *Dread History*, 18.

93. Chevannnes, *Rastafari*, 124–25; Post, *Arise Ye Starvelings*, 239, 164–68. See also "Among the Lodges: The Mystic Masons," *Limón Searchlight*, Nov. 2, 1929, 3.

94. Hill, *Dread History*, 21–28; Lee, *First Rasta*, 27–52.

95. "Courting Abyssinia," *Pittsburgh Courier*, Sept. 22, 1928, 20.

96. J. A. Rogers, "The Coronation of a King," *Pittsburgh Courier*, Dec. 13, 1930, A7.

97. Daniel Alexander, "Impressive Ceremony," *Pittsburgh Courier*, Nov. 8, 1930, 2.

98. "Anthropology a la Caucasian," *Pittsburgh Courier*, June 14, 1930, 10.

99. Police report quoted in Hill, *Dread History*, 29.

100. "Leonard Howell, On Trial Says Ras Tafari Is Messiah Returned to Earth."

101. Ibid.; Hill, *Dread History*, 25–27.

102. Chevannes, *Rastafari*, 115. She went on: "Most of the people saw the photograph say, 'But look, Christ change! This one is black.'"

103. Ibid.

104. Lee, *First Rasta*, 46.

105. Similarly, L. F. C. Mantle published extensive and supposedly firsthand reports on Ethiopia in the Kingston press in 1935 confirming Selassie's divinity. He was soon revealed to be a returnee from Cuba who had relied on *National Geographic* articles for his accounts. Reports further claimed that Mantle had gained occult knowledge from specialists in "ñañiguismo" or "VOODOOISM" while in Cuba. Quoted in Post, *Arise Ye Starvelings*, 169. See Chevannes, *Rastafari*, 43; Lee, *First Rasta*, 207–8; and Hill, *Dread History*, 20–21.

106. CO 318/425/15, Italian Conquest of Abyssinia: W. I. Reaction; Ottley, *New World*, 105–12; Yelvington, "War in Ethiopia and Trinidad."

107. Hill, *Dread History*, 21.

108. Ibid., 33.

109. Ibid., 35.

110. "A Public Danger."

111. Chevannes, *Rastafari*, 133–34.

112. Stoddard, *Rising Tide*, vi.

113. Pettersburgh, *Royal Parchment Scroll*.

114. Hill, *Dread History*, 18–20, 43–45.

115. Post, *Arise Ye Starvelings*, 172–73 (footnote 56), 197–98; Hill, *Dread History*, 40–41. On the actual history of Nyabingi mediums within anticolonial movements in East Africa, see Feierman, "Colonizers, Scholars."

116. Chevannes, *Rastafari*, 134–36 (quote on 135).

117. "Advises Joe to Pray," *Pittsburgh Courier*, Sept. 4, 1937, 15.

118. Chevannes, *Rastafari*; Chevannes, "Origins of Dreadlocks"; Homiak, "Dub History."

119. Warner, "Publics and Counterpublics," 80. "The individual struggle with stigma is transposed to the conflict between modes of publicness" (87).

120. Quoted in Chevannes, *Rastafari*, 136. Compare to the *Limón Searchlight* editors' plaint that "the coloured man" now "dare not go to certain countries, even though he was instrumental in making that country with his Brawn, his Brain, and his Blood." "24th MAY," *Limón Searchlight*, May 31, 1930, 1.

121. Ottley, *New World*, 86.

122. Marable, *Life of Malcolm X*, 30–37; X and Haley, *Autobiography*, 12–27 (quote on 186); Turner, *Islam*, 177–84.

123. Turner, *Islam*, 71–146; Slate, *Colored Cosmopolitanism*, 54–56.

124. Quoted in Turner, *Islam*, 151. See Marable, *Life of Malcolm X*, 81–90; Allen, "Religious Heterodoxy"; and Turner, *Islam*, 147–73.

125. Quoted in Post, *Arise Ye Starvelings*, 188–89.

126. Chevannes argues, though, that Rastafarianism came to differ from the "Black nationalism of the United States" in "allow[ing] the possibility of salvation for Whites, based on inward acknowledgement and rejection of the evil of White society." Chevannes, "Introducing," 29.

127. "Why the Sedition Bill Is Necessary," *Port of Spain Weekly Guardian*, Mar. 27, 1920, 11; "Anarchists in Flight" and "Conspirator Banished," *Port of Spain Weekly Guardian*, Apr. 3, 1920, 9.

128. Samaroo and Girvan, "Trinidad Workingmen's Association"; "Debate on Sedition Bill," *Port of Spain Weekly Guardian*, Mar. 27, 1920, 7–9.

129. Quoted in Martin, *Pan-African Connection*, 112.

130. Letter published in *Plain Talk*, 1937, quoted in Post, *Arise Ye Starvelings*, 177.

131. Post, *Arise Ye Starvelings*, esp. 5–6, 176–78; Carnegie, *Some Aspects of Jamaica's Politics*, esp. 147–50; Bolland, *Politics of Labour*, 299–333, esp. 305–9; Hart, *Rise and Organise*, esp. 18–28, 95–96.

132. Bolland, *Politics of Labour*, 309–24; Hart, *Rise and Organise*, 52 (quote).

133. Richard Hart, letter of 1938, quoted in Bolland, *Politics of Labour*, 325.

134. "Unrest Seethes in West Indies," *Pittsburgh Courier*, July 16, 1938, 1, 4.

135. Bouknight-Davis, "Chinese Economic Development," 84–85.

136. CO 950/44, Mr. Marcus Garvey (Universal Negro Improvement Association): Letter from Marcus Garvey, Sept. 21, 1938.

137. Ibid.

138. Thomas, *Trinidad Labour Riots*; Bolland, *Politics of Labour*, 252–57; Reddock, *Women, Labour*, 136–42. Padmore resigned from the Communist International in 1933 and moved to London, where he and fellow Trinidadian C. L. R. James

would found the International African Service Bureau. Makalani, *Cause of Freedom*, 165–224.

139. Meanwhile, in British Guiana, prominent organizers included Barbadian A. A. Thorne, Hubert Critchlow (the son of a Barbadian immigrant), and locally born East Indian leaders of the Manpower Citizens Association (a sugar workers' union). Cross, "Political Representation"; Bolland, *Politics of Labour*, 336–56; Lewis, *Labour*, 24–26.

140. Beckles, *History of Barbados*, 164–68; Bolland, *Politics of Labour*, 281–88; Brown, "1937 Disturbances"; Worrell, "Pan-Africanism"; Reddock, *Women, Labour*, 137; Chamberlain, *Empire and Nation-Building*, 3–5.

141. McKay, *Harlem*, 181.

142. Classically, see Post, *Arise Ye Starvelings*.

143. Jacobs, *Butler versus the King*; Bolland, *Politics of Labour*, 254–55; Singh, "June 1937," 61–62.

144. The *Courier* identified Butler as "a patriot, a hero and a martyr," "the leader of the great wave of strikes which has shaken the West Indies from Trinidad to Barbados," and "an outcast from the ranks of organized labor in Trinidad, and yet the island's greatest labor leader." Edgar T. Rouzeau, "Great Britain Bows When Her Might Is Defied by Uriah Butler, Negro Labor Organizer," *Pittsburgh Courier*, Oct. 16, 1937, 24.

145. Clemy George, quoted in Obika, *T. U. B. Butler*, 50.

146. "We're Sorry, Joe," *Pittsburgh Courier*, Aug. 8, 1936, 14.

147. Lion and Attila, "Louis-Schmeling Fight," recorded Feb. 24, 1937, *Joe Louis, American Hero* (Rounder 82161-1106-2, 2001).

148. Duke, "Diasporic Dimensions"; Parker, "Capital of the Caribbean"; Chamberlain, *Empire and Nation-Building*, 45–46.

149. Proctor, "Development of the Idea of Federation," 87 et passim; Braithwaite, "Federal Institutions"; Lewis, *Labour*, 42–43, 49–56; Bolland, *Politics of Labour*, 366–68.

150. See related analyses in Thomas, "The Violence of Diaspora," and Bogues, "Nationalism," as well as the documentary *Bad Friday: Rastafari after Coral Gardens*, produced by Deborah Thomas and codirected by Deborah Thomas and John Jackson (2011).

CONCLUSION

1. Just a small sampling must mention Von Eschen, *Race against Empire*; Gaines, *American Africans in Ghana*; Edwards, *Practice of Diaspora*; Makalani, *In the Cause of Freedom*; and Slate, *Colored Cosmopolitanism*.

2. Davies, *Left of Karl Marx*; Richards, *Maida Springer*.

3. The same point is made in different ways in Cooper, "What Is 'Globalization' Good For?"; Scott, "Small-Scale Dynamics"; and Manning, *African Diaspora*, 225, 243 et passim.

4. For a sampling of recent initiatives, see Corpis and Fletcher, "Two, Three, Many Worlds"; Brock, Kelley, and Sotiropoulos, "Transnational Black Studies"; Bayly,

Beckert, Connelly, Hofmeyr, Kozol, and Seed, "AHR Conversation: On Transnational History"; Fink, *Workers across the Americas*.

5. Lamming, *Castle of My Skin*, 295.

6. Palmer, "Defining and Studying the Modern African Diaspora"; Kelley, "But a Local Phase of a World Problem"; Bennett, "The Subject in the Plot"; Lemelle and Kelley, "Imagining Home"; Manning, "Africa and the African Diaspora"; Edwards, "The Uses of Diaspora"; Makalani, "Diaspora and the Localities of Race"; Scott, "An Obscure Miracle of Connection"; Guridy, *Forging Diaspora*. Partially connected to the trajectory of theorization of the African diaspora have been debates over the utility and analytic implications of the concept of diaspora more broadly. See Clifford, "Diasporas"; Axel, "Time and Threat"; Brubaker, "'Diaspora' Diaspora."

7. E.g., West and Martin, "Contours of the Black International"; Kelley and Patterson, "Unfinished Migrations."

8. Bosma, "Beyond the Atlantic"; McKeown, "Regionalizing World Migration"; McKeown, "A World Made Many"; McKeown, *Melancholy Order*; Lake and Reynolds, *Global Colour Line*.

9. Lucassen, "Migration and World History"; Hoerder, *Cultures in Contact*; Hoerder and Gabaccia, *Connecting Seas and Connected Ocean Rims*; Kelley and Patterson, "Unfinished Migrations," 25–26.

10. The classic statements of each position are Herskovits, *Myth of the Negro Past*, and Mintz and Price, *An Anthropological Approach*. Among recent analyses revisiting this formative era are Mintz, "Melville J. Herskovits and Caribbean Studies" and "Introduction"; Price and Price, *Root of Roots*; Scott, "Modernity That Predated the Modern" and "That Event, This Memory"; Carnegie, "Anthropology of Ourselves"; Yelvington, "Introduction" and "Invention of Africa"; and Harrison, "Building on a Rehistoricized Anthropology." On the related debate over creolization and its relation to hierarchies of power, see Trouillot, "Caribbean Region"; Bolland, "Creolization and Creole Societies"; Puri, *Caribbean Postcolonial*; Khan, "Journey to the Center of the Earth"; Price, "On the Miracle of Creolization"; and Mintz, "Enduring Substances, Trying Theories."

11. See, e.g., Edwards, *Practice of Diaspora*, Seigel, *Uneven Encounters*; Guridy, *Forging Diaspora*; Andrews, "Afro-World"; Alberto, *Terms of Inclusion*; and James, "Culture, Labor, and Race."

12. "Trinidad Protests against Venezuela Ban on West Indians," *Kingston Daily Gleaner*, Oct. 14, 1930, 10.

13. "Better Service," *Limón Searchlight*, Jan. 18, 1930, 2.

14. Similarly, see Palmié, *Wizards and Scientists*, 208 et passim.

15. Patterson and Kelley, "Unfinished Migrations"; Makalani, "Diaspora and the Localities of Race"; Chude-Sokei, "Foreign Negro Flash Agents." For early attention to class dynamics in the making of diaspora, see Lemelle and Kelley, *Imagining Home*.

Bibliography

MANUSCRIPT COLLECTIONS

Alajuela, Costa Rica
    Biblioteca Central, Universidad Nacional
        "Autobiografías campesinas" (transcripts)

Caracas, Venezuela
    Archivo del Ministerio de Relaciones Exteriores
        Archivo Antiguo
        Dirección de Política Internacional
    Archivo General de la Nación
        Sección Interior y Justicia

College Park, Maryland
    U.S. National Archive
        Record Group 84: Consular Posts, Bridgetown, Barbados: Correspondence,
            American Consulate, Barbados
        Record Group 84: Consular Posts, Kingston, Jamaica: Correspondence,
            American Consulate, Kingston, Jamaica

Cumaná, Venezuela
    Archivo Histórico del Estado de Sucre
        Documentos Sueltos

Kew, London, United Kingdom
    National Archives of the United Kingdom
        Colonial Office Series
        Foreign Office Series

Mona, Jamaica
    Sir Arthur Lewis Institute of Social and Economic Studies Documentation and
        Data Centre, University of the West Indies
        "Life in Jamaica in the Early Twentieth Century: A Presentation of Ninety
            Oral Accounts" (unpublished transcripts)

Panama City, Panama
    Archivo Nacional

San José, Costa Rica
    Archivo Nacional de Costa Rica

Spanish Town, Jamaica
    Jamaica National Archive

Abrahams, Roger D. "Afro-Caribbean Culture and the South: Music with Movement." In *The South and the Caribbean*, edited by Douglass Sullivan-González and Charles Reagan Wilson, 97–125. Jackson: University Press of Mississippi, 2001.

Actas de la Primera Conferencia Panamericana de Eugenesia y Homicultura de las Repúblicas Americanas. Habana, Cuba: n.p., 1928.

Adams, Frederick Upham. *Conquest of the Tropics*. Garden City, New York: Doubleday, Page, 1914.

Adi, Hakim. "The Negro Question: The Communist International and Black Liberation in the Interwar Years." In *From Toussaint to Tupac: The Black International since the Age of Revolution*, edited by Michael O. West, William G. Martin, and Fanon Che Wilkins, 155–78. Chapel Hill: University of North Carolina Press, 2009.

Adi, Hakim, and Marika Sherwood. *Pan-African History: Political Figures from Africa and the Diaspora since 1787*. London: Routledge, 2003.

Adriani, Alberto. "Venezuela y los problemas de la inmigración." In *Labor Venezolanista*, 143–53. 6th ed. Caracas: Academia Nacional de Ciencias Económicas, 1989.

Alarico Gómez, Carlos. *El poder andino: De Cipriano Castro a Medina Angarita*. Caracas: El Nacional, 2007.

Alberto, Paulina. *Terms of Inclusion: Black Intellectuals in Twentieth-Century Brazil*. Chapel Hill: University of North Carolina Press, 2011.

Allen, Ernest, Jr. "The New Negro: Explorations in Identity and Social Consciousness, 1910-1922." In *1915: The Cultural Moment*, edited by Adele Heller and Lois Rudnick, 48–68. New Brunswick, N.J.: Rutgers University Press, 1991.

———. "Religious Heterodoxy and Nationalist Tradition: The Continuing Evolution of the Nation of Islam, 1930–1996." *Black Scholar* 26, nos. 3–4 (1996): 2–34.

Alleyne, Mervyn C. *Roots of Jamaican Culture*. London: Pluto Press, 1988.

Allsopp, Richard, ed. *Dictionary of Caribbean English Usage*. Mona, Jamaica: University of the West Indies Press, 2003. Originally published, 1996.

Amador de Jesus, José. "The *Plena*'s Dissonant Melodies: Leisure, Racial Policing, and Nation in Puerto Rico, 1900–1930s." In *Honor, Status and Law in Modern Latin America*, edited by Sueann Caulfield, Sarah Chambers, and Lara Putnam, 249–71. Durham, N.C.: Duke University Press, 2004.

Anderson, Benedict. *Imagined Communities: Reflections on the Origins and Spread of Nationalism*. Rev. ed. New York: Verso, 1991.

André, Eugène. *A Naturalist in the Guianas*. London: Smith, Elder, 1904.

Andrews, George Reid. *Afro-Latin America, 1800–2000*. New York: Oxford University Press, 2004.

———. "Afro-World: African-Diaspora Thought and Practice in Montevideo, Uruguay, 1830–2000." *The Americas* 67, no. 1 (2010): 83–107.

Anshan, Li. "Survival, Adaptation, and Integration: Origins and Evolution of the Chinese Community in Jamaica (1854–1962)." In *The Chinese in the Caribbean*, edited by Andrew Wilson, 41–68. Princeton, N.J.: Markus Weiner, 2004.

Appelbaum, Nancy, Anne Macpherson, and Karin Rosemblatt, eds. *Race and Nation in Modern Latin America*. Chapel Hill: University of North Carolina Press, 2003.

Arreaza Arana, Laura V., and Daniel Blanco. "Relaciones Diplomáticas entre Venezuela y Gran Bretaña, Parte I (1830–1912)." *Boletín del archivo de la Casa Amarilla*, Año 13, no. 13 (2007): 9–166.

Atkins, E. Taylor. "Towards a Global History of Jazz." In *Jazz Planet*, edited by E. Taylor Atkins, xi–xxvii. Jackson: University Press of Mississippi, 2003.

Austin-Broos, Diane. *Jamaica Genesis: Religion and the Politics of Moral Orders*. Kingston: Ian Randle Publishers, 1997.

Axel, Brian Keith. "Time and Threat: Questioning the Production of the Diaspora as an Object of Study." *History and Anthropology* 9, no. 4 (1996): 415–43.

Barbados. *Report of the Census of Barbados, 1911–1921*. Compiled by Henry W. Lofty. Bridgetown, Barbados: Advocate Co., 1922.

Barrow, Christine. *Family in the Caribbean: Themes and Perspectives*. Princeton, N.J.: Markus Weiner, 1998.

Barry, William Francis. *Venezuela: A Visit to the Gold Mines of Guyana, and Voyage up the River Orinoco during 1886*. London: Marshall Bros., 1886.

Baud, Michiel. "Sugar and Unfree Labour: Reflections on Labour Control in the Dominican Republic, 1870–1935." *Journal of Peasant Studies* 19, no. 2 (1992): 301–25.

Baxter, Ivy. *The Arts of an Island: The Development of the Culture and of the Folk and Creative Arts in Jamaica, 1494–1962*. Metuchen, N.J.: Scarecrow Press, 1970.

Bayly, C. A., Sven Beckert, Matthew Connelly, Isabel Hofmeyr, Wendy Kozol, and Patricia Seed. "AHR Conversation: On Transnational History." *American Historical Review* 111, no. 5 (2006): 1441–64.

Beckles, Hilary. *A History of Barbados, from Amerindian Settlement to Nation-State*. New York: Cambridge University Press, 1990.

Beckwith, Martha Warren. *Black Roadways: A Study of Jamaican Folk Life*. New York: Negro Universities Press, 1969. Originally published, 1929.

Becu, Horacio Zorraquín. *El problema del extranjero en la legislación latino-americana reciente*. Buenos Aires: Editorial Guillermo Kraft, 1943.

Bennett, Herman L. "The Subject in the Plot: National Boundaries and the 'History' of the Black Atlantic." *African Studies Review* 43, no. 1 (2000): 101–24.

Berglund, Susan. "Las bases sociales y económicas de las leyes de inmigración venezolanas." *Boletín de la Academia Nacional de Historia* 260 (1982): 951–62.

Bergquist, Charles. *Labor in Latin America: Comparative Essays on Chile, Argentina, Venezuela, and Colombia*. Stanford, Calif.: Stanford University Press, 1986.

Bernhardt, Clyde, with Sheldon Harris. *I Remember: Eighty Years of Black Entertainment, Big Bands, and the Blues*. Philadelphia: University of Pennsylvania Press, 1986.

Besson, Jean. "Religion as Resistance in Jamaican Peasant Life: The Baptist Church, Revival Worldview, and Rastafari Movement." In *Rastafari and Other*

African-Caribbean Worldviews, edited by Barry Chevannes, 43–76. The Hague: Institute of Social Studies/Macmillan, 1995.

Bhabha, Jacqueline. "The 'Mere Fortuity of Birth'? Children, Mothers, Borders, and the Meaning of Citizenship." In *Migrations and Mobilities: Citizenship, Borders, and Gender*, edited by Seyla Benhabib and Judith Resnik, 187–227. New York: New York University Press, 2009.

Bogues, Anthony. "Nationalism and Jamaican Political Thought." In *Jamaica in Slavery and Freedom: History, Heritage, and Culture*, edited by Kathleen E. A. Monteith and Glen Richards, 363–87. Mona, Jamaica: University of the West Indies Press, 2002.

Boittin, Jennifer Anne. "In Black and White: Gender, Race Relations, and the Nardal Sisters in Interwar Paris." *French Colonial History* 6 (2005): 120–35.

Bolland, O. Nigel. "Labor Protests, Rebellions, and the Rise of Nationalism during Depression and War." In *The Caribbean: A History of the Region and Its Peoples*, edited by Stephan Palmié and Francisco Scarano, 459–74. Chicago: University of Chicago Press, 2011.

———. *The Politics of Labour in the British Caribbean: The Social Origins of Authoritarianism and Democracy in the Labour Movement*. Kingston: Ian Randle, 2001.

Bosma, Ulbe. "Beyond the Atlantic: Connecting Migration and World History in the Age of Imperialism, 1840–1940." *International Review of Social History* 52 (2007): 116–23.

Bosniak, Linda. *The Citizen and the Alien: Dilemmas of Contemporary Membership*. Princeton, N.J.: Princeton University Press, 2006.

Bouknight-Davis, Gail. "Chinese Economic Development and Ethnic Identity Formation in Jamaica." In *The Chinese in the Caribbean*, edited by Andrew Wilson, 69–92. Princeton, N.J.: Markus Weiner, 2004.

Bourgois, Philippe. *Ethnicity at Work: Divided Labor on a Central American Banana Plantation*. Baltimore: Johns Hopkins University Press, 1989.

Boza, Alejandra, and Juan Carlos Solórzano. "El estado nacional y los indígenas: El caso de Talamanca y Guatuso. Costa Rica, 1821–1910." *Revista de Historia* 42 (2000): 45–79.

Bradley, Lloyd. *Bass Culture: When Reggae Was King*. New York: Viking Press, 2000.

Braithwaite, Lloyd. "'Federal' Associations and Institutions in the West Indies." *Social and Economic Studies* 6, no. 2 (1957): 286–328.

———. "Social Stratification in Trinidad: A Preliminary Analysis." *Social and Economic Studies* 2, nos. 2–3 (1953): 5–175.

Brereton, Bridget. *A History of Modern Trinidad, 1783–1962*. London and Port of Spain: Heinemann, 1981.

Brock, Lisa, Robin D. G. Kelley, and Karen Sotiropoulos, eds. "Transnational Black Studies." Special issue of *Radical History Review* 87 (2003): 1–243.

Bronfman, Alejandra. *Measures of Equality: Social Science, Citizenship, and Race in Cuba, 1902–1940*. Chapel Hill: University of North Carolina Press, 2007.

Brooks, A. A. *History of Bedwardism; or, The Jamaica Native Baptist Free Church*. 2nd ed. Kingston: Gleaner Co., 1917.

Brooks, Tim. *Lost Sounds: Blacks and the Birth of the Recording Industry, 1890–1919.* Urbana: University of Illinois Press, 2005.

Brown, David. *Palmerston and the Politics of Foreign Policy, 1846–55.* Manchester, UK: Manchester University Press, 2002.

Brown, Jacqueline Nassy. *Dropping Anchor, Setting Sail: Geographies of Race in Black Liverpool.* Princeton, N.J.: Princeton University Press, 2005.

Brubaker, William Rogers. "The 'Diaspora' Diaspora." *Ethnic and Racial Studies* 28, no. 1 (2005): 1–19.

———. "Immigration, Citizenship, and the Nation-State in France and Germany." *International Sociology* 4 (1990): 379–407.

———. "Membership without Citizenship: The Economic and Social Rights of Noncitizens." In *Immigration and the Politics of Citizenship in Europe and North America*, edited by William Rogers Brubaker, 145–62. Lanham, Md.: University Press of America, 1989.

———. "Migration, Membership, and the Modern Nation-State: Internal and External Dimensions of the Politics of Belonging." *Journal of Interdisciplinary History* 41, no. 1 (2010): 61–78.

Bryan, Patrick. *The Jamaican People: Race, Class, and Social Control, 1880–1902.* Mona, Jamaica: University of the West Indies Press, 2000.

———. "The Question of Labor in the Sugar Industry of the Dominican Republic in the Late Nineteenth and Early Twentieth Centuries." In *Between Slavery and Free Labor: The Spanish-Speaking Caribbean in the Nineteenth Century*, edited by Manuel Moreno Fraginals, Frank Moya Pons, and Stanley Engerman, 235–54. Baltimore: Johns Hopkins University Press, 1985.

Burton, Richard D. E. *Afro-Creole: Power, Opposition, and Play in the Caribbean.* Ithaca, N.Y.: Cornell University Press, 1997.

Bury, Herbert. *A Bishop amongst Bananas.* Milwaukee: The Young Churchman, n.d. [1911?].

Butler, Jon, Grant Wacker, and Randall Balmer. *Religion in American Life: A Short History.* New York: Oxford University Press, 2011.

Calliste, Agnes. "Race, Gender, and Canadian Immigration Policy: Blacks from the Caribbean, 1900–1932." *Revue d'études Canadiennes/Journal of Canadian Studies* 28, no. 4 (1993/4): 131–48.

Campbell, John. *Obeah Yes or No? A Study of Obeah and Spiritualism in Guyana.* Georgetown, Guyana: n.p., 1976.

Carew, Jan. *Ghosts in Our Blood: With Malcolm X in Africa, England, and the Caribbean.* Chicago: Lawrence Hill Books, 1994.

Carmichael, Stokely, with Ekwueme Michael Thelwell. *Ready for Revolution: The Life and Times of Stokely Carmichael.* New York: Charles Scribner's Sons, 2003.

Carnegie, Charles V. "The Anthropology of Ourselves: An Interview with Sidney W. Mintz." *Small Axe* 19 (2006): 106–79.

———. "Reaching for the Border." *Small Axe* 19 (2006): v–ix.

Carnegie, Charles V., and Samuel Martinez, eds. "Crossing Borders of Language and Culture." Special issue of *Small Axe* 19 (2006): 1–229.

Carnegie, James. *Some Aspects of Jamaica's Politics, 1918–1938*. Kingston: Institute of Jamaica, 1973.

Carr, Barry. "Identity, Class, and Nation: Black Immigrant Workers, Cuban Communism, and the Sugar Insurgency, 1925–1934." *Hispanic American Historical Review* 78, no. 1 (1998): 83–116.

Casey, Matthew. "Haitian Migrants in Cuba, 1902–1940." Ph.D. diss., University of Pittsburgh, 2012.

Cassidy, F. G., and R. B. LePage. *Dictionary of Jamaican English*. Cambridge, UK: Cambridge University Press, 1967.

Chadbourne, Eugene. "Vernon Andrade's Biography." All Music Guide, http://www.allmusic.com/artist/vernon-andrade-p552590. April 3, 2012.

Chamberlain, Mary. *Empire and Nation-Building in the Caribbean: Barbados, 1937–66*. Manchester, UK: Manchester University Press, 2010.

———. *Family Love in the Diaspora: Migration and the Anglo-Caribbean Experience*. New Brunswick, N.J.: Transaction Publishers, 2006.

———, ed. *Caribbean Migration: Globalized Identities*. London: Routledge, 1998.

Chambers, Glenn. *Race, Nation, and West Indian Immigration to Honduras*. Baton Rouge: Louisiana State University Press, 2010.

Chang, Kevin O'Brien, and Wayne Chen. *Reggae Routes: The Story of Jamaican Music*. Kingston: Ian Randle Publishers, 1998.

Charlton, Audrey K. "'Cat Born in Oven Is Not Bread': Jamaican and Barbadian Immigrants in Cuba between 1900 and 1959." Ph.D. diss., Columbia University, 2005.

Charters, Samuel Barclay. *A Trumpet around the Corner: The Story of New Orleans Jazz*. Jackson: University Press of Mississippi, 2008.

Chen, Yuan-Tsung. *Return to the Middle Kingdom: One Family, Three Revolutionaries, and the Birth of Modern China*. New York: Sterling Publishing Co., 2008.

Chevannes, Barry. "Introducing the Native Religions of Jamaica." In *Rastafari and Other African-Caribbean Worldviews*, edited by Barry Chevannes, 1–19. The Hague: Institute of Social Studies/Macmillan, 1995.

———. "The Origins of the Dreadlocks." In *Rastafari and Other African-Caribbean Worldviews*, edited by Barry Chevannes, 77–96. The Hague: Institute of Social Studies/Macmillan, 1995.

———. *Rastafari: Roots and Ideology*. Syracuse, N.Y.: Syracuse University Press, 1994.

Chomsky, Aviva. "'Barbados or Canada?' Race, Immigration, and Nation in Early Twentieth-Century Cuba." *Hispanic American Historical Review* 80, no. 3 (2000): 415–62.

———. *West Indian Workers and the United Fruit Company in Costa Rica, 1870–1940*. Baton Rouge: Louisiana State University Press, 1996.

———. "West Indian Workers in Costa Rican Radical and Nationalist Ideology, 1900–1950." *The Americas* 51, no. 1 (1994): 11–40.

Chude-Sokei, Louis. "Foreign Negro Flash Agents: Eric Walrond and the Discrepancies of Diaspora." In *Eric Walrond: A Critical Heritage*, ed. Louis J.

Parascandola and Carl A. Wade. Mona, Jamaica: University of the West Indies Press, forthcoming [2012].

————. *The Last "Darky": Bert Williams, Black-on-Black Minstrelsy, and the African Diaspora*. Durham, N.C.: Duke University Press, 2006.

Clifford, James. "Diasporas." *Cultural Anthropology* 9, no. 3 (1994): 302–38.

Colby, Jason M. *The Business of Empire: United Fruit, Race, and U.S. Expansion in Central America*. Ithaca, N.Y.: Cornell University Press, 2011.

Collier, Ruth Berins, and David Collier. *Shaping the Political Arena: Critical Junctures, the Labor Movement, and Regime Dynamics in Latin America*. Princeton, N.J.: Princeton University Press, 1991.

"Concerning Negro Sorcery in the United States." *Journal of American Folklore* 3, no. 11 (1890): 281–87.

Conniff, Michael. *Black Labor on a White Canal: West Indians in Panama, 1904–1980*. Pittsburgh: University of Pittsburgh Press, 1985.

Cook-Martín, David, and David FitzGerald. "Liberalism and the Limits of Inclusion: Race and Immigration Law in the Americas, 1850–2000." *Journal of Interdisciplinary History* 41, no. 1 (2010): 7–25.

Cooper, Frederick. "What Is 'Globalization' Good For? An African Historian's Perspective." *African Affairs* 100 (2001): 189–213.

Cooper, Frederick, Thomas C. Holt, and Rebecca J. Scott. *Beyond Slavery: Explorations of Race, Labor, and Citizenship*. Chapel Hill: University of North Carolina Press, 2000.

Corbould, Clare. "Streets, Sounds, and Identity in Interwar Harlem." *Journal of Social History* 40, no. 4 (2007): 859–94.

Corinealdi, Kaysha. "Redefining Home: West Indian Panamanians and Transnational Politics of Race, Citizenship, and Diaspora, 1928–1970." Ph.D. diss., Yale University, 2011.

Corpis, Duane J., and Ian Christopher Fletcher, eds. "Two, Three, Many Worlds: Radical Methodologies for Global History." Special issue of *Radical History Review* 91 (2005): 1–190.

Costa Rica. *Colección de Leyes y Decretos*. San José: Imprenta La Paz, 1872.

Cowley, John. *Carnival, Canboulay, and Calypso: Traditions in the Making*. Cambridge, UK: Cambridge University Press, 1999.

————. "'Cultural Fusions': Aspects of British West Indian Music in the USA and Britain, 1918–51." *Popular Music* 5, "Continuity and Change" (1985): 81–96.

————. "L'Année Passée: Selected Repertoire in English-Speaking West Indian Music." *Keskidee: A Journal of Black Musical Traditions* 3 (1993): 2–9.

————. "West Indies Blues: An Historical Overview, 1920s–1950s." In *Nobody Knows Where the Blues Come From: Lyrics and History*, edited by Robert Springer, 187–263. Jackson: University Press of Mississippi, 2006.

Craine, W. Ralph Hall. *The Cruise of the Port Kingston*. London: Collier and Co., 1908.

Crawford, Sharika. "'Under the Colombian Flag': Nation-Building on San Andrés and Providence Islands, 1886–1930." Ph.D. diss., University of Pittsburgh, 2009.

Cronon, E. David. *Black Moses: The Story of Marcus Garvey and the Universal Negro Improvement Association*. Madison: University of Wisconsin Press, 1955.

Cross, Malcolm. "The Political Representation of Organised Labour in Trinidad and Guiana." In *Labour in the Caribbean*, edited by Malcolm Cross and Gad Heuman, 285–308. London: Macmillan Caribbean, 1988.

Cuba, Comité Estatal de Estadísticas. *Memorias Inéditas del Censo de 1931*. Habana: Editorial de Ciencias Sociales, 1978.

Cuba, Dirección general del censo. *Censo de 1943*. Habana: P. Fernández y cía., 1945.

Cuba, Secretaría de Hacienda, Sección de Estadística. *Informe y movimiento de pasajeros*. Habana, 1916–21.

Da Costa, Emilia Viotti. *Crowns of Glory, Tears of Blood: The Demerara Slave Rebellion of 1823*. New York: Oxford University Press, 1997.

Dalrymple, Daniel. "In the Shadow of Garvey: Garveyites in New York City and the British Caribbean, 1925–1950." Ph.D. diss., Michigan State University, 2008.

Dalton, Leonard. *Venezuela*. London: T. Fischer Unwin, 1912.

Daniels, Roger. *Guarding the Golden Door: American Immigration Policy and Immigrants since 1882*. New York: Hill and Wang, 2004.

Dankey, James, and Wayne Wiegand, eds. *Print Culture in a Diverse America*. Champagne: University of Illinois Press, 1998.

Davie, Maurice Rea. *A Constructive Immigration Policy*. New Haven, Conn.: Yale University Press, 1923.

Davies, Carole Boyce. *Left of Karl Marx: The Political Life of Black Communist Claudia Jones*. Durham, N.C.: Duke University Press, 2008.

Dawahare, Anthony. *Nationalism, Marxism, and African American Literature between the Wars: A New Pandora's Box*. Jackson: University Press of Mississippi, 2003.

DeCaro, Louis A., Jr. *On the Side of My People: A Religious Life of Malcolm X*. New York: New York University Press, 1996.

De la Fuente, Alejandro. *A Nation for All: Race, Inequality, and Politics in Twentieth-Century Cuba*. Chapel Hill: University of North Carolina Press, 2001.

Del Castillo, José. *La inmigración de braceros azucareros en la República Dominicana, 1900–1930*. Santo Domingo: Centro Dominicano de Investigaciones Antropológicas, 1978.

De Lisser, Herbert G. *In Jamaica and Cuba*. Kingston: The Gleaner Co, Ltd., 1910.

———. *Jane's Career*. New York: Africana Publishing Corp., 1971. Originally published, 1913.

Derby, Lauren. "Haitians, Magic, and Money: Raza and Society in the Haitian-Dominican Borderlands, 1900 to 1937." *Comparative Studies in Society and History* 36, no. 3 (1994): 488–526.

Domingo, W. A. "The Tropics in New York." *Survey Graphic*, "Harlem: Mecca of the New Negro" (March 1925): 648–50.

Dominica, Registrar General's Office. *Census of 1921*. Roseau: n.p., 1921.

Dominican Republic, Dirección General de Estadística. *Población de la República Dominicana distribuida por nacionalidades. Cifras del censo nacional de 1935*.

Ciudad Trujillo: Sección de Publicaciones de la Dirección General de Estadística, 1937.

Drake, St. Clair. "Diaspora Studies and Pan-Africanism." In *Global Dimensions of the African Diaspora*, edited by Joseph Harris, 359–66. Washington, D.C.: Howard University Press, 1982.

Duke, Eric. "The Diasporic Dimensions of Caribbean Federation in the Early Twentieth Century." *New West Indian Guide* 83, nos. 3–4 (2009): 219–48.

Duncan, Quince. "El negro antillano. Inmigracion y presencia." In *El Negro en Costa Rica*, by Carlos Meléndez Chaverri and Quince Duncan, 97–148. 10th ed. San José: Editorial Universidad de Costa Rica, 1993. Originally published, 1972.

Echeverri-Gent, Elisavinda. "Forgotten Workers: British West Indians and the Early Days of the Banana Industry in Costa Rica and Honduras." *Journal of Latin American Studies* 24, no. 2 (1992): 275–308.

Edwards, Brent Hayes. *The Practice of Diaspora: Literature, Translation, and the Rise of Black Internationalism*. Cambridge, Mass.: Harvard University Press, 2003.

———. "The Uses of Diaspora." *Social Text* 66, vol. 19, no. 1 (2001): 45–74.

Eisner, Gisela. *Jamaica, 1830–1930: A Study in Economic Growth*. Manchester, UK: Manchester University Press, 1961.

Elkins, W. F. "Hercules and the Society of Peoples of African Origin." *Caribbean Studies* 11, no. 4 (1972): 47–59.

———. "William Lauron DeLaurence and Jamaican Folk Religion." *Folklore* 97, no. 2 (1986): 215–18.

El Salvador. *Ley y reglamento de migración*. San Salvador: Imprenta Nacional, 1933.

Erman, Samuel. "Puerto Rico and the Promise of United States Citizenship: Struggles around Status in a New Empire, 1898–1917." Ph.D. diss., University of Michigan, 2010.

Euraque, Darío. "The Banana Enclave, Nationalism, and Mestizaje in Honduras, 1910s–1930s." In *Identity and Struggle at the Margins of the Nation-State: The Laboring Peoples of Central America and the Hispanic Caribbean*, edited by Aviva Chomsky and Aldo Lauria-Santiago, 151–68. Durham, N.C.: Duke University Press, 1998.

Evans, David. *Ramblin' on My Mind: New Perspectives on the Blues*. Chicago: University of Illinois Press, 2008.

Ewell, Judith. *Venezuela: A Century of Change*. Stanford, Calif.: Stanford University Press, 1984.

Fahrmeir, Andreas. *Citizenship: The Rise and Fall of a Modern Concept*. New Haven, Conn.: Yale University Press, 2007.

Fahrmeir, Andreas, Olivier Faron, and Patrick Weil, eds. *Migration Control in the North Atlantic World: The Evolution of State Practices in Europe and the United States from the French Revolution to the Inter-War Period*. Oxford and New York: Berghahn Books, 2003.

Feierman, Steven. "Colonizers, Scholars, and the Creation of Invisible Histories." In *Beyond the Cultural Turn: New Directions in the Study of Society and Culture*, edited by Victoria Bonnell and Lynn Hunt, 182–216. Berkeley: University of California Press, 1999.

Ferenczi, Imre, and Walter Willcox, eds. *International Migrations*. Vol. 1, *Statistics*. New York: National Bureau of Economic Research, 1929.

Ferreira, Jo-Anne S. "The History and Future of Patuá in Paria." *Journal of Pidgin and Creole Languages* 24, no.1 (2009): 139–57.

Fiehrer, Thomas. "From Quadrille to Stomp: The Creole Origins of Jazz." *Popular Music* 10, no. 1 (1991): 21–38.

Figueroa Ibarra, Carlos. "Marxismo, sociedad y movimiento sindical en Guatemala." *Anuario de Estudios Centroamericanos* 16, no. 1 (1990): 57–86.

Fletcher, Leonard P. "The Decline of Friendly Societies in Trinidad and Tobago." *Caribbean Studies* 24, nos. 3–4 (1991): 59–78.

————. "The Friendly Societies in St. Lucia and St. Vincent." *Caribbean Studies* 18, nos. 3–4 (1978–79): 89–114.

Flores Bolívar, Francisco. "Beyond the White Republic: Afro-Descendant Elites, Race, and Citizenship in Cartagena, Colombia, 1900–1945." M.A. thesis, University of Pittsburgh, 2011.

Foerster, Robert F. "The Racial Problems involved in Immigration from Latin America and the West Indies to the United States." In *Hearings of the Committee on Immigration and Naturalization, House of Representatives, March 3, 1925*. Washington, D.C.: Government Printing Office, 1925.

Ford, Jos. C., and Frank Cundall. *The Handbook of Jamaica for 1908*. Kingston: Institute of Jamaica, 1908.

Forde, Maarit. "The Moral Economy of Spiritual Work: Money and Rituals in Trinidad and Tobago." In *Obeah and Other Powers: The Politics of Caribbean Religion and Healing*, edited by Diana Paton and Maarit Forde, 198–219. Durham, N.C.: Duke University Press, 2012.

Forde, Maarit, and Diana Paton. "Introduction." In *Obeah and Other Powers: The Politics of Caribbean Religion and Healing*, edited by Diana Paton and Maarit Forde, 1–44. Durham, N.C.: Duke University Press, 2012.

Fraser, Cary. "The Twilight of Colonial Rule in the British West Indies: Nationalist Assertion vs. Imperial Hubris in the 1930s." *Journal of Caribbean History* [Barbados] 30, nos. 1–2 (1996): 1–27.

Fraser, Nancy. "Rethinking the Public Sphere: A Contribution to the Critique of Actually Existing Democracy." *Social Text* 25–26 (1990): 56–80.

————. "Transnationalizing the Public Sphere: On the Legitimacy and Efficacy of Public Opinion in a Post-Westphalian World." *Theory, Culture and Society* 24, no. 4 (2007): 7–30.

Fredrickson, George M. *Black Liberation: A Comparative History of Black Ideologies in the United States and South Africa*. New York: Oxford University Press, 1996.

Gaines, Kevin. *American Africans in Ghana: Black Expatriates in the Civil Rights Era*. Chapel Hill: University of North Carolina Press, 2006.

Garvey, Marcus. *The Philosophy and Opinions of Marcus Garvey*. Edited by Amy Jacques Garvey. Dover, Mass.: Majority Press, 1986. Originally published, 1923–25.

Gates, Henry Louis, and Evelyn Brooks Higginbotham, eds. *Harlem Renaissance Lives*. New York: Oxford University Press, 2009.

Gilroy, Paul. *Ain't No Black in the Union Jack: The Cultural Politics of Race and Nation*. Chicago: University of Chicago Press, 1991.

———. *The Black Atlantic: Modernity and Double Consciousness*. Cambridge, Mass.: Harvard University Press, 1993.

———. "Sounds Authentic: Black Music, Ethnicity, and the Challenge of a *Changing Same*." In *Imagining Home: Class, Culture, and Nationalism in the African Diaspora*, edited by Sydney J. Lemelle and Robin D. G. Kelley, 93–118. New York: Verso, 1994.

Giovannetti, Jorge. "Black British Caribbean Migrants in Cuba: Resistance, Opposition, and Strategic Identity in the Early Twentieth Century." In *Regional Footprints: The Travels and Travails of Early Caribbean Migrants*, edited by Annette Insanally, Mark Clifford, and Sean Sheriff, 103–20. Kingston: Latin American-Caribbean Centre, University of the West Indies, 2006.

———. "Black British Subjects in Cuba: Race, Ethnicity, Nation, and Identity in the Migratory Experience, 1898–1938." Ph.D. diss., University of North London, 2001.

———. "Caribbean Migration." In *Encyclopedia of Cuba: People, History, and Culture*, vol. 1, edited by D. H. Figueredo, Luis Martinez-Fernández, Louis A. Pérez Jr., and Luis González, 141–42. Westport, Conn.: Greenwood Press, 2003.

———. "The Elusive Organization of 'Identity': Race, Religion, and Empire among Caribbean Migrants in Cuba." *Small Axe* 19 (2006): 1–27.

Giovannetti, Jorge, and Reinaldo Roman, eds. "Garveyism in the Hispanic Caribbean." Special issue of *Caribbean Studies* 31, no. 1 (2003): 1–259.

Glenn, Evelyn Nakano. *Unequal Freedom: How Race and Gender Shaped American Citizenship and Labor*. Cambridge, Mass.: Harvard University Press, 2004.

Gómez, Carlos. *Contribución al estudio de la inmigración en Venezuela*. Caracas: Universidad Central de Venezuela, 1906.

Gordon, Edmund. *Disparate Diasporas: Identity and Politics in an African Nicaraguan Community*. Austin: University of Texas Press, 1998.

Gordon, Rev. Ernle. "Garvey and Black Liberation Theology." In *Garvey: His Work and Impact*, edited by Rupert Lewis and Patrick Bryan, 135–44. Trenton, N.J.: Africa World Press, 1991.

Gorman, Daniel. *Imperial Citizenship: Empire and the Question of Belonging*. Manchester and New York: Manchester University Press, 2006.

Great Britain, Foreign Office. "Report for the Year 1886 on the Trade of the Great State of Bolivar and the Mines of Yuruary." Diplomatic and Consular Reports on Trade and Finance, Venezuela, issue no. 138. *Annual Series*, 1887.

Great Britain, West India Royal Commission. *Report of the West India Royal Commission*. London: H.M.S.O., 1897.

Greene, Julie. *The Canal Builders: Making America's Empire at the Panama Canal*. New York: Penguin, 2009.

Griffiths, David. *Hot Jazz: From Harlem to Storyville*. Studies in Jazz, no. 28. Lanham, Md.: Scarecrow Press, 1998.

Grubb, Kenneth. *Religion in Central America*. London: World Dominion Press, 1937.

Guatemala, Dirección General de Estadística. *Censo de la República de Guatemala, 1921*. Guatemala: Talleres Gutenberg, 1924.

Guilbaut, Jocelyn. *Governing Sound: The Cultural Politics of Trinidad's Carnival Musics*. Chicago: University of Chicago Press, 2007.

Guridy, Frank. *Forging Diaspora: Afro-Cubans and African Americans in a World of Empire and Jim Crow*. Chapel Hill: University of North Carolina Press, 2010.

Hahamovitch, Cindy. *The Fruits of Their Labor: Atlantic Coast Farmworkers and the Making of Migrant Poverty, 1870–1945*. Chapel Hill: University of North Carolina Press, 1997.

———. *No Man's Land: Jamaican Guestworkers in America and the Global History of Deportable Labor*. Princeton, N.J.: Princeton University Press, 2011.

Hamilton, Beverly. "Marcus Garvey and Cultural Development in Jamaica: A Preliminary Survey." In *Garvey: His Work and Impact*, edited by Rupert Lewis and Patrick Bryan, 87–112. Trenton, N.J.: Africa World Press, 1991.

Hammar, Tomas, ed. *European Immigration Policy: A Comparative Study*. Cambridge, UK: Cambridge University Press, 1985.

Harpelle, Ronald. "Ethnicity, Religion, and Repression: The Denial of African Heritage in Costa Rica." *Canadian Journal of History* 29 (1994): 95–112.

———. "Racism and Nationalism in the Creation of Costa Rica's Pacific Coast Banana Enclave." *The Americas* 56, no. 3 (2000): 29–51.

———. *The West Indians of Costa Rica: Race, Class, and the Integration of an Ethnic Minority*. Montreal: McGill-Queen's University Press, 2002.

Harris, LaShawn. "Dream Books, Crystal Balls, and 'Lucky Numbers': African American Female Mediums in Harlem, 1900–1930s." *Afro-Americans in New York Life and History* 35 (2011): 74–110.

Harrison, Faye. "Commentary: Building on a Rehistoricized Anthropology of the Afro-Atlantic." In *Afro-Atlantic Dialogues: Anthropology in the Diaspora*, edited by Kevin Yelvington, 381–98. Santa Fe, N.Mex.: School of American Research Press, 2006.

Hart, Richard. *Rise and Organise: The Birth of the Workers and National Movements in Jamaica, 1936–1939*. London: Karia Press, 1989.

Henry, Frances. *Reclaiming African Religions: The Socio-Political Legitimation of the Orisha and Spiritual Baptist Faiths*. Mona, Jamaica: University of the West Indies Press, 2003.

Hernández González, Rafael. "Raza, inmigración e identidad nacional en la Venezuela finisecular." *Contrastes: Revista de Historia Moderna* [Universidad de Murcia, España] 9–10 (1997): 35–48.

Hersch, Charles. *Subversive Sounds: Race and the Birth of Jazz in New Orleans*. Chicago: University of Chicago Press, 2008.

Herskovits, Melville. *The Myth of the Negro Past*. New York: Harper and Brothers, 1941.

Herskovits, Melville, and Frances Herskovits. *Trinidad Village*. New York: Alfred A. Knopf, 1947.

Hill, Robert A. *Dread History: Leonard P. Howell and Millenarian Visions in the Early Rastafarian Religion*. Chicago and Jamaica: Research Associates School

Times Publications/Frontline Distribution Int'l and Miguel Lorne Publishers, 2001.

————, ed. *The Marcus Garvey and Universal Negro Improvement Association Papers.* Vols. 1–11. Berkeley: University of California Press, 1983–2010.

Hoerder, Dirk. *Cultures in Contact: World Migrations in the Second Millennium.* Durham, N.C.: Duke University Press, 2002.

Hoerder, Dirk, and Donna Gabaccia, eds. *Connecting Seas and Connected Ocean Rims: Indian, Atlantic, and Pacific Oceans and China Seas Migrations from the 1830s to the 1930s.* Leiden: Brill, 2011.

Homiak, John P. "Dub History: Soundings on Rastafari Livity and Language." In *Rastafari and Other African-Caribbean Worldviews*, edited by Barry Chevannes, 127–81. The Hague: Institute of Social Studies/Macmillan, 1995.

Honduras. *Reglamento para la Ley de inmigración, 1929.* Tegucigalpa: Tipografía Nacional, [1929?].

Honduras, Dirección General de Estadística y Censos. *Resumen del Censo General de Población . . . de 1930.* Tegucigalpa: Tipografía Nacional, 1932.

Houk, James. *Spirits, Blood, and Drums: The Orisha Religion in Trinidad.* Philadelphia: Temple University Press, 1995.

Hoyos, F. A. *Our Common Heritage.* Bridgetown, Barbados: Advocate Press, 1953.

Hu-DeHart, Evelyn. "Indispensable Enemy or Convenient Scapegoat? A Critical Examination of Sinophobia in Latin America and the Caribbean, 1870s to 1930s." *Journal of Chinese Overseas* 5 (2009): 55–90.

Hunte, Keith. "Protestantism and Slavery in the British Caribbean." In *Christianity in the Caribbean: Essays on Church History*, edited by Armando Lampe, 86–125. Mona, Jamaica: University of the West Indies Press, 2001.

Hurston, Zora. "Hoodoo in America." *Journal of American Folklore* 44, no. 174 (1931): 317–417.

Hurwitt, Elliott. "Renaissance Casino." In *Encyclopedia of the Harlem Renaissance*, vol. 2, edited by Cary Wintz and Paul Finkelman, 1043–44. New York: Routledge, 2004.

Hutton, Clinton. "The Cuban Influence on Popular Jamaican Music." In *Regional Footprints: The Travels and Travails of Early Caribbean Migrants*, edited by Annette Insanally, Mark Clifford, and Sean Sheriff, 155–82. Kingston: Latin American-Caribbean Centre, University of the West Indies, 2006.

Hutton, Clinton, and Garth White. "The Social and Aesthetic Roots and Identity of Ska." *Caribbean Quarterly* 53, no. 4 (2007): 81–95.

Jackson, Luther P., Jr. "Ottley, Roi." In *Dictionary of American Biography*, supplement 6, 1956–1960, edited by John Garraty, 489–91. New York: Charles Scribner's Sons, 1980.

Jacobs, W. Richard, ed. *Butler versus the King: Riots and Sedition in 1937.* Port of Spain: Key Caribbean Publications, 1976.

James, Winifred. *Mulberry Tree.* London: Chapman and Hall, 1913.

————. *Out of the Shadows.* London: Chapman and Hall, 1924.

James, Winston. "Culture, Labor, and Race in the Shadow of U.S. Capital." In *The Caribbean: A History of the Region and Its Peoples*, edited by Stephan

Palmié and Francisco Scarano, 445–58. Chicago: University of Chicago Press, 2011.

———. "Explaining Afro-Caribbean Social Mobility in the United States: Beyond the Sowell Thesis." *Comparative Studies in Society and History* 44, no. 2 (2002): 218–62.

———. *Holding Aloft the Banner of Ethiopia: Caribbean Radicalism in Early Twentieth-Century America*. New York: Verso, 1998.

Johnson, Howard. "The Anti-Chinese Riots of 1918 in Jamaica." *Immigrants and Minorities* 2 (1983): 50–63.

Jones, R. Clifford. *James K. Humphrey and the Sabbath-Day Adventists*. Jackson: University Press of Mississippi, 2006.

Kelley, Robin D. G. "'Afric's Sons with Banner Red': African American Communists and the Politics of Culture, 1919–1934." In *Imagining Home: Class, Culture, and Nationalism in the African Diaspora*, edited by Sydney J. Lemelle and Robin D. G. Kelley, 35–54. New York: Verso, 1994.

———. "'But a Local Phase of a World Problem': Black History's Global Vision, 1883–1950." *Journal of American History* 86, no. 3 (1999): 1045–77.

———. *Thelonious Monk: The Life and Times of an American Original*. New York: The Free Press, 2009.

Kelley, Robin D. G., and Tiffany Patterson. "Unfinished Migrations: Reflections on the African Diaspora and the Making of the Modern World." *African Studies Review* 43, no. 1 (2000): 11–45.

Khan, Aisha. "Journey to the Center of the Earth: The Caribbean as Master Symbol." *Cultural Anthropology* 16, no. 3 (2001): 271–302.

Killingray, David. "'A Good West Indian, a Good African, and, in Short, a Good Britisher': Black and British in a Colour-Conscious Empire, 1760–1950." *Journal of Imperial and Commonwealth History* 36, no. 3 (2008): 363–81.

King, Desmond. *Making Americans: Immigration, Race, and the Origins of the Diverse Democracy*. Cambridge, Mass.: Harvard University Press, 2000.

Kingsley, Charles. *At Last: Christmas in the West Indies*. New York: Harper and Brothers, 1871.

Kramer, Paul. "Power and Connection: Imperial Histories of the United States in the World." *American Historical Review* 116, no. 5 (2011): 1348–91.

Kuczynski, R. R. *Colonial Population*. New York: Negro Universities Press, 1969. Originally published, 1937.

———. *Demographic Survey of the British Colonial Empire*. Vol. 3, *West Indian and American Territories*. London: Oxford University Press, 1953.

Kuska, Bob. *Hot Potato: How Washington and New York Gave Birth to Black Basketball and Changed America's Game Forever*. Richmond: University of Virginia Press, 2004.

Lake, Marilyn, and Henry Reynolds. *Drawing the Global Colour Line: White Men's Countries and the International Challenge of Racial Equality*. Cambridge, UK: Cambridge University Press, 2008.

Lamming, George. *In the Castle of My Skin*. Ann Arbor: University of Michigan, 1991. Originally published, 1953.

Latimer, James. "The Foundations of Religious Education in the French West Indies." *Journal of Negro Education* 40, no. 1 (1971): 91–98.

Laughlin, Harry. "The Codification and Analysis of the Immigration-Control Law of Each of the Several Countries of Pan America, as expressed by their National Constitutions, Statute Laws, International Treaties, and Administrative Regulations, as of January 1, 1936." Mimeo, Eugenics Record Office, Carnegie Institution of Washington, October 1936.

Lee, Erika. "The 'Yellow Peril' and Asian Exclusion in the Americas." *Pacific Historical Review* 76, no. 4 (2007): 537–62.

Lee, Hélène. *The First Rasta: Leonard Howell and the Rise of Rastafarianism.* Translated by Lily Davis. Chicago: Lawrence Hill Books/Chicago Review Press, 2003.

Lemelle, Sydney J., and Robin D. G. Kelley. "Imagining Home: Pan-Africanism Revisited." In *Imagining Home: Class, Culture, and Nationalism in the African Diaspora,* edited by Sydney J. Lemelle and Robin D. G. Kelley, 1–16. New York: Verso, 1994.

———, eds. *Imagining Home: Class, Culture, and Nationalism in the African Diaspora.* New York: Verso, 1994.

Lent, John A. "Commonwealth Caribbean Mass Media: Historical, Social, Economic, and Political Aspects." Ph.D. diss., University of Iowa, 1972.

Lewis, Alvin. *Orinoco! God at Work in Venezuela.* Self-published, 2005.

Lewis, David Levering. *W. E. B. Du Bois, 1919–1963: The Fight for Equality and the American Century.* New York: Henry Holt and Co., 2000.

———. *When Harlem Was in Vogue.* 2nd ed., with a new preface. New York: Penguin, 1997.

Lewis, Rupert. *Marcus Garvey: Anti-Colonial Champion.* Trenton, N.J.: Africa World Press, 1987.

Lewis, Rupert, and Patrick Bryan, eds. *Garvey: His Work and Impact.* Trenton, N.J.: Africa World Press, 1991.

Lewis, W. Arthur. *Labour in the West Indies: The Birth of a Workers' Movement.* London: New Beacon Books, 1977. Originally published, 1938.

Liverpool, Hollis Urban. "Researching Steelband and Calypso Music in the British Caribbean and the U.S. Virgin Islands." *Black Music Research Journal* 14, no. 2 (1994): 179–201.

———. *Rituals of Power and Rebellion: The Carnival Tradition in Trinidad and Tobago, 1763–1962.* Chicago: Research Associates School Times Publications/ Frontline Distribution International, 2001.

Look Lai, Walton. *The Chinese in the West Indies, 1806–1995: A Documentary History.* Mona, Jamaica: Press of the University of the West Indies, 1998.

Lucassen, Leo. "Migration and World History: Reaching a New Frontier." *International Review of Social History* 52 (2007): 89–96.

Luis-Brown, David. *Waves of Decolonization: Discourses of Race and Hemispheric Citizenship in Cuba, Mexico, and the United States.* Durham, N.C.: Duke University Press, 2008.

Macdonald, Roderick J. "'The Wisers Who Are Far Away': The Role of London's Black Press in the 1930s and 1940s." In *Essays on the History of Blacks in Britain: From Roman Times to the Mid-Twentieth Century*, edited by Jagdish Gundara and Ian Duffield, 150–72. Aldershot, UK: Avebury, 1992.

Macpherson, Anne. "Colonial Matriarchs: Garveyism, Maternalism, and Belize's Black Cross Nurses, 1920–1952." *Gender and History* 15, no. 3 (2003): 507–27.

Magid, Alvin. *Urban Nationalism: A Study in Political Development in Trinidad*. Gainesville: University of Florida Press, 1988.

Magloire, Gérarde, and Kevin Yelvington. "Haiti and the Anthropological Imagination." *Gradhiva*, n.s., 1 (2005): 127–52.

Makalani, Minkah. "Diaspora and the Localities of Race." *Social Text* 98, vol. 27, no. 1 (2009): 1–9.

———. *In the Cause of Freedom: Radical Black Internationalism from Harlem to London, 1917–1939*. Chapel Hill: University of North Carolina Press, 2011.

Makin, William James. *Caribbean Nights*. London: R. Hale, 1939.

Makonnen, Ras. *Pan-Africanism from Within*. Edited by Kenneth King. London: Oxford University Press, 1973.

Malone, Jacqui. *Steppin' on the Blues: The Visible Rhythms of African American Dance*. Urbana: University of Illinois Press, 1996.

Manning, Patrick. "Africa and the African Diaspora: New Directions of Study." *Journal of African History* 44 (2003): 487–506.

———. *The African Diaspora: A History through Culture*. New York: Columbia University Press, 2009.

Manuel, Peter, with Kenneth Bilby and Michael Largey. *Caribbean Currents: Caribbean Music from Rumba to Reggae*. Philadelphia: Temple University Press, 1995.

Marable, Manning. *Malcolm X: A Life of Reinvention*. New York: Viking, 2011.

Marable, Manning, and Vanessa Agard-Jones, eds. *Transnational Blackness: Navigating the Global Color Line*. New York: Palgrave Macmillian, 2008.

Marshall, Dawn. "A History of West Indian Migrations: Overseas Opportunities and 'Safety-Valve' Policies." In *The Caribbean Exodus*, edited by Barry B. Levine, 15–31. New York: Praeger, 1987.

Marshall, Oliver. *The English-Language Press in Latin America: An Annotated Bibliography*. London: Institute of Latin American Studies, 1996.

Marshall, Paule. *Brown Girl, Brownstones*. New York: The Feminist Press at the City University of New York, 1981. Originally published, 1959.

———. *Triangular Road: A Memoir*. New York: Basic Civitas Books, 2009.

Marshall, T. H. *Citizenship and Social Class, and Other Essays*. Cambridge, UK: Cambridge University Press, 1950.

Martin, Tony. *The Pan-African Connection: From Slavery to Garvey and Beyond*. Dover, Mass.: The Majority Press, 1983.

———. *Race First: The Ideological and Organizational Struggles of Marcus Garvey and the Universal Negro Improvement Association*. Westport, Conn.: Greenwood Press, 1976.

Martinez, Samuel. *Peripheral Migrants: Haitians and Dominican Republic Sugar Plantations.* Knoxville: University of Tennessee Press, 1995.

Martínez Vergne, Teresita. *Nation and Citizen in the Dominican Republic, 1880–1916.* Chapel Hill: University of North Carolina Press, 2005.

Mathurin, Owen Charles. *Henry Sylvester Williams and the Origins of the Pan-African Movement, 1869–1911.* Westport, Conn.: Greenwood Press, 1976.

Maughan, Basil. "Some Aspects of Barbadian Emigration to Cuba, 1919–1935." *Journal of the Barbados Museum and Historical Society* 37 (1985): 239–76.

McDuffie, Erik S. *Sojourning for Freedom: Black Women, American Communism, and the Making of Black Left Feminism.* Durham, N.C.: Duke University Press, 2011.

McGillivray, Gillian. *Blazing Cane: Sugar Communities, Class, and State Formation in Cuba, 1868–1959.* Durham, N.C.: Duke University Press, 2009.

McGraw, Jason. "Neither Slaves nor Tyrants: Race, Labor and Citizenship in Caribbean Colombia, 1850–1930." Ph.D. diss., University of Chicago, 2006.

McKay, Claude. *Banjo: A Story without a Plot.* San Diego, Calif.: Harvest Book/Harcourt Brace, 1957. Originally published, 1929.

———. *Gingertown.* Salem, N.H.: Ayer Company, 1991. Originally published, 1932.

———. *Harlem: Negro Metropolis.* New York: E. P. Dutton, 1940.

McKeown, Adam. *Melancholy Order: Asian Migration and the Globalization of Borders.* New York: Columbia University Press, 2008.

———. "Regionalizing World Migration." *International Review of Social History* 52 (2007): 134–42.

———. "A World Made Many: Integration and Segregation in Global Migration, 1840–1940." In *Connecting Seas and Connected Ocean Rims,* edited by Dirk Hoerder and Donna Gabaccia, 42–64. Leiden: Brill, 2011.

McLeod, Marc C. "Undesirable Aliens: Race, Ethnicity, and Nationalism in the Comparison of Haitian and British West Indian Immigrant Workers in Cuba, 1912–1939." *Journal of Social History* 31, no. 3 (1998): 599–623.

Mehta, Uday Singh. *Liberalism and Empire: A Study in Nineteenth-Century British Liberal Thought.* Chicago: University of Chicago Press, 1999.

Mendes, Alfred H. *The Autobiography of Alfred H. Mendes, 1897–1991.* Edited by Michèle Levy. Mona, Jamaica: University of the West Indies Press, 2002.

Miller, Herbie. "Marcus Garvey and the Radical Black Music Tradition." *76 King Street—Journal of Liberty Hall: The Legacy of Marcus Garvey* 1 (2009): 102–25.

———. "Syncopating Rhythms: Jazz and Caribbean Culture." *Jazz Studies Online,* http://jazzstudiesonline.org/?q=node/596. September 29, 2010.

Miller, Norma, with Evette Jensen. *Swingin' at the Savoy: The Memoir of a Jazz Dancer.* Philadelphia: Temple University Press, 1996.

Mills, Lady Dorothy. *The Country of the Orinoco.* London, UK: Hutchinson, 1931.

Mintz, Sidney W. "Enduring Substances, Trying Theories: The Caribbean Region as *Oikoumen.*" *Journal of the Royal Anthropological Institute* 2, no. 2 (1996): 289–311.

———. "Introduction." In *Myth of the Negro Past,* by Melville Herskovits, ix–xxi. Boston: Beacon Press, 1990.

———. "Melville J. Herskovits and Caribbean Studies: A Retrospective Tribute." *Caribbean Studies* 4, no. 2 (1964): 42–51.

Mintz, Sidney W., and Richard Price. *An Anthropological Approach to the Afro-American Past: A Caribbean Perspective*. Philadelphia: Institute for the Study of Human Issues, 1976.

Molina Duarte, Simón. "Impacto cultural y socioeconómico producido por las poblaciones caribeñas en Venezuela." In *Las inmigraciones a Venezuela en el siglo XX: Aportes para su estudio*, edited by Fundación Mercantil/Fundación Francisco Herrera Luque, 95–108. Caracas: Fundación Francisco Herrera Luque, 2004.

Monestel, Manuel. *Ritmo, canción e identidad: Una historia sociocultural del calypso limonense*. San Jose, Costa Rica: EUNED, 2005.

Mongia, Radhika. "Historicizing State Sovereignty: Inequality and the Form of Equivalence." *Comparative Studies in Society and History* 49, no. 2 (2007): 384–411.

———. "Race, Nationality, Mobility: History of the Passport." *Public Culture* 11, no. 3 (1999): 527–55.

Moore, Brian L., and Michele A. Johnson. *Neither Led nor Driven: Contesting British Cultural Imperialism in Jamaica, 1865–1920*. Mona, Jamaica: University of the West Indies Press, 2004.

Moore, Richard B. "The Critics and Opponents of Marcus Garvey." In *Marcus Garvey and the Vision of Africa*, edited by John Henrik Clarke, 210–35. New York: Random House, 1974.

Moore, Robin. *Nationalizing Blackness: Afrocubanismo and Artistic Revolution in Havana, 1920–1940*. Pittsburgh: University of Pittsburgh Press, 1998.

Moses, Wilson Jeremiah. "Introduction." In *Classical Black Nationalism: From the American Revolution to Marcus Garvey*, 1–44. New York: New York University Press, 1996.

Mosquera Aguilar, Antonio. "Regulación jurídica de la migración en Guatemala." http://www.angelfire.com/mo/squera/derecho.html. April 4, 2012.

Moya, José C. *Cousins and Strangers: Spanish Immigrants in Buenos Aires, 1850–1930*. Berkeley: University of California Press, 1998.

Neely, Daniel. "Mento, Jamaica's Original Music: Development, Tourism, and the Nationalist Frame." Ph.D. diss., New York University, 2008.

Neptune, Harvey. *Caliban and the Yankees: Trinidad and the United States Occupation*. Chapel Hill: University of North Carolina Press, 2007.

Newton, Velma. *The Silver Men: West Indian Labour Migration to Panama, 1850–1914*. Mona, Jamaica: UWI-ISER, 1984.

Ngai, Mae. *Impossible Subjects: Illegal Immigrants and the Making of Modern America*. Princeton, N.J.: Princeton University Press, 2004.

Nicaragua, Dirección General de Estadística. *Censo General de 1920*. Managua: Tipografía Nacional, 1922.

Obika, Nyahuma. *An Introduction to the Life and Times of T. U. B. Butler, the Father of the Nation*. Port Fortin, Trinidad: Caribbean Historical Society, 1983.

Opie, Frederick Douglas. *Black Labor Migration in Caribbean Guatemala, 1882–1923*. Jacksonville: University Press of Florida, 2009.

O'Reggio, Trevor. *Between Alienation and Citizenship: The Evolution of Black West Indian Society in Panama, 1914–1964*. Lanham, Md.: University Press of America, 2006.

Ottley, Roi. *"New World A-Coming": Inside Black America*. New York: Houghton Mifflin, 1943.

Oxford English Dictionary Online. Oxford University Press, 2009. www.oed.com.

Palmer, Colin. "Defining and Studying the Modern African Diaspora." In *Perspectives: American Historical Association Newsletter* 36, no. 6 (1998): 1, 22–25.

Palmer, Paula. *"What Happen": A Folk-History of Costa Rica's Talamanca Coast*. San José, Costa Rica: Ecodesarrollos, 1977.

Palmié, Stephan. "Afterword: Other Powers: Tylor's Principle, Father Williams's Temptations, and the Power of Banality." In *Obeah and Other Powers: The Politics of Caribbean Religion and Healing*, edited by Diana Paton and Maarit Forde, 316–40. Durham, N.C.: Duke University Press, 2012.

———. *Wizards and Scientists: Explorations in Afro-Cuban Modernity and Tradition*. Durham, N.C.: Duke University Press, 2002.

Panama, Secretaría de Agricultura y Obras Públicas, Dirección General del Censo. *Censo Demográfico de 1930*, vol. 2. Panamá: Imprenta Nacional, 1931.

Parascandola, Louis J., ed. *Look for Me All around You: Anglophone Caribbean Immigrants in the Harlem Renaissance*. Detroit: Wayne State University Press, 2005.

———. *Winds Can Wake Up the Dead: An Eric Walrond Reader*. Detroit: Wayne State University Press, 1998.

Parker, Jason. "'Capital of the Caribbean': The African American–West Indian 'Harlem Nexus' and the Transnational Drive for Black Freedom, 1940–1948." *Journal of African American History* 89, no. 2 (2004): 98–117.

Paton, Diana. "The Trials of Inspector Thomas: Policing and Ethnography in Jamaica." In *Obeah and Other Powers: The Politics of Caribbean Religion and Healing*, edited by Diana Paton and Maarit Forde, 172–97. Durham, N.C.: Duke University Press, 2012.

Paul, Kathleen. *Whitewashing Britain: Race and Citizenship in the Postwar Era*. Ithaca, N.Y.: Cornell University Press, 1997.

Pearcy, Thomas L. "Panama's Generation of '31: Patriots, Praetorians, and a Decade of Discord." *Hispanic American Historical Review* 76, no. 4 (1996): 691–719.

Pellegrino, Adela. *Historia de la inmigración en Venezuela siglos XIX y XX*. Caracas: Academia Nacional de Ciencias Económicas, 1989.

Pennybacker, Susan. *From Scottsboro to Munich: Race and Political Culture in 1930s Britain*. Princeton, N.J.: Princeton University Press, 2009.

Perry, Jeffrey B., ed. *A Hubert Harrison Reader*. Middletown, Conn.: Wesleyan University Press, 2001.

Peterson, Bernard L. *The African American Theatre Directory, 1816–1960*. Westport, Conn.: Greenwood Press, 1997.

———. *A Century of Musicals in Black and White*. Westport, Conn.: Greenwood Press, 1993.

Petras, Elizabeth MacLean. *Jamaican Labor Migration: White Capital and Black Labor, 1850–1930.* Boulder, Colo.: Westview, 1988.

Pettersburgh, Fitz Balintine. *The Royal Parchment Scroll of Black Supremacy.* Kingston, Jamaica, and Brooklyn, N.Y.: Headstart Books/Roots Groundation, 1996.

Pinckney, Warren R., Jr. "Jazz in Barbados." *American Music* 12, no. 1 (1994): 58–87.

Pollak-Eltz, Angelina, and Cecilia Isturiz. *Folklore y cultura de la Península de Paria (Sucre) Venezuela.* Estudios Monografias y Ensayos, no. 127. Caracas: Biblioteca de la Academia Nacional de la Historia, 1990.

Pollitt, Brian H. "The Cuban Sugar Economy and the Great Depression." *Bulletin of Latin American Research* 3, no. 2 (1984): 3–28.

Porter, Christopher. "Jazz to Ska Mania." *Jazz Times* (July/August 2004), http://jazztimes.com/articles/14829-jazz-to-ska-mania. September 29, 2010.

Post, Ken. *Arise Ye Starvelings: The Jamaican Labour Rebellion of 1938 and Its Aftermath.* The Hague: Martinus Nijhoff, 1978.

Prais, Jinny. "Imperial Travelers: The Formation of West African Urban Culture, Identity, and Citizenship in London and Accra, 1925–1935." Ph.D. diss., University of Michigan, 2008.

Price, Richard. "On the Miracle of Creolization." In *Afro-Atlantic Dialogues: Anthropology in the Diaspora,* edited by Kevin Yelvington, 115–47. Santa Fe, N.Mex.: School of American Research Press, 2006.

Price, Richard, and Sally Price. *The Root of Roots; or, How Afro-American Anthropology Got Its Start.* Chicago: Prickly Paradigm Press/University of Chicago Press, 2003.

Proctor, Jesse H., Jr. "The Development of the Idea of Federation of the British Caribbean Territories." *Revista de Historia de América* 39 (1955): 61–105.

Proudfoot, Malcolm J. *Population Movements in the Caribbean.* Caribbean Commission Central Secretariat: Port of Spain, Trinidad, 1950.

Puri, Shalini. *The Caribbean Postcolonial: Social Equality, Post/Nationalism, and Cultural Hybridity.* New York: Palgrave Macmillan, 2004.

———, ed. *Marginal Migrations: The Circulation of Cultures within the Caribbean.* London: Macmillan, 2003.

Putnam, Lara. *The Company They Kept: Migrants and the Politics of Gender in Caribbean Costa Rica, 1870–1960.* Chapel Hill: University of North Carolina Press, 2002.

———. "Contact Zones: Heterogeneity and Boundaries in Caribbean Central America at the Start of the Twentieth Century." *Iberoamericana* [Ibero-Amerikanisches Institut, Berlin] 6, no. 23 (2006): 113–25.

———. "Eventually Alien: The Multigenerational Saga of British West Indians in Central America and Beyond, 1880–1940." In *Blacks and Blackness in Central America: Between Race and Place,* edited by Lowell Gudmundson and Justin Wolfe, 278–306. Durham, N.C.: Duke University Press, 2010.

———. "Ideología Racial, Práctica Social y Estado Liberal en Costa Rica." *Revista de Historia* [San José, Costa Rica] 39 (1999): 139–86.

———. "'Nothing Matters but Color': Transnational Circuits, the Interwar Caribbean, and the Black International." In *From Toussaint to Tupac: The Black International and the Struggle for Liberation*, edited by Michael O. West, William G. Martin, and Fanon Che Wilkins, 107–29. Chapel Hill: University of North Carolina Press, 2009.

———. "Rites of Power and Rumors of Race: The Circulation of Supernatural Knowledge in the Greater Caribbean, 1890–1940." In *Obeah and Other Powers: The Politics of Caribbean Religion and Healing*, edited by Diana Paton and Maarit Forde, 243–67. Durham, N.C.: Duke University Press, 2012.

———. "The Ties Allowed to Bind: Kinship Legalities and Migration Restriction in the Interwar Americas." *International Labor and Working-Class History*. Forthcoming.

———. "To Study the Fragments/Whole: Microhistory and the Atlantic World." *Journal of Social History* 39, no. 3 (2006): 615–30.

———. "Undone by Desire: Migration, Sex across Boundaries, and Collective Destinies in the Greater Caribbean, 1840–1940." In *Connecting Seas and Connected Ocean Rims: Indian, Atlantic, and Pacific Oceans and China Seas Migrations from the 1830s to the 1930s*, edited by Dirk Hoerder and Donna Gabaccia, 302–37. Leiden: Brill, 2011.

———. "Unspoken Exclusions: Race, Nation, and Empire in the Immigration Restrictions of the 1920s in North America and the Greater Caribbean." In *Workers across the Americas: The Transnational Turn in Labor History*, edited by Leon Fink, 267–93. New York: Oxford University Press, 2011.

———. "Work, Sex, and Power in a Central American Export Economy at the Turn of the Twentieth Century." In *Gender, Sexuality, and Power in Latin America*, edited by Katherine Bliss and William French, 133–62. Lanham, Md.: Rowman and Littlefield, 2006.

Reddock, Rhoda. *Women, Labour, and Politics in Trinidad and Tobago*. Kingston: Ian Randle, 1994.

Reid, Carlos. *Memorias de un criollo bocatoreño/Light in Dark Places*, edited by Stanley Heckadon Moreno. Panama: Asociación Panameña de Antropología, 1980.

Reid, Ira de Augustine. *The Negro Immigrant: His Background, Characteristics, and Social Adjustment, 1899–1937*. New York: Arno Press, 1969. Originally published, 1939.

Richards, Yevette. *Maida Springer: Pan-Africanist and International Labor Leader*. Pittsburgh: University of Pittsburgh Press, 2000.

———, ed. *Conversations with Maida Springer: A Personal History of Labor, Race, and International Relations*. Pittsburgh: University of Pittsburgh Press, 2004.

Richardson, Bonham. "Caribbean Migrations, 1838–1985." In *The Modern Caribbean*, edited by Franklin Knight and Colin Palmer, 203–28. Chapel Hill: University of North Carolina Press, 1989.

———. "The Migration Experience." In *General History of the Caribbean*, vol. 5, *The Caribbean in the Twentieth Century*, edited by Germán Carrera Damas and Bridget Brereton, 434–64. Paris and London: UNESCO and Macmillan, 2004.

————. *Panama Money in Barbados, 1900–1920*. Knoxville: University of Tennessee Press, 1985.

Roberts, George W. *The Population of Jamaica*. Cambridge, UK: Conservation Foundation at the University Press, 1957.

Rogers, J. A. "Jazz at Home." *Survey Graphic*, "Harlem: Mecca of the New Negro" (March 1925): 665.

————. *World's Great Men of Color*. New York: J. A. Rogers, 1947.

Rolinson, Mary G. *Grassroots Garveyism: The Universal Negro Improvement Association in the Rural South, 1920–1927*. Chapel Hill: University of North Carolina Press, 2007.

Roman, Reinaldo. *Governing Spirits: Religion, Miracles, and Spectacles in Cuba and Puerto Rico, 1898–1956*. Chapel Hill: University of North Carolina Press, 2007.

Rouse, Don. "New Orleans Jazz and Caribbean Music." http://www.prjc.org/roots/nojazzandcarribe.html. April 4, 2012.

Runstedtler, Theresa. "Visible Men: African American Boxers, the New Negro, and the Global Color Line." *Radical History Review* 103 (2009): 59–81.

Samaroo, Brinsley, and Cherita Girvan. "The Trinidad Workingmen's Association and the Origins of Popular Protest in a Crown Colony." *Social and Economic Studies* 21, no. 2 (1972): 205–22.

Schuler, Monica. *"Alas, Alas, Kongo": A Social History of Indentured African Immigration into Jamaica, 1841–1865*. Baltimore: Johns Hopkins University Press, 1980.

Schwarz, Bill, ed. *West Indian Intellectuals in Britain*. Manchester, UK: Manchester University Press, 2003.

Scott, David. "Modernity That Predated the Modern: Sidney Mintz's Caribbean." *History Workshop Journal* 58 (2004): 191–210.

————. "An Obscure Miracle of Connection." In *Refashioning Futures: Criticism after Postcoloniality*, 106–28. Princeton, N.J.: Princeton University Press, 1999.

————. "That Event, This Memory: Notes on the Anthropology of African Diasporas in the New World." *Diaspora* 1, no. 3 (1991): 261–84.

Scott, Rebecca J. "Small-Scale Dynamics of Large-Scale Processes." *American Historical Review* 105, no. 2 (2000): 472–79.

Seigel, Micol. *Uneven Encounters: Making Race and Nation in Brazil and the United States*. Durham, N.C.: Duke University Press, 2009.

Senior, Olive. *Encyclopedia of Jamaican Heritage*. St. Andrew, Jamaica: Twin Guinep Publishers, 2003.

Seymour, Walter. *Ups and Downs of a Wandering Life*. New York: D. Appleton and Company, 1910.

Shakes, Nicosia, ed. *76 King Street—Journal of Liberty Hall: The Legacy of Marcus Garvey* 1 (2009): 1–160.

Shanahan, Suzanne. "Scripted Debates: Twentieth-Century Immigration and Citizenship Policy in Great Britain, Ireland, and the United States." In *Extending Citizenship, Reconfiguring States*, edited by Michael Hanagan and Charles Tilly, 67–96. Lanham, Md.: Rowman and Littlefield, 1999.

Shipton, Alyn. *A New History of Jazz*. Rev. ed. New York: Continuum, 2007.

Singh, Kelvin. "June 1937 Disturbances." In *The Trinidad Labour Riots of 1937: Perspectives 50 Years Later*, edited by Roy Thomas, 57–80. St. Augustine, Trinidad: Extra-Mural Studies Unit, University of the West Indies, 1987.

Skurski, Julie. "The Ambiguities of Authenticity in Latin America: Doña Bárbara and the Construction of National Identity." *Poetics Today* 15, no. 4 (1994): 605–42.

Slate, Nico. *Colored Cosmopolitanism: The Shared Struggle for Freedom in the United States and India*. Cambridge, Mass.: Harvard University Press, 2012.

Smith, C. Calvin. "John E. Bush: The Politician and the Man, 1880–1916." *Arkansas Historical Quarterly* 54, no. 2 (1995): 115–33.

Smith, Faith. *Creole Recitations: John Jacob Thomas and Colonial Formation in the Late Nineteenth-Century Caribbean*. Richmond: University of Virginia Press, 2002.

Smith, Glanville. *Many a Green Isle*. London: The Travel Book Club, 1942.

Soto Quirós, Ronald. "Inmigración e identidad nacional: Los 'otros' reafirman el 'nosotros.'" Licenciatura thesis, Escuela de Historia, Universidad de Costa Rica, 1998.

Southern, Eileen. *The Music of Black Americans: A History*. 3rd ed. New York: W. W. Norton, 1997.

Squires, Catherine. "Rethinking the Black Public Sphere: An Alternative Vocabulary for Alternative Public Spheres." *Communication Theory* 12, no. 4 (2002): 446–68.

Stein, Judith. *The World of Marcus Garvey: Race and Class in Modern Society*. Baton Rouge: Louisiana State University Press, 1986.

Stepan, Nancy Leys. *"The Hour of Eugenics": Race, Gender, and Nation in Latin America*. Ithaca, N.Y.: Cornell University Press, 1991.

Stephens, Michelle Ann. *Black Empire: The Masculine Global Imaginary of Caribbean Intellectuals in the United States, 1914–1962*. Durham, N.C.: Duke University Press, 2005.

Stern, Alexandra Minna. *Eugenic Nation: Faults and Frontiers of Better Breeding in Modern America*. Berkeley: University of California Press, 2005.

Stewart, Robert. *Religion and Society in Post-Emancipation Jamaica*. Knoxville: University of Tennessee Press, 1992.

Stoddard, Lothrop. *The Rising Tide of Color against White World Supremacy*. New York: Charles Scribner's Sons, 1920.

Stokes, W. Royal. *Growing up with Jazz: Twenty-Four Musicians Talk about Their Lives and Careers*. New York: Oxford University Press, 2005.

Sullivan, Frances Peace. "'No Surrender': Migration, the Garvey Movement, and Community Building in the U.S.-Caribbean World." Unpublished manuscript.

———. "Radical Solidarities: U.S. Capitalism, Community Building, and Popular Internationalism in Cuba's Eastern Sugar Zone, 1919-1939." Ph.D. diss., New York University, 2012.

Szwed, John. "World Views Collide: The History of Jazz and Hot Dance." In *Crossovers: Essays on Race, Music, and American Culture*, edited by John Szwed, 191–94. Philadelphia: University of Pennsylvania Press, 2005.

Szwed, John, with Morton Marks. "The Afro-American Transformation of European Set Dances." In *Crossovers: Essays on Race, Music, and American*

Culture, edited by John Szwed, 153–67. Philadelphia: University of Pennsylvania Press, 2005.

Tabili, Laura. *"We Ask for British Justice": Workers and Racial Difference in Late Imperial Britain*. Ithaca, N.Y.: Cornell University Press, 1994.

Taylor, Ula Yvette. *The Veiled Garvey: The Life and Times of Amy Jacques Garvey*. Chapel Hill: University of North Carolina Press, 2002.

Thomas, Deborah. *Modern Blackness: Nationalism, Globalization, and the Politics of Culture in Jamaica*. Durham, N.C.: Duke University Press, 2004.

———. "The Violence of Diaspora: Governmentality, Class Cultures, and Circulations." *Radical History Review* 103 (2009): 83–104.

Thomas, Roy, ed. *The Trinidad Labour Riots of 1937: Perspectives 50 Years Later*. St. Augustine, Trinidad: Extra-Mural Studies Unit, University of the West Indies, 1987.

Thomas-Hope, Elizabeth M. "The Establishment of a Migration Tradition: British West Indian Movements to the Hispanic Caribbean in the Century after Emancipation." *International Migration* 24 (1986): 559–71.

Thompson, Rev. H. P. *Into All Lands: The History of the Society for the Propagation of the Gospel in Foreign Parts, 1701–1950*. London: S.P.C.K., 1951.

Thoywell-Henry, L. A., comp. *Who's Who Jamaica, British West Indies (1941–1946)*. Kingston: Who's Who (Jamaica) Ltd., 1946.

Tilly, Charles. "Citizenship, Identity, and Social History." In *Citizenship, Identity, and Social History*, edited by Charles Tilley, 1–18. Cambridge, UK: Cambridge University Press, 1996.

Tinker Salas, Miguel. *The Enduring Legacy: Oil, Culture, and Society in Venezuela*. Durham, N.C.: Duke University Press, 2009.

Torpey, John. *The Invention of the Passport: Surveillance, Citizenship and the State*. New York: Cambridge University Press, 1999.

Toussaint, Michael. "George Numa Dessources, the Numancians, and the Attempt to Form a Colony in Eastern Venezuela, circa 1850–54." In *Beyond Tradition: Reinterpreting the Caribbean Historical Experience*, edited by Heather Cateau and Rita Pemberton, 197–223. Kingston: Ian Randle, 2006.

Trinidad and Tobago. *Debates in the Legislative Council of Trinidad and Tobago* [Hansards], 1920–1936. Port of Spain: Government Printing Office, 1921–37.

Trinidad and Tobago, Registrar General's Department. *Census of the Colony of Trinidad and Tobago, 1921*. Port of Spain: Government Printing Office, 1923.

Trotman, David V. "The Yorùbá and Orisha Worship in Trinidad and British Guiana, 1838–1870." *African Studies Review* 19, no. 2 (1976): 1–17.

Trouillot, Michel-Rolph. "The Caribbean Region: An Open Frontier in Anthropological Theory." *Annual Review of Anthropology* 21 (1992): 19–42.

Turits, Richard Lee. *Foundations of Despotism: Peasants, the Trujillo Regime, and Modernity in Dominican History*. Stanford, Calif.: Stanford University Press, 2003.

———. "A World Destroyed, a Nation Imposed: The 1937 Haitian Massacre in the Dominican Republic." *Hispanic American Historical Review* 82, no. 3 (2002): 589–635.

Turner, Joyce Moore. "Richard B. Moore and His Works." In *Richard B. Moore: Caribbean Militant in Harlem*, edited by W. Burghardt Turner and Joyce Moore Turner, 19–122. Bloomington: Indiana University Press, 1992.

Turner, Joyce Moore, with W. Burghardt Turner. *Caribbean Crusaders and the Harlem Renaissance*. Urbana: University of Illinois Press, 2005.

Turner, Mary. *Slaves and Missionaries: The Disintegration of Jamaican Slave Society, 1787–1834*. Mona, Jamaica: The Press, University of the West Indies, 1998. Originally published, 1982.

Turner, Richard Brent. *Islam in the African American Experience*. 2nd ed. Bloomington: Indiana University Press, 2003.

Turner, W. Burghardt, and Joyce Moore Turner, eds. *Richard B. Moore: Caribbean Militant in Harlem*. Bloomington: Indiana University Press, 1992.

Ueda, Reed. "Introduction: State Development and International Migration." *Journal of Interdisciplinary History* 41, no. 1 (2010): 1–6.

Underhill, Edward Bean. *The West Indies: Their Social and Religious Condition*. London: Jackson, Walford, and Hodder, 1862.

U.S. Bureau of the Census. *Fifteenth Census of the United States, 1930*. Vol. 2, *Population*. Washington, D.C.: Government Printing Office, 1933. http://www.census.gov/prod/www/abs/decennial/1930.html. April 4, 2012.

———. *Fifteenth Census of the United States, 1930: Report on Outlying Territories and Possessions*. Washington, D.C.: Government Printing Office, 1932.

U.S. Bureau of Immigration. *Annual report of the Commissioner General of Immigration to the Secretary of Labor for the Fiscal Year Ended . . . June 30, 1925*. Washington, D.C.: Government Printing Office, 1925.

U.S. Department of State. *Admission of Aliens into the United States: Notes to Section 361 Consular Regulations*. Washington, D.C.: Government Printing Office, 1932.

Uslar Pietri, Arturo. "Introducción a la Primera Edición." In *Labor Venzolanista*, by Alberto Adriani. 6th ed. Caracas: Academia Nacional de Ciencias Económicas, 1989.

Vallenilla Lanz, Laureano. "Disgregación e integración." In *Cesarismo democrático y otros textos*, by Laureano Vallenilla Lanz, with prologue and notes by Nikita Harwich Vallenilla, 215–359. Caracas: Biblioteca Ayacucho, 1991. Originally published, 1930.

Venezuela, Ministerio de Fomento, Dirección de Estadística. *Sexto Censo de Población, 1936*, vol. 3. Caracas: Tipografía Garrido, 1940.

Venezuela, Ministerio de Relaciones Interiores. *Memoria (1929–1937)*. Caracas: Litografía del Comercio, 1930–38.

Verdery, Katherine. "Ethnicity, Nationalism, and State-Making: Ethnic Groups and Boundaries: Past and Future." In *The Anthropology of Ethnicity: Beyond "Ethnic Groups and Boundaries,"* edited by H. Vermeulen and C. Govers, 33–58. Amsterdam: Spinhaus, 1994.

Verrill, Alpheus Hyatt. *The Book of the West Indies*. New York: E. P. Dutton, 1917.

———. *Jamaica of Today*. New York: Dodd, Mead, 1931.

Vincent, Theodore. *Black Power and the Garvey Movement*. Berkeley: Ramparts Press, 1971.

Von Eschen, Penny. *Race against Empire: Black Americans and Anticolonialism, 1937–1957*. Ithaca, N.Y.: Cornell University Press, 1997.

Vogel, Todd. *The Black Press: New Literary and Historical Essays*. New Brunswick, N.J.: Rutgers University Press, 2001.

Wade, Peter. *Music, Race, and Nation: Música Tropical in Colombia*. Chicago: University of Chicago Press, 2000.

Walker, Klive. *Dubwise: Reasoning from the Reggae Underground*. Toronto: Insomniac Press, 2005.

Walrond, Eric. *Tropic Death*. New York: Boni and Liveright, 1926.

Warner, Michael. "Publics and Counterpublics." *Public Culture* 14, no. 1 (2002): 49–90.

Washburne, Christopher. "The Clave of Jazz: A Caribbean Contribution to the Rhythmic Foundation of an African American Music." *Black Music Research Journal* 17, no. 1 (1997): 59–80.

Watkins-Owens, Irma. *Blood Relations: Caribbean Immigrants and the Harlem Community, 1900–1930*. Bloomington: Indiana University Press, 1996.

Waxer, Lise. "Of Mambo Kings and Songs of Love: Dance Music in Havana and New York from the 1930s to the 1950s." *Latin American Music Review/Revista de Música Latinoamericana* 15, no. 2 (1994): 139–76.

West, Michael O. "The Seeds Are Sown: The Impact of Garveyism in Zimbabwe in the Interwar Years." *International Journal of African Historical Studies* 35, no. 2/3 (2002): 335–62.

West, Michael O., and William G. Martin. "Introduction: Contours of the Black International, from Toussaint to Tupac." In *From Toussaint to Tupac: The Black International since the Age of Revolution*, edited by Michael O. West, William G. Martin, and Fanon Che Wilkins, 1–44. Chapel Hill: University of North Carolina Press, 2009.

West, Michael O., William G. Martin, and Fanon Che Wilkins, eds. *From Toussaint to Tupac: The Black International since the Age of Revolution*. Chapel Hill: University of North Carolina Press, 2009.

Westerman, George W. *Los inmigrantes antillanos en Panama*. Panama: n.p., 1980.

West Indian Census 1946. Part A. General Report on the Census of Population. Kingston: Government Printer, 1950.

White, Garth. "The Evolution of Jamaican Music, Part 1: 'Proto-Ska' to Ska." *Social and Economic Studies* 47, no. 1 (1998): 5–19.

White, Luise. *Speaking with Vampires: Rumor and History in Colonial Africa*. Berkeley: University of California Press, 2000.

White, Timothy. *Catch a Fire: The Life of Bob Marley*. New York: Holt, Rinehart and Winston, 1998.

Wickham, Henry Alexander. *Rough Notes of a Journey through the Wilderness: From Trinidad to Pará, Brazil, by way of the Great Cataracts of the Orinoco, Atabapo, and Rio Negro*. London: W. H. J. Carter, 1872.

Wiggins, David Kenneth, and Patrick B. Miller. *The Unlevel Playing Field: A Documentary History of the African American Experience in Sport*. Urbana: University of Illinois Press, 2003.

Wimmer, Andreas, and Nina Glick Schiller. "Methodological Nationalism and Beyond: Nation-State Building, Migration, and the Social Sciences." *Global Networks* 2, no. 4 (2002): 301–34.

Winks, Robin. *The Blacks in Canada: A History*. New Haven, Conn.: Yale University Press, 1971.

Worrell, Rodney. "Pan-Africanism in Barbados." In *The Empowering Impulse: The Nationalist Tradition of Barbados*, edited by Glenford Howe and Don Marshall, 196–220. Mona, Jamaica: Canoe Press, University of the West Indies, 2003.

Wright, Winthrop R. *Café con Leche: Race, Class and National Image in Venezuela*. Austin: University of Texas Press, 1990.

Wynter, Cadence. "Jamaican Labor Migration to Cuba, 1885–1930, in the Caribbean Context." Ph.D. diss., University of Illinois at Chicago, 2001.

X, Malcolm, and Alex Haley. *The Autobiography of Malcolm X*. New York: Ballantine Books, 1964.

Yanow, Scott. *Swing*. San Francisco: Miller Freeman Books, 2000.

Yelvington, Kevin. "Introduction." In *Afro-Atlantic Dialogues: Anthropology in the Diaspora*, edited by Kevin Yelvington, 3–32. Santa Fe, N.Mex.: School of American Research Press, 2006.

———. "The Invention of Africa in Latin America and the Caribbean: Political Discourse and Anthropological Praxis, 1920–1940." In *Afro-Atlantic Dialogues: Anthropology in the Diaspora*, edited by Kevin Yelvington, 35–82. Santa Fe, N.Mex.: School of American Research Press, 2006.

———. "The War in Ethiopia and Trinidad, 1935–1936." In *The Colonial Caribbean in Transition: Essays on Postemancipation Social and Cultural History*, edited by Bridget Brereton and Kevin A. Yelvington, 189–225. Gainesville: University Press of Florida, 1999.

———, ed. *Afro-Atlantic Dialogues: Anthropology in the Diaspora*. Santa Fe, N.Mex.: School of American Research Press, 2006.

Young, Sidney A., ed. *Isthmian Echoes: A Selection of the Literary Endeavors of the West Indian Colony in the Republic of Panama*. Panama: n.p., 1928.

Zolberg, Aristide. "The Archaeology of 'Remote Control.'" In *Migration Control in the North Atlantic World: The Evolution of State Practices in Europe and the United States from the French Revolution to the Inter-War Period*, edited by Andreas Fahrmeir, Olivier Faron, and Patrick Weil, 195–222. Oxford and New York: Berghahn Books, 2003.

———. "Matters of State: Theorizing Immigration Policy." In *The Handbook of International Migration*, edited by Charles Hirschman, Philip Kasinitz, and Josh DeWind, 71–93. New York: Russell Sage, 2000.

———. *A Nation by Design: Immigration Policy in the Fashioning of America*. New York: Russell Sage Foundation and Harvard University Press, 2006.

Zumoff, Jacob. "American Communist Party and the 'Negro Question' from the Founding of the Party to the Fourth Congress of the Communist International." *Journal for the Study of Radicalism* 6, no. 2 (2012): 53–90.

Index

Abyssinia. *See* Ethiopia

Achong, Tito, 206–7, 208, 236

Africa: as source of music, 5, 5, 154, 159, 167–68, 176; as source of religion, 12, 50, 52–54, 59–60, 76–77; as contested symbol, 20, 77–78; within UNIA program, 36, 78, 125, 145, 216; indentured immigrants from, 52, 53; within Rastafarian thought, 216, 217, 219, 221

African Blood Brotherhood, 79, 133

African diaspora: scholarship on, 15, 233–34, 242 (n. 14); popular understandings of, 77, 234–39

African Methodist Episcopal Zion, 55, 72

African Telegraph, 133, 136

African Times and Orient Review, 124, 133, 221

Afro-Americans: internationalism among, 5–6, 16–17, 124, 141, 230; connections to Caribbean religions, 52, 54, 74, 221–22, 237–38; reactions to immigrants among, 91–92, 162; performers tour Caribbean, 173–76. *See also* Harlem

Alhambra Ballroom, 157, 162

Ali, Dusé Mohammed, 133, 221

Anarchists, 86–87, 99

Anderson, Benedict, 6

Andrade, Vernon, 161–62, 163, 164, 165

Anglican Church, 52, 53, 54, 55, 71

Antigua, 27; emigrants from, 32, 37, 61, 72, 157, 162, 200, 213

Anti-immigrant laws. *See* Immigration laws; Racism

Asian exclusion: by American republics, 85, 101; debated in Jamaica, 110–15;

complications for British Empire, 116–20, 146, 263 (n. 141)

Associations. *See* Civic associations

Assyrians. *See* Syria, immigrants from

Banana exports, 22, 27–28, 98, 108–9, 110. *See also* United Fruit Company

Baptists, 52, 53, 55, 71. *See also* Native Baptists; Spiritual Baptists

Barbados, 23, 112; emigration from, 13, 22, 26–37 passim, 85–95 passim, 128–29, 200; religion in, 52, 54, 56; anti-immigrant agitation in, 115; return migration to, 202, 204, 213; popular protests in, 196, 225

Barbados Weekly Herald, xiii, 124, 132, 136

Bedward, Alexander, 57–58, 74, 79, 249 (n. 5)

Belafonte, Harry, 4

Belize. *See* British Honduras

Belsidus, Dr. Henry, 134, 219

Benbow, William, 173–76

Black internationalism, 3–8, 123–24: scholarship on, 15–17, 124, 230; class divides within, 81, 154, 238; and international press, 126–37, 140–41, 145–52; and civic associations, 138–39, 163; and sport fandom, 140–41, 226; and performative realm, 153–54, 172–82 passim, 192, 193, 195; and conceptualization of diaspora, 233–34

Black nationalism, 5–6, 16, 284 (n. 126)

Bogle, Paul, 57, 79

Border control. *See* Immigration laws

Boston, 27, 28, 31, 32, 132

Brams, 184–86

Briggs, Cyril, 80, 127, 133, 136

British Empire: questioning of, 3, 8, 14, 125, 145–55, 199; loyalty to, 136–37, 147–48

British Guiana, 23, 27, 37, 139, 196; immigration to, 22, 26, 31, 53, 111, 199, 200; emigrants from, 24, 32, 72, 222; boundary dispute with Venezuela, 40, 42–43, 48

British Honduras, 27, 55, 102, 132, 136, 196

British subjects: British West Indians claim rights as, 3, 21, 39–47, 114, 125, 147–48, 150; joke about lack of status as, 3, 47, 150; rights defended by Palmerston, 41–42, 147; consuls distinguish among by race, 117–18; criteria for inheriting status as, 203–5. See also British Empire

British West Indies Regiment (BWIR), 136, 193, 232

Brooklyn, 29, 31, 32, 72, 87, 124, 166. See also New York City

Brown, E. Ethelred, 79

Brujería, accusations of, 60, 63, 64, 70

Bustamante, Alexander, 223–24, 228

Butler, Tubal Uriah "Buzz," 196, 224, 225–26

Cain, Herbert Hill, 132

Calypso, 14, 159, 161, 170

Campbell, Grace, 79, 254 (n. 127)

Canal Zone, 37, 55, 90, 95, 99, 128, 132, 140, 199. See also Panama

Caracas, 24, 31, 55, 200

Carmichael, Stokely, 213–14, 222

Carúpano, 24, 48

Catholicism, 49, 52, 54, 55, 71

Central American Express, 131–32, 134, 137

Chen, Eugene, 116–17

Children: and migration, 37, 90, 93–94; vulnerability to supernatural assault, 50, 64–70, 81; citizenship or subject status of, 94, 104, 203–4, 210

China, immigrants from, 13, 112, 207, 234; legislation against, 83–85, 101, 102, 113, 119, 208, 209; hostility toward, 84, 100, 111–12, 114–15, 223, 224; sending state reacts to laws against, 116–19, 281 (n. 63)

Churches. See Religion; specific denominations

Cipriani, Captain Arthur, 148, 209

Citizenship: scholarship on, 9, 18–19; social, historical expansion of, 9–10, 238; social, struggles over in British Caribbean, 83, 199, 226, 228–29; birthright, in United States, 94; birthright, in Panama, 104, 203

Ciudad Bolivar, 21, 24, 44, 55, 131, 169, 239

Civic associations, 1, 17, 35–36, 80, 138–39, 151, 163, 186, 225; insular loyalties and, 143–44, 200, 268 (n. 80)

Colombia, 27, 37; British West Indian migration to, 22, 33; anti-immigrant laws in, 100, 102, 103, 148

Color categories, 20

Communist activists, 50, 99, 196, 223, 225

Communist International (Comintern), 79, 80, 224

Consuls: role in migration control, 13, 85, 86, 87, 88–95 passim, 102, 104, 106, 109, 119, 121, 204, 211; migrants seek support from British, 40, 44, 47, 48, 63; attitudes toward British West Indians, 88, 118, 150, 205

Costa Rica, 60; British West Indian migration to, 1, 18, 26, 29, 35, 199; black internationalist organizing and debate in, 16, 37, 145–51 passim; British West Indian religious practice in, 49, 56, 58–63 passim, 77, 214; anti-immigrant laws and abuses in, 97, 98, 104, 108, 110; literacy in, 128; return migration from, 156; labor movement in, 197. See also Limón

civic life, 138–39; and questioning of British Empire, 145–53; and debates over youth and music, 154, 160, 170–72, 179, 180, 182–93. *See also specific titles*

Price-Mars, Jean, 76

Print culture. *See* Press

Psalm 68, 72–73, 215

Public sphere: scholarship on, 126, 151–52, 154; generated by international black press, 126–28, 137–39, 141, 151–52, 194–95

Pukumina. *See* Pocomania

Race: as social construct, 3, 5, 104, 117, 142–45; ideologies of, 3, 6; essentialist understandings of, 125, 142–44, 168, 228–29, 239

Racism: scientific, 2, 9; and mestizo populism, 9, 95–100, 103–4, 125; denunciations of, 13–14, 123, 130, 141, 145–52; antiblack, inverted by Rastafarianism, 216–21

Ras Tafari. *See* Rastafarianism; Selassie, Haile

Rastafarianism, 3, 15; originators of, 73, 75, 215, 237–38; relation to reggae music, 155, 238; relation to ideologies of race, 198, 214, 218–19, 221; early development of, 215–20

Reggae, 193; origins of term, 155–56, 187–88, 269 (n. 7); evolution of music, 155, 238. *See also* Regge dances (Limón)

Regge dances (Limón), 15, 153, 186–92, 238

Religion: development and diversity within British Caribbean, 49, 51–54; and class divides, 50, 55, 71–72, 74, 76, 81, 228; spread by migrants, 54–58, 72–76; and Garveyism, 72–73, 78, 80; rejected by Harlem radicals, 78–80; and Labour Rebellions, 196, 225; and race in 1930s, 214–22. *See also* Rastafarianism; Supernatural beliefs and practice; *specific denominations*

Renaissance Ballroom, 157

Restrictionism. *See* Immigration laws

Revival (Jamaican religion), 53, 54, 72

Richards, Alfred, 206

Rienzi, Adrian Cola, 224

Rodney, Walter, 10

Rogers, Joel Augustus, 78, 160, 183, 215

St. Kitts and Nevis, 27, 196; emigrants from, 32, 37, 82, 133, 157, 162

St. Lucia, 23, 27, 54, 61, 129, 170, 196, 201; witchcraft accusations in, 64, 67

St. Vincent, 23, 27, 52, 54, 129, 140, 196, 211; emigrants from, 24, 31, 82, 108, 200, 224; obeah in, 60, 61, 74

Salvation Army, 37, 49, 56, 57, 138, 139, 186

Santo Domingo. *See* Dominican Republic

Savoy Theater, 157

Schuyler, George, 134, 219

Segregation, formal, 55, 127, 132, 177, 207

Selassie, Haile, 78, 196, 214, 215, 216–17, 218, 221

Seventh-Day Adventists, 56, 72, 139

Shakers (St. Vincent), 54

Shouters, 49, 54, 196, 225

South Asian. *See* East Indians

Spiritual Baptists, 49, 54, 196, 225

Springer, Maida, 4, 230

Standard Oil Company, 121

State formation, 2, 9, 11, 18–19, 125

Stoddard, Lothrop, 87, 218

Subjects, British. *See* British subjects

Supernatural beliefs and practice: circulation and recombination of, 51, 59–62, 70–71, 74–76; and long-distance kinship, 62–63; and children's vulnerability, 64–70, 81; British West Indian leaders denounce, 77–79. *See also* Obeah; Religion; Witchcraft, fear of